The Palestinian People

The Palestinian People

Seeking Sovereignty and State

Mustafa Kabha

BOULDER
LONDON

This book is a revised, expanded, and updated version of
The Palestinians: A People Dispersed, published in Hebrew
by the Open University of Israel in 2010, translated by Rachel Kessel.

Published in the United States of America in 2014 by
Lynne Rienner Publishers, Inc.
1800 30th Street, Boulder, Colorado 80301
www.rienner.com

and in the United Kingdom by
Lynne Rienner Publishers, Inc.
3 Henrietta Street, Covent Garden, London WC2E 8LU

© 2014 by Lynne Rienner Publishers, Inc. All rights reserved

Library of Congress Cataloging-in-Publication Data
Kabha, Mustafa, author.
 The Palestinian people : seeking sovereignty and state / Mustafa Kabha.
     pages cm
 Includes bibliographical references and index.
 ISBN 978-1-58826-882-2 (alk. paper)
 1. Palestinian Arabs—History—20th century. 2. Palestinian
Arabs—History—21st century. 3. Arab-Israeli conflict. I. Title.
 DS113.6.K32 2013
 956'.0049274—dc23
                                                                                                    2013010904

British Cataloguing in Publication Data
A Cataloguing in Publication record for this book
is available from the British Library.

Printed and bound in the United States of America

∞ The paper used in this publication meets the requirements
   of the American National Standard for Permanence of
   Paper for Printed Library Materials Z39.48-1992.

5 4 3 2 1

Contents

	Introduction	1
1	The 1936–1939 Revolt and the Legacy of Disintegration	9
2	1939–1945: Times of Confusion and Stagnation	25
3	1945–1948: First Signs of Revival Before the Tempest	39
4	The War of 1948: The Nakba	85
5	From Nakba to Naksa: 1948–1967	141
6	In the Wake of the June 1967 Defeat	221
7	The Confrontation with Jordan	237
8	Establishing "Fatahland"	255
9	The PLO at Home and Abroad	263
10	In the Lebanese Maelstrom: Arafat Loses Ground	279
11	The Move to Tunisia	293
12	The First Intifada and Advancing Toward Oslo	315
13	The Oslo Accords: Leading Where?	331

14 The Struggle Between Fatah and Hamas   337
15 The Palestinians in the Whirlwind of the Arab Spring   347
    Afterword   361

List of Acronyms   363
Bibliography   365
Index   379
About the Book   399

Introduction

Most historians investigating the history of the Palestinian people begin their analyses with one of two major events in the annals of the Zionist-Arab conflict: the commencement of Jewish-Zionist immigration from Europe in 1882, or the Balfour Declaration and the promise given by the British to the Zionists in 1917 that they would assist efforts to construct a Jewish national homeland in Palestine. Recognition of these events as a focal point has at its root the assumption that the unique Palestinian national consciousness developed in response to the budding Zionist enterprise. Other historians choose starting points indicative of more authentic origins. One such option is the local revolt initiated in 1834, aimed against the tyrannical regime established in Palestine by Ibrahim Pasha, son of Egyptian ruler Muhammad 'Ali.[1] In a more far-reaching attempt, others identify Dahir al-'Umar, the eighteenth-century ruler of the Galilee, as the founder of the first "Palestinian national state."[2]

These scholars thus tie development of the modern Palestinian identity to that of the wider regional and modern Arab identity, a disputable viewpoint. We have no evidence that a nationalist Palestinian doctrine existed at these earlier times, whether declared or implied, nor evidence of intrinsic manifestations of local-nationalist identity, as distinguished from the affiliation with other parts of Greater Syria, Bilad al-Sham. On the contrary, contemporary sources show that feelings of alliance with the regional Ottoman system remained intact until the demise of the empire following World War I. This traditional Islamic sense of identification was retained during the prewar years, increasingly manifested by conspicuous displays of Arab consciousness, which evolved despite the policy of "Turkification" introduced by the Young Turks. Many contemporary pioneers of Arabism and Palestinian consciousness were in fact Arabic-speaking Christians, whose ties to the Muslim Ottoman Empire had been shaky to begin with.

It is indeed possible to recognize the initial development of both an Arab and a Palestinian modern identity as occurring in the transition between the nineteenth and twentieth centuries. The Arab dimension of this identity evolved as an inseparable part of shifts occurring in the entire region, and the local Palestinian dimension as a result of unique problems involving Palestine and the growing conflict with the Zionist movement. The first signs of this local dimension included, among other things, the emergence of exceptional modern newspapers, *Al-Karmil*, established in Haifa in 1908 by Najib Nassar, and *Filastin*, established by cousins 'Issa Daoud al-'Issa and Yusuf Hanna al-'Issa in Jaffa in 1911. The newspapers' names reflect familiarity with the scenery of the homeland. Articles published in these and similar newspapers reveal the gradual formation of a Palestinian consciousness, in acknowledgment of the threat posed by Jewish immigration to Palestine and its Arab residents.[3] Jewish immigrants, arriving in the second immigration that began in 1904, declared goals of "conquering the land" and "conquering labor." These declarations undoubtedly contributed to the consolidation of an Arab movement based on nationalist, local-patriotic, *watani* foundations.[4] At this point, an Arab-Palestinian national consciousness began to develop, and it has continued to motivate its adherents to this very day. From the beginning, these sentiments were anchored in pan-regional Arab identity, and so they remain. The Arab dimension of the Palestinian entity derived both from its purely historical-cultural affiliation and from its need for support from the Arab world in its battle for Palestine. The history of the Palestinians in the twentieth century manifests a gradually changing emphasis from pan-Arab to uniquely Palestinian, a shift facilitated by the permutations of the fight for Palestine and deeply affected by intrinsic transformations, both social and political in nature.

It is possible to contend that in the years prior to World War I only a fairly limited number of intellectuals possessed this complex, modern national identity. The working classes were the first to come into contact with Zionist immigrants, but they probably interpreted the threat inherent in the presence of the newcomers in traditional terms of protecting the pan-Islamic and pan-Arab region. After the war an Arab government was established in Damascus, headed by Faisal Ibn al-Husayn and leaders of the Arab revolt, resulting in the enhancement of modern Arab aspects among the intelligentsia and the elite. Faisal's supporters, who were made up, among others, of Palestinians, recognized Palestine as the southern part of Greater Syria, and many local Palestinians deferred to the government in Damascus. This is evident from the newspaper *Surya al-Janubiyya*, published at the time in Jerusalem, not the least from its name (Southern Syria). Newspaper names regularly reflected the spirit of the times and the different emphases of the new modern identity. Aside from *Surya al-Janubiyya*, edited by 'Arif al-'Arif and Hasan al-Budayri, another newspaper published in Jerusalem during these years was *Mir'at al-Sharq* (Mirror of the East) edited by Boulos Shihada. The newspaper reflected a general Eastern sense of identity, seeking to blur ethnic-national and religious differences between all residents of the East. The Palestinian local-patriotic dimension was consistently manifested by the newspaper *Filastin*, which renewed its publication after World War I, edited by 'Issa al-'Issa. The names of new organizations, for example, the Muslim-Christian Associations and the Arab Palestinian General Congress, were another mark of the newly forming modern Arab-Palestinian identity. In addition to its association with pan-Arabism, and its contemporary Damascus focus, the Palestinian entity derived some of its motivation from objection to the Balfour Declaration, the assurances it gave, and its threat to the future of Palestine. As early as 1918, members of the Muslim-Christian Association in Jaffa voiced a "protest against the aspirations of the Jews" and a submission of the Arabs' demands. The "protest" included statements specifically emphasizing the uniqueness of the Arab population of Palestine and the fundamental connection of this population to the land as a disparate territory: "Palestine, the homeland of our fathers."[5]

The emphasis on any one dimension of the Arab-Palestinian (or Palestinian-Arab) identity has always been related to social, political, and strategic processes within Palestinian society. With the beginning of the British Mandate in 1920 and the internationally distinct political definition of Palestine, the Arabs of Palestine abandoned the idea of Greater Syria and a pan-Eastern identity. From this point on they gradually became focused on the Arab-Palestinian identity, increasingly stressing the national dimension. A glance at books published in this period, primarily educational textbooks, shows that most of the writers used the name "Palestine" and defined its Arab residents as "Palestinians." For example, 1923 saw the publication of Husayn Rawhi's book *Concise Geography of Palestine*.[6] Educator Khalil al-Sakakini published a *History of Palestine following the Great War* in 1925.[7] Two other educators, 'Umar al-Salih al-Barghuti and Khalil Tawtah, composed a *History of Palestine*.[8] They wrote in the introduction, "In attempting to document the history of Palestine we fulfill the duty of each and every person to learn the history of his country and his nation before studying that of others."[9]

In the political sphere as well, institutions and organizations emphasizing national identity and its Arab and Palestinian dimensions were established in the 1920s. While the British attempted to address the Arab population of Palestine as a conglomerate of variegated religious groups, this approach was countered by the nonspecific Muslim-Christian Associations, precursors of the Arab Palestinian General Congress (al-Mu'tamar al-'Arabi al-Filastini al-'Am).[10] Members of the Executive Arab Committee, an organization demanding recognition of the nationalist ideology and its rights, headed by Mousa Kathim al-Husayni, were chosen from among this congress. Although the British never acknowledged the Executive Arab Committee (as they did its rival, the Jewish Agency), they did occasionally hold dialogues with its president and members, and some say that it was indeed recognized de facto.

Under the new circumstances formed by the British Mandate, in light of the conflict with Zionism and with no autonomous, official governmental Arab systems (which existed in other Arab countries), the Palestinian-Arab national movement found it difficult to become stabilized. The family-based factions of the traditional elite became further entrenched, hampering attempts at founding a modern system. These conflicting factions had existed for many years but were dormant during the late Ottoman period and reemerged in force during the first decade of the British Mandate. The British encouraged traditional factionalism and rivalries between the families of the elite. In 1921, the British authorities initiated the Muslim Higher Council, an organization created to provide religious leadership, which they then proceeded to recognize as representing the Arabs of Palestine, as opposed to the Executive Arab Committee, which was a nationalist organization. The Muslim Higher Council succeeded in aggravating the factionalism. British authorities directed the Nashashibi-led group to municipal positions and awarded the rival Husayni-led group precedence on the religious council. In 1912 Haj Amin al-Husayni was appointed mufti of Jerusalem, and a year later he became head of the Muslim Higher Council. This set in motion the development of strong rivalries and factionalism at the expense of modern national forms of organization.

The elements of national politics introduced by families of the Palestinian elite, together with the relative stability enjoyed in the region and in the world in general in the 1920s, helped calm matters during this decade. However, with the transition to the 1930s a new era began. Facing the crises emerging both globally and regionally, the existential need to form modern organs of a national movement—political parties, popular committees, journals, and armed units—arose once again. This coincided with a process of social change that strengthened Arab sentiments at the expense of local Palestinian identity. Establishment of the al-Istiqlal (Independence) Party (officially in 1932, but unofficially as early as 1930) marked the advent of a new generation of intellectuals becoming active in national politics, most originating from the middle class. This generation began developing a modern political system as an alternative to the old elite with its family-based rivalries. In contrast to the hegemony of the 1920s elite, the 1930s generation espoused a new national agenda in which a more patent attempt was made to use concepts incorporating pan-Arab modern unity. Efforts to achieve liberation from British rule replaced the apportioning of positions under British patronage.

In addition, the Zionist-Palestinian conflict in the 1930s deteriorated and became more violent. Fortification of the Jewish settlement by waves of immigrants escaping declining circumstances in Europe, in addition to impoverished conditions in Arab villages due to the economic crisis, led the extensive lower classes of Palestinian society to begin taking part in political activities from the onset of this decade. The new members were mostly organized in armed bands that operated clandestinely and attacked British and Jewish targets. The one leader most identified with the attempts of villagers and members of the urban proletariat to take to arms and terrorize their opponents was Shaikh 'Izz al-Din al-Qassam. Born in Syria in 1881, al-Qassam was a teacher at the Islamic School in Haifa and a preacher and imam at a local mosque. He was killed on November

19, 1935, in a battle with British forces near Jenin. He has remained a symbol, not only of armed participation of popular groups in Palestinian politics but also of the development of political Islam as an additional dimension and component of the Palestinian movement.

The history of the Palestinian people in the twentieth century was shaped by three triangles. One was external, and consisted of Britain (and the other superpowers), prestate Zionism and the State of Israel, and the Arab world, encompassing Arab countries and their vested interests. The second triangle relates to aspects of national identity: the pan-regional Arab dimension, the national Palestinian dimension, and the political Islamic dimension. The third triangle is social and intrinsic: the veteran, traditional family-based elite, the intellectual middle class that entered politics mainly from the 1930s, and working-class groups whose young armed representatives burst into the political sphere at crucial junctures, taking advantage of both traditional and modern leadership. These triangles remained in force throughout the modern history of the Palestinian people, albeit in different contexts and with different players, in light of the changing political and historical circumstances.

The 1936–1939 revolt, which is summarized in the next chapter of this book, was the first episode to demonstrate the relationship between these elements and their disastrous outcome for the Palestinian people. In the rest of the book I discuss processes that occurred subsequently, from the defeat of 1948 and the creation of a Palestinian diaspora, to attempts—led mainly by the Fatah movement—to reconstruct an independent modern Palestinian and secular Arab national movement. My analysis focuses on the efforts of the Palestinian people to become united and free, while becoming entangled in internal rivalries; the conflict with Israel; and the paternalistic and interest-based involvement of the Arab countries.

The book's final chapters discuss a new phase in the history of the Palestinian national movement in terms of active strategies and operative mechanisms. Land Day, which was initiated by the Palestinian citizens of Israel in late March 1976, was an early development heralding the reintroduction of popular civil disobedience over land issues to the operative mechanisms of the movement, as had occurred during the general strike of April–October 1936. This element received still greater emphasis following the outbreak of the First Palestinian Intifada in December 1987. As in the case of the general strike of 1936, the First Intifada emerged from below and forced the senior political leadership to jump on the bandwagon when it felt that the rug of leadership was being pulled out from under it. The Palestine Liberation Organization (PLO) had been expelled from Beirut and relocated to Tunis, whence it regarded the return to Palestine as further away than ever. Now it found itself struggling tooth and nail to preserve its preeminent status in the leadership of the Palestinian national struggle. Its efforts to do so drew it into the whirlwind of the intifada, creating an oppositional dynamic of external leadership versus leadership on the ground.

The tension between the new generation of intifada leaders in the occupied territories and the old guard in Tunis on the one hand, and the meteoric rise of the Islamist stream on the other hand, generated pressure on the senior leadership. This pressure, in conjunction with Arafat's international isolation after his support of Saddam Hussein in Iraq's war against the United States in 1991, caused the PLO leadership, with Arafat at the helm, to begin to display greater flexibility and to enter into secret negotiations with Israel in the Norwegian capital city of Oslo, culminating in the signing of the Oslo Accords on the White House lawn in September 1993. This process resulted in the mutual recognition of the PLO and Israel and paved the way for Arafat's return to the occupied territories and the establishment of the Palestinian Authority in May 1994. Although this maneuver liberated Arafat from isolation and provided a profound resolution to the tension existing between the leadership in Tunis and the leadership in the occupied territories, it failed to curb the Hamas-led Islamist stream's rise to a position of influence and to prevent it from challenging the PLO's three decades of nearly complete control of the Palestinian national movement. Arafat's death in November 2004 also contributed to the increasing power of Hamas, which reached its height in the group's victory in the parliamentary elections of January 2006. From that point on, all-out war was waged between the PLO, which controlled the West Bank, and Hamas, which set up a government of its own in the Gaza Strip. In the course of these events, through bloody street battles, Hamas forcefully ejected members of the PLO and its security forces from the Gaza Strip.

These developments brought the Palestinian national movement to an unprecedented low point. It now emerged as a deeply divided movement facing continued Israeli control of most of the West Bank; Israeli reinforcement of existing settlements and the establishment of new settlements that, over time, have made the idea of a Palestinian state unfeasible; and a delicate international situation that does not serve Palestinian interests and that precludes the possibility of American pressure on Israel, which is currently ruled by a right-wing government. Even the events of the Arab Spring failed to improve the situation of the Palestinians and actually made it more difficult in some Arab countries with large concentrations of Palestinian refugees, such as Syria. In conclusion, the Palestinian yearning for a fully autonomous independent state appears to be an aspiration that will remain unfulfilled for the foreseeable future.

Notes

1. See, for example, Kimmerling and Migdal, *Palestinim, 'Am Behivazruto* [Palestinians: The Making of a People].
2. See, for example, "The Palestinian national movement developed in resistance to Ottoman rule, and was headed for eighty years by Dahir al-'Umar and his sons," Palestinian National Information Center, http://www.pnic.gov.ps.
3. On the role of the press in forming a national consciousness in this period, see Kabha, *Palestinian Press*, ix–xiii.
4. See Rashid Khalidi, *Palestinian Identity*.
5. Zu'aytir, *Watha'iq al-Haraka al-Wataniyya al-Filastiniyya, Min Awraq Akram Zu'aytir* [Documents of the Palestinian National Movement: From the Papers of Akram Zu'aytir], 1.
6. Rawhi, *Al-Mukhtasar fi Gughrafiyyat Filastin* [Concise Geography of Palestine].
7. Al-Sakakini, *Filastin Ba'd al-Harb al-'Uthma* [Palestine After the Great War].
8. Al-Barghouti and Tawtah, *Tarih Filastin* [History of Palestine].
9. Al-Barghouti and Tawtah, *Tarih Filastin* [History of Palestine], 5.
10. The congress was part of the General Syrian Congress, and it received its new name once the concept of "Greater Syria" gradually diminished and was replaced by that of "Palestine for the Palestinians."

1

The 1936–1939 Revolt and the Legacy of Disintegration

The Palestinian revolt of 1936–1939, in Palestinian terms the Great Palestinian Revolt (Thawrat Filastin al-Kubra), is considered one of the most important events affecting the emergence of the Palestinian people and national movement to date.[1] It is possible to distinguish four stages in the history of the revolt: the general strike, diplomatic efforts, the height of the revolt, and finally, the stage of disintegration.

April–October 1936: General Strike

During the first stage of the revolt—the general strike—the local Arab population ceased all economic, trade, and transportation activities. Some of the younger intellectual leaders, assisted by Arab volunteers, organized modern guerrilla warfare against the British and the Jews.

The strike was instigated by national committees organized specifically for this purpose and consisted mainly of members of the al-Istiqlal (Independence) Party, hailing from the intermediate generation and representative of the new intelligentsia.[2] Committee activists tried to shape Palestinian public opinion and to direct the course of the strike through announcements and newspaper articles.[3] The veteran Palestinian leadership joined the action only about two weeks after the events began, aroused by the national committees and their initial success in inciting the public to strike. Once the leadership had joined, an inclusive political organization was established, named the Arab Higher Committee (al-Lajna al-'Arabiyya al-'Ulya), consisting of the leaders of the two veteran rival camps, the Husaynis and the Nashashibis, both prominent, elite clans. The activities of the Arab Higher Committee throughout the strike reflected a time of maximal internal consensus within the Palestinian national movement. However, the strike (and the "honeymoon") lasted only several months, ending when Arab leaders appealed to the Palestinians to desist, in return for negotiations with the British on the future of Palestine. This followed the recommendations of the Palestine Royal Commission (also known as the Peel Commission), which the British dispatched to Palestine in the fall of 1936.[4]

During the final two months of the strike, the Palestinians, reinforced by volunteers from neighboring Arab countries, who were led by Fawzi al-Qawiqji, engaged in an unsuccessful attempt to combine civil rebellion with guerrilla warfare. The volunteer force was deployed in the mountainous area of the Large Triangle, encompassing Nablus, Jenin, and Tulkarm. On September 3, an ambush was planned against the British at the Bal'a Junction (east of Tulkarm). Guerrilla forces cut off a British column of armored vehicles, causing losses and even shooting down airplanes that came to the rescue. However, in three other battles, which took place in the vicinity shortly afterward, the British succeeded in destroying much of Qawiqji's forces. The remaining guerrillas were maneuvered eastward toward the Tubas Valley, and from there retreated, crossing the Jordan River and leaving the country in mid-October 1936.

October 1936–July 1937: Diplomatic Efforts

The second stage of the revolt was characterized by numerous diplomatic efforts, eventually culminating in the Palestinian rejection of the Peel Commission's plan to divide the country. Initial rifts began appearing in the façade of solidarity displayed throughout the general strike. The main problems stemmed from two major coalitions formed in the interim. The first coalition joined young intellectuals, mostly from prominent urban (*a'yan*) and rural families, with field operatives belonging to the national committees, who represented intellectual and popular groups in the cities and villages. This coalition fell apart when intellectuals and members of the lower classes objected to the conduct of their allies (members of the bourgeoisie and the urban aristocracy), accusing them of joining forces with the senior leadership in Jerusalem and preferring their own agendas to those of the people. They also blamed them for agreeing to cease striking in response to the appeal of neighboring Arab rulers.[5] The assassination attempt on Fakhri al-Nashashibi, a nephew of Raghib al-Nashashibi—leader of the National Defense Party (Hizb al-Difa' al-'Arabi) and a major activist and organizer of the general strike—provided proof of the coalition's demise.[6]

Immediately prior to publication of the Palestine Royal Commission's recommendations, Palestinian opinion shapers accused Fakhri of "betraying the national cause," by "collaborating with Britain and the Zionist Movement" and "deviating from the ranks of national solidarity."[7] Such accusations were leveled at many other activists as well, mainly from the Nashashibi camp, or affiliated families, including Hasan Sidqi al-Dajani, attorney Mustafa Irshid, and attorney Mahmoud al-Madi. Many of those denounced as traitors had been influential in organizing the strike; for example, attorneys who volunteered to appear in court and represent those arrested by the British. Nonetheless, their association with the "opposition" (al-mu'arada), and their willingness to accept the recommendations of the Palestine Royal Commission and the partition plan it proposed, put them at risk of being targeted by supporters of Mufti Haj Amin al-Husayni and of al-Istiqlal. The criticism rapidly deteriorated to assassination attempts. Some of those denounced were forced to flee to Syria and Lebanon.

The dissolution of the first coalition led to the disintegration of the alliance between the Husaynis and the Nashashibis. Prior to publication of the Palestine Royal Commission's recommendations, the Nashashibis had initiated a process of withdrawal from the Arab Higher Committee. They were evidently aware of the commission report's main points, and they must have calculated that a majority of the committee would be unable to consent to them. The historian Muhammad 'Izzat Darwaza claims that this decision was coordinated with Emir Abdullah of Transjordan.[8] Indeed, in early July 1937, the Nashashibis' National Defense Party announced its withdrawal from the Arab Higher Committee. Now the rift between the camps widened. Members of the National Defense Party, as well as Emir Abdullah, were generally vilified, adding to the existing animosity and foiling any future possibility of cooperation between the two camps. Haj Amin maintained his control of the Arab Higher Committee despite the Nashashibis' withdrawal, which in fact served to reinforce the alliance between the Husaynis and al-Istiqlal.

August 1937–September 1938: The Height of the Revolt

During the third stage of the revolt, the armed conflict escalated. Many armed bands were created during the first two months after dissolution of the Arab Higher Committee. Dozens of fighter cells, each numbering about fifteen guerrillas, emerged throughout the country, from Safed in the north to Gaza and the Negev in the south.[9] Some had formed during Qawiqji's operations in the country (August 26 to October 13, 1936) and some were initiated by Shaikh 'Izz al-Din al-Qassam before the revolt broke out. Most of the band chiefs came from the villages and often lacked military training but nonetheless filled the void created in the absence of a supreme political leadership and the de facto elimination of modern guerrilla warfare. In late September 1937, following the assassination by Arab guerrillas of Lewis Andrews, British district commissioner for the Galilee, and until the mufti's escape to Lebanon, all remaining members of the Arab Higher Committee were arrested or deported. The young intellectual leadership was unable to fill this void. Some left the country and followed the mufti; others were branded traitors due to their willingness to accept the recommendations of the Peel Commission. At this point, the band chiefs assumed leadership of the entire Arab population, at first in the villages and then in the urban sector as well, where they became a major force in the summer of 1938.[10] The country was divided into regions, each headed by a regional commander (*qa'id mintaqa*) in charge of the band chiefs. The entire system was headed by the supreme commander of the revolt, 'Abd al-Rahim al-Haj Muhammad, who led from the spring of 1938 until his death in March 1939.

The major regional commanders (from north to south) included the following:

- Khalil al-'Issa (Abu Ibrahim al-Kabir) and Tawfiq al-Ibrahim (Abu Ibrahim al-Saghir) of Lower Galilee, Tiberias, and the northern valleys
- Fawzi Rashid, 'Abdallah al-Sha'ir, and 'Abdallah al-Asbah of Safed and the vicinity
- Yusuf Abu Durra and 'Atiyya 'Awad of the Carmel and Wadi 'Ara
- 'Arif 'Abd al-Raziq of the Large Triangle (Jenin, Nablus, and Tulkarm)
- 'Ali Hasan Salameh of the central region (Jaffa, Lydda, and Ramle)
- 'Abd al-Halim al-Julani of Hebron and Beer Sheva
- 'Abd al-Qadir al-Husayni of Jerusalem and the vicinity[11]

The leaders of the revolt established an independent court system as an alternative to that of the British Mandate government. It consisted of a five-member supreme court, headed by retired judge Salim 'Abd al-Hadi, and regional courts headed by approximately twenty-five judges.[12] There was also a "higher committee" located in Damascus and called the Holy Jihad Committee. Members of this committee were made up of activists from both the Husaynis and the Istiqlalis: Ishaq Darwish, Mu'in al-Madi, Akram Zu'aytir, Muhammad 'Izzat Darwaza, Khalil al-'Issa, and for a while, Jamal al-Husayni as well. The committee dealt with matters of recruitment, munitions, and supplies and ruled on complex legal issues referred to it by the courts of the revolt.[13]

During this period of revolution, a pattern emerged that would repeat itself throughout the history of the Palestinian people; it took the form of a leadership in exile directing activities through a "leadership in the field." In this specific case the format proved inefficient. Tensions among activists in the field promptly surfaced, as well as disagreements with the Holy Jihad Committee in Damascus and the mufti's entourage in Lebanon. The relationship between these organizations was often characterized by conflicting directives, personal contests, and internecine clashes between clans. The situation rapidly became violent and a bloody struggle ensued, involving liquidations that mainly targeted the opposition camp and those accused of acting "in contradiction to the nation's interests," for example, by the sale and transfer of land to Jewish institutions or collaboration with the British Mandate authorities and the exposure of rebels.[14] Thus a new state of affairs was created. While the revolt had initially been characterized by attacks against British and Jewish targets, now these were often aimed at parts of the Palestinian population as well, which were originally intended to be a supportive home front, providing refuge and assistance.

This decline was worsened by heavy British pressure on the Palestinian population, manifested by the operation of emergency regulations, as well as oppressive individual and collective sanctions imposed on entire villages and families.[15] The simultaneous British and internal pressures led to the emergence of Palestinian forces objecting to the revolt, mainly in families targeted by the fighting bands. The British encouraged opposition to the revolt and organized objectors in armed groups called "peace bands" (*fasa'il al-salam*).[16]

Fall 1938–Mid-1939: Disintegration

The fourth and final stage began with the establishment of these peace bands headed by Fakhri al-Nashashibi and Fakhri 'Abd al-Hadi (previously Qawiqji's deputy and a senior commander of the armed bands). Internecine clashes between the rebels and the peace bands created a hostile environment for the rebels in their home court. The situation deteriorated to a murderous civil war, caused grievous harm to the effectiveness of the revolt, and eventually brought about its demise. All this was accompanied by British military pressure on both the rebel bands and on the villages that continued to provide the rebels with support. The British, assisted by the peace bands, pursued the rebels and attacked them in their hill-based hiding places. The number of deserters gradually rose and the rebels' operations and hiding places were revealed. Toward the end of 1938 and early 1939 the rebels became less competent and many of the band chiefs left the country. In March 1939 the rebel forces received a blow from which they never recovered: the commander of the revolt since spring 1938, 'Abd al-Rahim al-Haj Muhammad, was killed in the village of Sanur upon returning from Syria to reorganize the forces.[17] His death led to complete disintegration. Entire bands deserted and joined the opposition, and the remaining chiefs, among them Yusuf Abu Durra, 'Arif 'Abd al-Raziq, and Hassan Salameh, fled the country. Even the appointment of a new commander did not put an end to the general deterioration. Finally, in late 1939, the few bands remaining in the mountainous areas ceased all activity.

Legacy of the Revolt

Although the Palestinians did not benefit politically from the revolt of 1936–1939 (in terms of the White Paper of 1939), and the final stages of the revolt are considered a traumatic event in collective Palestinian recollection, its legacy has nonetheless inspired the efforts of the Palestinian people ever since. It created a course of action, national rhetoric, and symbols, later utilized in future phases of the Palestinian national struggle, in operations of the Palestine Liberation Organization (PLO), and in the First and Second Intifadas.

The Failed Leadership of Mufti Haj Amin al-Husayni

The aftermath of the revolt continued to affect the strategic decisions of the Palestinians up to the Arab-Israeli War of 1948, and possibly even until the present. One example of the inadequacy of the revolt's leaders may be seen in the conduct of the Palestinian national movement's figurehead and prominent leader, Mufti Haj Amin al-Husayni. Two major errors were indicative of his narrow outlook, his focus on self-interests, and his incorrect appraisal of the situation and balance of powers.

First, his flight from the country and his attempt to control the battle from his location in Lebanon, as well as the disintegration of the Arab Higher Committee, which he headed, left the Palestinian people with no guiding leader. Moreover, even from afar, the mufti attempted, through violence and intimidation, to prevent anyone else from filling the void created by his departure. In addition, he encouraged exclusive dependence on his own camp and suppression of the opposition. When Haj Amin fled the country, he resumed his former position as leader of the Husayni camp and was no longer perceived as the leader of all Palestinians, a role he had succeeded in attaining during the general strike and the establishment of the Arab Higher Committee.

Second, the mufti's inflexibility and his inability to modify the goals of the revolt led to further errors. The two main goals of the revolt—to uproot four hundred thousand Jews from the country and to terminate the British Mandate—were unrealistic when considering the balance of powers. He did not take into account the Palestinians' inadequacy in comparison to the well-organized Jewish settlement and British power. Haj Amin misjudged the situation and was not able to exploit it to the people's benefit, in compensation for their perceived pain, sacrifice, and suffering. He was completely unwilling to accept a partial success, even if this could have been considered a substantial achievement. After the partition proposal presented by the Peel Commission in 1937, the mufti and his doctrine also led the Arabs to reject the White Paper of May 1939, in which Britain, in all respects, withdrew its support of a Jewish national home and imposed restrictions on Jewish immigration to Palestine. Instead, the mufti chose to take on both the British Empire and the Zionist movement simultaneously. This resulted in enhanced British-Jewish cooperation and facilitated the process of mobilization and the arming of the Jewish settlement, which would have crucial consequences in the Arab-Israeli War of 1948.[18]

Leadership Clash and Social Schisms

The revolt ended with disastrous results, manifested mainly in two spheres: the political and the socioeconomic. At the end of the revolt the Palestinian people were left with no locally based political leadership. The mufti, who had fled the country in the fall of 1937, orchestrated events from Lebanon, and later from Baghdad, Rome, and Berlin—focusing on directing Palestine-based activists from his camp to employ violence against local opponents. After the murder of Lewis Andrews, the British commissioner of the Galilee, in late September 1937, the British banned the Arab Higher Committee, and its members were arrested and deported. Only a handful of minor activists remained in Palestine, and these were forced to cooperate with the polarized and disintegrating military leadership, which controlled the Arab population using intimidation and violence.

During the years of revolt, social processes that had gathered momentum in the 1920s and early 1930s came to a standstill. The most significant of these developments was the urbanization along the coastline, mainly in the vicinity of Jaffa and Haifa. Young people from rural villages who had flocked to the suburbs of these two cities in the early 1930s, as a result of the economic crisis and decline of the rural economy, began returning to their villages at the outset of the revolt. These young people formed the core of the fighting bands that assumed leadership of the revolt, driven by their economic troubles and the ideological consciousness they had acquired in the cities, mainly from Muslim or communist activists. When they took command of the population, at first in the rural sector and in 1938 in the cities as well, tensions and social conflicts emerged. The rise of these young leaders, particularly uneducated villagers, aroused the resentment of prominent urban families and even wealthy rural familics. The new forces asserted their control using violence, which extended to settling scores and resolving their own personal and social conflicts with the upper classes.

Palestinian scholar May Sayqali summarized the situation in Haifa during this period:

> Most of the notable figures from Haifa belonging to the radical (Husayni) camp were in exile, and thus the fellahin and lower classes assumed control. These circumstances reduced the available pool of experienced leaders and all responsibility was transferred to fellahin with fewer organizational skills from a political and social perspective. In fact, the fellahin had almost complete control of the revolt, while the urban middle-class bourgeoisie and lower class had minimal influence. The impact of urban radical nationalists on the revolt amounted to mere words and organizational support and they took almost no part in the actual fighting.[19]

A common consequence of fellahin subordination of the cities was their socially based, disparaging attitude toward local residents. The situation reached a climax when men in the cities were forced to wear the kaffiyeh and agal, the traditional head covering of the fellahin, instead of the contemporary urban fez headgear. Revolt commanders justified the edict as an operational necessity, aimed at making the rebels more difficult to spot, but city locals were certain that its ultimate purpose was their humiliation. The "new rulers" aroused sectarian tensions in the rural sector as well, creating deep schisms within the social fabric. Nimr Murqus, a communist-affiliated intellectual from the village of Yassif in the Galilee, described the problem:

> Large landowners and the urban aristocracy, forced to fund the purchase of weapons for the rebels—their servants and hired laborers in normal times—were concerned about both the English and the

rebels, for whom they displayed forced empathy. In our village, for example, they would secretly ridicule the rebels, and they called the revolt "the butt revolt" (thawrat 'akkuz). 'Akuz was the name of a man who worked as a simple plowman for Abu Turki, and who was one of the first to join the revolt.[20]

Some of the new leaders of the revolt strove to amass money and become wealthy, often by confiscating the property of affluent people who had fled the country. Muhammad 'Izzat Darwaza, a member of the revolt's Central Jihad Committee, relates in his memoirs the story of the commander of the central region, 'Ali Hassan Salameh. Salameh had apparently taken over the orchard of Raghib al-Imam, who was out of the country at the time, renting it to others for 350 Palestine pounds.[21] Darwaza accused some of the band chiefs, whose families had been wealthy under the Ottomans, of attempting to restore their former status. As examples, Darwaza mentioned Fawzi Jarrar, from the village of Sanur, and Nayif Zu'bi, from the village of Sulam, who had been active in the Zu'biyya villages of the Ibn 'Amer Valley.[22]

The rampant disagreements and conflicts during the period of revolt had a disastrous effect on Palestinian society, tearing it apart and causing irreparable damage. British sanctions further aggravated the situation. Consequently, recently emerging modernization processes came to a halt, resulting in the collapse of systems that would have had the potential to unite Palestinian society.

The Revolt in Palestinian Recollection and Historiography

Palestinian writers and historians may be divided into two major groups, according to their views and assessments of the 1936–1939 revolt. The first group encompasses those who experienced the events firsthand, some even helping shape them. The second group consists of professional historians and critical writers.

Firsthand Accounts

The first group consists of authors such as Mufti Haj Amin al-Husayni, Akram Zu'aytir, Muhammad 'Izzat Darwaza, and others.

Their writings express a common contention: the Palestinians acted correctly and did their duty; however, they were up against stronger and larger forces—Britain, the Zionist movement, and even some of the Arab countries—which decided their fate and prevented the Palestinians from enjoying the fruits of their efforts. The mufti expressed such sentiments in his book *The Truth Concerning the Palestinian Problem*:

> Any seeker of the truth will recognize that the Palestinian jihad warriors (mujahedin) were undefeated on the battleground, although fighting a guerrilla war against both Jews and English simultaneously, which they did to the best of their ability. . . . The guerrilla war, which was based on self-sacrifice, devotion, and bravery, enabled the Palestinians to keep their enemies on edge for a lengthy period and to cause them significant losses. The Palestinian jihad movement succeeded during 1936–1939 in taking over most of the Palestinian lands, aside from a small number of cities—where the English soldiers were besieged for a not insignificant period of time in anticipation of reinforcements.[23]

The mufti obviously ignored his own conduct and that of his men during the revolt, the internal killings within the Palestinian camp, and mainly, the Palestinians' inflexibility in defining their goals and finding ways of achieving them. Akram Zu'aytir, in contrast, noted some deficiencies in his diary, but not before praising the revolt and rejecting accusations leveled against its leaders:

> Our great revolt has undoubtedly come to an end, perhaps only for the time being, as all circumstances have united to bring it to a conclusion. Who would have believed that Palestine could persist in its revolt for three years? Thousands of victims sacrificed themselves for the homeland, tens of thousands were arrested and exiled and hundreds of houses destroyed. I believe that no other nation as small as the Palestinian nation has made such sacrifices for its cause . . . but I cannot ignore some "negative" issues that disfigured the revolt in its final stages at the expense of public sympathy. I must stress that these "negative" issues did not exist at the first stage of the revolt, that is, during the great historical strike supported by the entire population, with no exceptions. The major issue in this respect was the inability of the supreme political leadership to prevent the rebels, or those posing as leaders of the revolt, from

implementing a policy of liquidation. I find no justification for assassinating those who were unquestionably loyal to their people.[24]

Zu'aytir tried to assign all responsibility for the "negative issues" to the supreme political leadership, that is, the mufti, and to exonerate himself and his al-Istiqlal colleague 'Izzat Darwaza.[25] Attempts to clear Haj Amin and his accomplices of responsibility for the failure of the revolt continued into the 1960s, 1970s, and 1980s. They diminished slightly in the mid-1980s—perhaps influenced by the PLO—but toward the end of the decade and into the 1990s, additional attempts were made to absolve Haj Amin as a historical symbol and as a primary national leader.[26]

Professional and Critical Accounts

The second group of writers encompasses professional historians and critical left-wing writers. Their approach is characterized by praise for the people's conduct, their sacrifices and suffering during the revolt, and sharp criticism of the leadership's conduct, which they portray as reactionary-sectarian. This group includes 'Abd al-Wahab al-Kayyali, Bayan Nuwayhid al-Hout, Kamil Mahmoud Khalla, Boulos Farah, Salih 'Abd al-Jawad, and Ilyas Shufani. Al-Kayyali, for example, summarizes the outcome of the revolt as follows:

> The failure of the Palestinian revolt in the late 1930s was unavoidable, for which there are many reasons, primarily the disproportionate balance of powers between the Palestinians and their foes. The destitute, undeveloped, tiny Palestinian nation had no chance of prevailing in its fight against a coalition consisting of the British Empire and its awesome military power teamed with international Zionism and its political and financial influence, as well as the power of the Jewish settlers who were well organized and equipped with modern arms and a visionary leadership.[27]

The writer describes the Palestinian leadership:

> The leadership of the Palestinian people did not prove capable of coping with its challenges. It was characterized by narrow-mindedness, personal ambition, and submissiveness. It provided no real response to the comprehensive support provided by the British to the Zionist movement. . . . Rather, the Palestinian political lead-

ership perpetuated sectarian conflicts and objected to mobilizing the general public in a revolutionary format, a format that could have suited the confrontation with Zionism and colonialism.[28]

Salih 'Abd al-Jawad offers a summary of the failure of the revolt:

> The Palestinian national movement emerged from the battles mortally wounded; many were killed, entire neighborhoods destroyed. Haj Amin left the country following British attempts to have him arrested, most of the rural military leaders were killed, and the political leaders opted for a life in exile or were deported. The Palestinian economy, which had been no equal to its Jewish counterpart to begin with, was grievously harmed.[29]

The extent of historical interest and discussion concerning the revolt of 1936–1939 in subsequent years has corresponded directly to the level of tension surrounding the Arab-Israeli conflict. Periods of aggravation have seen more discussion of the revolt, both as a source of inspiration and as a lesson for contemporary times. The revolt's ultimate failure and the damage it caused notwithstanding, its legacy, symbols, and slogans have remained a cornerstone of Palestinian national rhetoric to this very day.

Notes

1. The word *thawra* is usually translated as "revolution," although it means revolt. In Israeli historiography the revolt is called the Events of 5796–5799 (Me'ora'ot Tartsav-Tartzat), although in recent decades the term Arab Revolt has become more prevalent.

2. Al-Istiqlal is a party open to members of all clans and established by intellectuals in 1932.

3. See Kabha, "Tafkida shel ha'itonut ha'arvit hafalestinit be'irgun hashvita hafalestinit haklalit, April–October 1936" [The Role of the Palestinian Arab Press in Organizing the General Palestinian Strike].

4. On attempts at mediation by Arab leaders, see Porat, *Mimehumot Limrida, Hatnu'ah Hale'umit Ha'arvit Hafalestinit, 1929–1939* [From Unrest to Uprising: The Palestinian Arab National Movement], 238–258; Zu'aytir, *Yawmiyyat Akram Zu'aytir, 1935–1939* [From the Diary of Akram Zu'aytir], 174–175.

5. Akram Zu'aytir wrote an article to this effect in the Palestinian newspaper published in Cairo, *Al-Shabab* [The Young], February 22, 1937.

6. On the attempted assassination, see Darwaza, *Muzakkarat* [Memoirs], 2:415.

7. This was probably the source of the title Khawarij (Seceders) bestowed on those accused of treachery or of acting against the Palestinian national cause. This term has religious significance as well: the Khawarij were the first group to secede from the main sect of Islam.

8. Darwaza, *Muzakkarat* [Memoirs], 2:418.

9. Kabha and Sirhan, *'Abd al-Rahim al-Haj Muhammad, al-Qa'id al-'Aam Lethawrat 1936–1939* ['Abd al-Rahim al-Haj Muhammad, General Commander of the 1936–1939 Revolt], 18–22.

10. Kabha and Sirhan, *'Abd al-Rahim al-Haj Muhammad, al-Qa'id al-'Aam Lethawrat 1936–1939* ['Abd al-Rahim al-Haj Muhammad, General Commander of the 1936–1939 Revolt], 18–22.

11. Kabha and Sirhan, *'Abd al-Rahim al-Haj Muhammad, al-Qa'id al-'Aam Lethawrat 1936–1939* ['Abd al-Rahim al-Haj Muhammad, General Commander of the 1936–1939 Revolt], 23.

12. On the courts of the revolt, see Kabha, "Batey hadin shel hamered ha'arvi-falestini" [Courts of the Palestinian-Arab Revolt].

13. For more details, see Darwaza, *Muzakkarat* [Memoirs], 3:741–860.

14. Many such announcements are cited by Zu'aytir, *Watha'iq al-Haraka al-Wataniyya al-Filastiniyya, Min Awraq Akram Zu'aytir* [Documents of the Palestinian National Movement: From the Papers of Akram Zu'aytir], 473–648.

15. Zu'aytir, *Watha'iq al-Haraka al-Wataniyya al-Filastiniyya, Min Awraq Akram Zu'aytir* [Documents of the Palestinian National Movement: From the Papers of Akram Zu'aytir], 473–648.

16. On this, see Porat, *Mimehumot Limrida, Hatnu'ah Hale'umit Ha'arvit Hafalestinit, 1929–1939* [From Unrest to Uprising: The Palestinian Arab National Movement], 298–304; Swedenburg, *Memories of Revolt*, 138–170.

17. For additional details, see Kabha and Sirhan, *'Abd al-Rahim al-Haj Muhammad, al-Qa'id al-'Aam Lethawrat 1936–1939* ['Abd al-Rahim al-Haj Muhammad, General Commander of the 1936–1939 Revolt], 81–90n9.

18. Kimmerling and Migdal, *Palestinim, 'Am Behivazruto* [Palestinians: The Making of a People], 110–113.

19. Sayqali, *Hayfa al-'Arabiyya, 1918–1939, al-Tatawwur al-Ijtima'i wal-Iqtisadi* [Arab Haifa, 1918–1939: Social and Economic Development], 306.

20. Murqus, *Aqwq min al-Nisyan* [Stronger than Forgetting].

21. Darwaza, *Muzakkarat* [Memoirs], 3:785–786.

22. Darwaza, *Muzakkarat* [Memoirs], 3:756.

23. Al-Husayni, *Haqa'iq 'an Qadiyyat Filastin* [The Truth About the Issue of Palestine], 15.

24. Zu'aytir, *Yawmiyyat Akram Zu'aytir, 1935–1939* [From the Diary of Akram Zu'aytir], 611n4.

25. Zu'aytir, *Yawmiyyat Akram Zu'aytir, 1935–1939* [From the Diary of Akram Zu'aytir]. Zu'aytir and Darwaza were members of the Central Committee of the Jihad.

26. See, for example, Abu Shaqra, *Al-Haj Amin al-Husayni wa-Thawrat 1936–1939* [Al-Haj Amin al-Husayni and the Revolt of 1936–1939]; and Jarrar, *Al-Haj Amin al-Husayni, Ra'id Jihad wa-Batal Qadiyya* [Al-Haj Amin al-Husayni: Pioneer of the Jihad and Hero of the National Cause].

27. Al-Kayali, *Tarikh Filastin al-Hadith* [Modern History of Palestine], 313.

28. Al-Kayali, *Tarikh Filastin al-Hadith* [Modern History of Palestine], 314.

29. 'Abd al-Jawad, "Tatawwur al-nidal al-watani al-Filastini munzu bidayat al-istitan al-Suhuoni wahatta al-taqsim" [Development of the Palestinian National Struggle from the Beginning of Zionist Settlement Until the Partition Resolution], 489.

2

1939–1945: Times of Confusion and Stagnation

Following Mufti Haj Amin al-Husayni's escape from the country during the armed Palestinian revolt, and after the Arab Higher Committee rejected the White Paper published by the British government in 1939, all remaining Palestinian political activities were centered around the mufti's current place of residence, the first of which was the Lebanese town of Zuq Mikha'il, where Haj Amin fled in the fall of 1937. Later, in October 1939, he furtively escaped to Baghdad, and in May 1941, when the Rashid 'Ali al-Kilani coup in Iraq reached its dismal conclusion, the mufti embarked on a wandering journey that encompassed Rome, Tehran, and Berlin. After World War II, he continued on to Paris, Cairo, Gaza, Baghdad, and finally Alayh and Beirut.[1] By 1964—when the PLO had emerged and Haj Amin began his decline—each of these places in turn had served as the virtual capital of a demolished system (see Chapter 5 on the establishment of the PLO and the rivalry between Ahmad al-Shuqayri and Haj Amin).

The Mufti: Leading from Afar

Activists who claimed to serve as mediators between the Palestinian public and their leader flocked to the mufti's distant roving headquarters. They delivered messages to minor activists based in Palestine and assumed responsibility for implementing the mufti's instructions. In practice, these merely amounted to the rejection of any solution or compromise and to foiling attempts at forming an alternate leadership capable of challenging his exclusive control. The mediators employed persuasion and offered inducements, as well as physical and verbal threats aimed at any who criticized the mufti's policy and the methods exercised by his representatives.[2] Operatives who dared object to this policy were targeted. The mufti's men accused them of treachery and questioned their loyalty and morality, fomenting a great deal of bitterness among the opposition and affiliated population groups. In a proclamation printed in Jerusalem and distributed throughout the country in May 1939, the mufti was described as "a butcher who slaughters his people after blessing them in the name of God."[3]

With Britain's Enemies in Iraq

Following Haj Amin's arrival in Baghdad, he set out to organize the Palestinian exiles residing in the Iraqi capital and to establish a pan-Arab political party based on al-Istiqlal operatives, including Akram Zu'aytir, Darwish al-Miqdadi, and Mu'in al-Madi. These longtime Palestinian associates of Sati' al-Husri's pan-Arab educational-ideological enterprise in Iraq had extensive connections within the local population. Renowned pan-Arab operatives, such as brothers Nabih and 'Adel al-'Azma, Amin Ruwayha, and Sa'id Thabit, were also members of pan-Arab movements such as the Iraqi al-Muthanna Club and the Syrian National Action League (Lajnat al-'Amal al-Qawmi). In addition, they were affiliated with senior officers in the Iraqi army known for their pan-Arab views, headed by Salah al-Din al-Sabbagh and his colleagues Fahmi al-Sa'id, Mahmoud Salman, and Kamil Shabib, known as the Golden Square.[4] When Haj Amin arrived in Baghdad these connections facilitated its emergence as the center of Palestinian political operations. Thus began a process in which the Palestinian national movement relinquished its status as a unique local movement, *haraka wataniyya*, in favor of gradual assimilation within wider pan-Arab concerns and as an integral part of the "Arab problem" (*al-qadiyya al-'Arabiyya*). Two underlying causes motivated this process: the mufti's ambitions to become a pan-Arab and pan-regional leader and pan-Arab support of Iraq's struggle against Britain throughout the Fertile Crescent.

As a result of the mufti's involvement in the Iraqi pan-Arab coalition, the Palestinian exiles became allied with veteran politician Rashid 'Ali al-Kilani, one of the leaders of the Iraqi national movement and longtime supporter of pan-Arab ideology, as well as a distinct rival of Nuri al-Said, fellow Iraqi politician and statesman. This alliance was a contributing factor in the nomination of al-Kilani as prime minister of Iraq and in the promotion of his anti-British political approach over and against Nuri Said's conciliatory one. The British military invasion of Iraq in May 1941 prompted the Rashid 'Ali al-Kilani coup, headed by officers of the Iraqi army and their ally, Mufti al-Husayni. The Palestinian exiles played a significant role in this coup. Akram Zu'aytir, for example, wrote anti-British declarations, and Palestinians who had accumulated experience in the 1936–1939 revolt were integrated into Iraqi combat units.

Following the failure of the Rashid 'Ali al-Kilani coup and the flight of all senior personnel involved, the Palestinian leadership lost its base of operations in Iraq. In addition, the alliance with Iraqi army officers against the local Hashemite establishment resulted in a split between the Palestinian national movement and its former allies in Iraq and Transjordan. As a crucial consequence of this split, the Palestinian leadership aligned itself with the Axis powers. This entire course of action was to influence Western public opinion and the British position, as well as the British role in the Zionist-Palestinian conflict during the crucial years subsequent to World War II.

Akram Zu'aytir, in his memoirs, lists some of the reasons for the failure of the Iraqi coup d'état: the shortcomings of the Iraqi army and its inferior status versus the British army, as well as the Germans and Italians, who reneged on their promise to provide assistance. Zu'aytir also mentions the animosity felt by part of the Iraqi population toward the "foreign" Arabs (Syrians, Lebanese, Egyptians, and Palestinians) who took part in the coup.[5] Haj Amin added that "Jewish officials working for the Iraqi Telephone Authority would record important official telephone conversations and report them to the British Embassy in Baghdad."[6] Zu'aytir and the mufti were careful to avoid scrutinizing their own part in the failure. They did not examine, even in retrospect, whether they had acted responsibly, as befitting those who held the fate of the Palestinian people in their hands, by betting so blatantly in favor of Rashid 'Ali and

Britain's enemies. Would it not have been preferable to invest in ties with other Iraqi elements as well, or at least to display a certain degree of neutrality? The mufti claimed that he had tried to mediate between rival factions in Iraq but that Nuri al-Said and the old guard foiled all his attempts. Nonetheless, Haj Amin emphasized the special relations between the Iraqi rebels and his men and particularly the integration of Palestinian soldiers in rebel military units headed by 'Abd al-Qadir al-Husayni.[7]

It is noteworthy that two members of al-Istiqlal, Akram Zu'aytir and 'Izzat Darwaza, at the time ardent followers of Haj Amin, posed no objection to his actions and criticized him only at a later stage. In their books they noted his conduct, his complex relationship with most of the Iraqi leaders, and the negative effect on the Palestinian cause. Yet during World War II they constantly supported his strategies and made an effort to coordinate their positions, even during his time in Berlin.

The Mufti in Germany

On May 29, 1941, upon the defeat of the Iraqi rebels, Haj Amin fled to Iran and then through Turkey to Italy. He was received by Mussolini on October 27, 1941, and then left for Berlin, remaining in Germany until the end of the war. In a meeting with Hitler on November 28, his host stressed that once the Axis forces were victorious, Haj Amin "would be the decisive factor in matters concerning Arab countries and their leader." The Germans did not explicitly involve Haj Amin in the extermination of European Jewry, and he himself denied all involvement. However in his memoirs he admitted to sending letters to German leaders and others as well, asking for their help in preventing Jews from leaving the Balkans. For the remainder of his life he repeatedly stated that the Jews had brought their fate upon themselves with their "manipulations and acts of aggression." The mufti's motives for collaborating with Hitler are puzzling. This choice of allies has tainted Palestinian history ever since, and it has been exploited by Palestinian adversaries over the generations.

Palestinian historians and writers have not dwelled much on the mufti's travels to Germany during World War II and his stay there. Even when mentioned, his version of events was accepted at face value:

The World War II context and the many victories won by Germany over Western colonial countries, which had oppressed the Arabs and had not kept their promises from World War I, must be taken into consideration. These countries were not content with the great injustice done to the Arabs and they proceeded to top their aggression and maltreatment by awarding the Balfour Declaration to the Jews. In this declaration, Britain expressed its commitment to support the Jews and to establish a national homeland for the Jews in Palestine, the objections of the entire Arab nation notwithstanding. It was only natural for the Arabs to shift their hopes to the Germans and perceive them as friends. These were the enemies of their enemies, the colonialists and the Jews. Moreover, Germany had never wronged the Arabs. Its policy had always been contrary to that of colonial Western countries, which is why the Ottoman state, headed by Sultan 'Abd al-Hamid II and his successors, offered a hand in friendship to Germany and became its ally in World War I.[8]

The mufti chose to ignore the Nazification of Germany, its aggression and racism, and to perceive Nazi Germany as an extension of nineteenth-century and World War I imperial Germany. He even suggested that his alliance with the Axis powers was in compliance with the people's wishes: "The Iraqi multitudes, much the same as their Arab brethren, appealed to Germany in their eyes and hearts, developed great expectations, and anticipated its help and assistance."[9]

Although most Palestinian writers choose to use these protestations to justify the alliance that the mufti sought to form with Hitler, the Palestinians did not necessarily yearn for a German victory or embrace the Nazi philosophy, as alleged in contemporary documents depicting Palestinian public opinion.[10] These contentions should be perceived as a lack of constructive self-criticism in confronting such a blatant and disastrous historical blunder.

The Palestinian Community During World War II

When the 1936–1939 revolt was finally repressed, Palestinian antagonism toward the British did not dissipate. The maltreatment inflicted by the authorities against Palestinian civilians—collective sanctions that included the destruction of homes, damage to crops, food, and possessions, as well as arrest, torture, and abuse—have remained engraved in their memory over seventy years later. Some of those interviewed for the current volume angrily displayed scars or deformities inflicted upon them at detention centers during the revolt, expressing their unwillingness to forgive and forget. These stories were passed from generation to generation and have become part of Palestinian collective memory. It is not surprising that during World War II not many Palestinians hastened to stand by Britain, all the more so since in its initial stages Britain seemed helpless in response to the massive German attacks. However the mufti's actions notwithstanding, the Palestinians cannot be said to have uniformly supported the Axis forces. Most opinion shapers writing for the Palestinian press mitigated and toned down any demonstrations of support for Germany and Italy. The failure of the Iraqi coup d'état and Germany's unwillingness to support the rebels reduced all interest in other concurrent German achievements.

Recognizing Britain's Might

In a document composed in October 1941 by an informant working for the Arab division of the Jewish Agency, the atmosphere among the Palestinian public was described as follows:

> It may be confidently assumed that recent events—beginning with the suppression of the Iraqi coup, the occupation of Syria, the Russian-German war, and ending with the invasion of Iran—have brought about a certain change among the Arab masses, as they have seen that (1) in Iraq the coup initiated by the Germans has been suppressed; (2) the Vichy government, a German ally, has been forced to withdraw from Syria and Lebanon in favor of the English; (3) Russia had the courage to lash out against such a mighty force and to fight back; (4) Iran, a large Muslim country previously under German control, was forced by circumstances to open its gates to two oppressive forces; and (5) there has been an elimination of all signs of war. All these, as stated, had a certain effect on the local atmosphere among the Arabs. As a result, (1) former threats against the Jewish settlement have disappeared; (2) cooperation between the authorities and the masses, and even— significantly—the leaders, has intensified; and (3) the extremists have cooled off, since most of the population would not comply with them as long as England was accumulating victories in the East.[11]

Supporting Allied Efforts

In spite of the hard feelings remaining from the suppressed revolt, and despite the harsh economic situation, many Palestinians responded to the call to mobilize in favor of Britain's war effort. When the war broke out, a group of second-line Palestinian leaders—in the absence of first-line leaders—met with High Commissioner for Palestine Harold McMichael. The leaders expressed their support for Britain and even appealed to the Palestinian public in the press to support Britain and forego all internecine disputes.[12] Palestinian Arabs contributed to the British war effort on two levels: (1) recruitment of service-age youngsters for active service, and (2) recruitment of skilled men to work in army camps, unload wares at the harbors, supply fruit and vegetables, and build roads. There are no precise data concerning Palestinian recruits, but estimates indicate nine thousand to seventeen thousand.[13] Some of the recruits were familiar with the British training regime from their previous role in the peace bands established by the British during the revolt. Prior experience expedited integration into the armed forces, while other recruits were sometimes found unfit for combat and employed as drivers, guards, and for other noncombatant jobs. Palestinian recruits formed three operational units. The major unit was Commando 51, which took part in the fighting in France, North Africa, Ethiopia, and Crete. Historian Bayan Nuwayhid al-Hout concludes, "Palestinian Arabs contributed to the war effort comparatively less than the Jews. However, considering their political and psychological circumstances the assistance they provided may even be said to have exceeded their capacity."[14]

Britain's reinforced might in Palestine and neighboring countries had a positive effect on the local economy. Residents of towns and villages in the vicinity of army camps enjoyed an improved standard of living, as related by Nimr Murqus in his memoirs:

> A new source of livelihood was now available to many younger and older men from our village employed in construction of a camp adjacent to the village. The English opened construction workshops for building military camps and preparing basic facilities for the forces stationed in the country. There was a demand for workers and guards. Our village supplied a growing number of workers and many of them could now afford to eat meat practically every week. My father's butchery became a good source of livelihood for my

family. It no longer required a big effort to market the mutton produced and sell it the same day it was butchered.[15]

Most villagers who did not find work at the harbors in the large cities of Haifa and Jaffa found work at the British army camps, and the Arab population slowly extricated itself from the economic hardships experienced following the revolt.

Collapse of Self-Leadership

Britain, and its allies among the Arabs, constantly sought ways of reducing the resentment aimed at the British Empire and improving its image in the region. These efforts were initiated as early as July 1940 by Colonel S. F. Newcomb, the emissary of Britain's secretary of state for the colonies, in his tour of the Middle East. In Baghdad, Newcomb met with two Palestinian representatives, Jamal al-Husayni and Musa al-'Alami, in the presence of Iraqi prime minister Nuri al-Said and Shaikh Yusuf Yasin, representing King Ibn Sa'ud, of Saudi Arabia. The agreement they reached stated that al-Husayni and al-'Alami would declare their support of Britain if the latter would act to implement the 1939 White Paper resolutions. However, these discussions led to no practical actions. Newcomb had not been assigned an official mandate, and the Palestinian representatives had a hard time persuading the mufti to negotiate with Britain. On the contrary, this meeting only served to heighten the mufti's allegations of British treachery.

Nonetheless, the British were not discouraged, and Arab leaders who supported them competed with each other to try to find a solution to the Palestinian problem. The resulting rivalry led to increasing Arabization of the Palestinian issue, with Arab countries expanding their patronage of the Palestinians. Three Arab proposals subsequently emerged; of these, King Ibn Sa'ud's plan was never publicized. He charged his Palestinian associate, 'Awni 'Abd al-Hadi, a member of the Arab Higher Committee, with the steps necessary to form a new Arab Higher Committee. The committee was indeed formed and its members reached understandings concerning the need to consolidate Arab efforts and reconcile their disagreements. However this did not result in any effective actions.[16] Much more significant were the Greater Syria Plan, initiated by Emir Abdullah, and the Blue Book Plan of Nuri al-Said.

The Greater Syria Plan

Since establishing his emirate in Transjordan in 1921, Abdullah (a scion of the Hashemite family governing Iraq, and Jordan as well, at this time) had constantly attempted to expand the area under his control. In particular, he had his eye on the remaining parts of Greater Syria (Bilad al-Sham). In June 1941, once Rashid 'Ali's coup in Iraq had been subdued and Free French Forces had entered Syria and Lebanon, Jordanian prime minister Tawfiq Abu al-Huda made an announcement on behalf of his government:

> The government of the Emir hereby clarifies its position . . . in order to put an end to the schemes of the Axis forces in the area, all countries of Greater Syria [Syria, Lebanon, Transjordan, and Palestine] must unite in complete unambiguous support of the allied forces. The government of Transjordan hereby requests that it be permitted to hold talks with the national governments of all Syrian countries with the aim of collaborating toward realization of national aspirations."[17]

The British government turned down Abdullah's proposal and clarified that he must not initiate any maneuvers in this direction. Abdullah then tried to garner support for his proposal within Arab circles advocating comprehensive unity. A Transjordanian delegation traveling to Cairo in 1943 to take part in consultations regarding the establishment of an Arab union submitted the proposal. It included a recommendation to support the Allies and Britain, while the latter "would do its best to correct its defective relationship with the Arabs subsequent to World War I." Concerning the Palestinian issue, the proposal stated, "In regard to the Palestinian problem, Great Britain announced its position on the matter in the White Paper, and it hasn't reneged on this promise to date. Palestine must be included in any united organization or Arab union to be established."[18]

Abdullah's men printed the proposal, titled "From Abdullah Ibn al-Hussein to all residents of Bilad al-Sham," and sought to disseminate it throughout the Arab world. Abdullah also invited all leaders, clerics, and influential figures "in the countries of Greater Syria" to convene in Amman and discuss the proposed union headed by himself.[19] However, once again British authorities made it clear to Abdullah that they objected to his plan and forbade him from promoting it in the media throughout Greater Syria and Egypt, thus sealing its fate.[20]

Nuri al-Said's Blue Book Plan

Prime Minister Nuri al-Said, who had been intervening in Palestinian matters for years, suggested uniting the entire Fertile Crescent. He sent his proposal, the Blue Book Plan, to the British minister resident in Cairo, R. G. Casey, in the summer of 1943. The plan resembled that proposed by Abdullah, but differed in several aspects, mainly the geographical scope involved: In al-Said's plan, Iraq was included in Greater Syria. Whereas Abdullah's plan was to establish one kingdom in all of Greater Syria, of which he would be sovereign, al-Said proposed that the union's citizens should determine the type of government and was in favor of establishing a confederation. As far as the Jewish question was concerned, Abdullah's Greater Syria Plan provided no clear definition of the Jews' status in his united kingdom, while al-Said's Blue Book proposed awarding the Jews autonomy in certain districts as part of the confederation, similar to the arrangement reached with the Maronite Christians in Mount Lebanon in 1864.[21]

The national movements in Syria and Lebanon rejected al-Said's proposal, which they considered a British attempt to take control of their countries and prevent them from attaining independence. However, a group of Palestinian leaders affiliated with al-Istiqlal, who had been demonstrating pan-Arab inclinations since the early 1930s, accepted the plan with two reservations: they demanded suspension of Jewish immigration to Palestine, as ensuring the validity of the White Paper seemed insufficient, and they also demanded that the degree of autonomy accorded to the Jews be restricted as much as possible.[22]

This marked a change in the modes of action employed by Palestinian political activists. Consistent rejection of all suggestion of compromise gradually evolved into more flexible strategies based on two new foundations: accepting pan-Arab involvement as long as it did not include patronage, and accepting some type of Jewish autonomy as long as it did not involve sovereignty. Unsurprisingly, it was al-Istiqlal, previously adamantly opposed to any agreement with the Zionist movement, which now expressed readiness, albeit reserved, to accept the plan. Minimal compromise on the issue of Jewish autonomy was perceived as a necessary price for the primary goal of establishing a pan-Arab union, particularly one that would include both Greater Syria and Iraq. In light of the suppression of the 1936 revolt, which managed to deteriorate into a state of civil war, at least some of the leaders must have understood that the Palestinians had no chance of repelling the Jewish settlement unassisted. Only a wider organization, including better-established and stronger Arab members, might increase their chances of success in the struggle against Zionism and a Jewish national home.

Al-Said's plan, however, did not receive the support of most Arab leaders and was never implemented. Both King Ibn Sa'ud and Mufti Haj Amin al-Husayni's distrust of al-Said was at the root of the general lack of response to the plan. In addition, Emir Abdullah, as the Hashemite ally of Iraq's royal family, perceived the Blue Book as an attempt to block his own plan.

The Arab League Takes Charge of the Palestinian Cause

During the last two years of World War II, the concept of Arab unity headed the agenda of Middle East consultants to the British secretary of state for the colonies. British historian John Marlowe contemptuously comments on this trend: "Arab unity became the fashion among British Middle East 'experts' much as the Jewish National Home had been the fashion twenty-five years previously."[23] This "fashion" attracted advocates throughout the Arab world. Consequently, Arab leaders began initiating actual procedures, and intellectuals displayed a rising interest in all aspects related to pan-Arab causes—first and foremost, the Palestinian issue.

British policy regarding Arab unity set itself two goals: (1) to neutralize the mufti as an independent influential Palestinian leader, isolating him and restricting his ability to act within a wider coalition of Arab countries; and (2) to silence their remaining opponents in the Arab world. On the Arab side, Prime Minister Mustafa al-Nahhas Pasha of Egypt took the lead. He laid the foundation for inter-Arab consultations, eventually culminating in the announcement of the establishment of the Arab League on March 22, 1945.[24]

The newly formed Arab League provided a major platform for activists from all divisions and levels of the Palestinian national movement. The mufti continued to serve as the movement's primary political figure; however, his dismal relationship with the British, as well as with their allies and major elements within the Arab League, prevented him from reassuming leadership of his people in his own land. Haj Amin remained strongly convinced that the Palestinians had nothing to gain from Britain or its Arab allies, particularly the Hashemites. He therefore consistently focused on thwarting any endeavor aimed at developing the institutions of the national movement and reorganizing them under a new leadership. The Palestinian people and their national movement continued to pay for the mufti's pretense of exclusive leadership and for his grim relationship with the British and the Hashemites. Haj Amin's drawn-out leadership was detrimental to Palestinian relations with Egypt and Saudi Arabia as well. The leaders of Egypt and Saudi Arabia resented the fact that the mufti viewed himself as a pan-Arab leader, as well as his custom of relating to Arab leaders as colleagues rather than patrons, despite his impotence and phenomenal blunders. In light of this state of affairs, Arab League involvement in the Palestinian issue only served to widen existing rifts within the national movement, hampering its efficiency in the newly reemerging national struggle against Zionism.

Haj Amin continued to enjoy a certain popularity among the Palestinians, but this could no longer be translated into political influence and could certainly not provide a solid, responsible leadership. Since its establishment, the Arab League had become known as the undisputed patron of the Palestinians. The Arab League decided which organizations would represent the Palestinians, determined the nature of Arab countries' involvement in Palestinian concerns, and held negotiations with Britain and the UN to decide the future of the Palestinian people. This patronage became critical after the UN partition resolution of November 29, 1947, when Arab-Jewish hostilities broke out.

Notes

1. On the mufti's wanderings, see al-Husayni, *Haqa'iq 'an Qadiyyat Filastin* [Truth About the Issue of Palestine]. See also the mufti's memoirs, edited by his assistant 'Abd al-Karim al-'Umar, *Muzakkarat al-Haj Muhhamad Amin al-Husayni* [Memoirs of Haj Amin al-Husayni]; Elpeleg, *Grand Mufti*; and Jbara, *Palestinian Leader Haj Amin al-Husayni*.
2. See for example, Shahin, *Sawt Min Qubur Filastin al-'Arabiyya, Zulm al-'Arabi Leakhihi al-'Arabi* [Voice from the Cemeteries of Arab Palestine: The Arab's Tyranny Toward Arab Brethren].
3. Central Zionist Archive, S/25/9333, Jerusalem.
4. See Zu'aytir, "Min ajl ummati" [For My Nation].
5. Zu'aytir, "Min ajl ummati" [For My Nation], 12–15.

6. Al-'Umar, *Muzakkarat al-Haj Muhhamad Amin al-Husayni* [Memoirs of Haj Amin al-Husayni], 69.
7. Al-'Umar, *Muzakkarat al-Haj Muhhamad Amin al-Husayni* [Memoirs of Haj Amin al-Husayni], 148–149.
8. Al-'Umar, *Muzakkarat al-Haj Muhhamad Amin al-Husayni* [Memoirs of Haj Amin al-Husayni], 148–149.
9. Al-'Umar, *Muzakkarat al-Haj Muhhamad Amin al-Husayni* [Memoirs of Haj Amin al-Husayni].
10. Archives of the Haganah (henceforth AH) 107/197. See at length, Kabha, "'Oyev oyvi haveri': Hatenu'ah hale'umit hafalestinit veyahasa el hafashizem vehanazizem, 1925–1945" ["My Enemy's Enemy Is My Friend": The Palestinian National Movement and Its Attitude Toward Fascism and Nazism].
11. AH 105/197.
12. B. N. al-Hout, *Al-Qiyadat wa al-Mu'ssasat al-Siyasiyya Fi Filastin, 1917–1948* [Leadership and Political Institutions in Palestine], 432.
13. For the first estimate, see Esco Foundation for Palestine, II, p. 1007; and for the latter estimate, see Palestinian Research Centre, file no. L/111, Document 4, cited by B. N. al-Hout, *Al-Qiyadat wa al-Mu'ssasat al-Siyasiyya Fi Filastin, 1917–1948* [Leadership and Political Institutions in Palestine], 432. Even the higher estimate is lower than the number of Jewish recruits; however, even the lower estimate indicates significant activity, particularly if we note that during the 1936–1939 revolt, the General Command succeeded in recruiting only fifteen thousand fighters. See the document cited above by the Palestinian Research Centre.
14. B. N. al-Hout, *Al-Qiyadat wa al-Mu'ssasat al-Siyasiyya Fi Filastin, 1917–1948* [Leadership and Political Institutions in Palestine], 434.
15. Murqus, *Aqwq min al-Nisyan* [Stronger than Forgetting], 56.
16. Qasmiyya, *'Awni 'Abd al-Hadi, Awraq Khassa* ['Awni 'Abd al-Hadi, Personal Documents], 124–128.
17. Nawfal, *Al-'Amal al-'Arabi al-Mushtarak, Madihi wa-Mustaqbaluhu* [Joint Arab Activity: Its Past and Future], 53–54.
18. Abdullah, *Muzakkirat Sahib al-Jalalah al-Hashimiyya* [Memoirs of His Majesty the Hashemite King], 209–210.
19. Abdullah, *Muzakkirat Sahib al-Jalalah al-Hashimiyya* [Memoirs of His Majesty the Hashemite King], 209–210.
20. Abdullah, *Muzakkirat Sahib al-Jalalah al-Hashimiyya* [Memoirs of His Majesty the Hashemite King], 219–222.
21. B. N. al-Hout, *Al-Qiyadat wa al-Mu'ssasat al-Siyasiyya Fi Filastin, 1917–1948* [Leadership and Political Institutions in Palestine], 438–439.
22. Qasmiyya, *'Awni 'Abd al-Hadi, Awraq Khassa* ['Awni 'Abd al-Hadi, Personal Documents], 129–130.
23. Marlowe, *Rebellion in Palestine*, 243.
24. Marlowe, *Rebellion in Palestine*, 243.

3

1945–1948: First Signs of Revival Before the Tempest

Historian Bayan Nuwayhid al-Hout summarized the situation of the Palestinian national movement following World War II:

> In Palestine the national movement suffered grievous damage linked to the failure of the revolt [1936–1939] in its final stages and to the absence of a political leadership, which had either become scattered between detention centers, deported, or left for Axis countries. The general decrepitude of the political institutions only served to aggravate this sad state of affairs. In the aftermath of the revolt the Arabs of Palestine were confronted with the challenge of rebuilding their national movement and the need to reconstruct from scratch modes of operation, mechanisms, and leadership.[1]

Al-Hout compares the situation of the Palestinian national movement unfavorably to that of the Jewish national movement: "The Jews had never been as strong politically and militarily as after World War II. In contrast, the Arabs had never been as weak as they were at that point in time."[2] Al-Hout's conclusion is a recurrent one within the Palestinian narrative, which endeavors to explain the tragedy that befell the Palestinians following the War of 1948 by identifying them as the victims of a host of contriving elements: the British, the Zionists, Arab countries, and other Arab leaders. However, this conception disregards the three years in which Palestinian society attempted to recover by renewing processes that had been halted by the revolt and that harbored potential for revitalization and development. In this chapter I will analyze these processes and discuss the evolvement of organizations that aspired to help the Palestinian national movement recover from the aftermath of the 1936–1939 revolt and to extract the local Palestinian populace from the stagnation dominating its political scene. In addition, I shall identify elements pursuing possible alternatives to the exiled Husayni leadership.

The Husaynis and the Obstruction of an Alternate Leadership

Throughout World War II, most of the senior Palestinian leadership, as well as members of the Arab Higher Committee, were absent from the country. Mufti Haj Amin al-Husayni spent the war in Germany. Jamal al-Husayni (1892–1982) was imprisoned in a British jail in Rhodesia. 'Izzat Darwaza and Akram Zu'aytir were in Turkey; Ahmad Hilmi 'Abd al-Baqi (1882–1963), Fu'ad Saba, Alfred Roke, and Husayn Fakhri al-Khalidi lived in Lebanon; and 'Awni 'Abd al-Hadi, Ya'qub al-Ghusayn (1900–1947), and 'Abd al-Latif Salah were in Egypt.

The first to request permission to return to Palestine were the political activists living in Lebanon, and Ahmad Hilmi wrote on their behalf to the British authorities. The British consented, stipulating that each of the returnees must sign a letter of commitment to refrain from taking part in any act of disorderly conduct or undermining public order, and that anyone who wished to become involved in politics should do so legally. Some members of this group signed and returned immediately, while others did so hesitantly and gradually.

Hampering the Recovery of al-Istiqlal

When it became clear that the war was approaching a turning point in early 1943, Arab political activities began revitalizing. The first of the six existing political parties to reveal signs of recovery and reorganization was al-Istiqlal. Two of its leaders, 'Awni 'Abd al-Hadi and Rashid al-Haj Ibrahim (1889–1953), and an independent associated politician, Ahmad Hilmi 'Abd al-Baqi, made efforts to revive the party's branch in Haifa and the vicinity, as well as the Nation's Fund (Sunduq al-Umma). Rashid al-Haj Ibrahim, a dominant Haifa public figure, acted to establish a "united Arab front" in order to provide "national guidance." An assembly held on February 19, 1943, announced the establishment of the front, and Rashid al-Haj Ibrahim was appointed chairman and Ilyas Kusa secretary. Participants of the constituent assembly sent a memorandum to the British high commissioner for Palestine, asking him to approve the convening of a general Arab congress to elect a new representative committee with responsibility for managing Arab matters in Palestine.

Supporters of the Husaynis, who perceived all political alliances precluding their leader as an unacceptable act of subversion, succeeded in foiling this initiative. They accused the initiators of coordination and collaboration with the British. As proof, they stated that some of these leaders had returned to Palestine with British permission, while the real defenders of the Palestinian people remained in British prisons or in German territory. The incendiary allegations proved more effective than even Rashid al-Haj Ibrahim's popularity in Haifa and his strong relationship in the past with Shaikh 'Izz al-Din al-Qassam, the religious-militant leader killed by the British in 1935, as well as with the Young Men's Muslim Association in Carmel City.

In Jerusalem as well, Istiqlal activists endeavored to reestablish a committee charged with representing the Palestinians. For this purpose, they contacted several exiled members of the Arab Higher Committee. This initiative, however, was also undermined by the Husayni camp. No political proposal could receive their cooperation as long as the mufti and their senior activists remained in exile. They also openly declared that anyone promoting policies based on acknowledgment of the White Paper of 1939 would be considered a traitor. Due to their vigorous opposition, the initiative fell through and the committee was dissolved. As we shall see, the Husaynis eventually succeeded in establishing a committee in which their former influence was maintained.

Unsuccessful Attempts to Send a United Delegation to the Arab League

The Husaynis were under great pressure as well, particularly as a result of hurried meetings and talks in preparation for establishing the Arab League and selecting a Palestinian delegate. The primary force behind the entire process, Nuri al-Said, even came to Jerusalem, where he met with representatives of Palestinian parties and movements at the Iraqi consulate. The Husaynis had no choice but to declare their participation in this process, and they authorized Tawfiq Salih al-Husayni to negotiate on their behalf with the other Palestinian organizations. The latter proposed establishing a new committee consisting of leaders of the six political parties and two members of the Husayni Arab Party. They also suggested that no one be appointed chairman, a position reserved for Haj Amin without identifying him by name. In response, the Husaynis suggested appointing those who had participated in the Palestinian delegation to the London Convention in 1939 as a new Arab Higher Committee. This proposal was unfeasible, as only eight of the fifteen original delegates were currently in the country, and of these, two (Fu'ad Saba and Musa al-'Alami) refused to be part of the new committee. Four others were abroad: Haj Amin in Germany, Amin al-Tamimi and Jamal al-Husayni in Rhodesia, and 'Izzat Darwaza in Turkey. Three had died: George Antonius (1892–1942), Ya'qub Farraj, and Alfred Roke.

From the perspective of the other parties, the Husayni proposal was a blatant provocation aimed at blocking the Palestinians from participating in inter-Arab consultations, as long as the mufti could not head and control the proposed delegation. These internecine conflicts led the discussions and Nuri al-Said's efforts at mediation to a dead end and they reached no outcome. However, other Arab mediators did not despair. In November 1945 a delegation sent by the Arab League, and headed by renowned Syrian politician Jamal Mardam, arrived in Jerusalem. The delegation met with the conflicting parties and succeeded in establishing a new committee consisting of party leaders and other influential politicians. Regretfully, this committee was short-lived and did not initiate any substantial activities.

Upon returning from Rhodesia on February 6, 1946, Jamal al-Husayni appealed to the various constituents of the national movement to forgo their former conflicts and unite. His appeal, accompanied by a demand to recognize the hegemony of the Husayni party, was rejected by the other parties. In response, Jamal al-Husayni announced the establishment of a new Arab Higher Committee made up of members exclusively of his own camp. At the same time, rivals of the Husaynis announced the establishment of a new organization, the Higher Arab Front (al-Jabha al-'Arabiyya al-'Ulya). These two rival organizations counteracted each other and did not manage to revitalize the national movement. Their activities were confined to Jerusalem and remained bogged down by former animosities and personal grudges.

Preventing Establishment of an Arab Front

In Jaffa, local activists founded an Arab front with the declared intention of "refraining from any political affiliation" and of distancing themselves from the factionalism paralyzing Palestinian society. The front's constituent assembly met on May 8, 1945, and elected attorney 'Abd al-Rahman al-Siksik as general secretary. The assembly announced five main goals:

1. To organize Jaffa's public affairs from a social, economic, and political perspective as part of the National Alliance[3]
2. To act to establish similar fronts in all Palestinian cities and districts
3. To act to forge Palestinian unity and establish an apolitical organization that would properly represent the Arab nation in Palestine
4. To defend Palestinian concerns as part of the National Alliance
5. To serve Palestinian concerns in general[4]

The strong pan-Arab sentiments prevalent at this time throughout the Palestinian public scene, mainly hoping for salvation by the Arab League, are clearly evident in the phrasing of these principles. Once again, the Husaynis expressed resistance and concern that establishing such a front and building on Arab leaders would compromise their position of power created during the mufti's leadership, as well as the Palestinians' freedom of action. Restricted by the Husaynis, the Jaffa front was incapable of successfully rehabilitating Palestinian political power locally or elsewhere. The Husaynis still enjoyed a great deal of influence in the public sphere, while other political parties and groups acted mainly within the elite echelons, with almost no contact with the people. Meanwhile, Haj Amin's imprisonment in France enhanced his image as the people's warrior and dissuaded his rivals from proposing a viable alternative. It was not long before the Husaynis' rivals announced the termination of all activities, leaving the entire stage to the Husayni party.

Founding the Arab Higher Institution

Tawfiq Salih al-Husayni's election as temporary president of the Arab Party notwithstanding, Husayni activists and their many supporters remained focused on the two great leaders of their camp, Haj Amin al-Husayni and Jamal al-Husayni. Tawfiq al-Husayni and minor operatives scored a major achievement by delaying all decisions pertaining to national leadership until the return of Jamal al-Husayni. Jamal disembarked at the Port of Haifa where he was received by an impressive welcoming ceremony attended by representatives of local commerce, members of the Palestinian Scouts Association, and many admirers. A reporter for the local newspaper, *Al-Difa'*, concluded his report by saying, "The Arab Party has proven that it is the strongest party. . . . The Palestinian people admire Haj Amin al-Husayni and do not miss any opportunity to sing his praise."[5] The political activities that ensued after Jamal al-Husayni's return were described by Bayan Nuwayhid al-Hout: "Now the land awakened to outstanding intensive activities led by the Arab Party, particularly when its president [Jamal al-Husayni] initiated a series of successive visits to cities and villages. Jamal al-Husayni's leadership succeeded in arousing, but not healing, political life. It did not result in national unity and was incapable of joining the disparate forces."[6]

When the optimism and enthusiasm surrounding Jamal's arrival had dissipated, many reassumed their faith in Haj Amin al-Husayni. The mufti had fled custody in France, but the British prevented him from returning to Palestine. He reached Cairo and began dealing with matters pertaining to the Palestinian national movement. By preventing his return to Palestine, the British reinforced his image as leader and victim.

Palestinian failure to come to a consensus regarding the composition of a representative committee was discussed at a special session of the Arab League Council, held in Bludan, Syria, on June 8–12, 1946. At this conference a decision was reached to appoint a new Palestinian committee and call it the Arab Higher Institution (al-Hay'ah al-'Arabiyya al-'Ulya), to distinguish it from previous committees. It consisted of four members: two representing the Husayni camp—Jamal al-Husayni and Emil al-Ghouri (1907–1984)—and two representing the Higher Arab Front—Ahmad Hilmi 'Abd al-Baqi and

Husayn Fakhri al-Khaldi. The Arab League Council awarded the role of president of the Arab Higher Institution to Haj Amin, who served in this position from August 1946 until his death in 1974.

Ideological Political Parties

Feeling powerless to challenge the mufti and unable to provide a serious alternative to his personal leadership, traditional rivals attempted to breach the Husayni monopoly through ideological confrontations. The increasing involvement of the Arab League and of prominent Arab politicians in Palestinian concerns, which gradually undermined the traditional rules of the game, was a facilitating factor. Some of the organizations and groups challenging the Husayni hegemony were local and some were branches of movements and parties active in neighboring Arab countries.

The National Liberation League: The Communists and the Partition of Palestine

The National Liberation League was formed in September 1943 in Haifa and headed by Radwan al-Hiliw ("Comrade Musa," 1906–1980), following a split in the Palestinian Communist Party (PCP), the only binational party to include both Arabs and Jews. The underlying discord within the PCP, its increasing nationalist tendencies, and the resulting split were not surprising in light of the 1936–1939 revolt.[7] In addition to Radwan al-Hiliw, the new movement's constituent assembly was attended by Jabra Niqula, Mukhlis 'Amr, Emil Toma (1919–1984), Tawfiq Tubi, Emil Habibi (1921–1996), Boulos Farah, and Fu'ad Nassar. The movement's headquarters remained in Haifa and it was popular among intellectuals, worker unions, and villagers. In May 1944 it published the journal *Al-Ittihad* (Unity; which eventually became the Arabic-language journal of the Israeli Communist Party), and the periodical *Al-Ghad* (Tomorrow).

In early 1946 the National Liberation League published its political platform, consisting of the three familiar principles of the Palestinian national movement: termination of the British Mandate, removal of all foreign armies, and establishment of a democratic Palestinian state espousing equality for all. Regarding the Jewish issue, the platform stressed the difference between Zionism and Judaism and emphasized the need to respect the rights of "Jews residing in Palestine." Zionism was described as an aggressive movement serving the interests of imperialism and hostile toward the Arab nation, and even toward the Jews themselves. Objection to the arrival of Jewish immigrants was emphasized as well. Immigration was considered to be an issue requiring an international solution and requiring the consent of all residents.[8]

The Arab League had a complicated relationship with the Husayni leadership. On the one hand, the Husaynis were perceived as reactionary and opportunistic, but they were also acknowledged as a possible facilitator of national unity. Their potential advantages eventually resolved the issue, in light of the inadequacy of all other existing forces. Musa al-Budayri, historian of the Palestinian labor movement, described the process:

> Although the League was aware of the traditional leadership's undesirable traits, its adverse impact on the nature of the popular struggle, and its hostility toward all things progressive, the League did not reject this leadership. We were not granted the privilege of membership on the Arab Higher Committee, but nevertheless we saw nothing wrong in supporting it as long as it acted to liberate the country and redeem it from the hands of Zionism and imperialism. Indeed, we constantly declared that rather than following people or institutions, we follow a plan.[9]

This positive approach toward the mufti's leadership was evident in the report published in *Al-Ittihad* when welcoming the mufti upon his return from France: "The Arab people, who remain loyal to their leaders, are celebrating this festive day throughout the country."[10]

However, the relationship with the mufti was far from harmonious. Some of the Arab League's activists, particularly those belonging to the radical Marxist left wing, were not inclined to forgive the mufti for his support of the Axis forces and his prolonged stay in Berlin during World War II. Other elements in the movement, mainly leaders of the Workers' Congress, objected to the Arab League's compliance with the boycott dictated by the mufti upon arrival of UN delegates in 1947 to report on the situation in Palestine. Mukhlis 'Amr and Boulos Farah, for example, did not abide by the Arab League's decision and proceeded to appear before the international commission.

This affair portended the split that occurred in the movement following the controversy regarding the UN resolution on the partition of Palestine on November 29, 1947. Articles appearing in *Al-Ittihad* during this period reflect rising internal tensions. Opponents of the partition plan were headed by Emil Toma and Fu'ad Nassar, who were more strongly affiliated with the leadership of the Palestinian national movement. The other faction was headed by Tawfiq Tubi and later also Emil Habibi, who were in favor of accepting the resolution, probably under Soviet influence. The conflict worsened when the Arab League gathered for meetings. At the first of these, held in January 1948 in Nazareth, participants found it difficult to reach any agreement whatsoever. At the second, held two months later in Jaffa, supporters of the UN resolution succeeded in enforcing their opinion. By this time, however, it had become irrelevant, as Palestinian urban centers had already been occupied and the debate surrounding the partition had become obsolete. Partition opponents, led by Emil Toma, decided to express their strong objection to the decisions reached at the Jaffa meeting. They won the support of the mufti and Arab Higher Institution activists, who attacked supporters of the partition plan and urged the people to voice their objection. When the faction supporting partition gained the upper hand, some of the Arab League's branches were torched.[11] Many league members, particularly those in favor of partition, remained silent during the War of 1948. When the war ended and the State of Israel was established, they rejoined the Communist Party, renamed the Israeli Communist Party.

The Arab Nationalist Party

The Arab Nationalist Party (al-Qawmiyyoun al-'Arab) was formed by a small group of students and faculty at the American University of Beirut in the 1920s and headed by Qustantin Zurayq and Fu'ad Mifrig. The Palestinians in the group, and particularly Farid Zayn al-Din, conveyed the movement's ideology to young people in Palestine. Zayn al-Din was appointed president of the al-Najah College in Nablus, a position that served him well in his advocacy and organizational efforts among Arab nationalists. The Palestinian branch of the movement operated independently until the mid-1930s, its members including graduates of the university in Beirut, among others.[12] All were part of the wealthy, urban *a'yan* class. In 1937 the Palestinian and Lebanese branches were united and the Palestinians received equal representation at the highest levels.

The idea of Arab nationalism was perceived by the movement as "expressing the Arab wish to extricate themselves from imperialism, tyranny, poverty, and all other signs of weakness. This wish should be fulfilled by establishing a strong modern Arab national state. Thus the Arabs will succeed in defending their material and spiritual entity and continue to enrich all humanity and global culture."[13] The movement's regulations included no mention of a social ideology, as "the struggle is above all and its purpose is independence. Only then may we speak of social ideology."[14] This attitude explains the movement's alliance with Haj Amin al-Husayni, despite his identification as a model of reactionary leadership. Two instances of such an alliance occurred: one during the 1936–1939 Palestinian revolt, when the movement's younger members joined the leaders of the armed bands and acted as advisers in charge of propaganda and publicity, and the other during the Rashid 'Ali al-Kilani coup in Iraq.[15] During the mufti's stay in Baghdad, members of al-Qawmiyyoun took part in his attempt to establish a pan-Arab national party. They also cooperated with al-Istiqlal, blurring the distinction between the two organizations; some activists, such as Wasif Kamal and Mamduh al-Sukhun, were members of both parties simultaneously.

Once al-Kilani's coup in Iraq was defeated, and following the arrest or flight of most Iraqi nationalist activists, the movement entered a period of hibernation. It reappeared at a meeting held on June 18, 1946, in Haifa, at the home of Dr. 'Umar al-Khalil, and headed by Farid al-Sa'd. Other meetings were held in Jerusalem, Jaffa, and Gaza, however, no organized leadership emerged. Farid al-Sa'd, leader of the Palestinian branch of the movement, wished to retire and to appoint a successor. Several possible candidates were proposed; for example, Yusuf Haykal, the mayor of Jaffa, and Khalusi al-Khayri of Ramle. Al-Istiqlal followers—for example, Ahmad al-Shuqayri and Musa al-'Alami—were considered as well. None of the candidates, however, was appointed to a leadership position. Consequently, a collective leadership was established, a choice that may have solved pressing problems but was detrimental to the movement's long-term efficiency.[16] Its major achievement was the founding of the newspaper *Al-Sha'b* in 1946, edited by the well-known Palestinian journalist Kan'an Abu Khadra (1920–1984), which soon proved good competition for the two more established Jaffa dailies, *Filastin* and *Al-Difa'*. Al-Qawmiyyoun never had more than several hundred members and it remained, as was al-Istiqlal in its time, a party of the intellectual elite, with no following among the wider population. Its members failed in their attempts to expand the movement's constituency in preparation for the challenges of 1948, and their influence remained marginal.[17]

The Muslim Brotherhood

Hasan al-Banna founded the Muslim Brotherhood in Egypt in 1928. Local development of the movement in the early half of the 1930s urged further expansion, particularly in the Fertile Crescent. At first, charitable societies and cultural clubs were established, followed by official branches of the movement. The first society founded by the movement in Palestine was Jam'iyat al-Mukarama (Society of Good Attributes), opened in Jerusalem in 1936.[18] An official branch was then founded in Jerusalem as well, in early May 1946, dedicated in the presence of the Egyptian representative, 'Abd al-Mu'iz 'Abd al-Sattar, and Jamal al-Husayni, president of the (Husayni) Palestinian Arab Party. Further branches were opened in Lydda, Haifa, Tulkarm, Nablus, and Bisan. In mid-October 1946, the Muslim Brotherhood held a general meeting in Haifa, attended by representatives from Syria, Lebanon, and Jordan.[19] In its final announcement, the mandate government was declared responsible for the deteriorating state of affairs in Palestine, and Britain was challenged to bring the Palestinian issue before the UN Security Council. In addition, the meeting expressed its support for the Arab League's involvement in Palestinian concerns and for Egypt's demand that the British army withdraw from its territory and that the Nile Valley be united.[20] In October 1947 a public statement was published on behalf of the Muslim Brotherhood Society in Palestine regarding the "insistence of the Muslim Brotherhood on defending their country with all means possible and their readiness to cooperate with all national organizations acting to achieve this goal."[21] Historical sources indicate that this seemingly independent Palestinian branch was in fact run by delegates of the head office in Cairo. For this reason, and due to the special relationship between Haj Amin and Hasan al-Banna, the "general guide" of the Muslim Brotherhood, the mufti and his sympathizers did not perceive this group as a threat to their domination of the Palestinian national movement and were even inclined to be cooperative.

From the founding of the first branch in Jerusalem until the UN partition resolution on November 29, 1947, the Muslim Brotherhood had focused on opening social clubs and libraries and organizing lectures. As of November 29, however, their activities shifted to military preparations. The Jerusalem branch now served as a headquarters for recruiting and arming young Palestinians and Arab volunteers from other countries and helped coordinate their efforts with those of the other forces.

In early October 1947, Hasan al-Banna appealed to the general secretary of the Arab League with a message that his movement was ready to send ten thousand volunteers to Palestine. At the same time, al-Banna appealed to the Egyptian government for permission for the volunteers to depart. The Egyptians refused but turned a blind eye to the infiltration of Palestine by members of the Muslim Brotherhood, beginning in February 1948.[22] In April 1948 volunteer regiments began operating openly, once Syria, Libya, Saudi Arabia, and Yemen permitted volunteers affiliated with the Muslim Brotherhood to leave their territories and take part in the fighting. The volunteers fought on two fronts: Jerusalem, Bethlehem, and Hebron constituted one front, and Gaza, Majdal (Ashkelon), and Ashdod formed the other.[23]

The Syrian Social Nationalist Party

The first Palestinians to join the Syrian Social Nationalist Party (al-Hizb al-Suri al-Qawmi al-Ijtima'i)—a nationalist movement espousing the unity of Greater Syria—did so on the eve of the 1936–1939 revolt. The first branch of the party opened in Haifa, home to many families of Syrian and Lebanese descent. Further branches opened in Jerusalem, Jaffa, and Acre. During World War II, contact with the headquarters in Beirut was severed but resumed in 1947 when the party head, Anton Sa'ada, returned from South America to Lebanon, and as the conflict between the Zionist movement and the Palestinians intensified. After the UN partition resolution, an autonomous headquarters was established in Palestine. It was headed by Yusuf Sayigh of Tiberias, who received the title "general legal representative of the party in Palestine." He was authorized to publish proclamations and public statements on behalf of the party without requiring the approval of the party's headquarters in Lebanon.[24]

The doctrine of the Syrian Social Nationalist Party decreed that Palestine was part of Syria, and it was called "southern Syria," a term used by al-Istiqlal and other Palestinian groups as well. The party had a pragmatic relationship with al-Istiqlal, the Husaynis, and the Arab nationalists. Its relationship, however, with the communists and the Muslim Brotherhood was hostile. The "nationalist Syrians" in Palestine tried to associate with Mufti Haj Amin al-Husayni and organized a series of meetings between him and Anton Sa'ada. These meetings fell through as a result of the ideological differences between the two. Relations with the mufti deteriorated in late 1947 and early 1948 when the Syrian party asked the mufti to arm their young volunteers. The mufti rejected the demand for two reasons: lack of weapons and his refusal to let foreigners, that is, anyone who had not been born in the country, bear weapons amid the Palestinian populace. In his opinion, such conduct would endanger future Palestinian sovereignty as well as his own control of the Palestinians. These conflicts did nothing to detract from the party's active hostility toward the Jewish settlement and the Zionist movement. It objected to the UN partition resolution and declared the next day, November 30, a day of national mourning. In a public statement the party declared, "We are preparing for the day on which we will take control of the fighting, realize the people's wishes and be unfettered by personal interests and foreign considerations. November 30 is a day of mourning for the Syrian national socialists and a day of reckoning for the entire Syrian nation."[25]

These words reflected the party's attitude toward the war and its sharp criticism of the Palestinian and Arab leadership. The statement presented its authors as actively engaged in the fighting and as criticizing the preparations made by the Arab and Palestinian leadership and the Arab League. In actuality, however, the party did not conduct itself any differently from those it criticized. Militarily, its members focused on the fighting that took place during the first months of 1948 in Haifa; however, they preferred to act independently and separately and refused to submit to the authority of the city's national committee. In early May 1948, Anton Sa'ada organized a meeting in Beirut to discuss the party's enhanced involvement in the war. The meeting was attended by about 100 members, and Sa'ada instructed them to prepare to leave for Haifa and decide the outcome of the battle. The next day, however, he announced that this move would be delayed due to a lack of weapons. Since that time there is no evidence of any organized involvement of the Syrian Social Nationalist Party in the war.

The Arab Revival Party (al-Ba'th al-'Arabi)

Unlike the Arab or Islamic movements reviewed, the Ba'ath Party, founded in Syria, did not succeed in opening branches in Palestine prior to 1948. Nonetheless, it was involved in the dissemination of propaganda urging mobilization to help the Palestinians and in the organization of Arab volunteer forces.[26] The party's headquarters issued a public statement in September 1947: "The al-Ba'ath party leading the Jihad warriors fighting for the salvation of Palestine calls upon all Arab popular forces taking part in the struggle to coalesce their plans and efforts and take responsibility for managing the war in order to attain victory and redeem the land from the errors and blunders of reactionary leaders and governments."[27] Meshel 'Aflaq, head of the Arab Revival Party, visited the battlefront in the Jenin-Haifa sector, from whence he sent an article to the *Al-Ba'ath* journal in early May 1948. In his article he stated that "the defects and errors that we have witnessed and seen on the internal front are dangerous and require prompt and serious attention."[28]

Throughout the war, the party published several public statements and declarations and accused the Arab League and Arab regimes of helplessness, powerlessness, and oversights on the subject of Palestine. It demanded the arming of all Palestinian youth and maximal mobilization in support of the war efforts. In practice, however, the party did nothing but make declarations and voice slogans.

Attempts to Organize Popular Forces: Youth, Workers, Women

The enhanced political activities typical of these years were accompanied by frequent calls, particularly by ideological groups and movements, to establish popular organizations aimed at furthering social, economic, and political processes and challenging the traditional forces. This trend may have been an attempt to emulate the Zionist movement's efficient approach. It was also influenced by processes occurring in the Arab Mideast and affecting Palestinian society's attempts at recovery at this time. For example, there was an increase in cultural activities, and dozens of cultural and sports clubs opened in cities, towns, and even large villages. Palestinian agents brought the very best performers and artists from Arab countries to perform and exhibit their work in Palestine, thus strengthening Palestinian cultural ties with the entire Arab region.

The al-Najjada Organization

The al-Najjada organization was inspired by the Lebanese al-Najjada, in response to the military organizations founded by the Jewish settlement.[29] It was also a way of recreating the Muslim-Christian associations founded in Palestinian cities following World War I. The first group was formed in October 1945 by merging the Islamic Sports Club of Jaffa and the Orthodox Scouts Society. It was headed by attorney Muhammad Nimr al-Hawwari, teachers Rashad al-Dabbagh and Rashad 'Arafa, former military officer Mousa Kathim al-Husayni, and attorneys Sa'id Zayn al-Din and Amin 'Aql. In order to receive the authorities' permission, the organization concealed its military goals and declared that it had been founded with the intention of working with youth and holding Scouting and sports activities.[30] The organization announced the following regulations:

> The reluctance of young Arabs to engage in sports detracts from a major component of national revival. Arabism ('Uruba) in its current predicament is in need of people with healthy thought processes, for which a healthy body is crucial . . . thus a decision has been made to establish the al-Najjada organization in Palestine . . . [in order to help] unite the Arab nation, disseminate principles of ethics, science, and sports among the young, with the aim of connecting the fate of Palestine to that of all other Arab countries, which together will raise the flag of Arabism, based on principles of freedom, fraternity, and equality.[31]

The organization's meetings and gatherings often utilized the slogan "The land of the Arabs for the Arabs" (*Bilad al-'Arab lil arab*).[32]

The organization emphasized that it would not be involved in internecine, religious, ethnic, and political disputes between clans and political parties in the national movement and within Palestinian society. Regarding Zionism, al-Najjada stated in its platform that "it is the biggest crime known to history, founded on hostility and aggression. All its founders, members, and supporters, are party to this crime."[33] The founding meeting of the organization's Haifa branch, held in early February 1946, declared that "al-Najjada troops were established as a defensive force in response to Jewish military organizations. They will be initially responsible for suppressing Jewish aggression upon its inception. They will also supervise implementation of boycott operations [of Jewish merchandise] and support any emerging local nationalist movement."[34]

In the latter half of 1946 al-Najjada gradually increased its presence. Twenty-six branches opened throughout the country—in major cities, towns, and large villages. In July 1946 there were sixteen hundred to two thousand members, according to Jewish sources, or about three thousand, according to the Arabic press.[35] Most of the senior leadership was from the middle class—intellectuals, teachers, and former army officers. A great majority did not hail from urban *a'yan* families, but rather from towns such as Tulkarm, Nazareth, Jenin, and Qalqilya. Some of the leaders were not Palestinian, such as one of the founders, Ibrahim Ramlawi, who was from Lebanon. The leadership was largely comprised of Muslims. According to an intelligence report from December 1946, by the Jewish paramilitary organization Haganah, funding consisted of "monthly donations by major merchants, voluntary donations received irregularly, membership fees and dues from al-Najjada members, and revenues from balls and parties held occasionally by the organization." The author of the report stressed that Christian donors usually contributed under duress.[36]

However, al-Najjada encountered the same fate as had the political organizations. Its increasing influence and expansion were intercepted by sympathizers of Mufti Haj Amin al-Husayni. The Husaynis, who blocked the development of all institutionalized party-oriented political operations, were even more apprehensive of the establishment of an armed youth movement. The mufti himself was concerned by the organization's meteoric rise. He feared the emergence of an alternative leadership, and in the case of al-Najjada would not listen even to the local leader of his camp, Jamal al-Husayni, who held a positive opinion of the organization and even spoke at several of its meetings.[37]

Al-Futuwwa and Suppressing al-Najjada

Al-Najjada's initial success and the thousands of youngsters whom it attracted hastened the mufti's decision to disrupt the organization's expansion by maligning it and by founding a rival youth organization, which he called al-Futuwwa (the Spirit of Youth).[38] In July–August 1946, the Husayni newspapers, particularly *Al-Wihda*, began a campaign vilifying al-Najjada and its leader, Muhammad Nimr al-Hawwari, for encouraging factionalism. Al-Najjada's reply to these accusations appeared in the widely circulated Jaffa newspaper *Al-Difa'*, and its leaders declared their commitment to running their patriotic struggle "efficiently, with no licentiousness, self-congratulatory acts, or utilitarian propaganda. All this in accordance with scientific, modern, and democratic principles, and as an organization that obeys God and His messenger, as well as our leader—the Arab Higher Institution."[39]

Al-Najjada's declarations of loyalty to the Arab Higher Institution and to the Husayni leadership notwithstanding, the mufti decided to establish al-Futuwwa as an alternate organization with no semblance of autonomy. Muhammad Nimr al-Hawwari related in a conversation with an Arab journalist from Haifa that Jamal al-Husayni had ordered him to subject his organization to the authority of the Arab Party on pain of death. Al-Hawwari agreed to merge al-Najjada with the new movement initiated by the Husaynis, stipulating that the new organization thus formed could not be under the influence of any political party and that it must have a coherent constitution.[40] The constitutive assembly of al-Futuwwa took place in September 1946, declaring a membership of 3,500 young people.[41] Al-Hawwari and his organization, who could not compete with the well-oiled mechanisms of the Husayni camp, submitted to their edicts. The two organizations were united in January 1947 and formed the Young Arab Organization (Munthamat al-Shabab al-'Arabi). The mufti appointed Mahmoud Labib, a former Egyptian officer and a close associate of the Muslim Brotherhood, to head the organization. Labib occupied this role in the joint organization until August 1948.[42] Thus the rise of al-Najjada was interrupted and the beginnings of an armed alternative to the mufti's leadership were eliminated. The united organization did take part in the battle for the land, but its contribution was mainly symbolic—aside from a minor part in the fighting in Jaffa and Haifa, it could boast of no significant achievements.⁴³

The Scouts

Arab Scouts (Jam'iyyat al-Kashaf al-'Arabi) first emerged in Palestine in the late Ottoman period. The organization grew with the commencement of World War I, following an Ottoman decision to promote its activities. During the British Mandate, Scouting groups were established alongside government schools, and these were supervised and led by the teachers. Controlled by the British Department of Education, these groups minimized manifestations of active nationalism. Scouting groups were also established by private schools, clubs, and societies—particularly those run by Christians. The number of Palestinian Arab Scouts associated with the international Scouting organization reached 1,900 in early 1946, about one quarter of them girls.⁴⁴ The British Mandate government's official recognition of the Palestinian Scouts is not to be taken lightly, particularly considering the role of the Scouts in the 1936–1939 revolt. Only after World War II—and due to the pressure brought to bear by leaders of the international Scouting organization on the mandate government and on representatives of the Arab League and the affiliated Arab Scouts organization—did the Palestinian Scouts receive government recognition. Its members could now wear their official Scout uniforms in local marches.

The first general meeting of local Scout leaders was held in mid-July 1945, and the establishment of the Palestinian Scout Association was thereby declared. Fawzi al-Nashashibi of Jerusalem was elected president of the association, assisted by Jamal al-Qaddumi of Jaffa and 'Atef Nurallah of Haifa. The meeting also confirmed establishment of the Palestinian Sports Association (al-Ittihad al-Riyadi al-Filastini). From this point and until the beginning of the violent clashes in November 1947, the number of Scouting chapters and members steadily rose. A total of 186 chapters were established, and about ten thousand members signed up.⁴⁵

The Scouting movement gradually became embroiled in politics and in the national struggle, as reported by Yaakov Shimoni, of the Jewish Agency's Arab Division:

These troops undoubtedly nurture extreme nationalism. They endeavor to enhance the pan-Arab spirit through organized visits and trips to neighboring Arab countries, where the Scouts of Arab Palestine are warmly welcomed. Scout troops engage in field training, drills, and physical education. Rumors say that they also receive some weapons training. Scout troops have been known to serve as organizational centers for activities of the national movement. At present the Arab national movement is oriented more toward political and diplomatic forms of action, particularly with the assistance of Arab countries and the Arab League. The revived Scouting movement may possibly serve in the future as a catalyst for other activities, if so directed by the leadership. It is noteworthy that the Scouts have many adult members as well.[46]

Cultural Clubs

Modern social clubs began emerging in Palestinian society from the early twentieth century, with the establishment of cultural and literary clubs affiliated with the Arab national associations of the Ottoman Empire in major cities, Jerusalem in particular. At the beginning of the British Mandate, in the 1920s, the British Council began establishing Anglo-Arab cultural clubs, with the aim of disseminating the English culture and promoting amicable relationships between the British and residents of their colonies. The clubs initiated cultural events among the local Arab population, including lectures, exhibitions, plays, and book fairs. British Council clubs were located in expansive buildings, which also housed libraries, reading rooms, and playgrounds. Most of the Arabs who frequented these clubs were high officials and British army and police recruits. However, in the early 1930s, as Arab antagonism toward the British increased in the aftermath of the events of 1929, more commonly known in Palestinian jargon as Habbat al-Buraq (the Tempest of the Western Wall), the Arab public began to keep its distance. The British tried to overcome local reluctance by using a new title, Unity Clubs, but it was not long before rumors began circulating that the clubs were in fact imperialist spy centers.

During the latter half of the 1930s the Arab clubs played an important role in national endeavors, particularly in organizing the Great Strike of 1936 and in providing information and propaganda during the armed revolt. In major cities and towns, club members served as "inspectors." They forced business owners to close their shops during the strike and reported strike violators to the national committees. The clubs may be divided into three categories: (1) nationally oriented (Palestinian or pan-Arab) clubs, (2) religious-ethnic clubs, and (3) family-centered clubs.

Nationally oriented clubs. Clubs in this category promoted concepts of local Palestinian nationalism (wataniyya filastiniyya) and pan-Arab nationalism (qawmiyya 'Arabiyya). Their names usually commemorated Arab scientists, military leaders, authors, and poets associated with Arab-Islamic classical culture, or had modern national Arab connotations, such as the Arab Club (al-Nadi al-'Arabi) or the Young Arab Club (Nadi al-Shabab al-'Arabi). They hosted Arab cultural icons: singers such as Um Kulthum, Muhammad 'Abd al-Wahab, and Farid al-Atrash; authors such as Ibrahim 'Abd al-Qadir and Khayr al-Din al-Zirakli; and movie and theater actors such as Najib al-Rihani and Yusuf Wahba. Visiting guests lectured and performed at the municipal centers of Jaffa, Haifa, and Jerusalem. The public flocked to these popular performances. Other clubs served groups of workers and immigrants from neighboring Arab countries, for example, the Syrian Club in Haifa and the Egyptian Club in Jaffa.

Religious-ethnic clubs. Clubs in this category served members of a single religious or ethnic group. Muslims operated a group of clubs incorporated in the Young Muslim Association (Jam'iyyat al-Shubban al-Muslimun), with branches in cities, towns, and large villages. Other associations were the Religious Adherence Association (Jam'iyyat al-I'tisam), the Association of Observers of Virtues (Jam'iyyat Ansar al-Fadila), and the Boys of Muhammad Association (Jam'iyyat Fityan Muhammad). These associations engaged in religious instruction and cultural activities and sometimes organized popular protests against British policy and Zionist activities.

Christian ethnic clubs were divided by churches and sects. Attempts to establish pan-Christian clubs were unsuccessful. Only the Young Men's Christian Association (YMCA), funded by European elements, held inclusive Christian activities. Christian clubs operated charitable, welfare, and educational societies. Most Christian clubs were less involved in politics than Muslim clubs, aside from the clubs of the Orthodox community and the Scouting troops and sports societies affiliated with them. These clubs engaged mainly in matters involving culture and sports.

Other ethnic groups held club activities as well, particularly in Haifa. The Druze operated a club of the Association for Helping Needy Druze. The Matwal Shiites and the Baha'i had their own clubs. These engaged mainly in religious instruction and issues related to culture and welfare.

Family-centered clubs. Family-centered clubs evolved from the generations-old tradition of the clan *diwan* (family council) located in villages and small towns. Palestinian modernization entailed the transition of some notable rural families to the cities, and they brought this patriarchal tradition with them. Some examples are the clubs of the 'Abd al-Hadi and Jarrar families in the Jenin and Nablus regions, al-Madi in the Haifa region, al-Zu'abi in the Nazareth region, and the al-Ayubi family in the Hebron region. These family-centered clubs reinforced familial cohesiveness within the new urban reality versus the urban families with historical roots, such as al-Dajani and al-Khalidi in Jerusalem, who established similar clubs. In March 1946, 'Abd al-Hamid Yasin, a member of the Arab Office in Jerusalem, estimated the number of cultural clubs at over 150. The city with the most clubs was Haifa with twenty-seven, followed by Jerusalem and Jaffa with ten each. Medium-sized cities such as Gaza, Hebron, Acre, Nablus, Ramle, and Lydda had six to eight clubs on average.[47] Cultural clubs existed in large villages such as Ijzem, 'Ayn Ghazal (Haifa District), Majdal (Gaza District), and Safuriyya (Nazareth District).

Labor Movement and Trade Unions

The first trade union to operate among the Palestinians was the Arab Workers' Union, Jam'iyyat al-'Ummal al-'Arabiyya, founded in 1925. The union was organized in Haifa by activists affiliated with the Arab Executive Committee. At its core were railway workers from Haifa and the north, led by its founder, 'Abd al-Hamid Haymour. The union later grew and opened branches in most cities and large towns.[48] In its first two decades, the union concentrated on trade matters. It attained significant achievements in 1942–1943 by holding gatherings and organizing strikes, and succeeded in improving employment conditions of Arab versus Jewish workers.[49]

The union was recognized by the British Mandate government in 1944, and based on this recognition it began negotiating with employers on behalf of the workers. It represented Palestinian workers at international gatherings and conventions as well, initially in London in 1945. Issues related to the union's representatives in London led to the first split: communist members who objected to sending Sami Taha (1911–1947, born in the village of 'Arrabe near Jenin) and attorney Hanna 'Asfur left the union and established a new workers' union, the Arab Workers' Congress (Mu'tamar al-'Ummal al-'Arabi). The founding meeting of the congress took place in Jaffa on August 19, 1945, and Mukhlis 'Amr, Boulos Farah, and Fu'ad Nassar were appointed to its executive committee.

In September 1945 the Second World Trade Union Conference was held in Paris. Palestine was represented by two delegations: Arab Workers' Union delegates Taha and 'Asfur, and Arab Workers' Congress delegates Farah and 'Amr. On this occasion Arab Workers' Congress representatives had the upper hand and were recognized as the formal representatives, while Arab Workers' Union members participated in the role of observers. The Zionist-Palestinian conflict was discussed at the conference, but despite the strong support received from other Arab and Islamic delegations, the two Palestinian delegations did not succeed in averting the favorable resolution reached with regard to the Jewish national home.[50]

Before the split, the workers' union numbered approximately 9,100. The number of members in each chapter is shown in Table 3.1. The split within the labor movement coincided with the two factions' political-national activities. The first to embark on this course was the Arab Workers' Congress. At their initial general meeting they declared several goals and demands in the spirit of the national movement: termination of the British Mandate rule, objection to the Zionist movement, awarding Palestine independence, establishing a democratic national government, a complete ban on Jewish immigration, a ban on the sale of land to Jews, the release of political prisoners, the return of the exiles, and recognition of the Palestinian labor movement as part of the international labor movement.[51]

The Arab Workers' Union, which competed with the Arab Workers' Congress for the privilege of representing the workers, convened a general meeting in late August 1946. 'Abd al-Hamid Haymour was elected chairman and Sami Taha general secretary. Debate conclu-

Table 3.1 Members of the Arab Workers' Union

	Number of Members
Haifa	4,000
Jaffa	1,700
Jerusalem	1,234
Nazareth	400
Bayt Lahm	90
Tulkarm	182
Acre	800
Ramle	300
'Anbata	200
Salame	100
Ramallah	100

Source: Data from Farah, *Al-Haraka al-'Ummaliyya al-'Arabiyya al-Filastiniyya, Jadaliyyat Ba'thuha wa Suqutuha* [The Arab Palestinian Workers' Movement: The Paradox of Its Rise and Fall], 137.

sions were patently political. They determined the union's "national-socialist orientation," depicting it as a "reform movement striving to realize social justice through just distribution of national resources and national products of the land among manufacturers and citizens. The union strives to deliver all members of society from the shame of poverty, ignorance, and disease, and to afford equal opportunity to all."[52]

The union's nationalism had a local focus and it demanded *istiqlal watani*, that is, Palestinian, and not necessarily pan-Arab, independence. The concluding document described their rivals, the Arab Workers' Congress, as affiliates of the Soviet Union. "Any attempt by a foreign element to rule us," concluded the meeting, "is an attempt to terminate the independence and identity of the national movement, and it endangers the nation and the homeland."[53] At the same gathering, the union's name was changed to Council of Trade Unions (Majlis al-Niqabat), and its recognition by the Arab Higher Institution was stressed, legitimizing its representation of the workers. The mufti chose Sami Taha, general secretary of the council, as a member of the Palestinian delegation that left for London in early 1947.

The relationship between the council and the Arab Higher Institution was, however, short-lived. The first conflict arose when the

Arab Higher Institution called for a boycott of the International Commission of Inquiry initiated by the United Nations and for a subsequent three-day strike by the entire Palestinian economy. The Council of Trade Unions was not in favor of the boycott and the strike. In order to avoid a split, the council agreed to refrain from appearing before the commission, but declared a symbolic strike of only one hour. It received the full support of the workers who indeed went on strike for only one hour.

Now the relationship reached a point of confrontation. The Second Trade Union Convention, on August 19, 1947, adopted a stricter attitude toward the political leadership on two of the issues on its agenda. The first issue involved three financial-economic projects designed to save the lands of Palestine—the Constructive Enterprise of Musa al-'Alami, the Arab League project, and the Sunduq al-Umma (Nation's Fund) project (all detailed below). The second issue involved presenting the recommendations of the international commission to the United Nations and rumors concerning the partition plan. On the first issue the trade unions declared their support of the three projects, although the mufti's followers supported only the third. The meeting reached the following conclusion regarding the concept of partition:

> We hereby declare our objection to the partition plan of Palestine and demand that the Palestinian people be granted full independence and permission to determine their own fate. Regarding the Arab Jews, who had been living in the country prior to 1918, and their descendants, we see them as our brothers, equal citizens in all rights and obligations. Anyone who has entered the homeland without receiving the permission of its residents will be removed.[54]

As a result of these statements a major attack was launched against the unions and their leader, Sami Taha, on behalf of the Arab Higher Institution. Taha was renounced as an agent of Zionism and imperialism, and his life was threatened. On the night of September 11, 1947, Taha was shot in a Haifa alley and died of his wounds. His funeral turned into a mass protest and harsh words were voiced against the political leadership. The murder of Taha was never solved, but it was attributed by many to the Arab Higher Institution. The next day the Arab Higher Institution hastened to denounce the murder, but it was never absolved.[55] The potential goal of the murder was indeed achieved, as the unions subsequently ceased attempting to influence the political agenda, and their professional activity gradually diminished, coinciding with the overall local state of decline prior to the partition resolution.

Women's Organizations

Similar to the trade unions, Palestinian women's organizations first began by convening ad hoc gatherings in response to national political events, or with the aim of public volunteer work.[56] The first gathering was held following the events of 1929, in late October of that year, at the home of politician 'Awni 'Abd al-Hadi. At its conclusion, participants traveled in a procession numbering about one hundred cars (an impressive sight in those days) to the castle of the high commissioner, where they read their resolutions to him in Arabic and English.[57]

Throughout World War II no action was taken in this sphere, but in its aftermath two rival women's organizations were founded, following the new trend of establishing political and popular institutions. The first was the Association of Arab Women (al-Ittihad al-Nisa'i al-'Arabi). It was headed by Zulaykha al-Shihabi, Tarab 'Abd al-Hadi (the wife of 'Awni 'Abd al-Hadi), Mitil al-Mughannam (the wife of attorney Mughannam Mughannam), and journalist Sadij Nassar (the wife of journalist Najib Nassar, editor of *Al-Karmil*). The second organization was the Society of Arab Ladies (Jam'iyyat al-Nisa' al-'Arabiyyat) headed by Shahinda Dizdar. The two organizations had chapters in cities and large towns, and their rivalry was mostly personal and family based. They both focused on improving the status of Palestinian women through workshops and lectures, encouraged parents to send their daughters to school, established schools to combat ignorance, and organized evening classes for girls with no formal education. They also dealt with social issues and cared for the poor. Here, too, the British Council had an impact on the modes of organization employed. For example, the council supported the Society of Female Solidarity established by Huda Abu al-Huda, who made efforts to disseminate British culture among intellectual women.

From 1945 to 1948, women's organizations became involved in national political activities as well. A testimony from that time discussing the involvement of women's organizations in the Arab boycott of Jewish goods in Haifa relates, "The women's organization headed by Sadij Nassar and the Fatat al-'Arab Society headed by Gurget Karkar suggested that they send representatives to the committee supervising the boycott. The committee decided to include women who would then exhort their friends to avoid buying Jewish wares."[58]

Economic and Social Aspects: Rehabilitation and Its Failure

The conclusion of World War II saw the resumption of important social and economic processes that had begun in the first half of the 1930s and were interrupted by the revolt in 1936. One of the most important of these was urbanization, accompanied by a resurgence in the construction of public economic-financial institutions, which for the first time succeeded in connecting urban centers with the rural periphery.

Rural Societies and Trade Bureaus

During most of the British Mandate period, Arab villages experienced no real economic-commercial development. In the early 1920s the mandate government initiated the establishment of rural credit unions, and these performed small investments and issued loans to peasants and small commercial businesses. However these efforts floundered due to village social structure, the disinterest and suspicious attitude with which uneducated and unskilled farmers greeted offers of financial credit, and the lack of perseverance by mandate authorities. Attempts by leading rural families in the early 1930s to found rural societies failed as well, due to internal conflicts. Objections were posed by some, among them the urban elite, who perceived a potential threat to their control of the national movement and its institutions.

After World War II the absence of a strong urban leadership made it possible for the mandate government and the villagers to establish cooperative agricultural societies. By early 1947 there were 135 agricultural societies. They dug wells, installed modern pumping and irrigation systems, organized animal sales, facilitated the supply of provisions to the villages, granted loans for purchasing seed, loaned tractors and agricultural machines, and so on. These activities improved mutual relations between the rural and urban sectors and facilitated the development of a national network and central system for integrating villages and cities.

Development of Arab villages had become a significant topic on the urban public agenda. In Haifa, for example, two commercial societies were founded for "developing and improving the Arab village," which incorporated urban and rural investors—the latter from Ijzem, Tira, Tantura, and Shafaʻamr. In Jaffa, a Society for Improvement and Development was established, headed by two villagers from the vicinity, Sayf al-Din Abu Kishk, from ʻArb Abu Kishk, and Saʻid Baydas from Shaikh Munis. Similar societies were established in the Gaza District, in the towns of Faluja and Majdal, and in the southern Carmel and Bilad al-Ruha in Ayn Ghazal and Subarin. These activities were mainly supervised by the trade bureaus (*al-ʻuraf al-tijariyya*) established in the large cities at the initiative of notable families. The major bureaus were naturally located in Jaffa, Jerusalem, and Haifa. Attempts to establish an inclusive association to coordinate between all the bureaus were unsuccessful despite several meetings held for this purpose.

Tough disputes over control of the trade bureaus and the many splits and rivalries that ensued attest to their significance. In Nablus, for example, two bureaus resulting from family-based discord proceeded to compete with each other. Aside from the trade bureaus, the various industries established merchant unions, such as the grocery store union, the cloth merchants union, the handicrafts union, and the bookstore and stationery union. Representatives of these unions belonged to the municipal trade bureaus. Professionals—doctors, engineers, and attorneys—established their own unions, and some belonged to the pan-Arab unions organized by the Arab League. In time, countrywide bureaus began dealing with national, political public matters in addition to issues pertaining to economy and trade.

Financial Institutions, Opposing the Sale of Land, and the Nation's Fund

Since the 1920s Palestinian opinion leaders had gradually arrived at the recognition that preventing the sale of land to Jews was the most efficient way of opposing the plan for a Jewish national home underlying the Balfour Declaration. This recognition was voiced openly and unequivocally in contemporary journalistic debate and in the writings of Palestinian intellectuals. It did not, however, prevent interested parties from further transferring Arab land to Jews, whether through direct sales or through mediation and speculation. These efforts did not cease despite warnings by the religious apparatus of the Muslim Higher Council, headed by the mufti, and its religious ruling (fatwa) from 1935 that this act would be punishable by death.

In the 1940s the political leadership reached the conclusion that by establishing financial organizations and funds similar to those founded by the Jews they could provide a solution to this fundamental problem. The idea was that land would be bought by these organizations from those in need of money, and then turned into *waqf*, consecrated lands, which would belong to the national institutions. However, these plans too were only minimally implemented. The splits and schisms within Palestinian society once again worked to its disadvantage, and the attempt was unsuccessful. The overall social and political decline and the outbreak of hostilities were another reason that the plan did not reach fruition.

An important organization founded in order to organize the financial aspects of the national struggle was Sunduq al-Umma (the Nation's Fund). Representatives of major groups within Palestinian society had registered the fund as a company as early as 1935. The company's director and driving force was Ahmad Hilmi 'Abd al-Baqi, manager of the Nation's Bank and affiliated with al-Istiqlal. Board members included Jamal al-Husayni, president of the Arab Party; the mufti's close assistant 'Omar al-Bitar, the future mayor of Jaffa and affiliated with the Nashashibi Defense Party; Salim 'Abd al-Rahman; Ya'qub al-Ghusayn, the mayor of Ramle and president of the Youth Congress Party; Fu'ad Saba, an economist from al-Istiqlal who was affiliated with the Husaynis and the son of the mayor of Tulkarm; and finally Sa'id al-Khalil, a businessman from Haifa, affiliated with the Nashashibis. When the armed revolt broke out, the Nation's Fund halted its activities. By then it had collected about 2,400 Palestine pounds and purchased approximately 1,000 dunams of land near Gaza.[59] In September 1943 the leaders of al-Istiqlal, 'Awni 'Abd al-Hadi, Rashid al-Haj Ibrahim, and Subhi al-Khadra, established a new management for the fund and renewed its activities.

The first incident involving the fund proved controversial. Arab landowners from the village of 'Ana in the Acre District offered to sell 827.5 dunams of their land to Jews. Tenant farmers working the land turned to the Nation's Fund for help. Ahmad Hilmi 'Abd al-Baqi recognized this as an opportunity to renew the fund's activities, and his Nation's Bank purchased the land and paid the tenant farmers as decreed by British law. This initiative by al-Istiqlal was consistent with their desire to resume political activities and assume control of the leadership abandoned by the mufti, who was in Berlin at the time. The new flurry of activities was expedited by the improved financial affairs of the two social classes involved in the land deals: peasants and landowners. At this point the financial justification that had formerly prompted the decision to sell land diminished, as did the available supply. Yaakov Shimoni described the renewal of the Nation's Fund:

> The renewed fund began by mediating between fellahin and banks and money lenders, but at first the fund itself did not buy land. At the time, committees of activists were formed in the different cities, and they began to collect donations in various ways: by distributing stamps on festivals and in the streets, hanging boxes in shops and restaurants, deducting donations from purchases of sugar, rice, cloth, and so on. Fund committees visited cities in their district and held gatherings and special celebrations in villages and cities. Fund officials tried to obtain regular monthly donations and loans in addition to one-time donations. However it seems that they had more success with one-time donations, particularly at festive gatherings accompanied by fervent public speeches. This has to do with the psychological nature of the popular Arab public, which is more receptive to one-time donations, even large ones, but is not used to committing to regular donations.[60]

Shortly after renewing its activities, the Nation's Fund succeeded in arousing strong Palestinian opposition to the sale of land to Jews—not by mere words and slogans, as had previously been the case, but by providing alternatives and means of enforcement. These included, among other things, updated reports and denouncement of sales, supported by a threatening atmosphere toward those involved.[61] The fund's endeavors were not fully successful, but their impact was much greater than before. It managed to raise nearly

100,000 Palestine pounds, an enormous sum at the time, and purchased nearly 15,000 dunams that otherwise would have been sold to Jews.[62]

The main problem for the Nation's Fund was its relationship with the Husayni leadership. In its initial form the fund management boasted a diverse membership, although the Husaynis and their associates were in the majority. By renewing the fund, the Istiqlalis were now trying to make their way to the center of the political stage. The Husaynis, who had begun to recover from the mufti's collaboration with the Germans, were not interested at this time in a frontal clash with al-Istiqlal and its extensive inter-Arab relationships. They also could not reject the Nation's Fund outright, which was acquiring public prestige. On the other hand, several al-Istiqlal leaders had been in contact with Haj Amin for some time and were reluctant to become involved in a confrontation. Nonetheless, the Husaynis showed their objection to the Nation's Fund by rejecting al-Najjada, that is, by establishing a rival organization and proposing a merger under their control. This process was effected through the Constructive Enterprise.

The Constructive Enterprise and Termination of the Nation's Fund

The Constructive Enterprise (al-Mashru' al-Insha'i) headed by Musa al-'Alami, who represented Palestine in the Arab League, was established in August 1945 and began operating in early 1946. Al-'Alami was allied with a group titled the Unaffiliated Young from the Husayni camp. Unlike the Nation's Fund, leaders of the Constructive Enterprise arrived at the conclusion that no system was capable of preventing the sale of land to Jewish organizations, and that the option of alternative purchase by Arab institutions would be of no help to tenant farmers. The solution they advocated was self-development of Arab lands and bettering the condition of farmers. Only by boosting their agricultural, social, and economic standards of living, as well as health care and employment options, could impoverishment of rural communities be avoided and the sale of land to Jews be prevented.[63] Thus, the enterprise aimed at facilitating development through loans, founding schools and clinics, professional training, and establishment of a model farm. These services would be provided free of charge, and in return the villagers would refrain from selling their land to Jews. In a speech held in Haifa in early February 1946 al-'Alami said that with a sum of one million Palestine pounds he could save about thirty Palestinian villages, and he appealed to wealthy Arabs, Arab countries, and the Arab League to help raise the necessary funds.

Although the Husayni leadership expressed its full support, leaders of the Constructive Enterprise did not manage to raise significant sums among the Palestinian public. From among Arab countries, only the government of Iraq pledged a donation of 150,000 Palestine pounds in early November 1946 and another 220,000 Palestine pounds about a month later. Those opposed to the Constructive Enterprise, among them leaders of the Nation's Fund, claimed that most of the lands sold to Jews had originally belonged to urban landowners, wealthy Palestinians, Lebanese, and Syrians, and that ultimately they would be the beneficiaries, while only 15 percent of the lands originated from the fellahin, the project's genuine target. Fund advocates presented al-'Alami's plan as a fantasy and doomed to failure and were certain that its sole purpose was to disrupt their own project. In response, Musa al-'Alami charged the Nation's Fund with troublemaking, and said that their rival fund-raising was undermining the truly worthy enterprise.

The dispute was publicly manifested in the press and accusations were also voiced at gatherings and conventions held by the two sides. At the height of the controversy, members of the Arab Party announced their resignation from the board of the Nation's Fund. This step forced the two leaders, Ahmad Hilmi and Musa al-'Alami, to reach an agreement whereby they would refrain from mutual accusations and consent to a joint authority to be called the Arab Treasury (Bayt al-Mal al-'Arabi). The Husaynis and their associates were in the majority on this board. The Palestinian public seemed to have perceived this consequent fund as a united effort, as witnessed by an Arab journalist in his diary:

> The Arabs expressed much interest in the Arab Treasury established by the Higher Committee. I do not think that they had a preference for this specific fund. At first everyone was enthusiastic and believed that this fund would indeed be used to save the lands and to serve the Palestinian cause. However they rapidly became disillusioned once they understood that the fund had in fact been founded for propaganda purposes and in order to hold gatherings promot-

ing the Arab (Husayni) Party. I had the feeling that many people were repulsed and that prominent citizens [of Haifa] were planning to challenge it once again.[64]

This rivalry was in fact detrimental to both organizations and had an adverse effect on their chances of success, which had been minimal to begin with.

Cultural Aspects

In the period between the end of World War II and the Nakba, Palestinian society underwent a basic transition. It readily submitted to a process of social and political reorganization and rallied in preparation for the anticipated confrontation with the Jews. In the educational and cultural spheres as well, this was a time of development and prosperity, evident in the revival of the press. These were all indications that local society was recovering from the terrors of the 1936–1939 revolt and its aftermath.

The Educational System

A crucial area that experienced far-reaching changes during the British Mandate period was the Palestinian educational system. The mandate government had instituted a modern educational system, which gradually reduced, but did not completely abolish, traditional practices. The new system began producing results in the early 1930s, when thousands of new graduates became integrated into administration, education, health, and other fields of life. In 1933 mandate authorities developed an extensive program that strived to significantly expand the government educational network. However, this program came to a standstill during the revolt and with the outbreak of World War II. During the 1941–1942 school year the program flourished once again. The number of students in the government system reached eighty thousand, versus approximately twenty-five thousand during the 1933–1934 school year. Local residents were now enthusiastic. In the countryside, villagers began building schools at their own expense, in certain cases even paying teachers' salaries out of their own pockets. In the 1944–1945 school year the demand for government schooling exceeded the number of slots available. In the cities 8,716 students applied but only 4,721 were accepted. In the villages 13,789 applied and only 9,574 were accepted. Most Arab students who reached the age of compulsory education studied at government schools. In 1946 there were 504 such schools—78 in the cities and 426 in the rural sector. Private educational networks evolved alongside the government educational system. These were founded by foreign missions and commercially based private institutions and operated within urban and rural communities and among both Muslim and Christian religious groups.[65]

Government schools were officially designated as "Arab schools" and the mandate government did not distinguish between ethnic groupings. All lessons were in Arabic, while in some private educational institutions European languages were used. In addition to universal studies in the sciences and humanities, the curriculum at government schools included subjects pertaining to Arab identity, such as Arabic language and grammar, Arab history, and Islamic heritage. English was studied as the primary foreign language.

Some scholars investigating the history of the Palestinian educational system during the mandate period are critical of the subjects taught at government schools. 'Abd al-Qader Yusuf claimed, "The curriculum was constructed for a stable conservative society, however Palestinian Arab society was none of those. It was a society in a period of transition, formation, and creation."[66] According to Muhammad 'Urabi Nakhla, "the curriculum of the mandate government made no effort to take into consideration Arab national ambitions and desires. It purposely neglected modern Arab history and emphasized ancient history and Arab and English literature. It attempted to encourage conservative reasoning among the students."[67] Yaakov Shimoni says that:

> Government Arab schools encounter many unique educational problems, in addition to the regular problems encountered in all schools worldwide. The main problem seems to be the large gap between the concepts taught at the schools, Western concepts with their novel Western essence and ideals, and the Eastern reality characteristic of the immediate environment. Arab educators and intellectuals further protest that the education provided is not aimed at the needs of local students—particularly the secondary educational system, which focuses mainly on passing the matriculation exams and creating new "effendis" for which the country has no use. Although this problem is felt acutely in Arab cities, the deep chasm

between the educational system and the real world is even more conspicuous—so much so that its benefit is doubtful—in the rural sector, where this conflict between home and school, between the child's future and present, is unconscionable.[68]

Despite the abyss described by Shimoni, villagers were impressively willing to open new schools and help finance them. Contributions even exceeded the schools' expenses: in the 1944–1945 school year, for example, the rural sector contributed 137,900 Palestine pounds to the establishment of schools and toward funding their activities and the activities of regional educational committees. Meanwhile, the entire budget of the educational system in the rural sector was only 82,360 Palestine pounds. The next year, contributions reached 187,098 pounds while the budget comprised 124,531 pounds.[69]

The secondary educational system grew significantly during that period. While in the early 1940s the government educational system consisted of only four high schools, two of which were a two-year format in which students were not eligible for matriculation, toward the end of the British Mandate the same system encompassed twenty-two Arab high schools, seventeen of them in a two-year format. Four institutions offered postsecondary studies, that is, a fifth year of high school for training teachers. During the 1944–1945 school year, forty-eight students (eighteen of them girls) studied in the postsecondary system. The most famous of these schools were the Arab College (al-Kuliyya al-'Arabiyya), managed by intellectual and educator Ahmad Samih al-Khalidi; the Teacher Training College (Kuliyyat al-Mu'alimat); and the al-Rashidiyya High School in Jerusalem.[70] Most of their students were from the urban sector. Some studied to acquire preacademic training before applying to universities in Arab countries, Britain, or the United States.

The Arab College in Jerusalem was considered the flagship, where the government sent the very best students from all Palestinian high schools. It was fully funded by the government, and the privilege of studying there was a source of competition.[71] The atmosphere at the college dorms was described by Ihsan 'Abbas, a Palestinian intellectual from the village of 'Ayn Ghazal:

> The college was managed in an orderly fashion, and students were expected to conduct themselves accordingly. The college adminis-

trator would design a full curriculum for each trimester, with a regular timetable. Daily sports activities followed the morning shower; tennis, soccer, table tennis in the gym hall. . . . Meals were served on a strict schedule. . . . At the front of the dining room there was a platform, where the teachers dined. Then came the students' tables, each student in his place. . . . All students wore a uniform: a green jacket with the college emblem on its left breast . . . the trousers were gray, the tie green.[72]

The government policy was to train teachers and clerks, rather than establish a university and higher education per se. Only people of means were able to send their sons to study abroad. The great majority of those who traveled to foreign universities were sons of urban families and a minority came from prominent rural families; however, there were also several cases of outstanding poor students whose studies were funded by donations. When the War of 1948 broke out, 1,133 Palestinian students were abroad at school: 500 in Lebanon, 435 in Egypt, 107 in Britain, and 91 in the United States. The preferred destinations were the American Universities of Beirut and Cairo, al-Azhar University in Cairo, Oxford and Cambridge in Britain, and Georgetown University in the United States.[73]

The Arabic Press

The Arabic press made its first local appearance in 1876, when the newspaper *Al-Quds al-Sharif* (Holy Jerusalem), was published in Jerusalem. By the end of the Ottoman Period, thirty newspapers of all types had been published. The most prominent were *Al-Karmil* (weekly, Haifa, from 1908), *Al-Nafa'is* (literary monthly, Haifa, 1908), and *Filastin* (weekly, Jaffa, 1911).[74] In the period before World War I and throughout the war, almost all newspaper activity ceased, but it resumed after the British occupation of the country. In the 1920s dozens of newspapers were published, but they were short-lived and had a limited impact. A major transformation occurred following Habbat al-Buraq (the Tempest of the Western Wall). At this time daily newspapers began appearing, and the press assumed a double role: it both disseminated information and shaped public opinion and the evolving public discourse.

Contemporary journalistic discourse may be said to have consisted of five major domains: intra-Palestinian issues, inter-Arab issues, relationships with the Jewish settlement, relationships with Britain, and attitudes toward the world at large.

The press managed to cover internecine conflicts and attempted to cope with the shortcomings of Palestinian society. It also led processes aimed at shaping a Palestinian national identity and creating national institutions. Aside from isolated cases the press was willing to help publicize the basic demands of the national movement—mainly, termination of the British Mandate, halting Jewish immigration, and founding an independent Palestinian state. It became integrated into the pan-regional Arab cultural expanse and developed a discourse with the press of neighboring countries, particularly Egypt, Lebanon, and Syria. Senior journalists from the area visited and helped develop and nurture local journalistic practices. Palestinian newspapers were dispatched to neighboring Arab countries, informing their residents of local happenings. Palestinian journalists published newspapers in Arab countries, including *Alef Baa* in Damascus and *Al-Shura* in Cairo, and thus tried to assist the Palestinian struggle. Most of the newspapers were hostile toward the Jewish settlement and objected to the Jewish national home plan. However, some, such as *Al-Nafir*, *Al-Akhbar*, and sometimes *Mir'at al-Sharq*, were sympathetic toward the Zionist enterprise and described it as a source of prosperity for the entire country. There were also attempts at cooperation between Arabic and Hebrew newspapers, such as the collaboration between the Jaffa-based *Al-Difa'* and the Tel-Aviv-based *Haboqer*, which lasted from 1934 to 1948. This consisted of mutual updates, transporting reporters between the sides to cover events, and accompanying reporters on both sides in times of tension. In addition, Arabic newspapers were published by Jewish organizations, for example *Al-Salam* (Peace), by Nisim Malul (which appeared irregularly in the early 1920s), and *Haqiqat al-Amr* (the Truth of the Matter), published by the Histadrut from 1937 to 1960.

The newspapers were consistent in their view of Britain. They constantly complained about the discrimination of British censors and authorities toward the Arabic versus the Hebrew press. Tensions surrounding this issue rose particularly during 1930–1936, when the Arabic press reached the height of its influence in the Palestinian public arena, often in advance of the political leadership. The press, for example, spearheaded the process leading to the Great Strike that preceded the revolt in 1936, when the leadership was still mostly hesitant. The British censors reacted strongly to these endeavors, issuing warnings to the newspapers and interrupting their publication, and even arresting and incarcerating journalists and editors (for example, Akram Zu'aytir, Munif al-Husayni, and 'Ajaj Nuwayhid).

The Palestinian press expressed interest in world events, particularly those with possible implications for the Palestinian cause. In the 1930s most Arabic newspapers underwent a significant transition from an attitude of admiration for the liberal West to one of estrangement and even hostility, coupled with enthusiasm for the achievements of totalitarian regimes in Italy and Germany. General Arab hostility toward Britain and France—the powers that had conquered and now controlled the Arab expanse—and the dictatorships' use of propaganda, rallying the young, and employing symbols of power, aroused Palestinian interest as well. The Arabic press also discussed fascist and Nazi doctrines and the ideology of these movements, as well as affairs in the center of Western conflicts, such as the confrontation between Italy and Ethiopia and the Spanish Civil War. However, initial enthusiasm for fascist ideology gradually gave way to criticism, as on the eve of World War II most local Arabic newspapers and the majority of their opinion leaders were already expressing distaste with the racist views of these regimes.[75]

During World War II the Palestinian press was strictly supervised by the British censor. The few newspapers that held on received information from the Arab News Agency, established by the British in 1941 for purposes of disseminating propaganda. After the war a rapid process of recovery occurred: press centers in Jaffa, Jerusalem, and to a certain degree Haifa as well, were revitalized, and the press resumed its role as a tool directing public opinion in preparation for the encroaching time of judgment. The two large daily newspapers, *Filastin* and *Al-Difa'*, were complemented by three more dailies: *Al-Wihda*, *Al-Sirat al-Mustaqim*, and *Al-Sha'b*. Newspapers with a leftist orientation, *Al-Ittihad*, *Al-Ghad*, and *Al-Mihmaz*, appeared as well, as did newspapers with an Istiqlali orientation, such as *Al-Huriyya* and *Al-Mustaqbal*. There were also sports- and leisure-focused newspapers such as *Al-Hadaf*, and newspapers that dealt with cinema and radio, such as the journal *Al-Muntada* that appeared on behalf of the British government press bureau, as well as dozens of weeklies, biweeklies, and monthlies of various types.[76] During the two to three years prior to the War of 1948 the Palestinian press succeeded in resuming its former status as opinion shaper on national political issues, affecting social, economic, and cultural processes.

Poetry and Literature

In the creative arts Palestinians were part of the general Arab world, centered on Egypt and Lebanon, with works aimed at consumers of literature and philosophy in the entire Arab region. However, there was also an internal circle of authors who wrote for local consumption, and some even attained a wider reputation.

Poetry was the most common and influential of the literary arts. During the mandate period four popular poets were known for their political ideological poetry: Mutlaq 'Abd al-Khaliq (1910–1937, born in Nazareth), Ibrahim Tuqan (1905–1941, born in Nablus), 'Abd al-Rahim Muhammad (1913–1948, born in the village of 'Anbata), and 'Abd al-Karim al-Karmi (Abu Salma, 1909–1982, born in Tulkarm). 'Abd al-Khaliq died young in a traffic accident in Haifa, but left several collections of poetry that helped shape Palestinian national consciousness in the 1920s. Ibrahim Tuqan died young as well, at the age of thirty-six. His poetry succeeded in reaching a wide audience throughout the Arab world. It reached the heart of Palestinian consciousness with the famous song "Black Tuesday," written on June 17, 1930, when the mandate government sentenced to death three of those involved in the Events of 1929 in Safed and Hebron. Verses from this poem became slogans, which have been used ever since at national events. The song describes the British and the Zionists:

Since their conquest disaster and tragedy have not ended
You have brought abuse and poverty, and all things accursed
You breached all order, and they are arriving in torrents
Sweeping away our people, the destitute, the fettered.[77]

He wrote of the rising Jewish immigration in the first half of the 1930s:

Some say that thirteen is the unlucky number
Not so, it is one thousand. And who can deny:
One thousand immigrants. One thousand illegals. One thousand tourists.
One thousand deceptions. Yes, one thousand is the number.[78]

After his early death in 1941 his poems continued to influence Palestinian nationalism. When the Palestinian Authority was founded in 1994 it chose one of his famous songs, "My Homeland," as the national anthem.

Poet 'Abd al-Rahim Muhammad also held an important place in Palestinian consciousness. He became known, among other things, for standing in the path of Emir Saud's convoy and reciting a long poem of condemnation against the Arab countries' indifference to the fate of Palestine when the Saudi king's son passed near his village in 1935.[79] In some of his well-known poems he demanded that the principle of armed struggle be embraced. One of these was "Poem of a Shahid":

> *I gather all my blood with my two hands*
> *I will carry it with me to the battlefield,*
> *Striving for life, a place in the world,*
> *A fighter for whom everyone's heart will beat,*
> *Or I will drop, die, and the heart will stop,*
> *But the shame will reach into the heart of the enemy.*[80]

'Abd al-Rahim Muhammad became a much-admired figure when he was killed and recognized as a *shahid* (martyr) in the War of 1948, in the battle for the village of Shajra, on July 10, 1948.

Poet 'Abd al-Karim al-Karmi of Tulkarm is better known by his literary epithet "Abu Salma." He is known among other things for his song of lamentation written in 1937 after the execution of Shaikh Farhan al-Sa'di, a senior leader of the armed bands during the revolt. The poem denounced Arab leaders for their impassiveness:

> *Oh Arab kings, cursed is the day you were born*
> *The blood of the shahid calls to you in vain*
> *Open your eyes—our people are once again tossed*
> *Between empty promises and futile threats.*[81]

Al-Karmi had Marxist leanings and was active in the Communist Party and among the circle of affiliated Arab intellectuals. His poetry was characterized by a pronounced social motif and he voiced a demand to resist social exploitation and to unionize the workers.[82]

Among writers of prose, Khalil Baydas, owner and editor of the literary journal *Al-Nafa'is* (Precious Things) is considered a pioneer of Palestinian story writing. He began his career by translating stories and novels written by great Western authors, and slowly proved his mettle as an author in his own right. In 1920 he wrote *The Heir*, considered the first Palestinian novel. The best-known Palestinian novel is *Muzakkarat Dajaja* (Memoirs of a Chicken), written by Ishaq Musa al-Husayni (1904–1990). This literary work is replete with symbols interpreted by some as referring to the Palestinian-Zionist conflict.[83] Others find associations with universal concepts in his work.[84] Literary critic Mahmoud Ghanayim summarizes the novel:

> This is the story of a wise chicken, who strives for good and attempts to implement ideals of justice, love, and avoiding aggression. She acts to impart these attributes to her daughters and friends. However other chickens attack her abode and take control of it. The wise chicken gives a long speech and suggests that her friends leave without resisting. She herself decides to remain in order to continue her mission and promote her ideals.[85]

Other noteworthy writers are political leader Jamal al-Husayni, who wrote two novels, *On the Hijaz Railway* and *Thurayya*, as well as Najati Sidqi, who in 1947 published the collection of stories *The Sad Sisters*, on the Palestinian-Zionist conflict and the "Hebraization" of the country. Some writers emerged in the rural domain as well and described life in this sector. The most conspicuous were Hassan Mustafa, from the village of Batir in the vicinity of Jerusalem, who published a collection of stories called *Village Views*, and 'Abd al-Hamid Yassin, from the village of Lifta near Jerusalem, who published a collection called *Stories*.

Research and Textbooks

The scientific fields of research that occupied Palestinian scholars during this period were Arabic literature and language, history, culture, and traditional Muslim-Arab society. A prominent figure in the field of Arabic literature and language was Muhammad Is'af al-Nashashibi (1882–1942), who authored approximately ten compositions on these topics. He was a major Arab intellectual and member of the Academy of Arabic Language in both Cairo and Damascus. Another important researcher in this field was Khalil al-Sakakini (1878–1953), who was also active in the educational sphere and was in charge of Arabic language studies in the educational administration of the British Mandate government. Worthy of mention in the field of history and culture are folklore researchers 'Umar al-Salih al-Barghuti (1894–1965) and Tawfiq Kan'an (1882–1964). They published articles that documented the image of Palestinian society during the mandate period in the *Journal of the Palestinian Oriental Society*.

Authors of textbooks, particularly books of history and culture, were influential during this period. The most significant included Khalil Tawtah (1887–1955) and 'Umar al-Salih al-Barghuti, who wrote the series *History of Palestine*; as well as Wasfi 'Anabtawi (1903–1985), supervisor in the British Mandate Department of Education; and Sa'id Saba' (1900–1967), who wrote the textbooks *The Ancient World*, *The New World*, and *Summary of the History of the Middle Ages and the Modern Era*. Saba' also wrote *History of the Ancient Cultures* and *History of Syria and Palestine*. Textbooks were also written by political activists Rafiq al-Tamimi (1889–1956), a close associate of the mufti and the Husaynis; Akram Zu'aytir; Darwish al-Miqdadi; and 'Izzat Darwaza, affiliated with al-Istiqlal.

Impending Disaster

On November 29, 1947, the UN Assembly approved the plan to partition the country into two states, a Jewish state and an Arab state. This resolution had a critical impact on the history of the two nations fighting for the country and on their respective evolution. The Palestinian leadership rejected the proposal. As did most Arab leaders, they embraced the concept of "everything or nothing." They sought to prevent implementation of the resolution by power of force, although such force was not at their disposal. Even the little that they managed to accumulate in the years discussed above was fragmented and wasted on entangled rivalries and internecine conflicts. They eventually paid a very steep price. The Arab world, whose leaders declared their patronage of the Palestinians, was of no avail. The Arab League sent an army of Arab volunteers—the Liberation Army—under the command of Fawzi al-Qawiqji. This army and the irregular Palestinian forces, the Holy Jihad Army, carried the brunt of the fighting against the partition plan until the Jewish state was declared on May 15, 1948. On that day the regular Arab armies became involved and fought on behalf of the Palestinians until the cease-fire in early 1949. In the course of the war the Palestinian nation underwent a complete transition. From a nation endeavoring to become united on its own land, it became a nation scattered among many countries.

Notes

1. B. N. al-Hout, *Al-Qiyadat wa al-Mu'ssasat al-Siyasiyya Fi Filastin, 1917–1948* [Leadership and Political Institutions in Palestine], 447.
2. B. N. al-Hout, *Al-Qiyadat wa al-Mu'ssasat al-Siyasiyya Fi Filastin, 1917–1948* [Leadership and Political Institutions in Palestine], 447.
3. The contemporary title of the Arab League.
4. Al-Gabha al-'Arabiyya. *Al-Qanoun al-Asasi wa al-Nizam al-Dakhili* [Arab Front, the Basic Constitution, and the Internal Regulations].
5. Al-Gabha al-'Arabiyya. *Al-Qanoun al-Asasi wa al-Nizam al-Dakhili* [Arab Front, the Basic Constitution, and the Internal Regulations].
6. B. N. al-Hout, *Al-Qiyadat wa al-Mu'ssasat al-Siyasiyya Fi Filastin, 1917–1948* [Leadership and Political Institutions in Palestine], 478.
7. On Radwan al-Hiliw and other party leaders' role in the Palestinian revolt, see Yasin, "Al-Hizb al-Shuyu'i al-Filastini wa al-qadiyya al-wataniyya" [The Palestinian Communist Party and the National Issue].
8. For more details on the platform, see al-Ghoul, *'Usbat al-Taharrur al-Watani fi Filastin, Nash'atuha wa Tatawwuruha wa Dawruha, 1943–1948* [National Liberation League in Palestine: Its Growth, Development, and Role], 77–80.
9. Al-Budayri, *Tatawwur al-Haraka al-'Ummaliyya al-'Arabiyya Fi Filastin, 1919–1948* [Development of the Arab Workers' Movement in Palestine], 294.
10. *Al-Ittihad*, November 6, 1946.
11. *Al-Ittihad*, November 6, 1946.
12. The group included Farid al-Sa'd, 'Izz al-Din al-Shawwa, Rashad al-Shawwa, Wasif Kamal, Khulusi al-Khayri, Mamduh al-Sukhun, Farid Ya'ish and Darwish al-Miqdadi.
13. *Kitab al-Qawmiyya al-'Arabiyya: Haqa'iq wa Nata'ij* [Book of Arab Nationalism: Truths and Results], pamphlet published by the movement, cited by B. N. al-Hout, *Al-Qiyadat wa al-Mu'ssasat al-Siyasiyya Fi Filastin, 1917–1948* [Leadership and Political Institutions in Palestine], 492.
14. *Kitab al-Qawmiyya al-'Arabiyya: Haqa'iq wa Nata'ij* [Book of Arab Nationalism: Truths and Results].
15. For example, Wasif Kamal and Mamduh al-Sukhun joined up with the general commander of the revolt, 'Abd al-Rahim al-Haj Muhammad. Farid Ya'ish often joined the band of Yusuf Abu Durra and 'Arif 'Abd al-

Raziq, while Darwish al-Miqdadi collaborated with 'Izzat Darwaza, secretary of the Central Committee of the Jihad, located in Damascus.

16. B. N. al-Hout, *Al-Qiyadat wa al-Mu'ssasat al-Siyasiyya Fi Filastin, 1917–1948* [Leadership and Political Institutions in Palestine], 496.

17. B. N. al-Hout, *Al-Qiyadat wa al-Mu'ssasat al-Siyasiyya Fi Filastin, 1917–1948* [Leadership and Political Institutions in Palestine], 496.

18. I. M. al-Husayni, *Al-'Ikhwan al-Muslimun* [Muslim Brothers], 25.

19. I. M. al-Husayni, *Al-'Ikhwan al-Muslimun* [Muslim Brothers], 125–133.

20. I. M. al-Husayni, *Al-'Ikhwan al-Muslimun* [Muslim Brothers], 125–133.

21. "Muqarrarat mu'tamar al-Ikhwan al-muslimin fi Haifa—1947" [Resolutions of the Convention of the Muslim Brothers in Haifa], cited by B. N. al-Hout, *Al-Qiyadat wa al-Mu'ssasat al-Siyasiyya Fi Filastin, 1917–1948* [Leadership and Political Institutions in Palestine], 503.

22. Al-'Arif, *Nakbat Bayt al-Maqdis wa al-Firdaws al-Mafquod, 1947–1952* [Nakba of Jerusalem and Lost Paradise], 2:398.

23. I. M. al-Husayni, *Al-'Ikhwan al-Muslimun* [Muslim Brothers], 33–35.

24. B. N. al-Hout, *Al-Qiyadat wa al-Mu'ssasat al-Siyasiyya Fi Filastin, 1917–1948* [Leadership and Political Institutions in Palestine], 497.

25. Sa'ada, *Marahil al-Mas'ala al-Filastiniyya, 1921-1949* [Stages of the Palestinian Question], 93–94.

26. Hizb al-Ba'th al-'Arabi [Arab Ba'ath Party], *Al-Ba th wa Qadiyyat Filastin, 1944-1948* [Al-Ba'ath and the Question of Palestine], 37–38.

27. "Bayan majlis hizb al-ba'th al-'arabi fi Filastin—1947" [Declaration of the Council of the Arab al-Ba'ath Party in Palestine], cited by B. N. al-Hout, *Al-Qiyadat wa al-Mu'ssasat al-Siyasiyya Fi Filastin, 1917–1948* [Leadership and Political Institutions in Palestine], 794–795.

28. Hizb al-Ba'th al-'Arabi [Arab Ba'ath Party], *Al-Ba th wa Qadiyyat Filastin, 1944–1948* [Al-Ba'ath and the Question of Palestine], 88–90.

29. Israeli historiography commonly refers to this as the Salvation Organization. *Al-Najjada* literally means people who hasten to help those in distress, and the adjective *najad* complements the qualities of *muru'a*— the pious qualities—in ancient Arab culture. On the emergence of the organization as a response to the military organizations of the Jewish settlement, see Kabha and Osatzky-Lazar, "Irgun hahagana be'aynay ha'aravim, hiquy shelo hisliah" [The Hagana Organization as Seen by the Arabs: An Emulation That Did Not Work Out], 303–342.

30. Kabha and Osatzky-Lazar, "Irgun hahagana be'aynay ha'aravim, hiquy shelo hisliah" [The Hagana Organization as Seen by the Arabs: An Emulation That Did Not Work Out], 318.

31. *Al-Difa'*, January 18, 1946.
32. B. N. al-Hout, *Al-Qiyadat wa al-Mu'ssasat al-Siyasiyya Fi Filastin, 1917–1948* [Leadership and Political Institutions in Palestine], 510.
33. *Al-Difa'*, January 18, 1946.
34. From the personal diary of a Haifa-based Arab journalist, in the Hashomer Hatza'ir Archives (hereafter HHA) 90–35.5 (4).
35. Archives of the Haganah (hereafter AH) 105/67, *Al-Difa'*, July 20, 1946.
36. AH 105/69.
37. B. N. al-Hout, *Al-Qiyadat wa al-Mu'ssasat al-Siyasiyya Fi Filastin, 1917–1948* [Leadership and Political Institutions in Palestine], 510.
38. The word *futuwwa* has been used in various fashions: to describe courageous young warriors, as the "lively spirit of youth," or the street bullies who served local masters in the cities (*Qabadayat*).
39. *Al-Difa'*, August 28, 1946.
40. From the personal diary of a Haifa-based Arab journalist, HHA 95–35.5 (5).
41. *Al-Difa'*, September 13, 1946.
42. *Filastin*, August 13, 1948.
43. Muhammad Nimr al-Hawwari's omission of the al-Najjada chapter in his life, in his book *Sir al-Nakba* [Secret of the Disaster], published in the early 1950s, is conspicuous. Having represented the Palestinian refugees at the Lausanne talks, he then returned to Israel. His integration into the legal system as attorney and judge is the basis for his subsequent reluctance to mention the "sins" of his past.
44. Shimoni, *'Arviyei Eretz Yisrael* [Arabs of Palestine], 375.
45. B. N. al-Hout, *Al-Qiyadat wa al-Mu'ssasat al-Siyasiyya Fi Filastin, 1917–1948* [Leadership and Political Institutions in Palestine], 515.
46. Shimoni, *'Arviyei Eretz Yisrael* [Arabs of Palestine], 376.
47. *Al-Wihda*, March 16, 1946.
48. For more information, see al-Khafsh, *Muzakkarat Hawl Tarikh al-Haraka al-'Ummaliyya al-Filastiniyya* [Memories of the History of the Palestinian Workers' Movement], 11–12.
49. Al-Khafsh, *Muzakkarat Hawl Tarikh al-Haraka al-'Ummaliyya al-Filastiniyya* [Memories of the History of the Palestinian Workers' Movement], 11–12.
50. B. N. al-Hout, *Al-Qiyadat wa al-Mu'ssasat al-Siyasiyya Fi Filastin, 1917–1948* [Leadership and Political Institutions in Palestine], 522–523.
51. Yasin, *Hamas, Harakat al-Maqawama al-Islamiyya fi Filastin* [Hamas: The Islamic Resistance Movement in Palestine], 124.
52. Al-Khafsh, *Muzakkarat Hawl Tarikh al-Haraka al-'Ummaliyya al-Filastiniyya* [Memories of the History of the Palestinian Workers' Movement], 32–33n48.

53. Al-Khafsh, *Muzakkarat Hawl Tarikh al-Haraka al-'Ummaliyya al-Filastiniyya* [Memories of the History of the Palestinian Workers' Movement], 34.

54. Al-Khafsh, *Muzakkarat Hawl Tarikh al-Haraka al-'Ummaliyya al-Filastiniyya* [Memories of the History of the Palestinian Workers' Movement], 48–50n48.

55. Al-Khafsh, *Muzakkarat Hawl Tarikh al-Haraka al-'Ummaliyya al-Filastiniyya* [Memories of the History of the Palestinian Workers' Movement], 53.

56. On women's activities in this period, see Moghannam, *Arab Woman*; and Fleischmann, *The Nation and Its "New" Women*.

57. For more information about this gathering, see Zu'aytir, *Bawakir al-Nidal* [First Fruit of the Struggle], 56.

58. Personal diary of an Arab journalist from Haifa, HHA 90–35.5 (4).

59. Al-Safri, *Filastin al-'Arabiyya Bayn al-Intidab wa al-Suhyuniyya* [Arab Palestine Between Mandate and Zionism], 1:251. A dunam measures approximately 1,000 square meters.

60. Shimoni, *'Arviyei Eretz Yisrael* [Arabs of Palestine], 354.

61. Diary of a Palestinian journalist, HHA 95.35.5 (1).

62. Shimoni, *'Arviyei Eretz Yisrael* [Arabs of Palestine], 358.

63. Shimoni, *'Arviyei Eretz Yisrael* [Arabs of Palestine], 358.

64. From the personal diary of a Palestinian journalist, HHA 90–35.5 (4).

65. All the data are from Shimoni, *'Arviyei Eretz Yisrael* [Arabs of Palestine], 381.

66. Yusuf, *Mustaqbal al-Tarbiya fi al-'Alam al-'Arabi fi Dou' al-Tajriba al-Filastiniyya* [Future of Education in the Arab World in Light of the Palestinian Experience], 155.

67. Nakhla, *Tatwwur al-Mujtama' fi Filastin* [Development of Society in Palestine], 359–360.

68. Shimoni, *'Arviyei Eretz Yisrael* [Arabs of Palestine], 384–385.

69. Gavish, *A Survey of Palestine*, 729.

70. Gavish, *A Survey of Palestine*, 729. {

71. On this competition, see 'Abbas, *Ghurbat al-Ra'i, Sira Zatiyya* [Foreignness of a Shepherd: An Autobiography], 109–110.

72. 'Abbas, *Ghurbat al-Ra'i, Sira Zatiyya* [Foreignness of a Shepherd: An Autobiography], 112–113.

73. Nakhla, *Tatwwur al-Mujtama' fi Filastin* [Development of Society in Palestine], 360n68.

74. For more on this period, see Kabha, *Palestinian Press*, x-xiii.

75. For more details see, Kabha, "'Oyev oyvi haveri': Hatenu'ah hale'umit hafalestinit veyahasa el hafashizem vehanazizem, 1925–1945" ["My Enemy's Enemy Is My Friend": The Palestinian National Movement and Its Attitude Toward Fascism and Nazism].

76. For information on the newspapers *Filastin, Al-Difa', Al-Wihda, Al-Sirat al-Mustaqim, Al-Sha'b, Al-Ghad, Al-Mahmaz, Al-Hiriyya, Al-Mustaqbal*, and *Al-Hadaf*, see Kabha, *Palestinian Press*.

77. Tuqan, *Diwan Ibrahim* [Ibrahim's Poetry Collection], 79.

78. Tuqan, *Diwan Ibrahim* [Ibrahim's Poetry Collection], 79.

79. 'Abd al-Rahim Muhammad, *Diwan 'Abd al-Rahim Muhammad* [Poetry Collection of 'Abd al-Rahim Muhammad], 79.

80. 'Abd al-Rahim Muhammad, *Diwan 'Abd al-Rahim Muhammad* [Poetry Collection of 'Abd al-Rahim Muhammad], 97.

81. al-Karmi, *Diwan* [Poetry], 23–24.

82. In addition to these four poets, others worthy of mention are Iskander al-Khouri al-Bitjali, Muhammad Hassan 'Ala al-Din, Burhan al-Din al-'Abbushi, and Fadwa Tuqan (1917–2004).

83. Abu al-Shabab, "Al-Qissa wa al-riwaya al-masrahiyya fi Filastin, 1900–1948" [The Theatrical Story and Novel in Palestine], Parts II–IV, 146–149.

84. Qanazi', "Qira'a jadida likitab muzakkarat dajaja" [New Reading of the Book *Memoirs of a Chicken*].

85. Ghanayim, *Al-Madar al-Sa'b, Rihlat al-Qissa al-Filastiniyya fi Isra'il* [Tough Journey: The Journey of Palestinian Short Stories in Israel], 27.

4

The War of 1948: The Nakba

During the years 1945–1947, attempts were made to recover from the destruction caused by the events of 1936 to 1939. These efforts were only partially successful, however, and the general state of affairs held no promise for the Palestinians in their confrontation with the Zionist settlement.

Arab Factionalism and the Partition Plan

In the international arena, the world at large, particularly the victorious Allies, expressed sympathy toward the aspirations of the Jewish people for a state of their own following the Holocaust. The Anglo-American Committee of Inquiry (appointed by the British government to examine the situation in the country after World War II) published its conclusions on April 20, 1946, which divested the White Paper of 1939 of its powers and motivated Britain to slightly ease restrictions on Jewish immigration to Palestine. The committee's recommendations were instrumental in the British decision to bring the Zionist-Palestinian conflict before the United Nations, where a resolution was approved to divide the country into two states: a Jewish state and a Palestinian state. The Jews were heartened by the resolution, known as the Partition Plan for Palestine of November 29, 1947, but it aroused great anger among the Arabs. The Palestinians remained constant in their objection to any compromise, particularly with regard to the idea of partition, as in their opinion the country was exclusively theirs and an inseparable part of the great Arab homeland. Any diminishing of this ideal was perceived as a conspiracy, *mu'amara* in Arabic, by those who would shift the Jewish problem from European shoulders to the Arabs and at their expense.[1] From this point, a common interpretation often employed by Arabs and Palestinians referred to a "hidden hand," which caused the world to identify with the Jewish people and secretly designed an "international conspiracy" to establish a Jewish state and prevent the establishment of an Arab state in Palestine.

Neither did the Palestinians encounter an ideal situation in the inter-Arab sphere. Arab countries competed with each other for dominance of Palestinian affairs, each striving to attain an exclusive influence. This was particularly evident in the attitude of the Arab League to selecting Palestinian representatives to serve in its institutions. Musa al-'Alami, chosen as a compromise between the various Palestinian camps, was not recognized by the Arab League as an official representative. His letter of appointment stated only that "he may appear before the League plenum and present the Palestinian cause."[2] When al-'Alami came to Cairo to take part in the constitutive convention of the Arab League, the Egyptian prime minister, Mustafa al-Nahas, received him with a stern expression, and he was not allocated a seat at the main table. Only following intervention by the British representative in Egypt, General Charles Clayton, was his presence recognized.

On March 30, 1946, the Arab League Council decided that it had "the exclusive right to select the representatives of Palestine on the League" and expropriated the Palestinians' right to select their own delegates.[3] The explanation given, that the jarring disputes among the Palestinians would make it difficult to choose a Palestinian representative who would receive the consent of all parties, was not far from the truth. As mentioned, two rival Palestinian delegations came to the convention of the League Council that convened in Bloudan, Syria, in June 1946, one on behalf of the Higher Arab Front and the other on behalf of the Arab Higher Institution, and both claimed to represent the Palestinian people. Participants of the convention became even more convinced that the Palestinians did not have sufficient political maturity and that they were incapable of independently managing their own affairs.[4] This was not far from the mark. Despite their embarrassment at having the Arab League institutions usurp their right to select their own representatives, the Palestinians were unable to overlook their disagreements and demolish the alignment of opposing camps, which continued to divide them and impair their strength and ability to act.

The mufti's return to the area and to the leadership of the national movement did not enhance Palestinian representation on the Arab League, even when discussing matters pertaining to them. Haj Amin's status and authority never resumed its former supremacy. This was particularly evident when he was not invited to a special meeting of the League Council convened in Alayh, in October 1947, to discuss developments in the Palestinian issue. The mufti came to the meeting without having been formally invited and entered the meeting room despite the objections of the organizers.[5] The mufti's efforts to counter Arab countries—mainly Hashemite Iraq and Jordan—in favor of "Palestinian independence of decision," had no chance of succeeding due to the power of the latter and the support they received from Britain, which was still influential in the league's institutions.

The United Nations and the Partition Plan

On April 2, 1947, Britain announced to the United Nations its request to discuss the issue of Palestine. When the special session of the UN General Assembly commenced, a major uproar promptly ensued following the authorization accorded to representatives of the Jewish Agency to appear before the debaters while the Arab Higher Institution received no such mandate as representative of the Palestinians. Arab delegates announced that they would boycott the deliberations if the Palestinian representatives were not invited as well. On May 7, 1947, after the British delegate declared that the Arab Higher Institution indeed represented the Palestinians, the assembly decided to invite its members to appear before the debaters.[6] The six delegates included Wasif Kamal and Rasem al-Khalidi, who had traveled with the mufti to Nazi Germany, remained with him there, and took part in disseminating propaganda against the Allies. Jewish Agency representatives raised an outcry and the United States prevented the two from entering its territory. The four other representatives, Raja'i al-Husayni, Emil al-Ghouri, Henri Katan, and 'Issa Nakhla, took part in the discussions, the Palestinian delegation received major coverage, and its members felt that their delegation had succeeded in "slightly breaching" the hostile walls of the media covering the debates of the UN Assembly's special session.[7]

However, this breach was insufficient, and the delegates felt that they were taking part in a "done deal." Historian Bayan Nuwayhid al-Hout best describes this sensation:

> Although the Arab Institution's representative presented a good legal foundation, and although his words were the absolute truth, they could not change any of the prior agreements, which were based on new vested interests involving the Middle East. The Arab delegates as well were unable to change a thing. The information eventually laid before the special investigative committee appointed by the UN, UNSCOP, was what was originally planned by the Americans.[8]

The United Nations Special Committee on Palestine

The special committee appointed by the United Nations to inspect, investigate, and provide recommendations on the partitioning of Palestine (UNSCOP) was comprised of representatives of eleven countries.[9] The Arab Higher Institution announced in a telegram to the Secretary-General of the United Nations, on June 13, 1947, that it would boycott the committee since the latter had not been requested to discuss Palestinian independence and had not been required to separate the issue of Jewish European refugees from the future of the land.[10] On June 17, 1947, when UNSCOP members arrived in Jerusalem, the Arab Higher Institution declared a general strike and it received full compliance. The political committee of the Arab League called for cooperation with UNSCOP, since Arab countries could not allow themselves to boycott the United Nations; instead, the Arab League submitted a memo to UNSCOP on behalf of all of its members and stressed Palestine's Arab character and its right to independence, as well as warning against the establishment of a Jewish state in the area. The memo stated that the only possible solution would be the establishment of an independent state in which Arabs and Jews would live as citizens with equal rights and responsibilities.[11]

In September 1947 UNSCOP completed its work and submitted its recommendations to the UN Secretary-General. These included cessation of the hostilities between Arabs and Jews, termination of the British Mandate, and granting independence to Palestine after a UN-supervised period of transition. The committee recommended that the future independent state should be democratic, and that its constitution should include UN principles, in addition to ensuring freedom of religion, honoring holy places and affording access to them, and finding a rapid solution to the 250,000 Jewish European refugees.[12] Members of the committee, however, did not reach an agreement regarding implementation of these recommendations, for which they submitted two proposals. The first (the majority report) was submitted by seven representatives, and the second (the minority report) by three representatives (the Australian representatives backed neither of the reports).[13] The majority report recommended that the country be divided into Jewish and Arab states, with a joint international regime in charge of economic unity and the administration of Jerusalem. According to this proposal, the partition would be implemented gradually and supervised by Britain and the United Nations. This proposal is known as the "partition plan." The minority report recommended establishing an independent federative state in the space of three years, with Jerusalem as its capital. This state would be managed by two autonomous governments, Jewish and Arab.[14]

The Jewish Agency announced its acceptance of the majority proposal, with some reservations. The Arab Higher Institution announced Palestinian objection to both proposals. The only solution acceptable to the Palestinians—as stressed in their announcement—was the establishment of an independent democratic state for all of Palestine. The Arab Institution intended to forcefully resist any attempt to implement either of the UN proposals.

The Partition Resolution

The debate that raged within UN corridors over these two proposals left no doubt as to the significant impact of the United States and the Soviet Union as the new superpowers. Britain, now in decline, sought to remain neutral. The United States did everything in its power to enlist support for UNSCOP's majority report. An important development occurred when the Soviet delegate to the United Nations, Andrei Gromyko, announced his country's support for the partition plan before the General Assembly. The minority proposal was rejected on November 24, 1947, and with it the Arab countries' proposal to bring the matter before the international court in The Hague. The partition plan as declared by the majority report, indicating the establishment of two states (Jewish and Arab) in Palestine, was submitted for a vote on November 29, 1947. It became an official UN resolution and was termed Resolution 181, having received the support of thirty-three countries. Thirteen countries objected and ten abstained.[15]

Initial Reactions

Palestinian representatives and Arab members of the United Nations rejected the partition resolution, as expected. The Arab world was swept by a wave of denouncements, strikes, and riots. The Arab Higher Institution declared November 29 a day of mourning. It also declared three days of strikes in which furious Arab teenagers initiated violent confrontations with Jews on intercity roads and in areas of mixed population, particularly Jerusalem and the neighborhoods connecting Tel Aviv and Jaffa.

The political committee of the Arab League held a special session during December 8–17, 1947, attended by Arab prime ministers, and published an announcement at its conclusion:

> The governments of Arab League countries are cooperating with the people to protect their Arab brethren [in Palestine], prevent the injustice threatening them, and achieve Palestinian independence and unity. The prime ministers declare the partition void and invalid. Supported by their people, they will take the firmest possible steps to thwart the exploitative partition resolution. They will embark on the battle enforced upon them and emerge victorious.[16]

This declaration signaled the beginning of preparations. Conflicting Arab concerns and problematic relationships between some of the Arab League countries and the mufti made collaboration difficult. They had no problem, however, announcing slogans and making speeches. A wave of demonstrations swept Arab countries in late December 1947. Foreign delegations, particularly of the United States and Britain, were attacked in Beirut, Damascus, and Baghdad. In Cairo, a giant demonstration was held on the campus of al-Azhar University, calling for jihad and inciting thousands of demonstrators who vociferously denounced partition and supported Palestinian independence.

The Palestinians, Arab Countries, and the Beginning of the Fight for the Land

Reactions to the partition plan among the Arab public had far-reaching implications for actions taken by Arab countries and the Arab League. The Palestinians clearly had no chance of winning the war on their own, the Arab countries were not ready from a military point of view, and none were ready for cooperation and real coordination. Nonetheless, public pressure, as well as the desire of Arab governments and leaders to promote their own interests by becoming involved in the Palestinian issue and improving their patriotic image, had the final word.[17] Bayan Nuwayhid al-Hout summarized the involvement of Arab countries and the Arab League in the first stage of the war in Palestine:

> The truth is that Palestinian Arabs could not have fought on their own from November 29, 1947, to May 15, 1948. The Palestinians were now joined by many volunteers from various Arab countries, and the Arab nations helped raise money and amass arms. This assistance was genuine and devoted, but it was not sufficient. The war in Palestine turned into a direct confrontation between Arabs and Zionists. The British, who had declared their neutrality, openly supported the Jewish fighters . . . the Arab warriors and volunteers had no chance of winning by force alone. They were fighting against the Jewish Agency, backed by international Zionism and the most powerful nations on earth, who had awarded it the partition plan. The Palestinian Arabs and their Arab Institution were backed merely by a few Islamic countries, whose only help was their words and certain sums of money, and by Arab countries whose governments calmed their agitated masses with speeches. The fighters and the volunteers were enticed by these speeches and thought that the Arab countries had

genuinely promised to rescue Palestine and would do more than hold ostentatious military parades.[18]

The Political Sphere: Between the League and the Mufti

In the political arena, the rivalry between the Arab League and its members on the one hand, and the Arab Higher Institution headed by Haj Amin on the other, was now obvious. This rivalry was clearly manifested in the animosity between the mufti and the secretary-general of the Arab League, 'Abd al-Rahman 'Azzam, as well as between the Palestinian leader and the Hashemite leaders of Transjordan and Iraq. It put an end to any attempt at joint inter-Arab efforts. The mufti believed that the conflict was, first and foremost, a Palestinian affair and that their Arab brethren should provide them with support and assistance. He refused to accept the authority of the Arab League and sought to leave his mark on every process pertaining to the Palestinian cause. The secretary-general of the Arab League, in contrast, claimed that the mere presence of the mufti was detrimental, as it aroused feelings of former hostility among his Palestinian rivals and Britain, and alienated his old rivals, the rulers of Iraq and Transjordan. Any initiative proposed by the mufti encountered the automatic rejection of the Arab League, and all his requests met with refusal. As previously mentioned, he had made a point of attending the league session in Alayh, Lebanon, without being invited. When Haj Amin entered the room unexpectedly, the Iraqi delegate, Prime Minister Salah Jaber, asked the hosting prime minister, Riyad al-Sulh, to have him forcibly removed. The host answered that traditional rules of hospitality prevented him from doing so.[19]

The mufti took the opportunity to suggest establishing an Arab government in Palestine that would manage Palestinian affairs upon conclusion of the British Mandate and withdrawal. His proposal met with strong criticism from the delegates of Transjordan and Iraq, who promptly rejected it, explaining that establishing such a government would provoke the United Nations and cause damage to the Arab image in world public opinion.[20] The mufti's demand that Palestinian civil and political affairs be managed by the institution he headed was rejected as well, based on the contention that he did not represent all Palestinians. His demand that donations made to the Arab

League fund for Palestine be supervised also met with rejection. The Arab League now assumed exclusive and absolute administration of all Palestinian political, civil, and military affairs.[21]

In light of the Arab League's consistent refusal to recognize the Arab Higher Institution as representing the Palestinians, and due to their vigorous efforts to deprive the mufti of any real influence, he decided that he would not bend to its authority. Haj Amin hoped that the presence of his activists in the field would enable him to realize his leadership even in defiance of the secretary-general of the league and the Hashemite kings. The mufti explained the motives of these rivals as resulting from US and British pressure:

> The political pressure brought to bear by Britain and America on some Arab leaders, intended to separate administration of Palestinian affairs from their true owners, led to deviation from the basic plan of the political committee of the Arab League, reached at Alayh in October 1947 with the purpose of defending Palestine. As a result of this deviation the league refrained from providing the Palestinians with essential assistance in the form of funds and arms. It weakened them and undermined their efforts and their warriors' efforts to continue their jihad.[22]

Historian Ilyas Shufani described the current state of affairs and its implications:

> On the Arab side there was almost no planning. The attitude of the Arab League toward the Arab Higher Institution suffered ups and downs. It ranged from recognition of the institution as representing the Palestinians to revocation of this fact for various reasons and causes. The common approach was to refrain from inserting Arab armies into Palestine as long as the British authorities remained in the country. This situation created two different military systems in addition to local Palestinian armed bands. The dominant Arab approach was to enable the Palestinians to defend their "country and honor" with the assistance of neighboring Arab countries but not under Palestinian command. The Arab Higher Institution's insistence on retaining its role and status, in addition to this Arab position, created duplicate activities and mechanisms.[23]

In Palestine, the mufti succeeded in reinstating his former status as the violence increased. His activists and representatives of the

Arab Higher Institution organized national committees (*lijan qawmiyya*) in the cities, towns, and villages. They ran and supervised fund-raising and aid campaigns, and organized armament and defense systems and the establishment of blockades and fortifications in border areas and within mixed cities where Arabs and Jews lived in close proximity. This activity won the Arab Higher Institution and its president popular backing. When the hostilities broke out, the mufti's popularity among the Palestinians rose once again, at the expense of his rivals, who gradually disappeared. The Nashashibi opposition was almost completely eliminated. The Istiqlalis, who had tangled with the mufti on the eve of the partition resolution, managed to reach an agreement and even cooperated with him. This was also true of leaders of the trade unions and the faction of the National Liberation League that had objected to the partition.

The Military Sphere: Forces and Rivalries

One of the confidential decisions that the Arab League political committee reached at its meeting in Alayh, Lebanon, in October 1947 was to establish a supreme military committee responsible for transferring funds, supplies, and arms to the Palestinians and supervising the war effort against the partition plan and establishment of a Jewish state. The committee was comprised of senior officers in the armies of Arab League members. It was headed by General Isma'il Safwat from Iraq, and its members were Shawkat Shuwqayr from Lebanon, Mahmoud al-Hindi from Syria, Subhi al-Khadra from Palestine, and Bahjat Tabbara from Transjordan. Later on, Iraqi general Taha al-Hashemi also joined the committee in the position of general inspector.[24]

The committee's initial report was submitted to the political committee of the Arab League even before the discussions at Alayh had been concluded. Its authors analyzed Arab-Jewish power relations and both sides' preparedness for war:

> The Zionists in Palestine have well-organized military, political, and administrative organizations and systems, and they will not find it difficult to establish a Zionist government. They have at their disposal a force based on fighters, arms, and reserve forces, with all means logistically necessary to wage a war, and large reserves are being organized for them abroad. In contrast, Palestinian Arabs do

not yet have forces comparable to the Zionist force. Those territories occupied by a Jewish majority are home to about 350,000 Arabs, who will be at risk of death and obliteration once the Zionists begin their military operations against the Arabs.[25]

This document indicates that even at such an early date the Arabs were already aware of the balance of power and of the Palestinians' military inferiority compared to Jewish forces. The Arabs also estimated that the Jewish side had advantages, both in the field and in potential reserves abroad (Jews residing elsewhere, maybe hinting at American support of the Jewish settlement). In light of this knowledge, the Arab League's confidential decision to choose to implement a military course of action is baffling. Those who initiated this decision may have acted according to one of two conflicting possibilities: they either knew that they were entering (and drawing the Palestinians into) a process whose destructive results were known in advance, or they may have estimated that despite obvious Arab shortcomings they would be able to improve their deficits, balance the power relations, or even change the balance of power. The words "do not yet" employed in the document may indicate this possibility, although it does not expressly state that regular Arab armies would operate in Palestine. Some military steps were indeed taken to protect the Palestinians, but these were incapable of balancing existing forces. The destructive outcome was rapidly evident.

Decisions for implementation reached at the Alayh meeting were summarized in seven sections:

1. It is necessary to immediately begin locating volunteers, recruiting, training, and arming them with the help of government elements and popular organizations, in accordance with the political views of the Arab countries.
2. Arab countries shall begin gathering their regular military forces near the borders of Palestine. Each force shall have its own military command.
3. An overall Arab command to which all separate commands will be subject should be established as quickly as possible.
4. It is necessary to transfer to the Arabs in Palestine sufficient quantities of arms—no less than ten thousand guns and enough machine guns, grenades, explosives, and the like.

5. It is necessary to provide the military committee of the Arab League with a sum of no less than one million dinars in order to finance Palestinian forces.
6. Arab countries must initiate the purchase of a very large quantity of arms that will be prepared for the fighters.
7. It is necessary to amass fighter planes and bombers at airfields in the vicinity of the Mediterranean in order to control sea routes and prevent the Jews from receiving reinforcements from abroad.[26]

Actual implementation of these decisions did not live up to expectations. The process of locating volunteers, as well as their recruitment, training, and arming, met with enthusiasm among Arab and Islamic countries, and young people were impressively cooperative. Recruitment offices were crowded. In Baghdad volunteers signed up at the Palestine Rescue Committee, and in Damascus at the offices of the military committee of the Arab League; in Beirut volunteers gathered at the offices of the Arab Higher Institution, and in Cairo at chapters of the Muslim Brotherhood. These centers also registered volunteers from other Arab and Islamic countries, such as Libya, Tunisia, Algiers, Morocco, Saudi Arabia, Yemen, Sudan, Turkey, and Yugoslavia (Bosnia). Many thousands applied, but much fewer were actually accepted and recruited to take part in the fighting. Historian 'Arif al-'Arif describes the situation in his book on the war:

> A week after the decision was reached, the Palestine Rescue Committee was established in Baghdad, headed by General Husayn Fawzi Ibrahim. Fifteen thousand volunteers responded to the call to enlist and most received basic military training in the army and police. Two regiments were founded, al-Qadsiyya and al-Husayn, as well as a commando company.... On January 7, 1948, the commando company left for Damascus, and a week later the two regiments arrived with their arms and ammunition. The committee was busy training a new regiment when it received notice from the military committee of the Arab League to refrain from sending any more volunteer forces to Damascus until further notice. When Prime Minister Salah Jaber returned from England he gave an instruction to send no more than five hundred volunteers. Taha al-Hashemi, general inspector of the volunteer forces, told the head of the committee: If you send more volunteers I will send them back

to Baghdad at your expense. Thus the committee stopped sending volunteers and focused on collecting donations.[27]

In Egypt the recruitment offices succeeded in attaining more impressive results, particularly at the center organized by the Muslim Brotherhood, where thousands of volunteers registered. However, the offices opened by the government rejected many of those who applied to help, claiming that there were too many soldiers willing to fight. Gamal Abdel Nasser, in his book *Philosophy of the Revolution*, attested to the recruiting dilemma:

> I remember how a day after the partition resolution, the Free Officers held a meeting and decided to help the Arab resistance in Palestine. The next day I went to the home of Haj Amin al-Husayni, the Mufti of Palestine who was residing in the Zayton neighborhood. I said to him: You must need officers to command the soldiers and train the recruits. Many in the Egyptian army are willing to volunteer and they will be at your disposal whenever you say the word. Haj Amin said that he would accept my offer after receiving the approval of the Egyptian government. I returned to him several days later. The government had not given its consent.[28]

According to the Alayh resolutions, the military committee of the Arab League was supposed to transfer arms and supplies to the Palestinians. Sources describing the fighting indicate that the arms purchased by the military committee and transported to the front were of poor quality and the number of guns did not reach the ten thousand promised. Most of these military supplies reached the Arab volunteers and not the Palestinian fighters. Constant bickering characterized the relationship between leaders of the Palestinian volunteer forces and those heading the military committee. The Palestinians accused those operating the military committee of negligence and of supplying few arms of poor quality, while the military committee complained that Palestinian commanders and fighters lacked professionalism and were incapable of receiving the arms supplied. For example, in a discussion in Damascus on April 8, a few days before he was killed at the battle for al-Qastel, 'Abd al-Qadir al-Husayni, commander of the Holy Jihad Army, who had come to Damascus straight from the battlefield in Palestine, asked the military committee to provide his men with weapons and ammunition.

> He told Taha Pasha [Taha al-Hashemi, commander in chief of the military committee]: "Why did you confiscate the weapons purchased by our people in Lebanon and prevent them from reaching us?" Taha answered: "These are cutting-edge weapons and we will give them to the regiments we recruited from among the 'Alawis and the Druze [who had received previous training in the French colonial army]." 'Abd al-Qadir answered: "Give them weapons from your own warehouses. We are entitled to the weapons purchased for us and more deserving than anyone to defend our land." However Taha did not comply with 'Abd al-Qadir's demands. In another incident . . . 'Abd al-Qadir presented maps describing the current military situation in Jerusalem and the vicinity, and the danger that the Jews would take control of the village al-Qastel. . . . He said that in order to rescue Jerusalem we must drive out the Jews, and for this purpose he needs cannons, machine guns, and ammunition. Taha answered that he has no cannons. 'Abd al-Qadir said: "You gave Qawiqji four cannons, you can lend us one of them." Taha answered him: "We're not giving them to you because you are old-fashioned irregular troops."[29]

The decision to allocate one million dinars to the military committee for arming the Palestinian forces was also not implemented. Those involved, among them non-Palestinians, indicate that the sum that was actually allocated was lower, and most of it was invested in the Arab volunteer forces and not in the Palestinian forces.[30] The supreme military committee was supposed to have ended its work upon establishment of the supreme military command of the Arab armies. In the absence of a supreme command, the committee shaped the Arab war effort. However, instead of using its authority to apply to Arab governments for support and coordinate their contributions, it operated against the Palestinians for personal or local reasons, neutralizing their activities, and destroying any display of independence on their part. The two main Arab military organizations—the pan-Arab Liberation Army and the Holy Jihad Army (controlled by the Arab Higher Institution)—operated within this jumble of tensions and distrust during the period prior to the declaration of the State of Israel, and before the Arab countries joined the war.

The Pan-Arab Effort: The Liberation Army

The military committee of the Arab League declared the establishment of the Liberation Army immediately after the partition resolution was accepted by the United Nations. The committee held intensive discussions about the composition of the command and its authority in the field. Fawzi al-Qawiqji was mentioned as a candidate for the post of supreme commander, and most of the delegates supported his candidacy due to his military experience in the Ottoman army and his active part in the Syrian revolts of 1920 and 1925, the Palestinian revolt of 1936, and the Rashid 'Ali al-Kilani coup in Iraq in 1941. Qawiqji was known for his pan-Arab views and was popular among pan-Arab circles in Greater Syria and Egypt. He also enjoyed a close relationship with King Abdullah of Transjordan, an influential figure in the Arab League at the time. However, the mufti objected to the nomination due to residual tensions from Qawiqji's first visit to Palestine, from August to October 1936, when Qawiqji commanded the Arab volunteer regiments. The strained relationship increased during the Rashid 'Ali coup in Iraq. In addition, the mufti himself had his eye on the position of supreme commander, and he had reserved the role of field commander for 'Abd al-Qadir al-Husayni. He tried to convince representatives of the military committee to declare these nominations, explaining that only the Palestinians should bear the brunt of the fighting and their Arab brethren should help by providing funding and logistical aid.[31] The military committee rejected this claim and decided to nominate al-Qawiqji as supreme commander and Iraqi general Isma'il Safwat as senior military commander. They were to command a staff consisting of members of the military committee of the Arab League and officers from the regular Arab armies.[32]

The Liberation Army was composed of eight regiments (*afwaj*, singular *fawj*). These were mostly named for battles symbolizing the beginning of Islamic military heritage, or for the fighters' geographic or ethnic origins:

> First al-Yarmuk Regiment—composed of three companies and numbering 500 troops
> Second al-Yarmuk Regiment—composed of three companies and numbering 430 troops
> Third al-Yarmuk Regiment—composed of two companies and numbering 250 troops
> Hittin Regiment—composed of three companies and numbering 500 troops
> al-Husayn Regiment (the Iraqi Regiment)—composed of three companies and numbering nearly 500 troops

Druze Regiment (Jabal al-Duruz)—composed of three companies and numbering 500 troops

Ajnadin Regiment—composed of three companies and numbering 200 troops

In addition, the army had four companies not connected to these regiments, numbering 450 troops. The Liberation Army consisted of a total of 3,830 troops.[33] The general headquarters of Qawiqji and his staff was located in the village of Jaba' between Nablus and Jenin.

These forces received a short training session at the Qatana camp in Syria and were then deployed in the parts of Palestine allocated to the Arab state by the partition resolution. On December 9, 1947, the Second al-Yarmuk Regiment, commanded by Adib al-Shishkali (later, president of Syria from 1949 to 1954), entered Palestine and was the first to be deployed. The regiment entered the Acre District through the Lebanese border with the Western Galilee. From there they were further deployed in the Upper Galilee, Safed District, and in the Lower Galilee, Nazareth District.

The First al-Yarmuk Regiment, commanded by Syrian Muhammad Safa, entered Palestine on January 22, 1948, and was deployed in the Jenin-Bisan area. In early February 1948 the al-Qadisiyya Regiment, commanded by Iraqi Mahdi Salah al-'Ani, joined the existing forces and was deployed in the Ramallah–Bab al-Wad sector. In early March 1948 the Hittin Regiment, commanded by Iraqi Madlul 'Abbas, arrived and was deployed at first in the Tubas Valley and then in the Tulkarm District. At the same time, the al-Husayn Regiment, commanded by Iraqi 'Aadil Najm al-Din, entered the city of Jaffa and its vicinity. In mid-April 1948 Najm al-Din was replaced by Palestinian Mechel al-'Issa who commanded the defense of Jaffa until its defeat on May 12, 1948. The other regiments served as a reserve force and were attached to the forces fighting on the front during May 1948.

The Liberation Army suffered from low motivation, extensive diversity of its recruits, and poor preparations, logistics, and supply systems. A glance at its documents reflects the prevalent disorder and lack of discipline.[34] Soldiers and commanders constantly complained of a lack of basic supplies, including food, clothing, and suitable sleeping equipment. What they lacked, they requisitioned by force from the local population, resulting in frequent confrontations with the villagers. The weapon situation was no better. For example, the commander of the company defending the city of Bisan wrote to members of the Arab League's military committee: "Since February 19, 1948, when I received the weapons and ammunition . . . I found only fifty rifle bullets. I found no dynamite fuses. Most of the ammunition is useless, as I saw upon examination. Some of the soldiers couldn't get even one good shot out of five bullets."[35] A severe lack of fuel often prevented the use of vehicles. Many of the commanders in the field complained that local residents were uncooperative. The same company commander from Bisan wrote, "Since receiving responsibility for Bisan I have not received any help whatsoever from the residents of the city. Neither with organization and aid, nor with guard duties." The forces of the Liberation Army suffered mainly from lack of discipline and desertion. The diary of Jordanian officer Muhammad Abu Sufa, who commanded the al-Sa'iqa Company of the First al-Yarmuk Regiment, indicates the procedures that were utilized. At first he imposed relatively lenient sanctions, such as canceling food rations or increasing guard duty. In time, punishments became stricter and included lengthy incarceration and even lashings. In one of the orders distributed among the regiment's soldiers he threatened, "Some soldiers have attempted to flee. They will be punished by incarceration and lashings. From here on any soldier who attempts to flee or asks to be released will be punished initially by lashings and imprisonment and at the next stage will be executed by firing squad. All who do so will be considered traitors and collaborators with the Jews."

When threats and reprimands did not help, and the number of soldiers in the regiment dropped due to escape and desertion, Abu Sufa tried other tactics. He tried to strike up friendships with the soldiers and expressed strong criticism of the Liberation Army. In a daily order distributed among his soldiers he wrote, "All the soldiers know that none of the senior officers wish them well. Most of the soldiers and privates who took part in the fighting in Palestine and showed impressive abilities were not commended for their work. You know that the company commander submitted a list of twenty soldiers for badges of honor . . . however!!!" This tactic too fell through. Abu Sufa confronted his commanders and abandoned his command, but he was forced to return. He brought reinforcements and suppressed the rebels. In the next daily order he concluded, "How accursed is this anarchist military system."[36] In light of the army's deficient functioning, the incident of Commander Abu Sufa and his company was probably not uncommon and surely reflects the circumstances and conduct of the Liberation Army.

The Liberation Army Fights for the Land: December 1947–May 1948

Liberation Army forces were deployed, as stated, in areas allocated in the partition plan to the Arab state. As long as they remained there, the British did nothing to intervene and even considered them responsible for securing their territory. The Liberation Army operated in two main regions: The central region was under the direct command of the supreme commander, al-Qawiqji; it included the Ibn 'Amer Valley, the "Large Triangle" (Nablus-Jenin-Tulkarm), and the Lydda-Ramle sector. The second region, commanded by al-Shishkali, was in the north and consisted of the Upper Galilee, Lower Galilee, and the Acre District along the coast.[37] This division remained in place until the regular Arab armies entered the country in May 1948, at which time Qawiqji retreated from the central region, handed it over to units from the Iraqi and Transjordan armies, and proceeded to command regiments of the Liberation Army in the Galilee, which he led until the Israeli army conquered the area in late October 1948.

At the beginning of the confrontations, the Liberation Army initiated attacks against Jewish towns and fortifications at strategic locations. At three such attacks the liberation forces suffered complete defeat. In the first attack, the Second al-Yarmuk Regiment assaulted Kibbutz Yehi'am in Western Galilee on the night of January 21, 1948. The attacking forces were unable to break into the kibbutz and had to make do with a siege. In the second attack the First al-Yarmuk Regiment assaulted Kibbutz Tirat Zvi in the Bisan Valley on the night of February 16, 1948. This time the failure was more evident. The attacking forces were repulsed and suffered severe losses— thirty-eight killed and a similar number wounded. The third and largest attack occurred between April 5 and 8, commanded by al-Qawiqji himself. Its target was Kibbutz Mishmar Ha'emeq, overlooking the road from Jenin to Haifa and blocking Arab reinforcements to the city on Mt. Carmel. The attack began as planned, and the kibbutz defenders evacuated all women and children and asked for a truce, which was attained with British intercession. Qawiqji was led to believe, and even announced, that the kibbutz would soon fall; however, he was surprised by a counterattack that rebuffed his forces, which withdrew in disorder and with acute losses.

Qawiqji's failed attack on Mishmar Ha'emeq had a disastrous effect on the morale of Liberation Army troops and of Arab fighters in the area. The Arab villages in the region of Mishmar Ha'emeq—Abu Shusha, Abu Zurayq, al-Ghubayya and Kafarin—were occupied by the Haganah and the Palmach (the Haganah's elite force) and destroyed the next day. Arab Haifa fell on April 22, 1948. Even the Arab villages on the Carmel and in the area of Bilad al-Ruha were overpowered in the period between the failed attack of the Liberation Army on Mishmar Ha'emeq and the entrance of Arab armies in mid-May 1948. An attempt at diversion by the Liberation Army in the Shafa'amr area, which reached its climax at the battle of Husha and Kasayer, failed as well. This defeat created a large gap in the lines of the Liberation Army defending the Lower Galilee.

In addition to his attempts to conquer towns, Qawiqji also tried to take over general transportation routes and to damage Jewish roads in order to isolate and weaken the towns. In March 1948 the liberation forces and Palestinian volunteer forces succeeded in isolating towns in Gush Etzyon and the Western Galilee and in blocking the road to Jerusalem and other isolated towns. They caused big losses to Jewish transport convoys traveling to isolated locations: forty-six Jews were killed in an attack on a convoy to Yehi'am in the vicinity of the Arab village of Kabri; twenty-four were killed on the way to Kibbutz Hulda; fourteen on the way to Atarot; and eleven at Hartuv.[38]

If the main task of the Liberation Army was to "liberate" Palestine and prevent implementation of the partition plan and establishment of a Jewish state, it failed. Its offensives were unsuccessful and its defense missions did not succeed in preventing the fall of Arab centers. In the period prior to arrival of the regular armies, the Jews took control of Haifa, Jaffa, Tiberias, Safed, Bisan, and many large and major villages. The presence of the Liberation Army did nothing to help the morale and the endurance of local fighters and the civilian population. Hani al-Hindi summarized the actions of the Liberation Army: "Despite the aura that had surrounded it since its arrival in Palestine, and although it took part in several important battles, this army had one big fault—the lack of a general headquarters. Qawiqji tried to solve the problem with the handful of officers and administration people who accompanied him, however this was not sufficient to correct the glaring deficiency."[39]

Palestinian Guerrilla Warfare: Army of the Holy Jihad

Finding himself marginalized by the Arab League and its military committee, the mufti's response to his poor relationship with the military committee was to found his own Palestinian military organization, the Holy Jihad Army. This army of volunteers was comprised of fighters and commanders from the 1936–1939 revolt and Palestinian World War II recruits to the British army. The Arab Higher Institution agreed to provide funding and the Arab League's military committee promised to help as well; however, only a small part of the promised allocations actually arrived. Despite the budgetary difficulties and obstacles created by the Liberation Army, the Holy Jihad Army won the sympathy of the local populace, and Palestinian youth preferred to enlist in this army rather than be discriminated against and disparaged by Qawiqji's men.

Forming the nucleus of the Holy Jihad Army was the group led by 'Abd al-Qadir al-Husayni during the revolt. 'Abd al-Qadir, son of Mousa Kathim al-Husayni, former president of the Executive Arab Committee, was one of the few members of the Palestinian urban elite to fight in the 1936–1939 revolt. He had accumulated much experience as leader of a guerrilla movement sustained by a sympathetic population, experience supplemented by formal command and staff studies at the military academy of Iraq, subsequently earning him the rank of officer in the Iraqi army. He also took part in the Rashid 'Ali al-Kilani coup. When the new units were declared, 'Abd al-Qadir was joined by his former cronies from the revolt and from the military academy, among them Ibrahim Abu Diyya, from Surif in the Hebron District; Bahjat Abu Gharbiyya, from Jerusalem; Hassan Salameh, from Qula in the Ramle District; Yahya Hawwash, from the village of al-Barwa in the Acre District; Hamad Zawati, from the village of Zawata in the Nablus District; Tawfiq al-Ibrahim (Abu Ibrahim al-Saghir), from the village of Andur in the Nazareth District; and Khalil al-'Issa (Abu Ibrahim al-Kabir), from the village of Mazra'a al-Sharqiyya in the Ramallah District. Some of these fighters had been active in the armed bands initially founded by Shaikh 'Izz al-Din al-Qassam in the early half of the 1930s. Now they were once again recognized as Qassamyiyoun (supporters of Qassam) and received the title of shaikh. They returned to the same areas in which they had operated during the revolt and promptly enlisted their former subordinates from 1936–1939 into the new bands.

Bahjat Abu Gharbiyya, commander of the Jerusalem sector, describes the formation of the Jihad Army and 'Abd al-Qadir's activities:

> In April 1947 I traveled to Cairo where I met commander 'Abd al-Qadir al-Husayni. He had called upon former warriors throughout Palestine with the intention of reorganizing them against Zionist forces in preparation for any future decision to initiate war against us. Together with 'Abd al-Qadir I devised a plan for the organization and arming of the Jerusalem sector. We determined the quantities of weapons and ammunition necessary for each neighborhood and appointed commanders. 'Abd al-Qadir promised to send us all the weapons we needed through Commander Ibrahim Abu Diyya, who would supervise the provision of supplies from Egypt to Palestine. I assumed responsibility for preparing necessary warehouses to store the weapons and people to help with their transfer. This, although the English had declared a death sentence for anyone caught with any type of weapons or ammunition.[40]

The document clearly shows that 'Abd al-Qadir al-Husayni and the Arab Higher Institution had begun preparing for a possible military confrontation with the Jewish settlement even before the partition resolution, certainly before the Arab League established its military committee. These initial actions were partly responsible for the rivalry with the Liberation Army, nurtured by the slogan declaring "Only Palestinians will fight best for Palestine."[41]

The founding of a Palestinian military force was not consistent with British and Hashemite vested interests. General Charles Clayton, the British military attaché in Egypt, who had been involved in Arab League activities since its establishment, was present at almost all meetings discussing the Palestinian issue and surreptitiously directed the Arab League's policy on the subject. British policy at the time objected to establishing a Palestinian state headed by the mufti, for several reasons. They wished to make the mufti pay for his support of the Axis forces; they were concerned that a state under his leadership would prove to be radical; and they were concerned that, confined between Transjordan and the Jewish state, it would develop irredentist ambitions toward them both and thus endanger both regional stability and British enterprises. In addition, Britain preferred to collaborate with the Hashemite Arabs, who had proven their loyalty in the difficult years of World War II and who had not forgiven the mufti for subverting the Hashemite regime in Baghdad and allying with Iraqi military officers and with Rashid 'Ali al-Kilani. The two Hashemite countries, Iraq and Transjordan, differed in their hopes for the future of the Fertile Crescent but were united in their strong antagonism toward Mufti Haj Amin al-Husayni and their rivalry with the Syria-Egypt axis at Arab League debates.

The Jihad Army Is Tested on the Battlefield

Contrary to the Liberation Army, which conducted itself as a regular army, the Jihad Army engaged in guerrilla warfare consisting of surprise attacks on transportation routes, camps, and bases. The methods and mechanisms used were very similar to those of the 1936–1939 revolt. A large majority of Jihad Army company commanders had commanded armed bands during the revolt. As was previously the case, the fighters established no civilian defense systems, of which they were totally ignorant. When necessary, mainly in mixed cities, they asked for the assistance of officers of the Arab volunteer forces or of Turkish or Bosnian officers.

Most of the Jihad Army forces were deployed in the center of the country, in the area of Jerusalem, Hebron, Jaffa, Lydda, and Ramle. The headquarters of the Jihad Army were located in the town of Bir Zayt near Jerusalem, where 'Abd al-Qadir based his command, and where Kamel 'Ariqat, from Abu Dis, and Qasem al-Rimawi, from Bayt Rima, were based as well. After 'Abd al-Qadir's death on April 8, 1948, his heir, Khaled al-Husayni, transferred the headquarters to the Old City of Jerusalem.

A total of nearly a thousand troops in fifteen companies operated in the Jerusalem area.[42] In the Ramallah sector there were five hundred troops organized in seven companies. In the Jaffa, Lydda, and Ramle sector, Hassan Salameh, from the village of Qula in the Ramle District, commanded Jihad Army forces in the area until he was killed when Palmach sappers bombed his headquarters in late May 1948. Hassan Salameh was in charge of the border neighborhoods of Jaffa—Manshiyya in the north and Abu Kabir in the southeast—and of villages in the city's vicinity—Yazur, Bayt Dajan, and Salameh—as well as of the region of Lydda and Ramle. His headquarters were located near Ramle, and Mahmoud Abu al-Khayr and Fakhri Maraka served on his staff. He had at his disposal nearly a thousand troops in twelve companies. Salameh had a more constrained relationship with Liberation Army forces deployed in his area than did 'Abd al-Qadir al-Husayni in the Jerusalem area, as he was forced to maneuver between Jihad Army headquarters in Bir Zayt, the high command of the Liberation Army, and representatives of the Arab League military committee.

In addition, several companies of the Jihad Army operated in the north: one company under the command of Subhi Shahin in the vicinity of Tiberias, three companies under the command of Tawfiq al-Ibrahim in the Nazareth area, and a company under the command of Fawzi Jarrar in the Jenin area. These companies consisted of nearly five hundred troops. The total of all operational soldiers of the Jihad Army in all sectors was about three thousand. These were assisted by several dozen more who took care of logistics such as recruitment; locating, purchasing, and dispatching weapons to the fighting companies; missions in Arab countries; and chiefly, maintaining contact with the mufti's headquarters in Cairo (and later on in Damascus and elsewhere).

The Jihad Army offered the only Arab forces immediately ready for action following the partition resolution. Their first operation was on December 14, 1947, under the command of Bahjat Abu Gharbiyya, commander of the Jerusalem sector. His men attacked a Jewish bus traveling to the Hebrew University on Mount Scopus. Two passengers were killed in the attack and nine were wounded. This was a response to a Haganah attack on Arab targets at the Hebron Gate, in which six people were killed and nearly twenty injured.[43] Other major operations were the attack on Kfar 'Etzyon, which controlled the Jerusalem-Hebron road, on January 14, 1948, and the same-day attack on a Jewish convoy on the Tel Aviv–Jerusalem road near the village of Bayt Nabala.[44] On January 16 the Surif company, commanded by Ibrahim Abu Diyya, attacked a Jewish convoy on the way to Kfar 'Etzyon. The convoy, later known as the Lamed Hey Convoy, suffered grave damages and thirty-five of its men were killed, while Arab sources relate that the attackers lost four men with a similar number injured. In addition, Jihad Army units detonated charges on two Jewish streets in Jerusalem, Hasolel Street on February 1, 1948, and Ben Yehuda Street on February 22. In the latter explosion seventy-four people were killed and nearly two hundred injured.⁴⁵ The response by Jewish forces and the counterresponse led to a deterioration of the situation in Jerusalem, and the ensuing bloody war in the neighborhoods continued throughout March. At the height of these clashes, during the first two weeks of April, several battles were waged for control of the Qastal on April 6–9, and Etzel and Lehi forces occupied the village of Dayr Yasin on April 9. These events had further implications for combat zones throughout the land.

'Abd al-Qadir al-Husayni, commander of the Holy Jihad Army, was killed in the battle for the Qastal. His death shocked the Palestinians and resulted in anarchy, particularly in the Jerusalem-Hebron sector. From then on the army seems to have focused on circling their wagons in an attempt at defense, in which state they remained until the invasion by the Jordanian Legion. The legion further restrained the movements of the Jihad Army and at a certain stage even detained 'Abd al-Qadir's successor, Commander Khaled al-Husayni. At Dayr Yasin the occupying forces proceeded to massacre the villagers, although the village was not recognized as a major combat base against Jewish towns and may have even signed a noncombat agreement with nearby Jewish towns, as has been claimed.⁴⁶ The massacre deeply shook Palestinian civil society. Villages and neighborhoods with no Palestinian or Arab military presence were now abandoned by terrified residents, who left until the situation calmed down. Stories of massacre, rape, and abuse by the occupiers of Dayr Yasin were spread by word of mouth and reached all parts of the country. Coming on top of rumors of 'Abd al-Qadir's death, they had a grave effect on the morale of the Palestinian civil population. This process of disintegration served to hasten the approaching disaster.⁴⁷

In the Jaffa and central sector, under the command of 'Ali Hassan Salameh, developments took a different turn. Arab forces in this sector focused more on defense, in light of the proximity to Tel Aviv and the Jewish capacity to recruit better forces. 'Ali Hassan Salameh was, as stated, subordinate to 'Abd al-Qadir al-Husayni; however, on March 6, 1948, General Isma'il Safwat, supreme commander of the volunteer forces and head of the Arab League military committee, officially informed Salameh that he would henceforth be under his direct command. In his letter of instruction, Safwat defined Salameh's jurisdiction as bordered by Sidna 'Ali (northwest of Herzlia) in the west, Hawwara (Nablus) in the east, and the Majdal-to-Faluja line to the south, as far as the Jerusalem-Nablus road to the east. In addition,

Safwat also restricted Salameh's methods of action and instructed him to avoid clashes with the British and contact with the commanders of other sectors, in other words, 'Abd al-Qadir and Qawiqji. His operational instructions included defense of Arab cities and villages, sorties against enemy bases and vulnerable towns, disruption of enemy means of transportation, and attacks against their convoys.[48]

All in all, 'Ali Hassan Salameh had at his disposal nearly a thousand troops, who were indeed involved mainly in defensive actions. Their most significant offensive achievement was the takeover of the Ras al-'Ayin Junction on March 8, 1948. However on April 5 they were hit hard when their headquarters, located in a building about three kilometers west of Ramle, were bombed.[49] An even more severe blow was the fall of Jaffa on May 12–14, and a third blow was the death of Hassan Salameh himself on May 31, in the battle at Ras al-Ayin. At that time, Iraqi forces and the Jordanian Legion took control of the remnants of Salameh's sector, whereupon the remainder of his forces scattered. The large majority returned to their villages or chose to follow their families and became refugees. Others joined the Iraqi forces and the Jordanian Legion, which upon arrival began recruiting young Palestinians as guides, guards, and logistics assistants.

The Jihad Army did not function any better than did the Liberation Army. It too suffered from deficient military combat supplies, lack of coordination with other Arab forces, and above all, constant rivalries and antagonism. The need to rely on a supportive local population was sometimes to their disadvantage. In many cases, the emergency enlistment system, the *faz'a*, assisted the Jihad Army units, often helping them evade Jewish or British capture.[50] But it was not uncommon for *faz'a* participants to be in a hurry to start looting, obstructing the fighters and giving them a bad reputation.[51] Nonetheless, the Jihad Army did not suffer from desertion or pronounced disciplinary problems as did the Liberation Army. The charismatic figures of 'Abd al-Qadir al-Husayni and 'Ali Hassan Salameh united the soldiers and served as a source of inspiration. However their deaths in combat had a rapid and significant impact on morale and discipline. This was apparently also a result of their successors' bland images, particularly that of Khaled al-Husayni.

The Arab volunteer forces—the Liberation Army, the Jihad Army, and representatives of other Arab organizations, such as the Muslim Brotherhood—failed their main test: defending the Arab population and keeping the Jewish forces at bay until the end of the

British Mandate and arrival of the regular Arab armies. Most of the Arab or mixed cities occupied by Jewish forces during the War of 1948 succumbed during this period. Tiberias was taken on April 11, Haifa on April 22, Safed on May 11, Bisan on May 12, Jaffa on May 12, and Acre on May 16, 1948. This was true of most of the coastal villages, from Haifa to Jaffa, as well as the villages on the Carmel and the Hills of Menashe, and those in the Jaffa and Ramle Districts.

Establishment of the State of Israel and Arrival of the Arab Armies

The first stage of the war continued until the end of the British Mandate, and in it the Jewish settlement crossed swords with Palestinians as well as with volunteer and semiregular Arab forces. At the conclusion of this stage the Arabs were in bad shape. The Liberation Army and volunteer forces had been defeated and the Palestinian Jihad Army was on the verge of collapse. The Palestinian civil front and the entire society, with all its organizations and towns, were in advanced stages of disintegration.

Vested Interests of Arab Countries and Their Involvement in the War

When the Jews declared the establishment of the State of Israel on May 15, regular Arab armies entered the war. However while the Jews were fighting for their newly established state, the Arab armies had no goal of establishing a comparable Arab state. They invaded the country to serve their own vested interests, and they operated within their own set of rivalries. Some countries, for example Jordan and Egypt, even planned to incorporate the territory allocated for an Arab state, and held by them, into their own countries, as indeed happened in the case of Jordan and the West Bank and Egypt and the Gaza Strip. Bayan Nuwayhid al-Hout summarized the historical frustration of the Palestinians: "While the Jewish forces fought, dreaming of their state, the Arab leaders ordered their armies to fight a limited war, dreaming of and praying for a cease-fire."[52] These words are not unjustified and reflect the Palestinians' bitterness and their sentiments regarding the military involvement of members of the Arab League.

The well-timed entrance of Arab armies into the country creates an impression that they were coordinated, operating according to an organized plan and under one supreme command. However, the overall command headed by King Abdullah of Transjordan was merely theoretical. Only Abdullah's own army, as well as the Iraqi army to a certain degree, accepted his authority. The armies of Egypt, Syria, Lebanon, and the remnants of the volunteer forces operated separately. Their cooperation went no further than a series of meetings between the liaison officers. Their main purpose was to avoid confrontation with Britain and the United Nations, and to be portrayed as nonaggressive in global public opinion. Thus, for example, the secretary-general of the Arab League sent the Secretary-General of the United Nations a memo explaining that Arab intervention was aimed at "restoring security, peace, and justice to this land, following Zionist aggression against the Arab population, which has resulted in the displacement of one million refugees."[53] The memo emphasized that the ideal solution would be "the establishment of a single democratic state in Palestine in which all citizens will be equal and minorities will enjoy their rights according to a democratic constitution guaranteeing preservation of, and free access to, the holy places."[54] However, the pretense that the Jews would be reinstated as a protected minority lacked a firm foundation, considering the victories they had won since November 1947.

The Arab armies entered the country without suitable preparation, with no clear, common, well-defined goals, and amid heavy mutual disagreements and suspicions. Egyptian journalist Muhammad Hasanin Haykal, who served during the war as a military reporter for the newspaper *Aakhir Sa'a*, saw for himself the lack of coordination. He described the relationship between the four kings—King Farouq of Egypt, King Abdullah of Transjordan, King 'Abd al-'Aziz Ibn Sa'ud of Saudi Arabia, and King Faisal II of Iraq, with the prince regent, 'Abd al-'Ilah—as a race in which the Egyptian and Saudi kings tried to block the two Hashemite sovereigns. Ibn Sa'ud wrote to Farouq: "Our associate in Transjordan has no good intentions and he may still have some bad surprises in store for us. He must not expand his kingdom at the expense of the Palestinian cause. He plays with the English and the English play with him. He should be taught a lesson. With God, we trust your wisdom, lest disaster shall befall us and not them."[55]

Prior to May 15, 1948, Saudi Arabia and Egypt had not intended to send any regular forces to the battlefield to supplement the volunteers previously sent. However, due to their rivalry with the Hashemites, and particularly with Abdullah, they could not afford to let him proceed alone and "expand his kingdom." Their decision to send armed forces to Palestine was hasty, stemming from political rivalries, and was not supported by strategic planning. Syria and Lebanon were dragged into the war next, fearing for their own independence and despising the Hashemites for their territorial aspirations. Haykal describes King Abdullah's behavior immediately before the regular Arab armies joined the war:

> One person was reasonably capable of foreseeing future events. His insight was based on understandings reached with the two most influential parties from his perspective, the Jews and the English. Nonetheless he was concerned and anxious, aware of his previous attempts and desires. . . . With all his knowledge, he could not imagine how the other Arab kings would surprise him and what they would scheme. . . . In these circumstances King Abdullah chose to adhere to his secret agreements with the Jews and the English while at the same time toeing the line with the other Arab kings. He carefully maneuvered between the different parties, nimble and tense, ready for any surprise and negative turn of events.[56]

The other Arab kings and leaders adapted themselves to the strategies employed by the King of Transjordan. They were not in favor of a scenario in which Abdullah alone would join the war effort and receive massive recognition as the "Redeemer of Palestine." However, they were well aware of their faults and of the risks they were taking. Consequently, they agreed that Abdullah would assume the title of supreme military commander of all Arab armies. The title had no real meaning, as it was backed by no interarmy coordination.

Egypt dictated the decisive strategy. Its position, from the initial military involvement of the Arab League and establishment of the military commission, was to avoid direct entanglement and focus instead on dispatching volunteers, funds, and ammunition. Egypt had no part in the Liberation Army and sent no delegates to the military committee. King Farouq was not unduly perturbed by the UN partition resolution and the violence that erupted in its aftermath. Until mid-March 1948, he presumed that local clashes between Jewish organizations and Arab volunteer forces would not escalate into a regional war. On March 13 Farouq received a letter from Ibn Saud warning of secret communications between Abdullah and the British on the one hand and between Abdullah and the Jewish Agency on the other.[57] The letter also requested that Farouq act to block Abdullah and prevent a possible takeover of territory allocated in the partition plan to the Arab state. From this moment, the king of Egypt began to show more interest in events occurring in Palestine. The next day he said to his prime minister, Mahmoud Fahmi al-Naqrashi, "I have reached no final decision, but I am now positive that we cannot remain indifferent to events in Palestine, as this is something that will affect our future and our security."[58] The palace's approach became attuned to the general popular mood of enthused rallying to help liberate the country. Al-Naqrashi himself also underwent a change of mind; once strictly opposed to military intervention, he now became an ardent supporter. In a moving speech on May 12, the prime minister announced in parliament the initiation of "direct military Egyptian involvement to help save our brethren in Palestine."[59]

Arab Armies and Fighting Zones

Armies representing six of the seven Arab League countries (Yemen only sent a few dozen volunteers rather than regular combat units) crossed Palestine's mandatory borders on the night of May 15, 1948. On that same night the Jewish state was established, but contrary to the UN resolution an Arab state was not established concurrently.

The six armies entered simultaneously, thus forming the impression of a coordinated effort. The truth of the matter was that they had only a vague plan, known to a mere few. Moreover, their supreme commander, King Abdullah, changed the plan to fit his interests. Rather than destroying the Jewish state, the basic plan was to take over the territories allocated to the Arab state and divide them between the six regular Arab armies. As the Palestinians saw it, this was more an arrangement aimed at preventing the establishment of an independent Arab-Palestinian state than a way of obstructing the partition plan. Declarations advocating the destruction of Israel were not followed up.

Combat forces. Historian 'Arif al-'Arif relates that the invading Arab armies, numbering about 23,000 troops and including the various forces already located in Palestine, were comprised of the following: Egyptian army—10,000 troops (including volunteer forces, consisting of about 2,000 men); Jordanian army—4,500 troops (some of them had been in the country since World War II, mainly in the Haifa Bay area); Iraqi army—1,500 fighters (besides the Iraqi regiments of the Liberation Army, another approximately 1,500 fighters); Syrian army—1,500 fighters (aside from the Syrian regiments of the Liberation Army, another approximately 1,500 soldiers); Lebanese army—1,000 soldiers; Saudi army—1,500 fighters (under Egyptian command).[60] The authors of *The Struggle for the Security of Israel* bring slightly different numbers, and also present information on contemporary Israel Defense Forces (see Table 4.1).

Plan of action. The Arab armies' initial plan of action, drawn up in the Jordanian city of Zarqa, called for the Lebanese army to cross the border near al-Naqoura and seize the coastline as far as Acre. Units of the Liberation Army, led by Fawzi al-Qawiqji, would attack the Jewish forces in the Haifa area. The Syrian army would cross the border in the area of Banyas and Bint Jubayl and occupy Safed, Nazareth, and Afula. On the central front, the Iraqi army would cross the Jordan River at the Damya Bridge, from where one detail would occupy the southern Bisan Valley and Jenin, as far as Afula. The remaining forces would head for Jerusalem. The units meeting in Afula would seize Hadera and Netanya with joint forces. On the southern front the Egyptian army would cross the border in the area of Rafah and 'Uja al-Hafit and proceed toward Majdal. Egyptian volunteer forces, the Muslim Brotherhood, and others would reach the Hebron-Bethlehem-Jerusalem road. Thus, Egyptian forces would arrive at Jerusalem from the southwest and Jordanian forces from the northeast. King Abdullah, as supreme commander, and Iraqi general Nur al-Din Mahmoud, as commander in chief, were responsible for execution of the plan.

This plan, however, was changed about forty-eight hours before it was to be implemented, apparently in order to let Abdullah's legion occupy as much territory as possible while delaying the other armies. The change also entailed deleting plans to occupy Netanya and

Table 4.1 Arab and Israeli Combat Forces, 1948

	Forces	Divisions	Infantry Corps Standard Regular	Reserves Other	Armed Combat Vehicles Light Tanks	Armed Combat Vehicles Other	Artillery Field	Artillery Other	Air Force Combat	Air Force Other
Iraq	4,500	3	7	2	—	40	48	12	13	15
Egypt	5,500	2	4	2	30	24	24	16	32	12
Jordan	6,500	3	4	2	—	120	24	16	—	—
Syria	6,000	3	7	—	12	35	36	30	—	16
Lebanon	2,000	—	4	—	—	12	16	—	—	—
Irregular	3,000	—	—	4	—	5	6	—	—	—
Liberation Army	5,000	—	—	—	—	—	—	—	—	—
Total	32,500	11	26	10	42	236	154	74	45	43
IDF[a]	32,000	—	27(+6)	—	13	15	25	20	2	32

Source: Benny Michalson et al., *Hama'avaq Lebithon Yisra'el* [The Struggle for the Security of Israel] (Tel Aviv: 1999), p. 55.
Notes: a. Israel Defense Forces.

Hadera in order specifically to avoid entering areas intended for the Jewish state. The new plan retained no mention of conducting activities beyond the territories allocated to the intended Arab state. According to the revised plan, the Syrian army was to cross the border south of the Sea of Galilee and occupy Tzemach. The Egyptian army would cross the border at Rafah, advance to Ashdod, and create a line of fortifications. Its subservient volunteer forces would advance from Beer Sheva on the Hebron-Bethlehem-Jerusalem axis. The Iraqi army would cross the border at the Shaikh Husayn Bridge and occupy the area in the vicinity of Rottenberg's power station and Kibbutz Gesher. The Jordanian army would operate in two sections: one would cross the Damya Bridge and advance toward Nablus and from there to Ramallah; the other would cross the border at the Allenby Bridge and from there proceed directly to Jerusalem. The Lebanese army would not cross the border at all and would remain stationed on the international border.

The First Stage of the Fighting: May 15 to June 10, 1948

Despite the faults and deficiencies in the preparation, arming, and logistics of the Arab armies, once they became involved in the war the Jewish forces found themselves up against a difficult challenge. They had no choice but to interrupt the momentum of their operations against the volunteer forces and the Liberation Army, which, as mentioned, were on the verge of defeat, and turn to defensive tactics. The Jewish plan was initially to put up with the attacks, while fortifying their defensive lines and preparing for counterattack. Overall this plan achieved its goals, although the Jewish side suffered some crippling losses during the first month of the Arab armies' invasion, even showing signs of crisis.

A parliamentary investigation commission established in Iraq after the war documented the fighting as it occurred in various sectors led by the following Arab armies:

Syria. The first target was Tzemach, attacked on May 15, 1948. After three days of fighting the Syrian forces succeeded in occupying the site, from where they proceeded to threaten and bombard the settlements of Deganya Alef and Deganya Bet. By June 10 the Second

Syrian Infantry Regiment had occupied Mishmar Hayarden, Sha'ar Hagolan, and Mas'ada.

Lebanon. Lebanese forces fought the Israelis at al-Malkiyya and Qadas, which were passed back and forth until they were finally occupied by the Lebanese forces (assisted by regiments of the Liberation Army and Syrian forces) on June 6, 1948.

Iraq. On May 15, Iraqi forces occupied the Rottenberg power station at Naharayim, but were unable to take control of the Shaikh Husayn Bridge and cross the Jordan River. They continued south and crossed the river at the Allenby and Damya Bridges, entered Nablus and Tulkarm, and on June 2 held a battle with Israeli forces, which had occupied the city of Jenin and its vicinity four days earlier. They succeeded in forcing the Israeli forces to withdraw from Jenin, and settled on the Lajun (Megido)–Wadi 'Ara line.

Transjordan. Arab Legion forces that had been in the country since the end of the British Mandate attacked Gush Etzyon on May 12. After a fierce battle lasting two days, they occupied the settlements and took about 230 people prisoner (who were detained at the military base at al-Mafraq until the prisoner exchange between Transjordan and Israel following the cease-fire agreement signed in February 1949). On the morning of May 15, Arab Legion forces crossed the Allenby Bridge and fought tough battles at the entrance to Jerusalem and on the roads leading to the city from the northwest, near Latrun and Sha'ar Hagay.

The battles in the Jerusalem sector divided the city in two. The eastern part and the Old City—including the Jewish Quarter, which surrendered on May 28, 1948—were under Jordanian control. The western part (including the Arab quarters emptied of their residents during the civil war) was under Israeli control. Legion forces entered Bethlehem as well, and also occupied the potassium plant north of the Dead Sea on May 19.

Egypt. From Rafah, Egyptian army forces advanced north, occupied Kfar Darom and attacked Kibbutz Nirim, which did not surrender. The Egyptians continued to advance, leaving Jewish enclaves in their wake. On the way they captured the Arab village of 'Iraq Suwaydan and the nearby junction. Another regiment reached the city of Majdal (Ashqelon) and remained there. On May 29 the forces took control of the village of Asdod and established a line of fortifications to its north, halting Israeli counterattacks on June 2 and 3. Concurrently, another Egyptian regiment, assisted by Saudi units, succeeded in occupying the city of Beer Sheva. The regiment advanced northward on the Hebron-Bethlehem road until it reached a position seven kilometers south of Jerusalem. This situation created tensions with the Jordanians. At the same time, the Egyptians occupied Nitzanim and isolated the Jewish settlements in the Negev. They were unable to occupy Kibbutz Negba, although many forces were amassed for this purpose.

The First Truce

The Arab consent to a break in the fighting is surprising considering that the Arab offensive had produced fairly significant victories. From a military standpoint, their situation did not justify complying with the UN initiative to declare a cease-fire. The report later issued by Iraq's parliamentary commission of inquiry relates that "the major powers applied heavy pressure on the Arab countries to agree to a cease-fire."[61] The same report also cited the statement of General Nur al-Din Mahmoud, commander in chief of the Arab forces, that "from a military standpoint there was no reason for the Arabs to either request or adhere to a cease-fire."[62] The only Arab country in favor of the détente, and influential in its acceptance, was Transjordan. Abdullah promoted the cease-fire, against the wishes of other Arab leaders and of the secretary-general of the League, 'Abd al-Rahman 'Azzam (who resigned in protest, but later reneged). Abdullah threatened to withdraw his army and the Iraqi army if the others would not accept the respite. Abdullah's insistence may have stemmed from his concern that the Arabs would not conform to his agreements with the Jews. Withdrawing the Jordanian and Iraqi armies, as threatened, would have critically harmed the joint war effort, and therefore Arab leaders were forced to agree to the truce.

Once the sides agreed on a month-long cease-fire, the détente went into effect, as of June 11. The United Nations appointed Count Folke Bernadotte in charge of mediation efforts; however, the parties rejected his proposals and four weeks later the fighting resumed. Abdullah tried to extend the détente, but the other Arab countries strongly objected.

Ten Days of Fighting: July 9–18, 1948

On July 8, 1948, Bernadotte instructed the UN observers to withdraw from their positions, and the hostilities promptly resumed. During the truce Israeli forces had succeeded in significantly enhancing their armaments and combat forces, and they now began a counterattack. They chose to initiate this attack in the sector covered by the Syrian army and Liberation Army units in the Western and Upper Galilee. On July 9, Israeli forces attacked the Syrians at Mishmar Hayarden but were unable to drive them from their position, where they remained until the end of the war. At the same time, the Iraqi force initiated an attack aimed at removing the Israelis from the Jenin sector, forcing them to withdraw to the British Mandate border between the Jenin District and the Haifa District, near the village of Lajun (Megido). On the other side, Israeli forces began a comprehensive combined attack in the Shafa'amr-Safuriyya sector. Safuriyya was taken on the night of July 16 and the city of Nazareth succumbed that same night. These incidents marked the collapse of the Arab military formation in the Lower Galilee and the Ibn 'Amer Valley. At the same time, the Israelis embarked on an operation to occupy the coastline south of Haifa. The village of Tirat al-Karmil, one of the last strongholds of the Arab volunteer forces and the Jihad Army, was captured on July 16.

In the sector covered by the Jordanian army, the Israelis initiated Operation Danny (Mivtza Dani) on the night of July 9–10. Historian Benny Morris explains: "Operation Danny was the crowning glory of the 'battles of the ten days.' Its purpose was to relieve the pressure on partly besieged Jerusalem, defend the road between Jerusalem and Tel Aviv, and end Arab Legion threats to Tel Aviv. The Legion's front units were based in Lydda and Ramle, a distance of less than twenty kilometers from the major Jewish city."[63] In this operation, the Israelis took Lydda and Ramle, which were not included in the territory originally allocated to them. Jordanian Legion forces positioned in this region retreated on July 10 in the direction of Ramallah and Latrun. The fifty thousand to seventy thousand residents of the two cities (who included refugees from villages previously occupied in the Jaffa sector) were driven eastward toward the line held by the Arab Legion forces.[64] At this time the Israelis resolved to expand their accessible corridor to Jerusalem. They captured the remaining Arab villages southwest of Jerusalem. Most of these villages were vacated as well.

Benny Morris describes the ten days of fighting in the southern sector:

> [The Israeli force] swept through the area from July 8 to 11. Most of its residents, their numbers assessed by the IDF as "over twenty thousand Arabs," fled when the Israeli columns approached their villages. The IDF estimated that the occupation of Tel al-Safi undermined the morale of residents in surrounding villages, since they now felt isolated from the Egyptian army and irregular Arab forces to the east and south. At the second stage of the attack by the Givati Brigade, parts of the villages of Bayt 'Affa, Hatta, and Jusayr were occupied, tightening the stranglehold on the area of Tel al-Safi–Masmiyya al-Kubra to the north.[65]

The Second Truce and Operation Policeman (Mivtza Shoter)

On July 15, 1948, the UN Security Council declared that the situation in Israel was a "threat to world peace" and decided on a cease-fire. It threatened sanctions on any party that would not abide by its decision. The truce came into effect on July 18, with no date of expiry. The political committee of the Arab League consented to the truce, but it also expressed its outrage at the Security Council's decision and the manner in which it had been reached. In a public statement it commented: "The Arab governments see no reasonable explanation for the position of the Security Council permitting the Jews to take control of Palestine at the expense of the Arabs and of all humankind. Therefore our governments have decided to maintain their armies as currently positioned, primed to continue the work for which they were dispatched."[66]

During the truce, which lasted until October 15, Israel instigated several military operations. According to Morris, their purpose was "to remove clusters of hostile Arab populations from areas in the home front and near the front lines."[67] One of these, Operation Policeman, was conceived when two Israeli passengers were killed by sharpshooters near the village of Jaba' in the vicinity of the Haifa–Tel Aviv road. The operation was aimed at the group of villages between the coast and the southern Carmel—Jaba', Ijzem, 'Ayn Ghazal, and 'Ayn Houd. It was a punitive operation, allegedly executed by the police against irregular forces and violators of the peace on the home front, and the Israelis claimed that it was not in contradiction of the truce.[68] Alexandroni, Carmeli, and Golani units took part in the operation. Residents of the villages were notified in advance that they could surrender or be evacuated, but the notice met with no response.[69] The villages were attacked on the night of July 18. When the first attack was repelled, Israeli forces began artillery bombardments and bombing from the air. Once the villages had been emptied of their residents, they were entered by Israeli forces on July 26.

The Arab League submitted a complaint to the United Nations and to Count Bernadotte, the UN mediator, alleging that Israeli forces had not only occupied the villages but also massacred their inhabitants. Morris summarized the conflicting accounts:

> Several dozen villagers and militiamen, as well as refugees from previously occupied Arab towns, were killed in the attacks on the three villages. The secretary-general of the Arab League, 'Azzam Pasha, complained to Count Bernadotte that the Israeli soldiers had committed atrocities during the attack and in its aftermath. Among other things, he claimed that in one incident twenty-eight people were burned alive. Israel rejected these accusations, claiming that this story may have originated from an incident in which soldiers burned twenty-five to thirty bodies found in advanced stages of decomposition near 'Ayn Ghazal.[70]

The evacuation of clusters of Arab population from areas occupied by Israeli forces continued during the second truce. On August 24–28, 1948, the Givati Brigade embarked on a "cleanup operation" along the coast, south of Rishon Lezion and west of Yavne. It was ordered to "purge" the area between Yabna, al-Nabi Rubin, and Khirbit Saqrir, home to the clan of 'Arab Saqrir and the current location of refugees from Yabna, al-Qubayba, and Zarnuqa.[71] The Hanegev and Yiftah Brigades as well were engaged in the "purging" of territories in the vicinity of Kufkha, Kibbutz Tze'elim, Mishmar Hanegev, and al-'Amara, from mid-September until mid-October 1948.[72]

The Israelis had the foresight to use the respite to amass modern weapons and increase their military might, while also concentrating on taking over Arab enclaves to form one cohesive stretch of territory.

The Murder of Bernadotte

On September 17, while preparing a new mediation plan to be presented at the UN General Assembly, Count Bernadotte was murdered by assassins from the Israeli organization Fighters for the Freedom of Israel (Lehi) in Qatamon, Jerusalem. His plan, consisting of seven recommendations, was announced in Paris three days later:

- The Arab countries would recognize the State of Israel.
- The borders between Israel and the Arab countries would follow the partition plan, with slight corrections.
- The area allocated to the Arabs would be annexed to Transjordan.
- The Port of Haifa and the airport at Lydda would be declared "free ports" for the relevant countries.
- Jerusalem would be placed under international supervision.
- The refugees would have the right to return to their homes.
- A UN commission would outline the borders and be in charge of strengthening ties between the countries.[73]

The main innovation introduced by this plan was the mediator's recognition of Abdullah's desire to annex the Arab territories to his kingdom and the king's vested interest in the country's sea and air ports. Its announcement deepened the rifts and conflict between Arab countries, particularly Transjordan and Egypt. In the field, this was manifested in friction between the two armies, mainly southwest of Jerusalem.

Bernadotte's murder was a crucial political burden for Israel. Nonetheless, Israel made good use of the days of respite in order to prepare for further military developments, particularly in light of the helplessness demonstrated by Arab countries and their armies in the field. Meanwhile, the Bernadotte document remained in the form of unimplemented recommendations, and efforts by his successor, Ralph Bunche, to reach an understanding between the rival parties were unsuccessful.

The Last Stage of the War

On October 15, 1948, the fighting resumed in full force. Israeli forces began a combined attack on two main fronts: in the Negev against the Egyptian army and in the Galilee against what remained of Fawzi al-Qawiqji's Liberation Army.

On the Negev front, a besieged enclave of twenty Jewish towns had been formed, surrounded by Arab towns and forces. The suggestion proposed by Bernadotte, the UN mediator, to give the Negev to the Arabs, only served to intensify Israel's desire to promptly change this state of affairs. The purpose of the Ten Plagues Operation, later named Operation Yoav (Mivtza Yo'av) was described by Benny Morris:

> As a consequence of the threat that the Negev would be given to the Arabs, the insufferable geo-military situation, and the hardships suffered by the besieged settlements, and in the absence of a political understanding, the truce was doomed. Indeed, in late September the Israeli government adopted the proposal to launch an offensive aimed at breaking through to the enclave in the Negev and defeating the Egyptian army. The IDF allocated three and a half brigades for this purpose. On October 15 a supply convoy was sent southward. The Egyptians attacked it, as expected, thus giving Israel an excuse to launch the offensive.[74]

The operation lasted about three weeks, from October 15 to November 9, 1948, and it managed to achieve a takeover of the cities of Beer Sheva and Majdal, and the villages of Asdod, Hamama, al-Qubayba, Bayt Jibrin, 'Ajjur, Bayt Tima, Kawkaba, and al-Dawaymeh. Immediately after the operation, the villages of Bayt Natif, Zakariyya, Dayr al-Dibban, and Bayt Jammal were captured as well.[75]

On the Galilee front, Israeli forces launched Operation Hiram (Mivtza Hiram) on October 29, 1948, after the Liberation Army occupied the Shaikh 'Abd military post overlooking Kibbutz Manara. At the culmination of three days of fighting, Israeli forces succeeded in taking over the territory stretching from Yanuh and Majd al-Krum to the west; Sakhnin, Dayr Hanna, and 'Aylabun to the south; Faradiyya, Qaditha, and al-Malkiyya to the east; and to the Lebanese border in the north.

November 9, 1948, marked a renewed focus on the southern areas. Operation Horev opened with the seizure of the villages of 'Iraq Suwaydan and 'Iraq al-Manshiyya, and the Faluja Pocket was surrounded, with a besieged Egyptian regiment in its midst. This operation continued until January 7, 1949. A full takeover of the Negev was completed in Operation 'Uvda, which began on March 15, 1949.

Israeli forces reached Eilat on March 19 and captured it from the Jordanian League.

Accusations later surfaced of alleged atrocities by Israeli forces at this time as well. Notable incidents were those perpetrated at the village of Dawaymeh in the Hebron region on the southern front. According to testimonies by some of the perpetrators, they wished to avenge the massacre at Gush Etzyon and the Hebron massacre of 1929. Avraham Vered related the details:

> When the tracked vehicles of the invading regiment appeared on the horizon, the villagers were not concerned . . . only when we started firing did they understand who we were: the Israeli army. Then confusion and flight took over. They must have remembered that their homes were full of the loot [of Gush Etzyon] and suddenly, in the midst of their dismay, they understood that we were capable of retaliating. Only few tried to resist but our fire was intense and deadly. We knew that we were headed for Mount Hebron. We remembered 1929 and Gush Etzyon. Here there was no order to cease fire . . . magazines were emptied and reloaded. We found four guns there, and we also found the military equipment of a Jewish soldier and a letter in Hebrew sent to one of the people of Gush Etzyon.[76]

The most conspicuous incident on the northern front occurred in the village of 'Aylabun in the eastern Galilee. It was described in a letter sent by village elders to Bechor Shitrit, the Israeli minister for minority affairs:

> When the populace gathered in the center of the village, the commander chose twelve young people and took them away. Then he instructed that all residents be brought to al-Maghar and the priest asked him to leave the women and babies and take only the men, but he refused, and led them all [about 800 people] to al-Maghar before the army vehicles. The people were in night clothes and had no food . . . he [the commander] himself remained with another two soldiers, and only when they had killed the twelve young men in the streets of the village did they join the army at al-Maghar.[77]

Arab Countries and Palestinian Independence

Count Bernadotte's two mediation proposals, presented during the July and September cease-fires, bore signs of British intervention.

They did their best to strengthen the position of their ally, Abdullah, and to facilitate the annexation of Palestinian territory to his kingdom. However, Abdullah's enthusiasm toward the recommendations only served to increase the disapproval of his rivals on the Arab League. The recommendations also led to a certain amount of coordination between some of the Arab League countries and the mufti and the Arab Higher Institution.

The Mufti and the Government of All Palestine

Ever since the regular Arab forces joined the war on May 15, 1948, the mufti had been trying to convince the rulers of Egypt, Syria, and Saudi Arabia, as well as the secretary-general of the Arab League, 'Abd al-Rahman 'Azzam, to establish an independent Palestinian state. His recurring proposals encountered the strict objection of Abdullah and his Iraqi allies and aroused doubts among the Egyptians and their allies. However, the announcement of Bernadotte's first mediation proposal on July 4, 1948, signaled the beginning of discussions on the topic and led to a decision by the political committee of the Arab League to establish a "Palestinian temporary civil administration." This administration was to include nine divisions headed by Palestinian figures, almost all from the Husayni camp. In actual fact nothing happened, but the debate had the effect of sowing discord among the residents of the Palestinian territories controlled by the Transjordanian army. Abdullah and his men accused Haj Amin of organizing demonstrations and inciting the masses. Faced with the Arab League's indecision, Abdullah campaigned among the Palestinians, promoting their loyalty to him, assisted by the Husaynis' rivals.[78] These actions roused Abdullah's Palestinian rivals. In early October they declared the establishment of a government, which they hoped would eventually have authority over the entire country. In order to dispel all doubts and make it perfectly clear that the partition plan and the Jewish state would never be recognized, the new government was called the Government of All Palestine (Hukumat 'Umum Filastin).

Mufti Haj Amin al-Husayni played a major role in this initiative, although he was careful not to take part in the declared government. The government was headed by Ahmad Hilmi 'Abd al-Baqi, and it also consisted of Jamal al-Husayni (minister of foreign affairs), Raja'i al-Husayni (minister of defense), Husayn Fakhri al-Khalidi (minister of health), Mishal Abkarius (minister of finance), Futi Furayj (minister of the economy), 'Ali Hasna (minister of justice), Yusuf Sahyun (minister of publicity), Amin 'Aql (minister of agriculture), and 'Awni 'Abd al-Hadi (minister of social affairs). Sulayman Tuqan was appointed minister of transportation but refused to accept the appointment. Anwar Nusayba was appointed secretary of the cabinet.[79]

The government was declared at a constitutive convention—called the Palestinian National Council (al-Majlis al-Watani al-Filastini)—at the al-Falah School in Gaza on October 1, 1948. The declaration of government included the following directives:

> Based on the natural and historical right of the Palestinian nation to liberty and independence, a sacred right for which it has shed blood and made sacrifices, and for which it fought the imperial forces and the Zionist Movement who contrived against it, we members of the Palestinian National Council convened in Gaza, the city of Hashem (grandfather of the Prophet) hereby declare today, 29 in the month of Zu al-Ki'dah, October 1, 1948, the independence of all Palestine within its borders: in the north Lebanon and Syria, in the east Syria and Transjordan, in the west the Mediterranean, and in the south Egypt. We declare our full independence, which is the foundation for the establishment of a free, democratic, sovereign state, whose citizens will enjoy full liberty. This state will develop together with its Arab brethren in a sense of fraternity, and together they will enhance Arab glory and serve all humankind in the spirit of the Arab nation and its magnificent history. We are determined to retain our independence and to defend it. God will bear witness to the justness of our words.[80]

As the declaration of government indicates, the city of Gaza is named "Hashem's Gaza," after Hashem Ibn 'Abd Manaf, Prophet Muhammad's great-grandfather, who died in the city and was buried there.

The Government of All Palestine Is Marginalized

After the government was established, the secretary-general of the Arab League, 'Azzam, attempted to appease King Abdullah. At first he denounced the new government and then denied its association with Haj Amin. Nonetheless, Abdullah was palpably enraged: "The Arab Legion army fighting in Palestine will not consent to any interruption of its efforts. This government was established in contradiction of the wishes of the Arabs of Palestine."[81] Abdullah's accusations against Haj Amin were not unfounded. The mufti was indeed the moving force behind the establishment of the Government of All Palestine. In contravention of advice offered by the Arab League's secretary, the mufti came to Gaza clandestinely and headed the discussions of the government's constitutive council. Ultimately, this initiative came too late, and all the declarations were no match for the facts on the ground created by Abdullah and Israel.

The mufti was the recurring target of harsh criticism. He did not return to the country in person to lead his people in times of crisis. After May 15, 1948, he could no longer use British harassment and retribution as excuses for his absence. In his memoirs, Haj Amin tried to answer his critics:

> My strongest passion was always to return to this beloved country to which my soul was bound. In the fall of 1948 I attempted to travel to Palestine, however the secretary-general of the Arab League asked me to wait, for the sake of general concerns and of the Palestinian issue. He said: "Your arrival in Palestine at this stage might turn the predicted Arab-Jewish war into a war between the Arabs and the Jews and British. Once the English Mandate in Palestine will end nothing will prevent you from traveling there." . . . On May 14, 1948, when I was planning to travel, I was surprised to discover that Britain was persuading the League and Arab foreign ministers to prevent me from going. These ministers said to me: "If you go now, when the Arab armies are on the verge of war, you will be accountable for failure of the operation for liberating Palestine, and you will spark disputes among Arab countries. You will be to blame for the failure." They also asked the president of the Syrian Republic to persuade me. Since I was unable to reach Palestine from Syria, I returned to Cairo. In Egypt I met with Ahmad Muhammad Khashaba, Egypt's foreign minister. He told me that King Abdullah had sent a messenger to King Farouq, demanding that I be prohibited from entering Palestine.[82]

The Egyptians removed Haj Amin from the Gaza Strip five days after the constitutive convention of the Government of All Palestine. They brought him to Cairo, where he was placed under strict supervision of the interior defense forces.[83] The mufti tried to operate the Palestinian national committees and the remnants of the Holy Jihad Army from his location in the Egyptian capital, and he even announced administrative appointments to replace former British officials. These moves rekindled Abdullah's rage. He wrote to Haj Amin, demanding the cessation of "announcements sowing confusion" and also thanking him for past services. By so doing he sought to identify himself as the person ultimately in charge of Palestinian concerns. On December 20, 1948, Abdullah appointed Shaikh Husam al-Din Jarallah as mufti of Jerusalem, instead of Haj Amin. Jarallah had earlier competed against Haj Amin for the role of mufti in 1921. Later on Abdullah also appointed Jarallah president of the Muslim Higher Council.[84] Abdullah explained Haj Amin's dismissal in a letter to the prime minister of Egypt, Mahmoud Fahmi al-Naqrashi: "I am taking these steps to prevent disintegration of the Arab League and to counter the damage to its unity caused by Haj Amin and his friends. I shall fight them as I fight the Jews."[85]

In contrast to Abdullah's determination, the Egyptians were hesitant. Although they wished to restrict Haj Amin, and perceived him as a threat to their control of Palestinian territory, they had no interest in quelling the antagonism between Abdullah and the mufti. They thus prevented a delegation consisting of Emir 'Abd al-Karim al-Khatabi (the exiled Moroccan leader in Egypt), Hasan al-Banna (leader of the Muslim Brotherhood), Ahmad Husayn (leader of the Young Egypt party), and Muhammad Salah Harb (president of the Young Muslim Society) from traveling to Amman to reconcile the two. Under orders from al-Naqrashi, the Egyptian Ministry of the Interior was forbidden to issue them exit permits.[86]

Although all members of the Arab League except Transjordan recognized the Government of All Palestine, its effect was minimal. Following the harsh blows sustained by the Egyptian army from mid-October 1948 and the siege on Gaza, the government ministers moved to Cairo and its officials operated from derelict buildings, mainly issuing Palestinian passports. The ministers gradually stopped attending meetings and took up private occupations. In the fall of 1952 the political committee of the Arab League decided to cancel the government ministries of the Government of All Palestine, leaving only the prime minister (Ahmad Hilmi 'Abd al-Baqi), the secretary of the cabinet (Jamil al-Sarraj), and four junior officials.[87]

Despite this marginalization, Mufti Haj Amin and Ahmad Hilmi continued to maintain the Government of All Palestine and occasionally to hold symbolic displays of its existence. But even these two were unable to work harmoniously and eventually became embroiled in petty fights about the right to represent Palestine in debates held by the Arab League and other Arab and Islamic organizations. In the 1950s their relationship was on the verge of a split, allegedly due to Haj Amin's support of Iraqi president 'Abd al-Karim Qasem in his rivalry with Egyptian president Gamal Abdel Nasser. Now the Egyptians started using Ahmad Hilmi against the mufti, and their rivalry henceforth shadowed all conduct of the Government of All Palestine.

The End of the War:
Jordan, Egypt, and the Palestinians

The war ended with a series of separate armistice agreements between Israel and neighboring Arab countries: first with Egypt in February 1949, then Lebanon in March, Jordan in April, and finally Syria in July 1949. These agreements were called *hudna* in Arabic, that is, a break in the fighting, rather than *sulh*—reconciliation.[88] Despite this choice of term, the Arab countries had no intention of resuming the fighting and realizing their previous goals, namely, to prevent implementation of the partition plan and establishment of a Jewish state. In reality, the Arab side was much worse off than at the time of the partition resolution. The borders of the Jewish state exceeded the partition borders and cut into the territory that had been allocated to the Arab-Palestinian state, which had not been established. The territory remaining in Arab hands was distributed between Egypt, which received the Gaza Strip, and Transjordan, which received the West Bank. Palestinian efforts to prove their existence as a nation, their right to self-definition and to a state of their own, expanded exponentially. The Palestinians now had to contend not only with a rival national movement, Zionism, which was striving to realize its claims to the same homeland, but also with other Arab nations that controlled part of this homeland and adamantly refused to grant them independence. This refusal, at least on the part of Transjordan, was manifested in its extreme form in attempts at erasing any trace of modern Palestinian identity.

The War of 1948 in Palestinian Historiography

Any attempt to compare the Zionist narrative of the War of 1948 with the Palestinian narrative is ludicrous. Until the war began they held a certain similarity; both developed as narratives of competing national movements. After the war their courses split and they developed in completely different situations and contexts, both regarding their ideological role and the means and tools at their disposal.

Ideologically, the Zionist historical narrative was responsible for glorifying the miraculous victory and concealing its darker sides. The Palestinian narrative attempted to comprehend the destruction and the dispersal of the Palestinian nation among exiles and communities in various political and social settings. From the narrative of a single community, until 1948, it became a "narrative of diasporas," in which each diaspora developed its own collective memory. Those who were able to write despite the shock—mainly those who had taken part in formulating Palestinian history during the British Mandate period and throughout the war—focused on denying their responsibility and laying it on others, on superpowers against whom no one stood a chance. These writers nurtured the "conspiracy concept" (*nathariyat al-muamara*) that dominated Palestinian historiography for many years.

The contrast was particularly evident in the means and tools available to those designing the narratives. Zionist historians enjoyed the support of new government and academic institutions, and of the state's vested interest in their research. They also had easier access not only to documents of the Zionist Movement and of Jewish prestate institutions but also to Arab documents. Palestinian researchers had no access, either to the latter or to documents left by the mandate government, its institutions, and offices. Even when Palestinian research progressed and engaged in a renewed debate of its history, it relied mainly on Israeli researchers, particularly the New Historians such as Simha Flapan, Benny Morris, Ilan Pappé, and Avi Shlaim, who challenged the established Zionist narrative.[89]

Recollections of the Nakba:
From Lamentation to Self-Criticism

The term *nakba* means "disaster." The first writer to use this term in the Palestinian context was the Lebanese historian Qustantin Zurayq who wrote his book *Ma'na al-Nakba* [The Meaning of the Disaster] in August 1948. 'Arif al-'Arif was one of the first Palestinians to use the concept: "How can I not call this event 'Nakba' after the awful disaster that befell us such as we had not experienced for centuries? Our homeland has been taken, we have been evicted from our homes, we lost many of our sons, and above all our honor has been grievously harmed."[90] 'Ali al-Khalili referred to the need to create and shape a collective Palestinian recollection in general, and a recollection of the Nakba in particular:

> It is clear to all that Palestinian consciousness has not lost its recollection of the Nakba. On the contrary, this recollection is engraved within us and continues to smolder. However smoldering does not manifest itself necessarily in actual or systematic deeds. Some think that this smoldering consciousness has sunk into the depths of horrifying recollections. These are experienced chapter by chapter, not used to produce hope and with no attempt to reshape the image of the suffering victim. Thus the Palestinian warrior has no respite and no opportunity to comprehend and cope with his legacy and to write his narrative.[91]

These words of al-Khalili are significant and provoke this basic question: Why has a community that lives its past so tangibly proven unable to shape this recollection in a professional and scientific manner, creating a Palestinian narrative that is separate from the focus on lamentation and on feelings of victimization? Is the only purpose of the historical consciousness to continue recycling this focus? By concentrating on displays of victimization, the Palestinian historical narrative does not allow itself to disengage from subjective and emotional writing. Al-Khalili hopes for some type of respite, a calm mental detachment that will afford an opportunity to observe, comprehend, and process history.

'Arif al-'Arif, the first Palestinian writer to describe the war in a comprehensive book, did so immediately after its conclusion. He emphasized the importance of documentation even in the absence of perspective and distance:

> It is our duty to document the events as they occurred and to describe them as they are, before time weaves its strands of forgetfulness. If we do so, subsequent historians will have basic documentation . . . detailed events, names, places, and numbers. This is what motivated me to document the events of the Nakba and I have depicted them devotedly and precisely in written form . . . although

I know that reliable history is written in retrospect in the space of a generation and not at the time of occurrence.[92]

Al-'Arif remained a solitary voice. His attempt to document the fighting, mainly in the Jerusalem area, was a one-time endeavor, and he was not emulated. Since no similar attempts were made in regard to other fronts, most of the Palestinian testimonies were, in fact, lost. Almost all the other books written by Palestinians on the War of 1948, and those published prior to 1967, consist of polemics, apologetics, or manifestations of anger and frustration. The great majority make no use of self-criticism. Rather, they stress their criticism of others: Jews, the British, the Arab countries, or local Palestinian rivals.

This group of writers includes Muhammad Nimr al-Hawwari, leader of the al-Najjada organization and representative of the Palestinian refugees at the Lausanne talks. In December 1949, Israeli representatives at the talks convinced him to return to Israel. Upon returning, he wrote a book titled *Secret of the Disaster* (Sir al-Nakba), which is merely a writ of accusation against Haj Amin al-Husayni, asserting that his conduct and leadership were the secret key to the disaster of the Palestinians in 1948. Haj Amin wrote his own version of events in a book called *Haqa'iq 'An Qadiyyat Filastin* (*Truth About the Issue of Palestine*), first published as a series in the Egyptian newspaper *Al-Misri* and later, in 1957, as a book. Several of the mufti's associates published similar versions. Two of these were the leaders of al-Istiqlal, Muhammad 'Izzat Darwaza and Akram Zu'aytir. Darwaza, a member of the Waqf administration and of the Arab Higher Institution, wrote history books even before World War II. During the 1936–1939 revolt he maintained strict cooperation with the mufti, as he did in 1948, particularly on issues of propaganda. In the 1950s Darwaza published a series of articles entitled "About the Palestinian Problem" ("Hawl al-Qadiyya al-Filastiniyya"). These articles were rich in detail but inaccurate and were intended to clear the Palestinian leadership from all responsibility for the defeat. The articles maintained that the disaster was caused only by Britain, the Zionist Movement, and the countries of the Arab League. Akram Zu'aytir, a radical activist and a speaker of the al-Istiqlal Party and of the Palestinian national movement headed by the mufti during the mandate period, switched sides after 1948 and became associated with the Hashemite regime in Transjordan, filling high-level diplomatic positions. In a book written in 1955, *Al-Qadiyya al-Filastiniyya* (The Palestinian Problem), he attempted to clear Abdullah and Transjordan from all blame and did his best to conceal the criticism aimed at them.[93] Abdullah al-Tal, commander of the Transjordan Legion in Jerusalem during the war, crossed the lines in the opposite direction. After defecting from Jordan to Egypt he published a book in 1959 entitled *Karithat Filastin* (Holocaust of Palestine), in which he tendentiously magnified Abdullah's responsibility for the disaster.

When the Arab armies were defeated in the War of 1967, another phase began in the Palestinian historiography of 1948. A new generation of writers joined the growing rejection of the pan-Arab vision and was inspired by the new, independent Palestinian struggle and guerrilla warfare that had replaced interarmy combat. The new writers did not hesitate to criticize the Palestinians and their leadership. This group included 'Abd al-Wahab al-Kayyali, Bayan Nuwayhid al-Hout, Kamil Mahmoud Khalla, and Khayriyya Qasmiyya. Most of them chose to begin their research with the Balfour Declaration, or the country's occupation by Britain toward the end of World War I, and to end it in 1939, with the fading of the revolt. Only a few, such as Bayan Nuwayhid al-Hout, covered a lengthier period, ending with the War of 1948, thus expressing greater caution. The professional writing of this generation was aided by the establishment of the Palestinian Research Center in Beirut in the mid-1960s, and the fact that some of the writers were graduates of Western universities who embraced scientific, historical writing.

Under Israeli occupation, historical writing developed in institutions of higher education in the West Bank as well. At the Bir Zayt University, for example, a series of reviews was published on Arab villages destroyed in 1948. Lacking archival material, writers based their work on oral testimonies. Seventeen reviews were published on seventeen destroyed villages; however, the project, originally intended to eventually cover most of the destroyed villages, was inexplicably interrupted.

In light of revelations by the New Historians over the last two decades of the twentieth century, Palestinian writers began expressing interest in archival material, particularly those documents located in Israeli archives. This material formed the basis for attempts to form an outline of Palestinian society prior to 1948, its experiences during the war, and to identify the remnants of destroyed villages and cities. The most famous of these studies is the book by historian Walid al-Khalidi, first published in English in 1992 under the title *All That Remains* and later in 1997 in an Arabic version titled *So That We Will Not Forget*, which became a best seller in the various Palestinian communities. Nur al-Din Masalha's books have also had a strong impact, particularly his book *More Land, Less Arabs: Israel's Transfer Policy 1949–1996*, published in Beirut in 1997.

Beginning in the late 1980s, after the main part of the Palestinian national movement recognized the June 1967 borders as a basis for solving the conflict, a profound historiographic dispute arose regarding the Palestinian response to the partition proposal in 1947–1948. From this point, the debate concerning the defeat of 1948 expanded to include criticism of the mufti and the Arab Higher Institution, contending that their refusal to accept the UN partition plan was not representative of Palestinian public opinion. They were thus held accountable for missing the opportunity to achieve more than was later offered, and certainly more than was actually achieved. This line of criticism was led in particular by communist writers, who claimed that at the time they had protested against the imprudent rejection of the partition plan.

This criticism, however, is basically unfounded. Until the establishment of the State of Israel the communists were a small part of Arab society, with minimal influence. Moreover, not all Palestinian communists supported partition: Fu'ad Nassar, Boulos Farah, and Emil Toma, for example, strongly objected to the resolution. Even those who claimed to have been forewarned of the disaster and to have supported partition, such as Emil Habibi, did so under the influence of the former Soviet Union, and thus, only when the actual decision was imminent and in accordance with the policy decreed by Moscow.[94] The decisions reached by the Palestinian leadership in 1947–1948, with all their consequences, were definitely not in contradiction to a more sober and realistic public opinion.

The process of forming a scientific, historical Palestinian narrative concerning the events of 1948 is still in development. This narrative may indeed have begun shedding its desire to commemorate the "victim" while renouncing the conspiracy theory and the inclination to lay all responsibility and blame on others. Nonetheless, it is taking time to construct self-critical mechanisms. The ongoing

Israeli-Palestinian conflict and its current inflammation are not conducive to the expansion of Palestinian research and academic institutions or to an atmosphere of balanced self-examination and unbiased criticism of the past.

Notes

1. On the development of this concept among Arab and Palestinian writers, see al-Naqib, *Al-Fikr al-Ta'amuri 'End al-'Arab* [Conspiracy Idea Among the Arabs].
2. B. N. al-Hout, *Al-Qiyadat wa al-Mu'ssasat al-Siyasiyya Fi Filastin, 1917–1948* [Leadership and Political Institutions in Palestine], 537.
3. Radwan, *Al-Lajna al-Siyasiyya lijami at al-Diwal al-'Arabiyya* [Political Committee of the Arab League], 106.
4. Qasmiyya, *'Awni 'Abd al-Hadi* ['Awni 'Abd al-Hadi, Personal Documents], 142.
5. On this see Elpeleg, *Grand Mufti*, 85–90.
6. Darwaza, *Hawl al-Haraka al-'Arabiyya al-Haditha* [About the New Arab Movement], 4:92.
7. Letter sent by Emil al-Ghouri to the mufti on May 16, 1947, and cited by B. N. al-Hout, *Al-Qiyadat wa al-Mu'ssasat al-Siyasiyya Fi Filastin, 1917–1948* [Leadership and Political Institutions in Palestine], 567.
8. B. N. al-Hout, *Al-Qiyadat wa al-Mu'ssasat al-Siyasiyya Fi Filastin, 1917–1948* [Leadership and Political Institutions in Palestine], 568.
9. Countries with representatives on the committee included Canada, Australia, Guatemala, India, Czechoslovakia, the Netherlands, Iran, Peru, Sweden, Uruguay, and Yugoslavia. In order to enhance the committee's neutrality and impartiality in the conflict emerging at the time between the Soviet Union and the United States and NATO, it did not include representatives of these powers.
10. Darwaza, *Hawl al-Haraka al-'Arabiyya al-Haditha* [About the New Arab Movement], 93n6.
11. Shufani, *Al-Mujaz fi Tarikh Filastin al-Sayasi* [Summary of the Political History of Palestine], 2:506.
12. John and Hadawi, *Palestine Diary*, 177–178.
13. The three countries who submitted the minority proposal were Yugoslavia, India, and Iran.
14. Shufani, *Al-Mujaz fi Tarikh Filastin al-Sayasi* [Summary of the Political History of Palestine], 507n11.
15. Shufani, *Al-Mujaz fi Tarikh Filastin al-Sayasi* [Summary of the Political History of Palestine], 507n11.

16. Shufani, *Al-Mujaz fi Tarikh Filastin al-Sayasi* [Summary of the Political History of Palestine], 510.

17. B. N. al-Hout, *Al-Qiyadat wa al-Mu'ssasat al-Siyasiyya Fi Filastin, 1917–1948* [Leadership and Political Institutions in Palestine], 578.

18. B. N. al-Hout, *Al-Qiyadat wa al-Mu'ssasat al-Siyasiyya Fi Filastin, 1917–1948* [Leadership and Political Institutions in Palestine], 611–612.

19. B. N. al-Hout, *Al-Qiyadat wa al-Mu'ssasat al-Siyasiyya Fi Filastin, 1917–1948* [Leadership and Political Institutions in Palestine], 16.

20. B. N. al-Hout, *Al-Qiyadat wa al-Mu'ssasat al-Siyasiyya Fi Filastin, 1917–1948* [Leadership and Political Institutions in Palestine], 16.

21. The secret report of the Iraqi parliamentary investigative commission on Palestine, pp. 100–101, is cited by B. N. al-Hout, *Al-Qiyadat wa al-Mu'ssasat al-Siyasiyya Fi Filastin, 1917–1948* [Leadership and Political Institutions in Palestine], 583.

22. Al-'Umar, *Muzakkarat al-Haj Muhhamad Amin al-Husayni* [Memoirs of Haj Amin al-Husayni], 349.

23. Shufani, *Al-Mujaz fi Tarikh Filastin al-Sayasi* [Summary of the Political History of Palestine], 515n11.

24. B. N. al-Hout, *Al-Qiyadat wa al-Mu'ssasat al-Siyasiyya Fi Filastin, 1917–1948* [Leadership and Political Institutions in Palestine], 827.

25. The report is cited by Hakim, *Tariq al-Nakba* [Way of the Nakba], 24. The emphasis is mine.

26. Al-'Arif, *Nakbat Bayt al-Maqdis wa al-Firdaws al-Mafquod, 1947–1952* [Nakba of Jerusalem and Lost Paradise], 1:19.

27. Al-'Arif, *Nakbat Bayt al-Maqdis wa al-Firdaws al-Mafquod, 1947–1952* [Nakba of Jerusalem and Lost Paradise], 1:51–52.

28. Nasser, *Falsafat al-Thawra* [Philosophy of the Revolution], 55. This story is also mentioned in the book by al-Husayni, *Haqa'iq 'an Qadiyyat Filastin* [Truth About the Issue of Palestine], 55.

29. Al-'Umar, *Muzakkarat al-Haj Muhammad Amin al-Husayni* [Memoirs of Haj Amin al-Husayni], 391.

30. See, for example, the words of the Egyptian representative at one of the subcommittees of the political committee of the Arab League, Ahmad Farraj Tayi', in his book *Safahat Matwiyya 'an Filastin* [Forgotten Pages About Palestine] (n.p., n.d.), 68–69.

31. Al-'Arif, *Nakbat Bayt al-Maqdis wa al-Firdaws al-Mafquod, 1947–1952* [Nakba of Jerusalem and Lost Paradise], 1:41.

32. Al-Hindi, *Jaysh al-Inqaz* [Army of Salvation], 40–44.

33. Khalidi, *From Haven to Conquest*, 860.

34. These documents are in the IDF Archives, file 94/57–1.

35. This letter was sent to the military committee on March 11, 1948, IDF Archives, file 1–57/80.

36. Letter from company commander to regiment commander, February 21, 1948, IDF Archives, file 1–57/ 84.

37. Shufani, *Al-Mujaz fi Tarikh Filastin al-Sayasi* [Summary of the Political History of Palestine], 518n11.

38. Shufani, *Al-Mujaz fi Tarikh Filastin al-Sayasi* [Summary of the Political History of Palestine], 519.

39. Al-Hindi, *Jaysh al-Inqaz* [Army of Salvation], 42–43n32.

40. Abu Gharbiyya, *Fi Khidam al-Nidal al-'Arabi al-Filastini, Muzakkarat al-Munadil Bahjat Abu Gharbiyya* [In the Whirlwind of the Palestinian Arab Struggle: Memoirs of Fighter Bahjat Abu Gharbiyya], 152. The Jihad Army was founded in December 1947, while the first units of the Liberation Army arrived in the country in January 1948.

41. On this see al-'Umar, *Muzakkarat al-Haj Muhammad Amin al-Husayni* [Memoirs of Haj Amin al-Husayni], 358–387.

42. Of the fifteen companies that operated in the Jerusalem area, ten were employed in the defense of Arab neighborhoods and five operated in adjacent villages (Abu Dis, al-'Izariyya, Sur Baher, 'Ayn Karem, and Bayt Safafa).

43. Abu Gharbiyya, *Fi Khidam al-Nidal al-'Arabi al-Filastini, Muzakkarat al-Munadil Bahjat Abu Gharbiyya* [In the Whirlwind of the Palestinian Arab Struggle], 158n40.

44. Abu Gharbiyya, *Fi Khidam al-Nidal al-'Arabi al-Filastini, Muzakkarat al-Munadil Bahjat Abu Gharbiyya* [In the Whirlwind of the Palestinian Arab Struggle], 175.

45. Abu Gharbiyya, *Fi Khidam al-Nidal al-'Arabi al-Filastini, Muzakkarat al-Munadil Bahjat Abu Gharbiyya* [In the Whirlwind of the Palestinian Arab Struggle], 190–193.

46. See, for example, al-'Arif, *Nakbat Bayt al-Maqdis wa al-Firdaws al-Mafquod, 1947–1952* [Nakba of Jerusalem and Lost Paradise], 1:170–171. See also al-Khalidi, *Dayr Yasin, al-Jum'a 9 bi'april 1948* [Dayr Yasin: Friday April 9, 1948], 11–14.

47. The Dayr Yasin massacre is a point of contention in Zionist historiography. In Palestinian and pan-Arab historiography the massacre has become a symbol of the War of 1948 and the Nakba.

48. Al-'Arif, *Nakbat Bayt al-Maqdis wa al-Firdaws al-Mafquod, 1947–1952* [Nakba of Jerusalem and Lost Paradise], 1:128.

49. This house was built by Zuhdi Abu al-Jibin, one of Jaffa's great citrus growers. Nationalist circles accused him of selling land to Jews and to avoid sanctions he contributed generously to nationalist and volunteer activities, including the house bequeathed in 1946.

50. The term *faz'a* originally meant providing help to a person or people in distress. During the 1936–1939 revolt it was used in order to appeal to

the villages to help the bands of the revolt besieged by the British. This system was utilized once again in the War of 1947–1948, particularly in Jihad Army sectors.

51. About such operations see, for example, al-'Arif, *Nakbat Bayt al-Maqdis wa al-Firdaws al-Mafquod, 1947–1952* [Nakba of Jerusalem and Lost Paradise], 1:48, and on p. 123, regarding unfair distribution of war spoils.

52. B. N. al-Hout, *Al-Qiyadat wa al-Mu'ssasat al-Siyasiyya Fi Filastin, 1917–1948* [Leadership and Political Institutions in Palestine], 622.

53. B. N. al-Hout, *Al-Qiyadat wa al-Mu'ssasat al-Siyasiyya Fi Filastin, 1917–1948* [Leadership and Political Institutions in Palestine], 641.

54. B. N. al-Hout, *Al-Qiyadat wa al-Mu'ssasat al-Siyasiyya Fi Filastin, 1917–1948* [Leadership and Political Institutions in Palestine], 641.

55. Haykal, *Al-'Urush wa al-Juyush, Kazalika infajara al-Sira' fi Filastin* [Chairs of Kings and Armies], 1:75.

56. Haykal, *Al-'Urush wa al-Juyush, Kazalika infajara al-Sira' fi Filastin* [Chairs of Kings and Armies], 32.

57. The truth of these rumors was proven in studies supported by documents and recollections of key personnel from this period. On Abdullah's secret contacts with the British, see Glubb, *Soldier with the Arabs*, 63–66; Nevo, *King Abdullah and Palestine*, 88–89.

58. Haykal, *Al-'Urush wa al-Juyush, Kazalika infajara al-Sira' fi Filastin* [Chairs of Kings and Armies], 47.

59. Haykal, *Al-'Urush wa al-Juyush, Kazalika infajara al-Sira' fi Filastin* [Chairs of Kings and Armies], 78–84.

60. The numbers are cited in the book by al-'Arif, *Nakbat Bayt al-Maqdis wa al-Firdaws al-Mafquod, 1947–1952* [Nakba of Jerusalem and Lost Paradise], 2:342.

61. Report of the Iraqi Parliamentary Commission of Inquiry, p. 201, cited by al-'Arif, *Nakbat Bayt al-Maqdis wa al-Firdaws al-Mafquod, 1947–1952* [Nakba of Jerusalem and Lost Paradise], 3:550.

62. Al-'Arif, *Nakbat Bayt al-Maqdis wa al-Firdaws al-Mafquod, 1947–1952* [Nakba of Jerusalem and Lost Paradise], 3:550.

63. Morris, *Laydata shel Be'ayat Haplitim Hafalestinim 1947–1949* [Birth of the Palestinian Refugee Problem], 272.

64. Morris relates (in *Laydata shel Be'ayat Haplitim Hafalestinim 1947–1949* [Birth of the Palestinian Refugee Problem], 277) that the eviction was performed by soldiers of the Qiryati unit under order of the commander of the operation, Yigal Alon (Fykowitz). He adds that Yigal Alon asked Ben-Gurion about the fate of residents of the two cities and was told, "Expel them." On this see also Zohar, *Ben Guryon: Biografya* [Ben Gurion: A Biography], 2:775.

65. Morris, *Laydata shel Be'ayat Haplitim Hafalestinim 1947–1949* [Birth of the Palestinian Refugee Problem], 284.

66. Shufani, *Al-Mujaz fi Tarikh Filastin al-Sayasi* [Summary of the Political History of Palestine], 535n11.

67. Morris, *Laydata shel Be'ayat Haplitim Hafalestinim 1947–1949* [Birth of the Palestinian Refugee Problem], 285.

68. Morris, *Laydata shel Be'ayat Haplitim Hafalestinim 1947–1949* [Birth of the Palestinian Refugee Problem], 285.

69. An inquiry by the UN mediator concerning occurrences in these villages, following a complaint by the Arab League, showed that representatives of the local population had expressed willingness to negotiate a surrender, while Israeli commanders in the field rejected their request. A summary of the inquiry may be found in a letter sent by Bernadotte to Israel's foreign minister, Moshe Shertok (Sharet), on September 9, 1948. The correspondence is located in the files of the Israel Ministry of Foreign Affairs, State Archives, file 11/2426.

70. Morris, *Laydata shel Be'ayat Haplitim Hafalestinim 1947–1949* [Birth of the Palestinian Refugee Problem], 285.

71. Morris, *Laydata shel Be'ayat Haplitim Hafalestinim 1947–1949* [Birth of the Palestinian Refugee Problem], 287.

72. Morris, *Laydata shel Be'ayat Haplitim Hafalestinim 1947–1949* [Birth of the Palestinian Refugee Problem], 287.

73. Shufani, *Al-Mujaz fi Tarikh Filastin al-Sayasi* [Summary of the Political History of Palestine], 536n11.

74. Morris, *Laydata shel Be'ayat Haplitim Hafalestinim 1947–1949* [Birth of the Palestinian Refugee Problem], 289.

75. Morris, *Laydata shel Be'ayat Haplitim Hafalestinim 1947–1949* [Birth of the Palestinian Refugee Problem], 290.

76. Cited by Morris, *Laydata shel Be'ayat Haplitim Hafalestinim 1947–1949* [Birth of the Palestinian Refugee Problem], 297.

77. Morris, *Laydata shel Be'ayat Haplitim Hafalestinim 1947–1949* [Birth of the Palestinian Refugee Problem], 305.

78. Elpeleg, *Grand Mufti*, 99.

79. Al-'Arif, *Nakbat Bayt al-Maqdis wa al-Firdaws al-Mafquod, 1947–1952* [Nakba of Jerusalem and Lost Paradise], 3:704–705.

80. Al-'Arif, *Nakbat Bayt al-Maqdis wa al-Firdaws al-Mafquod, 1947–1952* [Nakba of Jerusalem and Lost Paradise], 3:704.

81. Ahmad Farraj Tayi', *Safahat Matwiyya 'an Filastin* [Forgotten Pages About Palestine] (n.p., n.d.), 150–151n30.

82. Al-Husayni, *Haqa'iq 'an Qadiyyat Filastin* [Truth About the Issue of Palestine], 83–85.

83. Al-Husayni, *Haqa'iq 'an Qadiyyat Filastin* [Truth About the Issue of Palestine], 85–87.

84. Elpeleg, *Grand Mufti*, 98.

85. Al-'Arif, *Nakbat Bayt al-Maqdis wa al-Firdaws al-Mafquod, 1947–1952* [Nakba of Jerusalem and Lost Paradise], 3:708.

86. Al-'Arif, *Nakbat Bayt al-Maqdis wa al-Firdaws al-Mafquod, 1947–1952* [Nakba of Jerusalem and Lost Paradise], 3:708.

87. After the government ministries of the All-Palestine Government were cancelled, each minister developed a private career: Amin 'Aql (minister of agriculture) was employed as a senior official at the University of Cairo; Dr. Futi Furayj (minister of health) opened a private clinic at 'Ayn Shams; Mishal Abkarius (minister of finance) was employed as a lecturer at the American University of Beirut; Raja'i al-Husayni (minister of defense) was employed as adviser to the Ministry of Transportation in Saudi Arabia; Yusuf Sahyoun (minister of publicity) opened a medicine depot in Cairo; Anwar Nusayba moved to Jordan, where he served as minister of education and then minister of defense; 'Ali Hasna moved to Jordan as well and was assistant minister of the interior; while 'Awni 'Abd al-Hadi was the Jordanian ambassador to Egypt. See al-'Arif, *Nakbat Bayt al-Maqdis wa al-Firdaws al-Mafquod, 1947–1952* [Nakba of Jerusalem and Lost Paradise], 3:711.

88. The term *hudna* means a state of calm following frenzied activity. Later on it came to mean the temporary cessation of fighting until an agreement is reached regarding the conditions of reconciliation. See *Al-Munjid Fi al-Lugha wa al-'Alam* [Dictionary of Language and Biographies], 27:859.

89. On the New Historians see Morris, "Hahistoriografya hahadasha: Yisra'el pogeshet et 'avarah" [The New Historiography: Israel Meets Its Past], 23–41.

90. Al-'Arif, *Nakbat Bayt al-Maqdis wa al-Firdaws al-Mafquod, 1947–1952* [Nakba of Jerusalem and Lost Paradise], 1:3.

91. 'Ali al-Khalili, *Al-Waratha al-Ruwah, Min al-Nakbah ila al-Dawla* [Generation of Heirs of History Relaters: From the Nakba to the Establishment of Israel], 162.

92. Al-'Arif, *Nakbat Bayt al-Maqdis wa al-Firdaws al-Mafquod, 1947–1952* [Nakba of Jerusalem and Lost Paradise], 1:3.

93. Akram Zu'aytir, *Al-Qadiyya al-Filastiniyya* [The Palestinian Problem], Nazareth, 1955.

94. See, for example, *Al-Ittihad*, September 13, 1947.

5

From Nakba to Naksa: 1948–1967

After the Arab defeat in the War of 1948, the Arab-Palestinian side needed a significant interval within which to come to terms with its new circumstances. A large proportion of the Palestinian people were now refugees, both within and outside their own land. Those remaining in the former territory of Palestine under the British Mandate were either a minority living within the Jewish state, residents of the West Bank under Transjordanian rule, or residents of the Gaza Strip under Egyptian rule. The distinction between "locals" and "refugees" formed as a result of this division of territory has remained valid because both the refugees and the host towns see the current state of affairs as temporary, to be resolved by a final solution of the refugee problem. Any discussion of the Palestinian nation from this point requires attention to the dispersal of these people and comprehension of how this new state of affairs helped further the processes of both national cohesiveness and sectarian-based disintegration.

Annexation of the West Bank to the Kingdom of Transjordan

Since the beginning of King Abdullah's rule of Transjordan in 1921, he never concealed his aspirations to expand his dominion beyond the barren land awarded by the British and to extend his rule over all of Greater Syria. Once he understood that any attempt to realize this dream would end in a confrontation with Britain and France, he turned his gaze westward, toward mandatory Palestine, thus creating a continuous conflict with Mufti Haj Amin al-Husayni, leader of the Palestinian national movement.

After the UN partition resolution in late 1947, Abdullah began taking steps to realize his dream. He succeeded in drawing the Arab League states and their armies into the war and received supreme command of Arab armies to be deployed in Palestine. His well-trained army, the Arab Legion, took control of a more extensive territory than that originally designated for the Arab state. With Egypt's hesitant assistance, Abdullah even succeeded in blocking the mufti's attempt to establish an All-Palestine Government as a manifestation of Palestinian independence. The momentum acquired by the Israeli army after the second truce helped weaken the mufti's position and strengthen that of Abdullah. On the eve of Operation Yoav (which began in mid-October 1948 and culminated in the conquest of the southern coastal areas and wide swaths of the Negev, including the cities of Majdal and Beer Sheva), the British warned the secretary-general of the Arab League that the All-Palestine Government, located in Gaza, was in danger of being captured by the Jews, justifying Abdullah's demand that it be relocated to East Jerusalem, where it would be protected by the Arab Legion's soldiers.[1] Consequently, and as a result of the mufti's impotence, the ministers of the All-Palestine Government departed for Cairo, leaving Abdullah the strongest and most senior Arab element in those parts of Palestine not occupied by Israel. The mufti, to his chagrin, was forced to acknowledge this fact. Jamal al-Husayni, minister of foreign affairs in the All-Palestine Government, declared in Cairo after a meeting with Haj Amin that "the government of Palestine is ready to cede its territory to Transjordan if Abdullah will collaborate with the other Arab states to remove the Zionists from Palestine."[2]

Encouraged by this statement, on December 1, 1948, Abdullah convened several hundred Palestinian representatives from around the country in Jericho, receiving their approval to annex the territories of which he had gained control. Surprisingly, some of the mufti's chief sympathizers were now the first to support the king's move. The first of these was Shaikh Muhammad 'Ali al-Ja'bari, mayor of

Hebron and a major activist in the Husayni Arab Party, who was appointed president of the conference. He was joined by advocate 'Ajaj Nuwayhid, a Druze originally from Lebanon, who served as secretary of the conference and determined its general direction. In his summative speech, al-Ja'bari expressed doubt regarding the legality of the All-Palestine Government and called upon Abdullah to annex the West Bank to his kingdom. He depicted this step as the initial stage leading to eventual pan-Arab unity and entreated those present to entrust "His Highness King Abdullah Ibn al-Husayn with the responsibility for handling all Palestinian matters."[3]

The conference declared the unification of Palestine with Transjordan as the first step toward pan-Arabism, thanking the Arab states for their role in the War of 1948 and for their efforts to reinstate the refugees. It concluded with an oath of allegiance—*bay'a*—to Abdullah, as king of Palestine. However, the king was not satisfied with the resolutions formulated and broadcast on Radio Ramallah. The statement whereby "the Palestinians agree to the unification of Palestine with Transjordan in return for Abdullah's commitment to liberate all Palestine" seemed to him restrictive and problematic. His men quickly reconvened a considerable number of the participants and instructed them to change the statement, which now read, "The Palestinians authorize the king to solve the Palestinian problem as he sees fit."[4] The resolutions of the Jericho Conference were submitted to the Jordanian government, which ratified them on December 7, 1948.

The annexation aroused agitation both within the Arab League and elsewhere. The secretary-general of the league, 'Abd al-Rahman 'Azzam, published a renouncement, and the move was criticized on Syrian and Egyptian radio. The heads of the 'Ulama of al-Azhar urged objection to Jordan's one-sided move.[5] The wave of denouncements had no effect on Abdullah; neither did the riots incited by Haj Amin's people in Palestinian West Bank territories and even among Palestinians in the East Bank. Abdullah quickly regained his composure and ordered arrests that succeeded in calming the contentious atmosphere.[6] In order to persuade his opponents, the king awarded them government posts in the interior administration of the kingdom, the army, the foreign service, and the upper house of parliament. In the resulting lull, he managed to sign armistice agreements with Israel and hand over the Little Triangle unhindered.[7] This semblance of calm was retained until Abdullah was murdered by a Palestinian outside the al-Aqsa Mosque on July 20, 1951, in revenge for the annexation of the West Bank and the subsequent blow to Palestinian national aspirations, identity, and symbols.

The Gaza Strip Under Egyptian Rule

The area that became known as the Gaza Strip after the War of 1948 was at this time part of the Gaza District, which together with the Beer Sheva District formed the southern province of mandatory Palestine (encompassing about 50 percent of the country and 11 percent of its population).[8] The territory remaining under Arab rule after the war was placed under Egyptian management, but not annexed to Egypt. It measured forty-five kilometers in length, from Rafah in the south to about eight kilometers north of Gaza, with an average width of approximately six kilometers.[9] Before the war this territory was home to some ninety thousand people, and subsequently their number tripled with the arrival of nearly two hundred thousand Palestinian refugees, particularly from the vicinity of Jaffa, Majdal, and Beer Sheva.[10]

According to the cease-fire terms reached by Egypt and Israel in February 1949, the Gaza Strip was under the control of the Egyptian government, an arrangement approved by the Arab League. Consequently, Gaza was isolated from all other Palestinian territories, leaving Egypt as the only access route. At first, the commander of Egypt's border patrol was recognized as the governor of Gaza. The first person to hold this position was General Muhammad Najib, who eventually became first president of the Republic of Egypt. Later a general military governor was appointed, as well as an executive and a legislative council.

Emergence of the Palestinian-Arab Minority in Israel

Approximately nine hundred thousand Palestinian Arabs had been living in the territory allocated to the Jewish state by the partition resolution. Only some of them remained on their land throughout the war, particularly in two villages on the coastal plain, several villages and Bedouin encampments in the Ibn 'Amer Valley, and in mixed cities, such as Acre, Haifa, Jaffa, Lydda, and Ramle. In the second stage of the war, when Israel occupied territories not included in the partition plan, particularly in the Galilee and on the southern fronts, many Arab villages were added to its territory. At first Israel defined these as "occupied enemy territories," however, at the cease-fire talks with the Arab states it was already confident and strong enough to demand and receive other densely Arab-populated areas, such as the Little Triangle, granted to Israel in the third week of May 1949. By the time the annexation of these territories to the State of Israel had been completed, the number of Palestinian Arabs in the country had reached 156,000, or about 14 percent of its entire population. A new Palestinian group was thus formed, the Palestinian-Arab national minority in the State of Israel.

This minority group has received many definitions, depending on the times or on national-political views. Members of this group often use the terms "al-'Arab fi Isra'il" (the Arabs in Israel), "al-Filastiniyyun fi Isra'il" (the Palestinians in Israel) or "al-'Arab al-Filastiniyyun fi 'Isra'il" (the Palestinian Arabs in Israel). Some have embraced the common expression employed by the Jewish majority, "Israeli Arabs" ('Arab Isra'il). The Jewish majority sometimes uses the terms "Arabs of the Land of Israel," "the Arabs in Israel," "members of the minorities" (emphasizing their status as members of several religious minorities rather than one national minority), or "the Arab sector" (or related terms such as "the Druze sector" or "the Bedouin sector"). In the Arab world they have been called "'Arab 1948" (the Arabs of 1948), "'Arab al-dakhil" (the Arabs of the interior, evidently referring to the Israeli interior or the interior of the Green Line), and some have also used the term "'Arab al-yahud" (the Arabs of the Jews). The term used in the current book is "the Palestinian-Arab national minority in Israel."

The special status of this minority was described by Benny Neuberger:

> The Arabs in Israel are both a numerical and a sociological minority. They are a numerical minority since in 1996 they constituted only 18 percent of the country's population. They are a sociological minority since this sector is not represented among the country's political, military, and economic elite, and therefore feels deprived compared to the dominant national group. . . . Israeli Arabs are a new minority, since up to 1948 they formed two-thirds of the population governed by the British Mandate. Significantly, aside from

the status shift from majority to minority, vexing in its own right, the Arabs were also defeated in the War of Independence. The great majority of their towns were destroyed in battle, and they became separated from most Palestinian Arabs, who received refugee status in Arab countries or settled in the West Bank, occupied by Jordan, or in the Gaza Strip, occupied by Egypt. Moreover, the massive flight during the war left the Arab populace of Israel with no leadership—lacking the entire political, economic, social, religious, and cultural upper echelon of society. Urban centers were divested of their supremacy: some lost most of their Arab residents (Haifa, Jaffa, Lydda, and Ramle) and some remained, after the agreements were signed, on the other side of the armistice line (Gaza, East Jerusalem, Hebron, and Nablus).[11]

Apart from the mixed cities, Israel's Arab population resided in three geographically distinct clusters, in the Galilee, the Triangle, and the Negev. In January 1950 Israel formally imposed military rule on these Arab regions, based on regulations enacted by the British Mandatory authorities and termed the Emergency Defense Regulations (1945). The area under military rule was divided into northern, central, and southern regional commands. The officials in charge had significant power, including the authority to place people under house arrest, administrative arrest, deportation, to demolish houses, expropriate property, close newspapers, dissolve organizations, prohibit unionizing, determine traffic arrangements, close sectors, set curfews, and place employment restrictions.[12] The decision to impose military rule was justified by the need to maintain order and avoid potential threats, feared at the time by the country's leaders.

The state of military rule remained in place until November 1966. At first it was lifted from Druze and Circassian towns, as well as mixed cities, and finally from all other Arab towns. Its use clearly signified the Israeli establishment's perception of the Arab minority as a "time bomb." Israel's first prime minister, David Ben-Gurion, is credited with saying, "The Arabs must be judged by what they might do, and not by what they have done."[13] Neuberger interpreted this outlook: "The political and military establishment, and as a result most of the Jewish population of Israel, perceive the status of the Arab minority in Israel strictly as a security issue. Familial, cultural, linguistic, and national ties of the Arab sector with other Arab countries lead to its common perception as a hostile element, whether in theory or in practice, or even as a fifth column or potential Trojan horse."[14] This conception undoubtedly did not disappear upon the conclusion of military rule.

Palestinian Refugees in the Diaspora

Historians disagree as to the degree of disruption suffered by the Palestinian people in 1948. In addition to the controversy on how they became refugees to begin with—whether through expulsion, displacement, or because they fled their homes—there are different versions of the number of villages destroyed and the number of refugees who left: Benny Morris counts 385 villages.[15] Walid al-Khalidi mentions 418.[16] Salman Abu Sitta, who adds Bedouin encampments and places of residence in the Negev to previous lists, maintains that the number is 531.[17] This debate was not unexpectedly informed by ideological and political considerations, but it also derived from objective difficulties such as the problems inherent in categorizing nomadic places of residence or village extensions.[18]

The dispute regarding the number of refugees has political undertones; however, it is also supplemented by objective problems, such as defining and counting the refugees. It is easy to discern the political motives and the natural tendency of each side to cite the numbers most beneficial for its cause. The Palestinians tend to maximize and the Israelis are interested in minimizing the scope of those affected. UN institutions, which are seemingly neutral, have problems of their own. They understandably count only those who received aid from UN agencies, although this number presumably does not encompass all refugees. Nonetheless, UN documents can be assumed to be the most reliable source. As defined by the United Nations, a Palestinian refugee is "any person for whom mandatory Palestine was a permanent place of residence from about two years before the outbreak of the Arab-Israeli War in 1948, and who in the aftermath of this war lost his home and source of livelihood and was forced to leave his country."[19]

In the summer of 1949, the secretary-general of the United Nations established a mission chaired by Gordon Clapp to prepare a survey on the economic state of the Palestinian refugees and their living conditions. The mission report, submitted in mid-October 1949, stated that it was impossible to reach an exact number of refugees, but the mission estimated their number at 750,000: 70,000 in Transjordan, 96,000 in Lebanon, 75,000 in Syria, 4,000 in Iraq, 200,000 in the Gaza Strip, 280,000 in the West Bank, and 25,000 in Israel.[20] In 1950 the UN Relief and Works Agency, UNRWA, reported that it distributed aid to 960,000 refugees, a number not including refugees in Iraq, Israel, and Egypt.[21] This estimate may include certain duplications due to refugee movement between the various camps.

The condition and status of Palestinian refugees in Arab host countries varied. In the early 1950s, Palestinian camps established in Arab host countries largely became independent entities with their own social and economic characteristics. Mutual relations developed between the camps and their surroundings, despite efforts by host countries and UN representatives to prevent the development of such relationships and to block all possibility of refugee assimilation within the local society and economy. Camp residents constituted a workforce utilized by those in the immediate environs and gradually became a permanent part of the host economy. There was also some movement, albeit marginal, from the camps to the local community.

Palestinian and Arab discourse uses two terms, "integration" (*indimaj*) and "assimilation" (*insihar*), to describe the mutual relationship between Palestinian refugees residing in the camps and the host population. Most Palestinian authors and spokesmen were in favor of a certain amount of integration, to fulfill daily needs, but did not advocate assimilation. Palestinians avoided assimilating in order to preserve their identity, while the hosts objected for their own reasons. Both refugees and hosts alike have always been adamant in perceiving the refugees and their camps as temporary, insisting that they should remain thus until such time as the "right of return" to Palestine is realized. The declared pan-Arab consensus sees realization of this right as the solution that will enable the refugees to return to their homes and resume their former identities, consequently relieving the host countries of an economic, social, political, and demographic burden.

Palestinian Refugees in Jordan

After the West Bank was annexed to the Hashemite Kingdom of Transjordan, the entire country was renamed Jordan. It now encompassed thirty refugee camps, particularly in the vicinity of the large cities of Amman, East Jerusalem, Ramallah, Nablus, Irbid, Tulkarm, al-Zarqa, and Jenin. Twenty camps were located in the West Bank and ten in the East Bank. All Palestinians living within the kingdom, both refugees and permanent residents who expressed such a desire, were granted Jordanian citizenship with full political privileges as well as the right to receive government services.

Due to the strong relationship between residents of the two banks, which included marriage ties, patronage, and blood relations, Palestinian refugees had a better chance of becoming integrated into the Jordanian Kingdom than any other Arab country. The Jordanian government was interested in their integration as justification of the annexation and for purposes of legitimization. The refugees in the West Bank did not feel as estranged as did their brethren in other countries. Although they had been displaced from their homes and villages, they remained in their homeland and were not forced to cope with a hostile environment. Nonetheless, there were differences between the refugees' living conditions and integration in the East and West Bank. East Bank residents displayed less willingness than their West Bank counterparts to welcome the refugees into their lives. Nonetheless, the Jordanians were much more open toward the Palestinian refugees than other Arab governments and countries.

Integration in the East Bank

Refugee integration in Jordan was the most thorough of all Arab host countries. The proportion of those who left East Bank camps and became integrated into local society showed a steady rise, from 35 percent in 1949 to 81 percent in 1995. Most of these settled in the Jordanian cities of Amman, Irbid, al-Zarqa, and Jarash or their suburbs, moving to houses they had bought or rented, indicating their financial capabilities.[22]

Leaving the refugee camps led to an improved social status, and marriage ties with the local population became more frequent, augmenting the Palestinians' cultural integration into society. At first, most refugee families were dependent on UNRWA for their livelihood, through the "supply card" (*bitaqat al-tamwin*), but they gradually began searching for other sources of income by working, trying their hand at small commercial initiatives, and in the food and services industries.[23] The host society and the Jordanian government displayed flexibility and openness in this respect, permitting these initiatives to flourish. Another source of income was funds sent by the many relatives who had traveled to the Gulf countries, which became wealthy in the 1950s and attracted unemployed Palestinian youth.[24] Palestinians found various employment options in the Gulf states, from public service and physical labor to teaching and technical jobs.

Research on the integration of Palestinian refugees into Jordanian life indicates that once the economic state of refugee families improved, they tended to leave the camps and become an integral part of the host society. Nevertheless, they did not relinquish their unique Palestinian identity. Leaving the camps had no effect on the internal connections within refugee groups. Even when living in Jordanian cities and suburbs they maintained a shared community life according to their rural or regional origins in Palestine.[25]

The integration of Palestinian refugees into Jordanian politics was also greater than in all other Arab countries, and they became involved in local government and in the parliament.[26] This was further facilitated by the fact that nonrefugee Jordanians of Palestinian origin had reached senior government positions and served as ministers and even prime ministers. Beginning in 1950, animated debates on this subject were held from time to time in Jordanian newspapers, particularly in the informal press, indicating two trends: local Jordanians were concerned with the refugees' rate of integration into politics and the possibility that they would eventually take control of the government, while Jordanians of Palestinian origin and the refugees themselves were concerned that the government would rescind the inclusive Jordanian citizenship awarded to the refugees. This concern tended to emerge particularly when relationships between Jordan and the Palestinian national movement were in a state of decline.[27]

Palestinian Refugees in the West Bank

The refugees generally found integration easier in the West Bank. They were among their own people, sometimes in the vicinity of their extended families. The basic difference between the two banks was in the political realm: In the East Bank, refugees who wished to become integrated were obliged to act according to the rules of Jordanian politics. In the West Bank, however, integration followed more familiar rules. Some of the population had lived under the British Mandate and had experienced similar changes and processes as had populations in the coastal plains from where the refugees had originated, leaving pockets of Palestinian political activity not necessarily compatible with Abdullah's plans. The Jordanian government succeeded in co-opting some of the Palestinian leadership, even among the mufti's camp, and enjoyed the support of the Nashashibi camp, but its policy was perceived by many as an attempt to erase Palestinian identity. Many in the West Bank were angered, feeling that they were part of the Palestinian nation. This sense of hurt and insult increased, mainly among the refugees, and was further aroused by rumors of Abdullah's duplicity on the Palestinian issue and his agreements with the Zionists.

Undercurrents of opposition to the Jordanian government represented feelings prevalent among most residents of the West Bank. This opposition erupted in full force during the escalation of revolutionary pan-Arabism instigated by Egypt's Gamal Abdel Nasser.

Palestinian Refugees in the Gaza Strip

In the Gaza Strip, the arrival of the refugees had a dramatic demographic impact since they comprised a group twice as large as the local population. Moreover, the arrival of such a large number of refugees, most of whom were destitute, occurred at a time when the region's economic capacity had been severely reduced due to the war. The economy of Gaza and its environs was dependent on the entire southern province and based mainly on the agricultural industry, but after the war most of the agricultural lands remained in Israeli hands. For many Gazans—land owners and their vassals—this meant losing their only source of subsistence. The tens of thousands of refugees who wound up in the Gaza Strip did not become integrated into the local population, and both the indigent and the refugee population all began adapting to the new situation. The eight refugee camps in the Gaza Strip became centers of rampant unemployment, a status that rapidly encompassed the original residents as well. Many young people, tens of thousands of working-age Gazans, traveled to the Gulf states. Husayn Abu al-Nmil described their tribulations:

> Egypt, the Gaza Strip's neighbor and its only land route to the rest of the world, did not permit the refugees to work in its territory, with or without pay. Even traveling to Egypt was a problem. . . .

> Faced with these difficulties, Palestinian refugees had no option but to sneak into the West Bank on foot through the territories occupied in 1948, at the risk of being hit by Egyptian bullets on suspicion of spying, or by Israeli bullets on suspicion of being an "infiltrator" or feda'i. Even if they succeeded in evading the Egyptians and Israelis, it remained for them to evade the Jordanian blockades in order to reach the West Bank. From there they would make their way to the East Bank and then steal into one of the Arab Gulf States through the desert. All of this on foot or hiding in a truck crossing the border.[28]

Since young people were under such pressure to reach the Gulf, smuggling workers became a flourishing business, and stations for processing and guidance were erected in the West Bank, the East Bank, Iraq, and Saudi Arabia. Even the season of the hajj (the pilgrimage to Islamic holy places) was now seen as an opportunity to receive entrance permits to Saudi Arabia, from where they would cross the border illegally to the various Gulf states.[29] In this way many Palestinian workers left the Gaza Strip and succeeded in reaching the Gulf and finding jobs. The salaries sent to their families in Gaza supplemented UN aid money and made life a little more bearable.

Palestinian Refugees in Israel

The controversy surrounding the number of Palestinians in general is even more acute when debating the issue of those termed "refugees within the State of Israel" or "present absentees."[30] Historian Hillel Cohen explains the situation:

> One of the most complex questions related to the issue of the Palestinian refugees currently residing in Israel is how to determine their numbers. In the absence of fully verified data, any attempt to determine the number of internally displaced is merely an estimate. However the absence of formal data is significantly no coincidence. Population censes held by the Central Bureau of Statistics count the refugees as part of the total Arab population, and no official Israeli elements have published any information on this issue since the 1950s. Their motive seems to be a wish to avoid specifically referring to this population as a distinct group, in order to prevent its members from uniting around common demands, as well as rein-

forcement of the assertion that there is no longer an internal refugee problem.[31]

This policy enacted by Israeli authorities made it difficult to define the "internal refugees." Hillel Cohen distinguishes between two types: (1) those whose villages were destroyed and who remained in Israel in another town of refuge when prevented by the authorities from returning to their original villages, and (2) those whose towns were partially destroyed and who were permitted to return to them as "present absentees."[32] The latter were not permitted to realize ownership of their property, and their assets have since been managed by the Custodian for Absentees' Property. In many cases those returning were not permitted to return to their original homes, being required instead to live in the homes of others. Statistically, only those belonging to the first group were considered refugees. Sami Samooha estimated the number of internal refugees as 23.1 percent of the entire Arab population of Israel, while Ramzi Rabah estimated them at 40 percent.[33] A survey performed by the Jewish National Fund in the early 1950s and assessments by the Committee of Displaced (which seeks to represent this population) estimate the refugees as constituting about 25 percent of the entire Arab population of Israel. The great majority of internal refugees presently reside in the Galilee, with the remainder in mixed cities and in the Negev. In some villages they encompass nearly the entire population (for example, the village of Sha'b) and in other villages 50 percent or more (for example, the village of Jedida). They usually live in a separate neighborhood, which locals call "the refugee neighborhood" (*harat al-laji' in*).

The Israeli Government and Rehabilitation of the Refugees

The task of handling the internal refugee issue in Israel was entrusted to the Jewish National Fund, the government Authority for Rehabilitation of Refugees, and the authorities in charge of military rule—organizations that had no vested interest in helping the refugees return to their villages. Some of those in charge were even known for encouraging Arab migration from territories allocated to the Jewish state during the war. The Jewish National Fund managed the refugees' lands in such a way as to prevent them from returning. Its representatives visited the refugees and tried to convince them to sell the lands belonging to their villages. For example, Yosef Weitz visited refugee concentrations in Nazareth and tried to convince refugees from the villages of Mujaydel and Ma'lul to sell their lands or receive restitution.[34] He summarized his disappointment in his journal on September 9, 1948: "The Arabs show no sign of consenting to sell the land. They are evidently certain that everything will return to its original state and they will once again play the land game with us."[35] Similar attempts over the years were no more successful, and neither was an attempt to encourage immigration, for example, of refugees from the Upper Galilee village of Jish to Argentina.[36]

Hillel Cohen summarized the work of the governmental Authority for Rehabilitation of Refugees:

> An Authority for Rehabilitation of Refugees operated on behalf of the government of Israel for about four years (1949–1953). It settled hundreds of refugees in the various villages. . . . The authority operated mostly in semiofficial villages of refuge. These were villages abandoned by most of their residents and chosen to house refugees from other places. This category includes two villages in the Eastern Galilee, 'Akbara (near Safed)—which received refugees from Qaditha, Dalata, Mayron, and Qabba'ah, and the village of Wadi al-Hanan near Majdal—which received refugees from Khisas, Katya, and the Halahla clan, whose displacement aroused a parliamentary uproar. In the Western Galilee, the village Sha'b, from which most residents had fled, was chosen as a rehabilitative village. This is an unusual case, since most of its local residents remained in the country and themselves became internal refugees (particularly in Majd al-Krum). The authority planned to transfer to this village refugees from al-Damon. Later on, residents of villages from the demilitarized zone on the Israel-Syria border, Akarad al-Baqqara and Akarad al-Ghannameh, evacuated from their homes, were also transferred there. In the 1960s and 1970s some of its original residents were also reinstated in the village, but their lands were not returned to them. . . . Those handled by the Authority for Rehabilitation of Refugees constituted only a small percentage of all internal refugees. The authority seems to have given preference to particularly difficult cases and to people considered "positive elements," stipulating that the assistance provided is contingent on consenting to relinquish their property in the village of origin. All other refugees had to manage on their own, wherever they happened to be at the end of the war.[37]

During the war, refugees were expelled from villages occupied by the army. There are those who claim that this was done at the behest of an unofficial committee called the "transfer committee," composed of 'Ezra Danin, Moshe Sason, and Yosef Weitz, activists of the Jewish Agency's Arab Department from the British Mandate period and employees of the Jewish National Fund.[38] Weitz wrote to the deputy chief of the General Staff at the time, Major General Yig'al Yadin, suggesting that the army expel refugees from occupied territories.[39] It is not clear whether the army accepted his suggestion and acted accordingly; however, it clearly operated in this spirit in many of the conquered towns, such as Lydda and Ramle, where refugees were expelled along with most of the local residents, and the villages of Dayr al-Asad, Bi'na, Rama, and Faradis. Even after the cease-fire agreements were signed and after the Triangle was annexed to Israel, 8,500 refugees were removed, 4,000 of them to Baqa al-Gharbiyya and the vicinity.[40]

Two levels can be discerned in the integration of internal refugees: integration into the country in general, and into the Arab population in particular. Internal refugees never became fully integrated into the Arab population, and to this day many Arabs distinguish between "locals" and "refugees." Refugees lived in separate neighborhoods until the mid-1960s, often residing in temporary shacks and huts, apparently hoping to return to their villages of origin as soon as possible. The War of 1967 and the Arab defeat (*naksa*) seems to have extinguished these hopes, and refugees began moving to stone houses and becoming more integrated into the social and economic life of their villages of refuge. A lack of integration was evident in the political sphere as well. In villages with larger concentrations of refugees, they formed their own lists for election to local authorities; for example, the Refugees of Ma'lul Party (Laji'o Ma'lul), who for many years formed an independent list in Yafat al-Nasira. Sometimes these lists even won the elections and the head of the list was appointed mayor, as, for example, in Hudayda and Tamra in the Galilee, and in Umm al-Fahm and Jaljulye in the Triangle.

In contrast, other internal refugees became involved in the country and in Israeli politics as an integral part of Israel's Arab minority and were affiliated with a wide array of orientations. Some became members of the Knesset, such as Shaikh Salih Salim Sulayman from Safuriyya, a resident of Nazareth (in the satellite parties of Mapai); Rustom Bastuni from Tirat al-Karmel, a resident of Haifa (Mapam);

Hashem Mahamid from Lajjun, a resident of Umm al-Fahm; Ahmad Sa'ad from Birwa, a resident of Abu Snan (Hadash); Muhammad Mi'ari, born in Birwa and a resident of Maker and Haifa (the Progressive List for Peace); and Tawfiq Khatib, from Khuraysh, a resident of Jaljulye (the Islamic Movement). Several internal refugees also became senior government officials, for instance, Muwaffaq Khuri, deputy secretary-general of the Ministry of Education, Culture, and Sports. Some became famed authors and poets, including Taha Muhammad 'Ali from Safuriyya, a resident of Nazareth, and Muhammad 'Ali Taha from Mi'ar. Some became well-known soccer players for Israeli teams, such as 'Abbas Sawwan from Sakhnin, whose family originated from the village of Murassas near Bisan.

Palestinian Refugees in Lebanon

Fifteen refugee camps were established in Lebanon: six in the south, five in Beirut, two in the north, one in the Lebanon Valley, and one on Mount Lebanon. They were populated mainly with refugees from the vicinity of Acre, Haifa, and the Galilee.[41] The number of refugees who ended up in Lebanon is also disputed, and estimates range from 120,000 to 200,000. The most reliable estimate is that of the Department for Refugee Matters in the Lebanese Ministry of the Interior, from 1952, which mentions some 140,000 refugees.[42] Initially, Palestinian refugees settled in southern Lebanon as close as possible to the Israeli border, living in three camps: Burj al-Shamali, al-Bas, and al-Rashidiyya, near Tyre. Eventually, some refugees moved to other parts of Lebanon. According to one study, only 43.3 percent of the refugees lived in the camps, a proportion that diminished over time.[43]

Integration of Palestinian refugees into Lebanon was lower than in any other Arab country. The authorities perceived them as foreigners and strictly withheld Lebanese citizenship. According to Lebanese law, they were foreign individuals, rather than a collective, and subject to Lebanese sovereignty. The delicate ethnic balance typical of Lebanon was undoubtedly instrumental in shaping this policy, particularly from the Christian perspective, with its concern for an inflated Muslim population. Many laws were enacted, as well as strict regulations aimed at handling the presence of tens of thousands of Palestinians, restricting them to their places of residence and preventing them from becoming permanent residents. Refugees did not enjoy basic freedom of employment or fundamental social rights. Restrictions were imposed on developing infrastructure within the camps, allocating slots for students at institutions of higher education, purchasing land, and working in various professions.[44] Scholar Sulayman Natur states, "The policy of the Lebanese government regarding the refugees may be summarized as an attempt to make life difficult, forcing them to leave and to move elsewhere."[45] The restrictions and hardships aggravated existing tensions between the Palestinians and Lebanese authorities, particularly the local security establishment, who perceived the guests as a potential threat to the country's well-being. The Palestinians did nothing to quell these concerns. They eventually played a major role in the crises embroiling the country in the years 1958, 1968, and 1975, which increased the feelings of estrangement and hostility, particularly between Lebanese Christians and Palestinians who had found refuge in the country.

Palestinian Refugees in Syria

In Syria, fourteen refugee camps were established: seven in the Damascus District, two each in the Haleb and Dir'a Districts, and one each in the Hims, Hamat, and Lazikiyya Districts. Palestinian refugees comprised 2.4 percent of the entire population and 11 percent of all Palestinian refugees in the world.[46] Most of the Palestinian refugees in Syria originated from three areas: 40 percent from the city of Safed and its vicinity, 22 percent from the city of Haifa and its vicinity, and 16.5 percent from Tiberias and its surroundings.[47] Some came directly to Syria through the Golan Heights, while others came through Lebanon or through the West Bank and Transjordan.[48]

Most of the restrictions imposed on Palestinian refugees in other Arab countries, particularly in Lebanon, were not evident in Syria. The integration of Palestinian refugees into Syria is considered among the highest in the Arab world and many have since left the camps. On July 10, 1956, Law 260 was enacted in Syria, declaring, "The Palestinians are equal to Syrian citizens in all matters of work, residence, commerce, military service, education, and healthcare, at no cost to their national identity."[49] The Palestinians were also awarded the right to vote and to be elected to Syrian parliament and labor unions. In addition, they benefited from the law ensuring free education and there were no restrictions on admission of Palestinians to universities. The main restrictions imposed upon refugees were that each family head, if registered as a refugee, was allowed to own only one house, and refugees were forbidden to purchase agricultural land, in order to prevent permanent settlement in Syria.

Political integration in Syria was rapid.[50] Many of the Palestinian refugees joined local political organizations, movements, and parties. Only a few movements were hesitant to include Palestinians, a reluctance born of several instances of dual allegiance to both Syrian and Palestinian organizations. Although this was usually tolerated thanks to the pan-Arab orientation of Syrian politics, sometimes conflicts occurred. For example, after the Syrian-Egyptian United Arab Republic (UAR) was dissolved in 1961, Palestinian members of the Ba'ath Party were forced to choose between their loyalty to the party and to Palestinian organizations; many chose to ally with Palestinian organizations.

The economies of the Palestinian camps became well-integrated within the Syrian economy as a whole. The location of some 70 percent of the refugees in the vicinity of the capital, with others near other central towns, was a facilitating factor. When restrictions on the integration of Palestinians into the Syrian educational system were removed, the number of intellectuals and academics rose, as did their participation in the government administrative system and the private sector. Many Palestinian intellectuals began working in the Gulf, sending their salaries to their families in Syria.

Palestinian Refugees in Iraq

Opinions differ regarding the number of Palestinian refugees in Iraq as well. According to estimates, they numbered three thousand to five thousand in 1948.[51] The great majority came from the villages of Jaba', Ijzem, and 'Ayn Ghazal on the coastal plain, south of Haifa. The residents of these villages had originally formed friendships with Iraqi army forces fighting in the Triangle area, and when the villages were occupied and their residents expelled in July 1948, the Iraqis transported the refugees by truck to the East Bank and from there to Baghdad. In time, Iraqi authorities awarded the Palestinians refugee status based on two conditions: (1) that they came from a Palestinian town occupied in 1948, and (2) that they arrived in Iraq before September 25, 1958. The second condition was imposed once the number of infiltrators multiplied in the late 1950s, when Iraq's oil industry began flourishing. All Palestinians who arrived after this date were thus registered as foreigners.[52]

A special authority, established in 1950 in Iraq's Ministry of Labor and Social Affairs, was in charge of all refugee matters. Its role was essential, since no refugee camps had been erected in Iraq, and therefore the refugees received no assistance from UN aid agencies, a responsibility that was instead assumed by the government of Iraq. In 1958 the government formulated criteria for providing the refugees with financial aid. In the mid-1970s the government completed the construction of low-cost housing units and the refugees were given small flats in lieu of the financial aid previously awarded.[53]

Integration into Iraqi Society

Iraqi authorities permitted the full integration of Palestinians into Iraqi political movements and parties. The two major movements that attracted Palestinians were, naturally, the Nasser and Ba'ath movements. Both espoused pan-Arab unity and gave the Palestinian issue precedence, placing it in the center of their political platforms. The Iraqis also allowed the Palestinians to hold activities among the refugees and approved establishment of the Association of Sons of Palestine in Iraq in March 1960. After the Palestine Liberation Organization (PLO) was established in 1964, it received free rein to operate in Iraq and hundreds of youngsters joined. Other Palestinian organizations later followed suit and received the support of the Iraqi government.[54]

In the social and economic spheres there was less integration. Most of the Palestinian refugees preferred to remain distinct and separate from their hosts. A survey indicates that about 84 percent preferred to live with fellow Palestinians and only 16 percent were willing to live among other populations.[55] From an economic perspective, the rural-agricultural background of most of the refugees hampered their integration, and they lacked the ability to handle life in an urban setting such as Baghdad. Government support was their only source of subsistence. Research conducted two or three decades after they arrived in Iraq showed that 57 percent still lived exclusively off the subsidy received from the Iraqi government, which offered very poor subsistence.[56]

Nevertheless, a few of the refugees managed to become culturally integrated. Some Palestinian authors and writers became incorporated within the Iraqi cultural elite, among them the author, artist, poet, and playwright Jabra Ibrahim Jabra (1919–1994); the author, poet, and journalist Sulafa Hajjawi; and Khaled 'Ali Mustafa. Musicians Jamil Qushta and Rawhi Khammash and journalist Muhammad Wahid, editor of the journal *Iraq Observer*, became well integrated in their fields as well.[57] There were also some athletes who became an integral part of the local scene: the Haifa Club played in the top Iraqi soccer league and its players formed part of the Palestine Team.[58]

Aftermath of the Nakba: Rehabilitation Efforts and the Inter-Arab Domain

After the shock of the war and its outcome, and in light of the new state of affairs, leaders of the Palestinian national movement attempted to act on two spheres: the Arab and Islamic, and the Palestinian spheres. Leaders made efforts to keep the Palestinian cause on the agenda of both the Arab and the Islamic world. At the same time, they did their best to help Palestinian communities in the diaspora recover and to reorganize them in their varied locations, with the aim of reviving the armed struggle.

The Mufti and the Arab Realm

Although the Palestinians and their leaders were deeply disappointed with the role of Arab regimes in the War of 1948, they did not choose to disengage from the Arab world. Leaders of the Palestinian national movement, and particularly the mufti, could not afford to take such a step. Their status was in decline in the entire region, as well as among their own people. Any attempt at rehabilitation of the Palestinian communities in the diaspora would have to go through Arab channels, and the latter did not wish to revive the power formerly wielded by Haj Amin al-Husayni and his cronies. The mufti continued to draw apart from his people, as his vision of a Greater Palestine, on which he had gambled, gradually faded away. Many of those who had joined him prior to 1948 left, and most turned to other political endeavors. Haj Amin, an ambitious leader in the early 1940s who aspired to lead the Arab and even the Islamic world through his Palestinian vision, was now a defeated politician who had "gambled it all" and lost, with nothing to show for his efforts. The mufti, however, neither gave up nor relinquished his position. He continued his endeavors in the pan-Arab realm, particularly in Arab League institutions, his efforts directed mainly against Jordan and its rule of the West Bank, and against Egypt and its rule of the Gaza Strip.

The mufti contends with King Abdullah. The mufti objected to King Abdullah's attempts to revoke specific Palestinian representation in the Arab League and was opposed to Abdullah's plan to hold general elections for a joint East and West Bank parliament. In both cases, Haj Amin suffered stinging defeats.

Prior to the Arab League's eleventh session, planned to commence on August 17, 1949, Ahmad 'Abd al-Baqi, prime minister of the Government of All Palestine, approached the political committee of the Arab League and demanded that representatives of his government be invited to attend. He threatened that if rebuffed, the Palestinians would sever their ties with the league. The Jordanians immediately countered by threatening to withdraw from the Arab League if a representative of the All-Palestine Government were to be invited to the committee's discussions. They also rejected a compromise proposed by the Egyptians, whereby the Arab League would continue to be in charge of appointing Palestinian representatives, while Jordan and Egypt would appoint representatives from the territory under their control. Ultimately, the committee decided to accept the Jordanian position and not invite a representative of the All-Palestine Government to the discussions. The prime minister of Lebanon, whose turn it was to serve as president of the political committee, explained, "The lack of Palestinian representation will cause much less damage than that accruing from a Jordanian absence."[59]

Abdullah's intention to include residents of the West Bank in Jordanian general elections was opposed by the mufti, whose sympathizers held a protest campaign. Despite their copious threats, they failed to convince the Palestinians to abstain from voting, since the Jordanian establishment used its power both to make counterthreats and to promise positions and benefits. The elections were held as planned on April 11, 1950, with a particularly high turnout of West Bank Palestinian voters (about 90 percent of the eligible population). The Palestinians were allocated half the seats in the lower house of parliament (Majlis al-Nuwwab). Abdullah appointed seven West Bank representatives from a total of twenty members of the upper house (Majlis al-Aayan). Some of those thus appointed had previously belonged to Haj Amin's camp, stressing the king's victory over the mufti.

The mufti and the Egyptian monarchy. Haj Amin's resistance was displayed less conspicuously in Egypt. He resided in Cairo and could not openly express his sentiments against the regime. He never concealed his discontent, however, at Egypt's conduct in the Arab League and its "capitulation" to Abdullah on the Palestinian issue. In one incident he even accused the prime minister of Egypt and his representative on the political committee of duplicity. The Egyptian government's strict and sometimes brutal actions in the Gaza Strip added to the tensions. The mufti maintained constant contact with opposition forces in Egypt in order to incite public opinion against the government's activities in Gaza. At the height of the crisis between the regime and the Muslim Brotherhood, following the murder of Egyptian prime minister Mahmoud Fahmi al-Naqrashi by a member of the movement on December 28, 1948, Haj Amin testified twice on behalf of the assassins. In his testimony he praised the "devotion and sacrifice displayed by warriors of the Muslim Brotherhood during the war in Palestine."[60]

Cooperation between the Arab Higher Institution and the Muslim Brotherhood resulted in the first group of Palestinian fighters anxious to correct the outcome of the War of 1948 and to avenge the defeat and the loss of Palestine. The mufti's alliance with the Muslim Brotherhood tainted his relationship with Egyptian authorities and dealt a fatal blow to his ability to influence their policy on the Palestinian issue. In addition, Egyptian authorities resented the mufti's recurring demands that they help finance the All-Palestine Government and the Arab Higher Institution.[61] This relationship remained unchanged until the end of the Egyptian monarchy and ascension of the Free Officers in July 1952.

The mufti and the Islamic world. After being repeatedly defeated in the inter-Arab realm, Haj Amin decided to try his luck in the wider Islamic world. The mufti had constructed a network of contacts in this realm ever since his days in Jerusalem, when he organized the Pan-Islamic Conference in December 1931. In late 1950, the Pakistani authorities approached him and requested that he lead the committee organizing the World Muslim Conference, planned to take place in Karachi on February 10, 1951, to be attended by representatives of thirty Muslim countries. Haj Amin did not pass up this opportunity; he was chosen president of the conference and in his speech he called upon Muslim states to "unite and pursue the liberation of Palestine."[62] He remained in Pakistan until May 1951 and worked on promoting his religious standing. The local Muslim council of sages even offered him the role of Shaikh al-Islam, but he preferred to return to Cairo, the epicenter for decisions on Palestinian matters, which was also in closer proximity to his rival, King Abdullah, and his allies in the Arab League.

In a short time, two events were to revive Haj Amin's hopes of resuming an influential role in the pan-Arab world: the murder of King Abdullah in Jerusalem on July 20, 1951, and the revolution of the Free Officers in Egypt on July 23, 1952.

The murder of Abdullah and maintaining continuity in the West Bank. Elements in Jordan and elsewhere attempted to implicate Haj Amin in Abdullah's assassination. One way or the other, the mufti did not hesitate to take advantage of the passing of his great rival. After the murder, the Jordanians imposed a strict regime in the West Bank, and Haj Amin came out strongly against their rule. His men incited those residing in the refugee camps and fomented riots in the West Bank to the best of their ability. Haj Amin lobbied against Jordan's hold on the West Bank among the Arab League as well, citing the inexperience of Abdullah's heirs, his brother, Talal, and his son, Husayn. However, these efforts proved unsuccessful. Part of the Palestinian elite in the West Bank had always been opposed to Haj Amin and the Husayni camp and now continued to ally themselves with the Hashemite Kingdom. As events would have it, even the murder of the kingdom's charismatic founder could not prevent annexation of the West Bank to Jordan and the increasing dependency of much of the Palestinian elite on the Hashemite Kingdom.

*The Mufti, Inter-Arab Rivalries,
and the Establishment of the PLO*

The mufti's relationship with Egypt's new rulers, the officers leading the revolution of July 1952, was based on prior connections, particularly with Gamal Abdel Nasser, who was familiar with Haj Amin from the War of 1948. The Free Officers saw their relationship with Haj Amin as an opportunity to bolster their image in the Arab League by declaring their support for the Palestinian cause and of the refugees. It took only two years for the relationship to go sour, particularly due to Haj Amin's close relationship with the Muslim Brotherhood, who clashed with the regime in 1954. Even so, the officers refrained from deporting the Palestinian leader, and he continued his talks with Nasser.

From his base in Cairo, Haj Amin often traveled to other Arab states to speak of the Palestinian issue. In Saudi Arabia he asked for financial assistance; in Lebanon and Syria he sought contact with the refugee camps. His maneuvering among the Arab leaders and regimes, however, produced only minimal dividends. He relentlessly pursued public opinion and kept the embers of Palestinian nationalism glowing but was perceived as a tactless inciter. The mufti intervened in rivalries between Arab states; first between Nasser and Iraqi prime minister Nuri al-Sa'id, and then between Nasser and Iraqi president 'Abd al-Karim Qasem; finally he even crossed swords with Nasser himself.

After the Czech arms deal between Egypt's Nasser and the Soviet Union in 1955, the Egyptian regime changed its attitude toward Palestinian activities originating in Gaza. Occasional operations by Palestinian infiltrators, under the auspices of the Arab Higher Institution, were now considered Fida'iyyun (Holy Fighters) activities, and encouraged by the Egyptians, who even helped publicize them in the media. Consequently, Haj Amin grew closer to the Cairo authorities and even took part in a fund-raising campaign in support of the Czech arms deal. The Egyptian media rewarded him by awarding prominent and positive coverage to his presence and activities.[63] Relationships with the authorities continued to improve until the fall of 1958. Haj Amin supported Nasser in his struggle against the Baghdad Alliance. He bore a grudge against the Hashemites in general and did not forget the assistance provided by their allies in Iraq to the British during the Rashid 'Ali coup in May 1941. His sympathizers incited riots in West Bank cities, supporting Nasser and renouncing the Hashemites and the Baghdad Alliance. The mufti continued to support Nasser when the latter nationalized the Suez Canal and in his war with Britain, France, and Israel in 1956. He interpreted the "triple attack" (*harb al-'udwan al-thulathi*) on Egypt as proof of his claims that the imperialists and the Jews had conspired against the Arab nation and claimed that the Palestinians were the spearhead of the Arab defense.[64]

The positive relationship between Haj Amin and the highest echelons of the Egyptian government did nothing to help the situation in Gaza, however. Following a short Israeli occupation of the Gaza Strip from October 1956 to March 1957, the former state of affairs was resumed. The Egyptians did not permit Haj Amin and his men to operate in Gaza and did not award local Palestinians even a semblance of self-government. Nasser preached pan-Arab unity, and even united his country with Syria, and therefore saw no need to award distinct marks of autonomy to a narrow territory populated by Palestinian refugees. Both these circumstances, as well as the failed attempt to include Iraq's new republican regime in the United Arab Republic (UAR), led Haj Amin to contemplate a closer relationship with the regime of General 'Abd al-Karim Qasem, who had defeated the Hashemite dynasty in Iraq on July 14, 1958. It was not long before Qasem refused to accept the dictates of Egypt, the "older sister," and when their relationship deteriorated he began goading Nasser—as did other Arab leaders—on the Palestinian issue. In November 1959 Qasem formulated the term "Palestinian entity" (*al-kayan al-Filastini*), asserting that it should have been established and recognized by Egypt and Jordan long before. He also demanded that a Palestinian army be founded, "to assume responsibility for the task of liberating Palestine," and declared the recruitment of about five thousand young Palestinian refugees in his country, who were then trained by the Iraqi army.[65] At the ceremony held at the conclusion of their training in August 1960, Qasem promised that soon they would embark on the holy war and congratulated them on the "birth of the eternal Palestinian republic."[66] As Haj Amin grew closer to Qasem, his relationship with Nasser deteriorated, and he transferred his residence and the offices of the Arab Higher Institution to Beirut. He frequently traveled from the Lebanese capital to Baghdad to discuss with Qasem the plan to establish the Liberation Army and the Palestinian republic.[67]

Now the Egyptian media began a campaign to vilify Haj Amin. He was depicted as living a life of luxury at the expense of the Palestinian people and as having been the person most responsible for the Nakba.[68] The Egyptian authorities acted to form Palestinian military units in the UAR and in the Gaza Strip. Institutions symbolizing local autonomy were established in Gaza. A legislative council operated alongside both the Egyptian governor and the Palestinian National Union (al-Ittihad al-Wattani al-Filastini), founded as a branch of the National Union, the political organization of the United Arab Republic.

More important, the Egyptians began searching for an alternate Palestinian leader to replace the mufti and found him in Ahmad al-Shuqayri, one of the mufti's many rivals. In late November 1962, on the fifteenth anniversary of the UN partition resolution, the Egyptian authorities organized a rally, but the mufti was not invited. The primary speaker was Naser al-Din al-Nashashibi, a son of the Nashashibi family, who had headed the main opposition to the mufti during the British Mandate. In June 1963, after the death of Ahmad Hilmi 'Abd al-Baqi, the Egyptians offered Ahmad al-Shuqayri, son of As'ad al-Shuqayri and one of the mufti's greatest opponents during the British Mandate, the position of head of the All-Palestine Government and representative to the Arab League. Once he agreed, the Egyptian authorities immediately demanded that he begin preparations for establishing the Palestine Liberation Organization, as well as units of the Palestine Liberation Army (PLA). At the Arab summit that convened in Cairo in January 1964, Nasser passed a resolution concerning establishment of the PLO.[69] Haj Amin was not invited to take part in this historical event. This was an unprecedented move: it was the first time since Haj Amin had assumed leadership that a formal Arab forum had made such an important decision on behalf of the Palestinian people with total disregard for the mufti.

In his time of need, Haj Amin turned in an unexpected direction—he tried to approach the Hashemite regime in Jordan. King Husayn was not as hostile toward Haj Amin as his grandfather, Abdullah, had been, but still, he was the current representative of the dynasty that the mufti had been fighting for decades, and which many Palestinians believed had done their nation much harm. At first the rapprochement was hesitant: In March 1960, Haj Amin sent King Husayn greetings in honor of 'Id al-Fitr, a gesture that was broadcast on Jordan's national radio. About a year later, a Palestinian delegation on behalf of the Arab Higher Institution, headed by Munif al-Husayni, the mufti's nephew, came to Amman to discuss "joining Arab efforts on the Palestinian issue."[70] Another Palestinian delegation came to Amman following the conclusion of the Arab summit that resolved to establish the PLO. At the time the mufti began this course of action, Husayn was interested in receiving his "stamp of approval," since Jordan and Egypt were at odds with each other. However, when Husayn's relationship with Egypt began to improve, he became less supportive of the mufti, only permitting the mufti's followers to hold a campaign against Ahmad al-Shuqayri in the West Bank.[71]

This campaign and other acts of the Arab Higher Institution among Palestinian refugees in Lebanon had no effect on Ahmad al-Shuqayri. In late March 1964 he announced a conference in preparation for a Palestinian national convention to be held in East Jerusalem in May. The mufti's attempts to prevent this convention were unsuccessful, and it took place on May 28, 1964, at the Intercontinental Hotel in Jerusalem. The Arab Higher Institution and other Palestinian organizations—including Fatah, led by Yasir Arafat, and Subhi Yasin's Pioneers of Self-Sacrifice (Tala'i al-Fidaa)—did not attend. They declared that Shuqayri's organization was a pawn of Egypt's Nasser, established by the Arab League and Arab governments in order to block the independent Palestinian organizations.[72] These boycotts, however, could not prevent the convention from taking place. It was opened by King Husayn and Secretary-General of the Arab League 'Abd al-Khaliq Hassunah and attended by prime ministers and foreign ministers of several Arab countries. Ahmad al-Shuqayri was chosen president and the convention declared itself the "first national Palestinian council" (*al-majlis al-watani al-Filastini al-awwal*), disregarding the founding council of the All-Palestine Government, which had convened in Gaza in early October 1948 under the leadership of Haj Amin. The concluding announcement of the convention confirmed the Palestinian National Charter (al-Mithaq al-Qawmi al-Filastini) and the basic statutes of the PLO.

The mufti's loss of face notwithstanding, this event in fact symbolized the success of all his endeavors: the declaration of the founding of the PLO, in Jerusalem of all places, continued the path that he had outlined for nearly forty years. For the first time, an entity representing Palestinian national sovereignty had been established, with actual inter-Arab approval. In addition to the guidance and blessings of Gamal Abdel Nasser, the founding convention was also under the patronage of King Husayn. For the first time since ascending the throne, the Hashemite king expressed support for the Palestinian national identity, and in his speech he offered his assistance: "I am one of you and a soldier in your army—the Army of Palestine, to which I have devoted my life."[73] Neither did the contents of the Palestinian National Charter, confirmed at the Jerusalem convention, deviate from Haj Amin's doctrine. He was incapable of accepting the blow to his supremacy, however, and continued to bicker with Ahmad al-Shuqayri and his organization until Shuqayri resigned after the defeat in the War of June 1967.

Aftermath of the Nakba: Attempts at Rehabilitating Self-Efficacy

The institutions of Palestinian society, only partially rehabilitated after World War II, were destroyed following the War of 1948. The political and social leadership scattered. Its remnants, headed by the mufti, engaged in unsuccessful attempts to contend with the inter-Arab patronage imposed upon the Palestinians.

The new postwar circumstances had the effect of almost completely blocking any process of rehabilitation. Palestinian society—until that time a single community, located in one place, with a common history—was divided into several communities distributed among numerous political entities. Each of these communities found itself in a different situation, and therefore each developed a unique history. For this reason, any discussion of attempts to recover from the Nakba (and of Palestinian history in general) requires a focus on two different dimensions—the local and the general. The first of these dimensions relates to each of the diasporas separately, and the second to the evolution of the general Palestinian issue and the place that it received within regional and global politics.

Discussion of the Palestinian diasporas requires a distinction between communities that remained in the territory of mandatory Palestine and refugee communities located in Arab countries. Those remaining in the country preserved organizational components from the British Mandate period, while Palestinian communities in other countries may be portrayed as islands in a foreign sea. As we have seen, they avoided assimilating among the local societies, which were reluctant to accept them. The identity of refugee communities in Arab countries depended on the existence of a comprehensive

Palestinian national organization, a unifying "national alignment of diasporas."

Political Organization and Activities in the West Bank

After the war, once the West Bank had been annexed to Jordan, its population consisted of two groups: (1) refugees from the coastal plain and (2) local residents. The two groups had always felt close to each other, and they both underwent the same political developments during the British Mandate period. These common experiences, which continued during Jordanian rule, created a measure of continuity, stemming among other things from the continuous activity of entities, movements, and political parties. The two large traditional camps that had controlled Palestinian political life during the mandate, the Husaynis and the Nashashibis, were now replaced by two ideological movements that occupied the center of the political map—the Communist Party and the Muslim Brotherhood. To these were added other ideological movements, such as the Islamic Liberation Party, and movements with an Arab-nationalist orientation, such as the Arab Ba'ath Movement and the al-Qawmiyyoun al-'Arab Movement.

The Communist Party and the National Liberation League. At the conclusion of the War of 1948, several Arab communist activists who were members of the National Liberation League ('Usbat al-Tahrrur al-Wattani) moved to Jordan. The most prominent of these were Fu'ad Nassar and former secretary-general of the Palestinian Communist Party Radwan al-Hiliw (Musa). Together with activists from among the refugees and from communist centers in the West Bank, they managed to revive the Communist Party, later known as the Jordanian Communist Party. Amnon Cohen writes about their activities:

> The upheavals that shook the Land of Israel during the years 1947–1948 served as a catalyst for activities of key figures in the communist movement, which had been active for several decades. Some of these activists moved to the territory occupied by Abdullah's army, where they could organize new or renewed activities, whether among the refugees, who were familiar with the party from their towns of origin, or among the population of the West Bank,

where communist activities had been taking place even prior to 1948, for example in Bethlehem. The communists believed that the new circumstances were conducive for amassing fans and members, both in light of the antagonism of at least part of the West Bank population toward Abdullah's regime, and in light of new problems created by the war: problems stemming from the strict occupation regimes of the Egyptian and Jordanian armies, and the problem of the multitudes of homeless refugees who sought a change and an answer to their economic as much as to their political situation. In the years 1949–1951 communist activities included the distribution of bulletins, organization of cells and chapters, and attempts to hold overt public activities in major cities.[74]

The first meaningful issue to occupy the National Liberation League was the annexation of the West Bank to Jordan. Members of the league announced their fundamental objection to the annexation and began distributing bulletins and demonstrating in both the West and East Bank against the elections. Their first show of force was a demonstration in Nablus attended by some fifty people, mostly senior activists. The Jordanian police arrested them all and led them, on foot and in handcuffs, to Amman. One of the detainees died on the way and the others remained in custody for about two months.[75] They then began focusing on attempts to infiltrate trade unions and the lower classes, but the Jordanian police again acted firmly to circumvent them. The league's activities had reached a crossroads. Some of the members, led by Radwan al-Hiliw, were convinced that activities must have a wide base among the workers and lower classes. Others, headed by Fu'ad Nassar, believed that the league should direct most of its efforts toward the intellectuals. This power struggle ended when Fu'ad Nassar gained the upper hand. In 1952, Radwan al-Hiliw was accused of undermining the authority of Fu'ad Nassar and his men, and his membership in the party was revoked.

In the first half of the 1950s, the party's activities expanded. It established new branches and cultural clubs in most West Bank towns and cities, and even began publishing a journal named *Al-Muqawama al-Sha'biyya* (Popular Resistance). The authorities responded with preventative arrests and by confiscating propaganda material. In late December 1951, Secretary-General Fu'ad Nassar was arrested and sentenced to ten years in prison, but the party was not silenced. In May 1954 it joined forces in a national front with other left-wing organizations, and in the October elections the front supported independent candidates and achieved a measure of success, for example, in the election of 'Abd al-Qader al-Salah in Nablus, despite the authorities' objections. Al-Salah was a property- and landowner, and his communist activity was more an expression of his opposition to the Jordanian regime than an attempt to represent workers' concerns. The party reached its zenith in the elections held on October 21, 1956, when three of its members were elected to parliament: Ya'qub Zayadin from the Jerusalem District, Fa'iq Warrad from the Ramallah District, and 'Abd al-Qader al-Salah from the Nablus District. In the new government headed by Sulayman al-Nabulsi, who had socialist left-wing leanings, 'Abd al-Qader al-Salah served as minister of agriculture.[76] The party began operating in the open and its imprisoned activists, particularly Secretary-General Fu'ad Nassar, were released. In January 1957 the party began publishing the journal *Al-Jamahir* (the Masses), edited by Rushdi Shahin, but it was not long-lived. Once it became a platform for attacks against the authorities, it lost its license and was closed. Prime Minister Nabulsi's flexible attitude toward the Communist Party (and the Soviet Union) was one of the reasons for his dismissal by King Husayn.[77] On April 25, 1957, the king dissolved all political parties, including the Communist Party, which was declared illegal. In a broadcast on Radio Jordan, the king attacked the party for its past and present contacts with Israel, for betraying the Arab cause by appealing for peace with Israel, and for endangering the unity of the Jordanian people, the integrity of the country, and religious principles.[78]

Government agencies castigated the party on religious grounds, claiming that it promoted "heretical elements."[79] Hundreds of the party's activists, including the two parliamentary representatives, were arrested and charged. Fa'iq Warrad was sentenced to sixteen years in prison and Ya'qub Zayadin to nineteen years. Some of the detainees escaped a severe sentence by publicly denouncing the party and swearing allegiance to the king.[80] In the late 1950s and early 1960s the Jordanian Communist Party disappeared and its activities remained negligible until Israel occupied the West Bank in June 1967.

The Islamic Liberation Party. The Islamic Liberation Party (Hizb al-Tahrir al-Islami) was established in Jerusalem in early 1952 by a group of clerics and former officials of the Muslim Higher Council during the British Mandate. Taqi al-Din al-Nabhani and Nimr al-

Masri led the initiative and began by founding a religious group objecting to the route taken by the Muslim Brotherhood.[81] The group expanded to include several remnants of the Husayni camp, and its significance rose when it was joined by senior clerics from the Hebron region, such as the As'ad brothers and Rajab Bayyud al-Tamimi, as well as 'Abd al-Qadim Zallum. In November 1952, members of the group submitted a formal request to the Jordanian minister of the interior to approve the establishment of a political party named the Islamic Liberation Party.

Two months later their request was rejected on the grounds that their platform contradicted Jordan's constitution, particularly the governing principle that the country shall forever be ruled by a king from the family of Hashem. The party founders tried to circumvent the prohibition by employing the Ottoman Law of Association and by reporting to the governor of Jerusalem that they had founded a society.[82] However the authorities were intent on putting an end to these activities from their onset: they arrested the leaders for two weeks and declared the movement itself illegal due to its subversive nature.[83] From then on, the founders "kept a low profile" and were not harassed by the regime. Amnon Cohen described their further activities:

> In their first year of activity they focused on the urban centers of Jerusalem and its environs, Hebron and Nablus, as well as the refugee camps near Jericho, 'Ayn al-Sultan and 'Aqbat Jabir. Propaganda was promoted in Hebron mostly after Friday prayers at the Cave of the Patriarchs, and organized in Jerusalem by teachers in the form of study groups, mainly in the evening. There were also attempts at clandestine activities aimed at circumventing government supervision. In Hebron, all propaganda material was distributed by foreigners rather than locals, who had been warned off by the authorities. Following instructions and generous funding from Lebanon, Taqiy al-Din tried to form disparate ten-member groups, but did not achieve much success, aside from a single group in Jerusalem.[84]

The regime eventually became aware of these activities and in 1955 published the "guidance and preaching" law limiting the freedom of imams to preach in the mosques and subjecting them to regulations. In 1959 party leaders once again tried to incite the public against King Husayn's support of US intervention in the Middle East and the authorities hastened to respond. Many activists were deported from Jordan and the party resumed its dormant status. At the same time, the party suffered from internecine conflicts, dismissals, and departures. By June 1967 it was no longer an influential political factor among Palestinians in the West Bank.

The Arab Nationalist Movement. The beginnings of the al-Qawmiyyoun al-'Arab Movement were described above. It probably resumed its activities in Jordan between the fall of 1952 and early 1953, led by George Habash (1926–2008) and Wadi' Haddad (1930–1978), who came to Amman from Beirut. Another version has West Bank activities resuming even before the arrival of Habash and Haddad and organized by two Palestinian physicians, Dr. Subhi Ghusha from Jerusalem and Dr. Salah 'Anabatawi from Nablus.[85] In any case, they achieved momentum only when Dr. Habash arrived in Amman in December 1952. He opened a private clinic in the Jordanian capital and treated Palestinian refugees, charging them very little. In time he was joined by Wadi' Haddad, and they both used the clinic as cover for their ideological activities among the refugees. They were not alone in revitalizing the movement's activities. 'Anabatawi and Ghusha's groups operated in the West Bank, and another group headed by Hamad al-Farhan operated in the East Bank.[86] In early 1953 the Habash-Haddad group united with the al-Farhan group, while the West Bank group continued to operate separately.

The East Bank al-Qawmiyyoun al-'Arab group was composed of two generations of the students of Qustantin Zurayq at the American University of Beirut: those born in the early 1920s, headed by Hamad al-Farhan and Wasfi al-Tal; and those born in the late 1920s, such as George Habash and Wadi' Haddad. First-generation members were Jordanians from wealthy families who attained influential positions within Jordanian government circles. Second-generation members were Palestinian refugees from the urban middle class who became influential among their peers. This group began their public activities in early 1955 by publishing the journal *Al-Ra'i* and distributing it for free in the West Bank. The journal attacked the Baghdad Alliance and Britain's influence in Jordan, leading the authorities to close it down eight months later. Three months after its closure, it renewed its appearance in Damascus, openly demanding termination of Jordan's "reactionary government."[87]

At this point, movement activists tried to conceal their intentions using two different approaches. On the one hand they operated through recognized legal associations, such as the Arab Club and the Institution for Objection to Reconciliation with Israel. The other tactic involved clandestine arrangements with the movement's branches in other Arab countries. These were the circumstances that led to the secret meeting organized by Habash in early 1954, later known as the "Amman meeting." Arab Nationalist activists from other countries, most prominent of whom was 'Ali Naser al-Din, one of the movement's spiritual leaders in Lebanon, were invited to this meeting, in addition to members of the founding group. They embraced a plan originally presented to the Arab League by Iraqi prime minister Muhammad Fadhel al-Jammali, proposing that Arab unity would take place by first uniting Syria, Iraq, and Jordan. Egypt and Saudi Arabia rejected this idea, claiming that it was designed to assert Britain's influence in the region, but *Al-Ra'i* gave its enthusiastic approval.[88]

Unsurprisingly, the Palestinian issue was of special significance to Jordan, which was also the hub of most of the movement's activities. A bulletin called *Al-Th'ar* (Revenge) was published in Jordan, and its slogan, "unity, liberation, revenge," indicated an actively militant approach to the Palestinian issue. The movement's theorists emphasized the principle of armed struggle as the solution to the Palestinian problem and the pursuit of unity on the pan-Arab level. Nonetheless, the leaders took care to avoid stressing a single local patriotic issue at the expense of pan-Arabism. Thus, they steered clear of the term "Palestinian people" (*sha'b Filastini*), preferring "Arab displaced" (*al-nazihun al-'Arab*) or "Arabs of Palestine" (*'Arab Filastin*).[89] This created a paradoxical concurrence between the Jordanian authorities, who wished to eliminate the Palestinian identity, and the Arab Nationalist Movement with its pan-Arab terms. Indeed, until the clash between Husayn and Gamal Abdel Nasser, the king strengthened his ties with former members of the movement, such as Wasfi al-Tal, and included in his governments figures with pan-Arab nationalist views, such as Akram Zu'aytir. Only when the movement began seeking to overthrow his regime and turn Jordan into a pan-Arab "forward operating base" for reviving Palestine was it declared illegal. At that point, its journal was closed and activists were arrested or went underground. After the political parties were dispersed in the spring of 1957, the movement collaborated with the communists and with Nabulsi's Socialist National Party in the national front. In 1959, however, when Iraqi ruler 'Abd al-Karim Qasem and Nasser split ways, and following the communists' support of Qasem, this collaboration ended as well.

The establishment of the PLO in 1964 and its conflict with King Husayn marked a new chapter in the deteriorating relationship between the authorities and the movement. Although al-Qawmiyyoun perceived the PLO as a reactionary organization, they took its side against the king. The conflict intensified as preparations for the third Palestinian National Council, planned for May 1966, proceeded. In late March and early April, Jordanian authorities began an extensive campaign, arresting members of the Arab Nationalists, the Communist Party, and other radical groups. Prime Minister Wasfi al-Tal explained that "these subversive and destructive groups have taken over leadership of the PLO and prevented it from reaching an agreement with Jordan regarding the definition of the Palestinian entity, its nature and authority."[90] Ghassan Kanafani, a member of the movement and among those responsible for publicity, responded: "The Jordanian battlefield is not only an important front, it is the Palestinians' only front. . . . Any Palestinian sacrificed in the struggle with Israel before resolving the conflict with Jordan will be sacrificed in vain. . . . The journey to Amman is equivalent to two-thirds of the journey to Tel Aviv."[91]

The movement longed to put an end to the Hashemite regime and to use Jordan as a guerrilla auxiliary base, similar to North Vietnam's war with South Vietnam. All these ideas were set aside after the War of 1967. Jordan did not collapse and al-Qawmiyyoun al-'Arab went through a major transformation, abandoning its pan-Arab theories in favor of Marxism.

The Muslim Brotherhood. The first Muslim group to emerge in mandatory Palestine was a branch of the Muslim Brotherhood (al-Ikhwan al-Muslimun). This movement was established in 1946 (see above for its history up to 1948). By 1948 it had twenty-five branches and somewhere between twelve thousand to twenty-thousand members. The branches were directly subordinate to the Brotherhood's center in Cairo, which declared Mufti Haj Amin al-Husayni to be in charge of the Palestinian chapters, despite his absence from the country.[92]

The involvement of volunteer fighters from the Muslim Brotherhood of Egypt and Syria in the War of 1948 was a major factor that helped encourage Palestinians, mainly from the area of Bethlehem and Hebron, to join the movement. During the first years of Jordanian rule, branches appeared in almost all cities, towns, and large villages in the West Bank. The appointment, in 1953, of 'Abd al-Rahman Khalifa as general supervisor (*muraqib 'aam*) in place of 'Abd al-Latif Abu Qawwara led to better coordination between the West and East Bank chapters.[93] Khalifa operated from Amman, arousing less suspicion than his predecessor, and held the position until 1965.[94]

Unlike most of the ideological political movements in Jordan, the Muslim Brotherhood operated legally and maintained a proper relationship with the regime. Its gatherings were public and convened with government permission. Sports events and Scouts activities were sanctioned by the authorities. Senior government officials and representatives of military leadership and security forces often took part in the movement's events.[95] The movement did not hasten to become involved in Jordan's parliamentary process, but it took part in the 1956 elections, and its representative, Dr. Hafiz 'Abd al-Nabi al-Natsha, was elected to parliament as one of the Hebron delegates. In the 1961 elections the movement supported the regime, and in doing so, enhanced the legitimacy of the elections, which were boycotted by the left wing under orders from Egypt. By supporting the king, the Muslim Brotherhood was doing itself no favor, as its delegates were perceived as collaborators with the regime and therefore lost votes. This fluctuating relationship was described by Amnon Cohen:

> The Brothers' attitude toward the regime fluctuated according to a combination of both intrinsic and foreign-policy considerations, causing them to seem inconsistent: In late 1956, after Glubb Pasha was suspended as commander of the Legion, the Brotherhood praised the king for his action that "unites Muslims, realizes Arab unity, and releases the Arab world from the burden of imperialism." Their support intensified after the Suez War, in which Jordan at least professed to stand by Egypt. In early 1957, when the Eisenhower Doctrine was publicized, it was strongly attacked by the Brotherhood, undoubtedly causing the king much discomfort. When the conflict between the king and his opponents, headed by Prime Minister–elect Sulayman al-Nabulsi, broke out in 1957, the Brothers were open and adamant in their support of the king. They held support rallies and spoke in praise of the king's proper Islamic course of action, attacking the mistakes and deceptions of the Nabulsi government. Although it was clear to all that the Jordanian

government was headed back toward its former Western orientation, this was not mentioned at all at this time, and the highest order of preference was to help destroy the Qawmiyyoun and the communists, the Brotherhood's dangerous rivals in the West Bank, and to support the king's anti-Nasser orientation.[96]

Yusuf al-'Azm, a senior leader in the movement, explained:

The king demonstrated tolerance toward our activities, in contrast to the brutality employed by Nasser's government in Egypt. Thus, the Brotherhood refrained from turning against the king and compromised with him, as they could not fight on all fronts simultaneously. . . . We stood by the king, since Nasser's attacks against us were irrational. . . . We stood by the king in order to defend ourselves. If Nasser had entered Jordan or established a local government loyal to him, he would have wiped out the Brotherhood as he had in Egypt."[97]

This ideal state of affairs did not last long. The ideological foundations of the Muslim Brotherhood have always been a threat to any government that does not fully implement Islamic law as they perceive it and that has a relationship with the West. At the conclusion of the 1957–1958 crisis, and once the government made a sharp turn toward the West, particularly the United States, the Brotherhood's publicity organs promptly embarked on a condemnation and protest campaign, and the government responded with harsh steps, arresting the general supervisor. From this point on, the Brotherhood reduced their scope of operations and focused on social and cultural activities and moral preaching. In 1965 their relationship with the authorities reached a temporary crisis, following attempts by several Brotherhood supporters to attack cinemas and places of entertainment. Generally speaking, however, the peace was kept until June 1967.

The Gaza Strip Under Egyptian Control

Politically, developments in the Gaza Strip resembled those in the West Bank. Here, too, refugees encountered a population consisting of their own people, under the auspices of an Arab government that had taken control of the area in the War of 1948, with one conspicuous difference: refugees in the Gaza Strip were much more numerous than the local population, and this had political, social, and economic implications. Moreover, the many refugees inflating the local population created crowding that did not exist in other areas. The overcrowding and the hardships thus created formed unique conditions that set it apart from other Palestinian communities. This was compounded by the obvious differences between the attitudes of the Jordanian and Egyptian governments to the Palestinian issue and their handling of the problem: the Egyptians saw themselves as guardians of the Palestinians but did not object to the development of a Palestinian identity, while King Abdullah, whose country had absorbed a large number of refugees compared to its original population, saw the forging of a distinct identity as an existential threat to his kingdom.

The Palestinian Communist Party in the Gaza Strip. One of the first actions of the Egyptian governor of Gaza following his appointment was to declare the dissolution of the National Liberation League and the Palestinian Communist Party in the Gaza Strip and the arrest of its members there, including Fakhri Makki, 'Ali 'Ashour, Muhammad Khas, Fayiz al-Wahidi, Mansour al-Haddad, and Hamed al-Husri. However, when Abu 'Agila, the jail in which they were held, was captured by Israeli forces in early 1949, some of the detainees chose to remain in Israel, particularly after being accused by Egyptian authorities of "disloyalty to the national cause," collaboration with Israel and the Soviet Union, and consent to the partition plan.[98] These accusations had a grave effect on the image of communists in the Gaza Strip, enabling the authorities to restrict their activities more than any other political movement. Only a small group continued operating there, focused on infiltrating teenage cadres and on writing propaganda. This group was led by Fakhri Makki, formerly the secretary of the National Liberation League's branch in Gaza during the British Mandate. Makki succeeded in recruiting dozens of students and publishing a newspaper, *Al-Muqawama* (the Resistance), for four years, until it was closed in 1953 by the Egyptian authorities. Bulletins such as *Kifah al-'Ummal* (Struggle of the Workers), *Rayat al-Shabab* (Flag of the Youth), and *Tali'at al-Talba* (Pioneers of the Students) were published as well. In August 1952, once the party had managed to recover, the authorities arrested Makki and nearly four hundred members and supporters. Mu'in Basisu, the famed Palestinian poet who had fled Iraq, subsequently assumed responsibility for its preservation. A skilled orator, Basisu succeeded in forming a group of young people and rejuvenating the party. He imbued them with a communist consciousness and introduced them to global left-wing literature. As secretary-general of the party during 1953–1964, Basisu organized demonstrations against the plan to settle refugees in their current countries of residence. After the Israel Defense Forces (IDF) attack on Gaza, on February 28, 1955, the party organized demonstrations against Israel and succeeded in rehabilitating its former image from the days of the partition plan. Its success led the authorities to arrest its leaders once again.

After Israel occupied the Gaza Strip in October 1956, the Communist Party established a Palestinian National Front, consisting of prominent national figures such as Hamdi al-Husayni, Hayder 'Abd al-Shafi, and Farid Abu Warda. Throughout Israel's short rule, however, the front did not achieve any successes. After Israel retreated on March 7, 1957, the communists, together with other opposition parties, initiated demonstrations against internationalization of the Gaza Strip and in favor of reinstating Egyptian rule. Any beneficial effect this may have had on their relationship with the Egyptians, who returned to rule the Gaza Strip, was reversed, however, when two years later Palestinian communists sided with Qasem's Iraq in its conflict with Nasser. This time the communists' allies in the national front, as well as the Muslim Brotherhood, backed the Egyptian government. Both groups demonstrated against the communists and their support of the Iraqi president.[99]

The communists in the Gaza Strip focused on national causes, rather than social causes that could have facilitated their development. The class struggle, the main issue occupying communist parties all over the world, remained second to the struggle for national liberation. Ziyad Abu 'Amru summarized communist activity during the period of Egyptian rule:

> Despite their relatively low numbers, and despite their persecution, arrest, and torture, the communists had a significant role in defending the Palestinian cause against attempts to silence and erase the national [Palestinian] identity of the Gaza Strip. They were effective in helping foil the Sinai Plan for settling refugees in the desert, in resisting the Israeli occupation in 1956, and in thwarting the "internationalization plan" [calling for international control of the Gaza Strip] in 1957.[100]

The Muslim Brotherhood in the Gaza Strip. During the first years of Egyptian rule of the Gaza Strip, which were also the last years of Egypt's monarchy, the authorities did not give the Muslim Brotherhood permission to operate in any way. As mentioned, members of the Brotherhood in Cairo murdered Prime Minister al-Naqrashi, and the authorities countered with the murder of Hasan al-Banna. The impact of this conflict remained in effect until the revolution of July 1952. The revolution of the Free Officers was a changing point. During the first two years of the Free Officers' rule, their relationship with the Muslim Brotherhood was fairly satisfactory. The movement's headquarters in Cairo sent an official delegation to the Gaza Strip, called the "Delegation for Exhortation and Direction." It was led by several Egyptian Brotherhood leaders, among them Shaikh Muhammad al-Ghazali and Shaikh Muhammad al-Abasiri, who served as links to the movement's leaders in Gaza. The Muslim Brotherhood in Egypt became responsible for running a government project named Train of Mercy, intended to provide refugees in Gaza with basic commodities. The situation worsened in October 1954 when the movement's activists in Egypt attempted to assassinate President Gamal Abdel Nasser. The authorities banned the movement and began a campaign of mass arrests among the Gaza branch as well.

Prior to the assassination, the Brotherhood had been the largest movement in Gaza, with one thousand registered members organized in eleven cells.[101] Most of the members came from UN Relief and Works Agency schools; some had studied at Egyptian universities and were members of the Palestinian Student Association in Cairo—among them future leaders of Fatah and the PLO, including Yasir Arafat, Salah Khalaf, and Salim al-Za'nun.[102] Most of the movement's leaders in the Gaza Strip were from the middle class: teachers, clerks, and merchants. The General Management Center was headed by Shaikh 'Umar Suwwan, a senior official at the Gaza Municipality and a sharia judge.[103]

After the clash with the authorities, most of the leaders and many activists fled to the Gulf and all subsequent activities became clandestine. When the Egyptian authorities forbade all political activity, most movements began searching for legal routes, mainly by operating through various societies and associations. The most active was the association of teachers employed by the UN aid agency. Of its nine board members, six were actually from the Muslim Brotherhood, including Secretary-General Fathi Bal'awi. This was the tactic that enabled the Brotherhood (together with the communists, who had two representatives on the association's board) to hold demonstrations in March 1955, in protest of Israel's operations in late February.

Israel's occupation of the Gaza Strip in late October 1956 marked the end of collaboration between the Muslim Brotherhood and the communists. The Brotherhood stressed the concept of armed struggle, while the communists preferred passive resistance. After Israel's retreat and the resumption of Egyptian rule, the Brotherhood's activities were halted once more by the Egyptian government and they were subjected to government persecution, as were their associates in the parent organization. The authorities were particularly strict during 1964–1966.

The Ba'ath Party. Following establishment of the Free Officers' regime in Egypt in July 1952, with its positive attitude toward the Ba'ath Party in Syria, a branch of the party was also set up in the Gaza Strip between 1953 and 1955.[104] The founders were two refugees, Shafiq al-'Ifranji and Sa'id al-Dajani, who arrived in Gaza after 1948 and were active in the refugee camps. They had both studied at Cairo University, where they were introduced to the ideology of the Ba'ath movement. They returned to the Gaza Strip as teachers and disseminated the party's philosophy among their colleagues and students. The founding group expanded to include eight members, of whom five were refugees and the remainder locals. They initiated a Palestinian Student Association in Egypt, as well as a women's organization headed by May Sayigh, who would later become president of the Union of Palestinian Women.

During the conflict between the Free Officers regime and the Muslim Brotherhood, Ba'ath members strengthened their alignment with the government, but they were consequently branded as collaborators with Cairo, thereby reducing their status among the refugees. Their influence was at its height during the unification of Egypt and Syria, and party members enjoyed benefits, positions, and scholarships in both Egypt and Syria. Once the union was dissolved, however, Ba'ath members in Gaza were no longer favored by the Cairo-centered regime.

Palestinian Arabs in Israel: The Political Dimension

Following establishment of the State of Israel, the country remained home to a frightened and divided Arab public, now a minority, whose social and political institutions had been shattered. The new state of affairs was described by Sabri Jiryis:

> The establishment of the State of Israel and of the Jewish regime led to severe upheavals within Arab society. Most of the traditional and social leadership, as well as most of the wealthy people, professionals, and intellectuals, had fled the country. Those remaining were transformed overnight from a majority to a minority ruled by others. They suddenly found themselves with no leadership, experience, or guidance.[105]

Two forces remained influential among this public: (1) the traditional leadership, composed of remnants of urban families and leaders of rural families and clans; and (2) the Communist Party, since most of its leaders had remained in the country. In this state of general disarray, and in the absence of most of the other leaders, the communists, who during the British Mandate period had lingered on the margins of Arab-Palestinian society, now occupied a central place.

Traditional leadership and Zionist parties. The traditional leadership, some of whom had sustained a lengthy interest-based relationship with Jewish institutions and with the British Mandate authorities, maintained this relationship with the new state. They helped the authorities establish control of the population in return for benefits and made an effort to assist the Zionist parties before elections, particularly by founding "satellite parties" that operated alongside the Jewish parties. Most Zionist parties were unwilling to include Arabs on their lists, and by using satellite parties they could receive Arab votes without asking the voters to commit to their ideology.[106] These satellite lists, particularly those affiliated with the current ruling party, Mapai (Party of Workers of the Land of Israel), gained parliamentary representation beginning with the first Knesset and continued until the political transfer of power in 1977.[107] Jiryis described the secret of the ruling party's success:

> Many Arabs supported these lists, which enjoyed the backing of Mapai's entire system, and particularly of the military government. Their supporters received many benefits from government ministries. They had no ideological basis and they operated in collaboration with the government, any government. They had previously supported British Mandate authorities, then the Arab League's

Liberation Army, and when the State of Israel was established they sided with the Israeli government.[108]

Mapam (United Workers' Party) tried to establish "auxiliary lists" as well, but did not succeed. On the eve of elections to the second Knesset, the party decided to award Arabs member status and to reserve a space for an Arab on its list for the Knesset (occupied initially by Rustom Bastuni, and later by Yusuf Khamis and 'Abd al-'Aziz Zu'abi). The remaining Zionist parties did not have Arabs run for the Knesset on their ticket. In this respect, Mapam preceded all other Zionist parties, even letting Arab members express their identity and culture in the literary journal *Al-Fajr*, where some of the greatest Arab poets and creators destined to emerge on the local scene took their first steps.[109]

The Communist Party. Once the State of Israel was established and the National Liberation League dissolved, most of the Arab communists united once again with their Jewish peers in the Israeli Communist Party (Maki). Some Arab members who objected to the partition, such as Boulos Farah, did not return to the party's ranks, while others, such as Emil Toma, returned but were not appointed to senior political positions. Maki defined itself as an anti-Zionist party, but accepted the principle of "two states for two nations." Nonetheless, Jewish and Arab members were conflicted on the issue of the border: the Arabs called upon the party to recognize the partition borders, while the Jews sought long-lasting recognition of the armistice lines.

During the years of military rule, 1948–1966, the party exhibited systematic resistance, objecting to the policy of discrimination against Arabs and expropriation of their lands. This led to the popular perception that the Communist Party was the only protest venue available to the Arab population. Local support of the party stemmed from its status as a mechanism of Arab national protest and not from its social communist platform.

Jewish-Arab discord within the party continued to fester and emerged in times of crisis. Similar to the state of affairs during the British Mandate, the party once again experienced a process of "Arabization," wherein the large Jewish majority gradually became a minority, although the leadership remained mostly Jewish. This was the result of a rise in the number of Arab members, following the growth of Nasserism and Arab national pride in the entire region, as well as the deteriorating relationship between the Soviet Union and Israel. These circumstances led to a split in the party in 1965. Most of Maki's Arab members, and some of its Jewish members, left and founded the New Communist List (Rakah). The circumstances leading to the split are described by Nessia Shafran:

> Once the party became a large popular force within the Arab population it was impossible to maintain the ideological uniformity characteristic of the party's Jewish branches. . . . An Arab communist could be an ardent Muslim . . . but such luxuries were not a prerogative of Jewish party members, of whom total ideological intractability was demanded. . . . Officially, Jews and Arabs had an equal standing in the party and movement, but morally Arabs were considered more virtuous. The Arabs in the party were at an advantage, as even Jewish party members perceived Arab justice as absolute, natural, and obvious, with no apologies or guilt feelings necessary. . . . At a certain stage the burden of loving the Arabs became overbearing. There was an uneasy sense that something had gone wrong. The craved brotherhood between Jews and Arabs gradually diminished, until not much was left. . . . None of us had imagined that our communism and that of our Arab peers were two parallel courses never to converge.[110]

Moshe Sneh voiced an opinion similar to Shafran's: "No thinking person would agree with the rationale whereby the Arab population holds significantly greater socialist beliefs and their Marxist outlook is a hundred times more prevalent than among the Jews. In other words, Rakah seems to attract Arabs and reject Jews. It is a known fact that Rakah is the party of Arab chauvinist nationalism."[111]

From the Arab side Nimr Murqus alleged that a Zionist faction was responsible for the split:

> In late 1964 signs of crisis began emerging in our party . . . someone fed the Zionist newspapers information that allowed them to incite against the universal views of the party. . . . The attacks and provocations focused particularly on the party's support of the Arab National Liberation movement and the role of its leader, Gamal Abdel Nasser, and the party's views on the endeavors of Arab citizens to resist the policy of tyranny and discrimination directed at them. This revealed a Zionist-national chauvinist opportunist faction within the party's leadership. . . . The facts revealed were [that the most prominent Jewish party leaders] were the leaders of that destructive opportunist faction.[112]

Several years later, Maqi disappeared and Rakah was officially designated the Israeli Communist Party. The party reached the height of its power during this era in the elections of 1955, when it received six mandates (occupied by four Jews and two Arabs). In all other election campaigns the party received between three and five mandates.[113]

The Popular Arab Front. While the Zionist parties, particularly Mapai, and the Communist Party, were busy contending for primacy among the Arab Israeli public, several movements with a pan-Arab and Palestinian nationalist orientation emerged as well, despite the heavy restrictions imposed by the military government on nationalist political organizations. The first was the Popular Arab Front (al-Jabha al-'Arabiyya al-Sha'biyya) founded in June 1958 by communists and nationalist activists from the British Mandatory period.[114] Its platform centered on the call to cancel the military regime and to cease the expropriation of lands and other acts of discrimination. The front also demanded the return of Palestinian refugees to their villages.[115]

Attempts at collaboration between the communists and the nationalists were not long-lived. The conflict between Gamal Abdel Nasser, supported by the nationalists, and President 'Abd al-Karim Qasem of Iraq, supported by the communists (as dictated by the Soviet Union), led to dissolution of the partnership. Disparate views on integration of the Arab minority in the country also caused a rift. While the communists emphasized Arab-Jewish cooperation and called for equality and integration, the nationalists were opposed to integration and in favor of Palestinian association with the entire Arab world.

The al-Ard Group. Upon dissolution of the Popular Arab Front, the seceding nationalists founded a new movement, which they initially called Family of the Earth ('Usrat al-Ard) and then Movement of the Earth (Harakat al-Ard). The circumstances of the movement's emergence are described by Jiryis:

> Cooperation with Maki lasted until 1958, when the Arab Nationalist Movement visibly dissociated itself from all Arab communist parties. . . . No more than five or six months later the Popular Front split in two. One section—which consisted of three or four people—continued the front's collaboration with Maki. The second section, which supported the Arab Nationalist Movement, left the front and continued operating independently. It established an

organization known as the al-Ard Group, and published its own political platform and newspaper.[116]

Israel's official in charge of the northern district rejected the movement's request to publish a newspaper, while its request for recognition as a limited cultural company, designed to preserve and spread Arab culture, was only approved following intervention of the Supreme Court.[117] The state banned the movement from participating in the Knesset elections of 1965, stating that it "was founded with the purpose of undermining the existence and integrity of the State of Israel."[118] The Supreme Court rejected the group's appeal in a decision with constitutional implications. For the first time since the establishment of the state, the Supreme Court disqualified a list of candidates from running for the Knesset based on the claim that it posed a risk to the state and its democratic system.[119] The movement never recovered from this ruling. Some of its senior members, Salih Baransi and Mansour Kardush, were arrested, charged with incitement and acting against state security, and convicted. Others, including Sabri Jiryis and Habib Qahwaji, left the country and joined the PLO.

Revival of Armed Conflict: Circumventing an Independent Palestinian Struggle

In the early 1950s, small clandestine groups of young Palestinians, including remnants of the forces that had fought in the Palestinian Revolt of 1936–1939 and in the War of 1948, began attacking Israeli civilians along the armistice line. They sought revenge for the humiliation and disaster inflicted on them by the Jews and felt frustrated by the restraint forced upon them by Arab states, Jordan in particular, as early as 1948.

The Jordanian government acted according to the express instructions of King Abdullah, who ordered that any independent Palestinian military force in the West Bank be disarmed. This was amplified when the All-Palestine Government announced in early October 1948 that it intended to reorganize the Holy Jihad Army units, which had been in a process of disintegration since the death of 'Abd al-Qadir al-Husayni. On December 18, 1948, Jordanian military authorities declared the Jihad Army illegal and initiated steps to disarm it. Some Jihad Army fighters, who numbered about 2,500 troops, joined the regular Arab forces, while others laid down their arms. The Egyptian authorities acted similarly in the Gaza Strip. They disarmed irregular Palestinian fighters and closed an improvised Palestinian radio station attempting to recruit fighters. Egyptian authorities also dismantled a volunteer company operating under the auspices of the Muslim Brotherhood and returned its recruits to Egypt. Egyptian and Jordanian authorities acted to neutralize efforts by the Arab Higher Institution and the All-Palestine Government to achieve dominance in areas under Arab control, seeking to prevent a renewed conflagration on the armistice line with Israel and to block the revival of an independent Palestinian enterprise and the emergence of a leadership that could also incite local public opinion against the current regimes.

In the first half of the 1950s most Palestinian operations against Israel consisted of individual infiltrations. Palestinian refugees or other Arabs crossed the armistice lines and entered Israel for several reasons. In addition to seeking revenge, some wished to return to their original villages in order to gather crops, belongings, and valuables hidden before they fled. A "smuggling industry" developed on both sides of the border, and according to Palestinian historian Yazid Sayigh, "The truth of the matter is that only a tenth of the incidents were nationally motivated. Nonetheless, they created dangerous circumstances. In 1952 there were 16,000 cases of infiltration, in 1953 the number dropped to about 7,000, and in 1955 to 4,351."[120] The decline may be attributed to three factors: Israel's strong response, prevention by Arab countries, and reduced motivation (for example, after the first year no crops remained to be gathered).

The Gaza Strip and the Fida'iyyun

On February 28, 1955, a week after the president of Egypt visited the Gaza Strip and promised to protect the population, Israel staged an extensive retaliation raid in response to the infiltrators' operations. Local residents responded with a series of demonstrations and riots against the government, demanding a fitting Egyptian response. These riots, known as the Intifada of March 1955, came at a difficult time for the Egyptian regime, which was engaged in an internal war against the Muslim Brotherhood.[121] From the government's perspective, instigators of the Gaza riots were operating on behalf of the

Brotherhood, and they were consequently forcefully suppressed. Nevertheless, the Egyptians were also aware of the spontaneous nature of the demonstrations and of the need to respond to Israel's operation.

Government circles were now intent on reconstructing the Palestinian border police. The new force was named Regiment 11. It consisted of about seven hundred soldiers under Egyptian command and was employed mainly to prevent infiltration of Israel's borders to avoid a conflagration for which it was not yet ready. Regretfully, the regiment did not fulfill its mission. It proved unable to prevent infiltration and Israel was not intimidated. Some of its officers were accused of contact with the Muslim Brotherhood and with actually encouraging infiltration. In October 1955, about six months after its establishment, Regiment 11 was dismantled, and its commander, 'Abd al-Mun'im 'Abd al-Ra'ouf, and other senior officers were accused of belonging to the Muslim Brotherhood.[122] 'Abd al-Mun'im was sentenced to death, but he succeeded in escaping to the West Bank, where he became involved in the reorganization of the Muslim Brotherhood.[123]

Egypt now entered a new stage in its approach to infiltrations. The Egyptian government embraced the infiltrators, calling them Fida'iyyun, and recognizing their acts as operations on behalf of the Arab national cause. Husayn Abu al-Nmil relates, "When the Egyptians officially recognized the activities of the Fida'iyyun, they were already a well-established fact. The infiltrators were well-trained and brave, familiar with the occupied territories and their transformation following the occupation, as well as with Jewish towns and guard posts. Their utilization facilitated relatively rapid operations with extensive and immediate results."[124] Mustafa Hafiz, an Egyptian officer who had taken part in the War of 1948 and was a former head of intelligence in the Gaza Strip, was charged with establishing these units. He promptly completed their organization, releasing from prison infiltrators familiar with Israeli territory. Special preference was given to Hebrew speakers. The guerrillas were trained at first in Gaza and then at national guard bases in Egypt. Egyptian authorities did not recognize them as regular soldiers and their salary was paid by the civil administration of the Gaza Strip, although they were directly subordinate to Egyptian military intelligence.[125] Fida'iyyun operations in the second half of 1955 resulted in severe retaliation by the Israeli army and extensive damage to the population of the Gaza Strip.

In December 15, 1955, 'Abd al-Hakim 'Amer, supreme commander of the Egyptian Army, announced that Fida'iyyun forces would become a military regiment. The unit, named Regiment 141, would later constitute the beginning of the Palestine Liberation Army.[126] Establishment of Regiment 141 increased infiltrations into Israel and attacks against Israeli targets. From December 1955 to March 1956, the United Nations listed some 180 Fida'iyyun operations, including shootings, placing mines, and arranging ambushes. On April 5, 1956, Israel entered Gaza, responding forcefully. The operation left fifty-nine dead and ninety-three wounded.[127] The severe response convinced Egyptian authorities to impose restrictions on Hafiz and his men, who subsequently limited their infiltrations through the Egypt-Israel border and began sending infiltrators through the Jordanian border in the West Bank. Infiltration operations in the West Bank were headed by Subhi Yasin, and Egypt's military attaché in Jordan, Salah Mustafa, was in charge of coordination with Egyptian authorities.[128] From the beginning of April until the end of October 1956, about ninety-five operations were executed through the Jordanian border. Israel responded by eliminating those responsible: On July 11, 1956, Hafiz was assassinated by a booby-trapped mail package, the blast killing him and one of his aides.[129] Salah Mustafa was similarly eliminated on October 14, 1956.[130] In addition, Israeli forces raided Gaza four times during the months of September–October 1956, leaving many wounded.[131] These raids served as a prelude to the Israeli attack on Egypt on October 29, 1956, in cooperation with Britain and France (Operation Sinai).

Before Israel began its attack, in which it was to occupy the Gaza Strip and the Sinai Peninsula, Israeli radio announced in Arabic that the Fida'iyyun had been identified and would be severely judged. Nearly 1,500 Fida'iyyun and a similar number of family members left the Gaza Strip following the announcement, passing through Israel and seeking refuge in the West Bank. Jordanian army forces arrested most of them for five months and then handed them over to Egypt's military attaché in Amman, who transported them to Egypt. In the Gaza Strip itself the Israeli invaders met with no serious Palestinian resistance. During the short period of Israeli occupation (October 29, 1956, to March 7, 1957), Israeli forces arrested nearly four thousand Fida'iyyun and members of the Palestinian National Guard. According to Palestinian sources, a few dozen were executed during the occupation.[132]

Egypt's attempt to establish Palestinian Fida'iyyun units as a means of quelling the population's rage and frustration toward Egypt and as a way of redirecting these feelings of rage toward Israel may be said to have boomeranged. As a result of this policy, Egypt became embroiled in a painful confrontation with Israel, exposing the impotence of its army and government. Nor did the Palestinians benefit from this course of action: the violence did nothing to promote their aspirations and instead further aggravated their hardships in the Gaza Strip and West Bank. The attempt to establish a militant Palestinian force under Egyptian auspices proved unsuccessful. The Egyptian authorities dismantled the Palestinian National Guard and replaced it with a Palestinian regiment (Regiment 107), which they stationed in the vicinity of the Suez Canal. Remnants of the national guard and the remaining Fida'iyyun in Gaza were forbidden from harassing Israel and charged with intelligence tasks or internal security missions.[133]

The Situation in the West Bank

After the Israel-Egypt armistice agreement was signed in Rhodes on February 24, 1949, and once the "Little Triangle" (from Kafr Salem in the north to Kafr Qasem in the south) had been annexed to Israel, the border between Israel and the West Bank remained unprotected. The villages appended to Israel were close to the border, and in three cases (Bart'ah and Baqa in the Little Triangle and Bayt Safafa in the Jerusalem area) the border cut through villages, leaving them divided.[134] Infiltrators crossed the border to visit relatives, smuggle goods, and sometimes also as envoys of the Fida'iyyun commander in the Gaza Strip. Lines were crossed in the West Bank in both directions. Young Arabs with Israeli citizenship left Israel for nationalist reasons, influenced by pan-Arab ideology and attracted to Gamal Abdel Nasser's leadership. Some became involved in Arab propaganda aimed at target populations in Israel, and their knowledge of Hebrew created a demand for their opinions as "experts" on Israel and the Jews.

In the West Bank, as in the Gaza Strip, Israel responded to infiltrator activities with 117 military operations from 1949 to 1951.[135] Following Israel's response, Jordan established a national guard, aimed at blocking infiltrations from its territory. This force encountered organizational problems and logistical deficiencies and employed citizens in return for a low salary. The national guard fought aggressively against individual infiltrators, but could not prevent organized acts of infiltration based on nationalist motives and directed by external elements, such as Egyptian Intelligence. The Jordanian army as well, was unable to prevent organized infiltration, and its commander at the time, General John Glubb, wrote, "Acts of infiltration are performed by a group of refugees residing in Damascus, all former terrorists acting by order of the mufti in Palestine. The government of Saudi Arabia funded the activities of anyone crossing the border from Jordan to Israel to kill Jews.[136]

Throughout 1951–1954, infiltrations resulted in 463 Israeli casualties.[137] During the first half of 1953, Israel carried out 200 retaliation raids, resulting in 295 Jordanian casualties, including an attack on the village of Qibya in October 1953, which has become particularly well known, in which dozens of homes were destroyed, 66 villagers killed, and 75 wounded.[138] Israel tried to apply pressure on Jordan, and its actions achieved their goal: During the first half of 1954 the Jordanian army reinforced its patrols along the border and arrested hundreds of Palestinians heading for Israel. During 1954–1955 the Jordanians arrested 997 Palestinians who were planning to infiltrate Israel.[139] But the consequent calm along the border did nothing to appease Israel and at the height of the lull, during the months of March through September of 1954, its army conducted four large operations: at Nahhalin, al-Rahwa, Husan, and Qalqilya. The rapid pace of events was not necessarily determined only by the Jordanian and Israeli armies. Syria and Egypt were involved in incidents in the West Bank as well. For example, in 1955, during the Baghdad Alliance crisis, Egyptian and Syrian authorities instructed their forces to increase the rate of entries into Israel and to stir up the border sector.

Infiltration Through the Syrian Border

In the early half of the 1950s the Israeli-Syrian border was relatively quiet, and only a few infiltration incidents were noted. The infiltrators were usually small Palestinian groups organized and armed by the Arab Higher Institution. Shaikh Tawfiq al-Ibrahim was in charge of these operations and commanded infiltration through the Syrian, Lebanese, and Jordanian borders.

Beginning in 1953, Syrian authorities used Palestinian infiltrators to gather information from the Israeli side of the border. In late

1955, when Israel attacked Syrian military posts overlooking the Sea of Galilee in response to forays by Palestinian fighters into its territory, the Syrians founded a Palestinian commando unit called Unit 68. Refugees were recruited, particularly those who had experience working with Syrian intelligence services. The unit's commander, Akram Safdi, was Syrian, as were its senior officers.[140] As in Gaza and the West Bank, this unit was not recognized as part of the regular army, and the salaries and rights of its members, which numbered about six hundred at its height, did not equal those of regular soldiers. The unit's operations mainly followed Syria's vested interests in the inter-Arab scene. In 1957, during the al-Nabulsi government crisis, the unit operated against Jordanian targets. It executed similar actions in Lebanon as well, against President Kamil Sham'un's government, which supported US policy in the region. The unit was also utilized for its impact on Syria's internal affairs, for example as part of the failed attempt to reinstate a regime supporting unity with Egypt, after dissolution of the United Arab Republic in September 1961. After this debacle, eighteen of the unit's fighters were accused of treason and executed.[141] Once the Ba'ath Party took control of Syria in 1963, Unit 68 was dismantled. New units were established in its stead to follow and supervise political activities among Palestinian refugees in Syria. These units were manned by members of Unit 68 who had proven their loyalty to the party.[142]

Independent Palestinian Activity

Side by side with activities backed by Arab states, small Palestinian military groups assembled in the field, operating secretly and independently. Most of their activities remained hidden, while some were attributed to the Fida'iyyun or to Unit 68. These activities were disregarded, among other things, due to Fatah's policy, after it was established in 1964, to take credit for all initial Palestinian ventures.

Battalions of Arab Sacrifice. Kata'ib al-Fida' (Battalions of Arab Sacrifice) was founded by elements from the Arab Nationalist Movement, headed by Palestinian George Habash and Syrian Amin al-Hindi. Both were recruited to the Liberation Army and witnessed its failure, as well as inter-Arab dissension and disputes. They concluded that Arab states had collaborated with Britain and with the Zionist movement to prevent establishment of a Palestinian state.[143]

Therefore, they decided to strike at Western and Zionist concerns and to punish any Arab leader striving for peace with Israel. The Battalions of Arab Sacrifice was instigated by a handful of Syrian and Egyptian activists affiliated with the Green Shirt Organization of Young Egypt who fled to Syria upon being indicted for attempting to assassinate an Egyptian minister. The military arm they established was headed by Egyptian Husayn Tawfiq.[144] Habash and al-Hindi sought to expand their circle of recruits, appealing largely to students from all over the Arab world. Their main goal was to "liberate Palestine," but they maintained that the first step in that direction was to change current Arab regimes. The third leader, Wadi' Haddad, even stated that "the road to Tel Aviv passes through Damascus, Baghdad, Amman, and Cairo."[145]

The organization began its activities in full force in August 1949, with approximately twelve operations against Western and Jewish targets in Beirut and Damascus. The first attack was planned for the opening day of the Lausanne Conference for conciliation between the Arab states and Israel. In an attack on a Damascus synagogue, twelve people were killed and twenty-seven were injured.[146] Other targets were the British and US consulates in Cairo and offices of the UN aid agency.

During the first half of the 1950s, the movement was paralyzed by internal divisions, but it managed to recover in the latter half, as Gamal Abdel Nasser enjoyed a rise in status throughout the region. His successful endeavors against the Baghdad Alliance, nationalization of the Suez Canal, and unification of Egypt and Syria (1958–1961) motivated movement leaders to join him. At the same time, they formed strong ties with Egyptian and Syrian intelligence services and subsequently found themselves used as tools in operations against Arab regimes. This state of affairs created animosity between the movement and other Arab regimes, diverting their attention from the Palestinian cause. Inspired by the Syrian commander of military intelligence, 'Abd al-Hamid al-Sarraj, and under his authority, the group initiated a series of bombings in Jordan at sites belonging to the government and to Western states once Sulayman al-Nabulsi's government had fallen. Jordanian authorities responded with an extensive wave of arrests, which included Wadi' Haddad and his cronies. George Habash, who had been planning to run for Jordan's parliament in the elections slated for fall 1957, succeeded in escaping at the last moment.[147] The group assisted Egypt's intelligence services as well, providing information on other Arab countries. During the Lebanese Civil War in the summer of 1958, members who had fled Jordan, such as Nayif Hawatmeh and Muhammad al-Zayyat, supported Kamal Junbalat and his allies who sided with Egypt. They also supported the Iraqi officers' revolt in March 1959 against 'Abd al-Karim Qasem, Nasser's rival.[148]

The group's entanglement in events involving other Arab states at the expense of the Palestinian cause intensified the dilemma for most members. Should they wait for full unity of the entire Arab nation before attempting to deliver their own people? On the one hand, they knew that Nasser had restricted military operations against Israel from Egyptian territory and the Gaza Strip; on the other, they admired and had become dependent on him for their existence, particularly after dissolution of the United Arab Republic and once the movement's senior leaders had left Syria for Lebanon, Iraq, and Egypt.

In the early 1960s, Palestinian members began demanding independent activity on the Palestinian front. They were inspired by Algeria's victorious, albeit bloody, struggle for independence in 1962. The popular coup waged in Yemen in September 1962, concluding with the establishment of an Arab National Republic, added to these sentiments. These two successes, backed by Nasser, prompted the movement to approach the Egyptian leader with a demand to focus on the Palestinian issue as well and to announce a clear plan for the "liberation of Palestine." Once Nasser admitted in early 1964 that he had no such operational plan, they decided to found an independent Palestinian branch of the movement, which was established that summer.

The tensions that emerged between the Egyptian regime and its organizations intensified, creating a split after the defeat of June 1967. In a show of protest against Nasser and his leadership of the pan-Arab struggle against Israel, Palestinian members, led by George Habash, founded the Popular Front for the Liberation of Palestine (PFLP). They announced an armed struggle against Israel through guerrilla warfare, thereby rejecting the Arab national realm with which they had become disillusioned and realigning themselves with the Palestinian realm.

Branches of the Muslim Brotherhood. Palestinian anger at the Arab regimes regarding their conduct in the War of 1948 was not directed at Muslim Brotherhood volunteers, who originated mainly from Egypt and Syria. On the contrary, these fighters were a source of inspiration for young people who sought a way to erase the disgrace and take their revenge on those responsible. In late 1951 and early 1952, about two hundred recruits began training at a camp near al-'Arish under the command of Egyptian officers affiliated with the Brotherhood. Among the group's leaders were future PLO leaders Khalil al-Wazir (Abu Jihad, 1933–1988), Muhammad Yusuf al Najjar (Abu Yusuf), and Salah Khalaf (Abu 'Iyad). Leaders of the Muslim Brotherhood in the Gaza Strip bowed to their pressure and decided to establish two clandestine Palestinian groups, Youth of Revenge (Shabab al-Thar) and Battalion of the Truth (Katibat al-Haq). The leadership of the Muslim Brotherhood in Cairo, which initially maintained contact with the Free Officers' regime in Egypt, was less enthralled with the initiative and aware of its potential dangers; they instructed the Gaza leadership to prevent activities in Israeli territories. When the Palestinians ignored these instructions and entered Israel from the Gaza Strip, this led to increasing tensions between them and the Brotherhood leadership.

Following the split between the Muslim Brotherhood and the Egyptian government, particularly after the failed attempt to assassinate Nasser, many of these activists chose the pan-Arab over the religious orientation. However, it was not long before they clashed with Nasser's government as well. An operation executed by infiltrators within Israel resulted in a harsh Israeli assault on the city of Gaza in late February 1955, and local residents subsequently held violent demonstrations, demanding an Egyptian response.[149] Most of the activists in these two groups were arrested, including Khalil al-Wazir and Muhammad Yusuf al-Najjar, followed by a lull in activities. Widespread immigration of young people from the Gaza Strip to the Gulf also contributed to the group's dwindling membership.

Establishment of Fatah

The failure of operations against Israel led Palestinian activists in favor of armed conflict to an extreme conclusion. They decided that it would be impossible to continue the struggle in the absence of independent systems, devoid of any connection to major Arab governments and their security systems. Since such an organization could only operate at a distance from these dominant systems, the center of the new initiative was now located in the Gulf, among groups of young Palestinians, and it was there that the most important Palestinian movement of the time—the Movement for the Liberation of Palestine (Harakat Tahrir Filastin; Fatah)—emerged.

Obscure Beginnings

Precise information regarding the establishment of Fatah is unclear.[150] There are differences of opinion concerning the context, time, place, and even identity of the founding members. Most sources agree that there were between five and seven founders. Two of these—Yasir Arafat and Khalil al-Wazir—are almost uncontested, while the rest are in dispute. Historian Yazid Sayigh, for example, includes 'Adel 'Abd al-Karim, 'Abd Allah al-Dannan, Khaled 'Amira, and Tawfiq Shadid. The first two arrived in Kuwait from Syria, and the latter two from Gaza. Sayigh relates that all six met in Kuwait in late 1957 and decided to establish an independent, clandestine Palestinian movement.[151] Sayigh asserts that many of those who would later become major figures in the movement joined at a later stage; for example, Salah Khalaf and Khaled al-Hasan, who joined in 1959, and Farouq al-Qaddumi, who joined in 1961 after leaving the Syrian Ba'ath Party.[152]

Sayigh's version of events is supported by Khalil al-Wazir.[153] But two other prominent Fatah leaders, Salah Khalaf and Khaled al-Hasan, claim that the movement's founding meeting took place on October 10, 1959, at a safe house in Kuwait City, with only a handful of participants in attendance.[154] Khalaf states that Fatah's initial organizational stage concluded only toward the end of 1961 with a gathering of activists from thirty-five to forty organizations espousing independent Palestinian activities.[155] In contrast, Khaled al-Hasan states that the initial entity drawing together the various groups that founded Fatah was formed in 1962. He considers all previous activities as local and unconnected.[156]

It is only natural that these two would offer dates coinciding with the dates they joined the organization, however, the ambiguity results in particular from the significant silence of Yasir Arafat. Throughout his years at the head of the PLO and the Palestinian Authority, Arafat encouraged the ambiguity enveloping all information concerning himself and the beginnings of the organization. This obscurity is conspicuous in the PLO's official publications and in the literature published by its research centers. For example, the *Palestinian Encyclopedia* describes the actual beginning of the organization as follows: "Fatah is a Palestinian organization first established in the month of October 1957, which operated clandestinely until 1968, when Yasir Arafat ('Abu 'Ammar') was declared its spokesman. Information on the organization, its founders, leaders, ideas, and plans, was publicized through public statements disseminated on his behalf, books written about him, and documents published on the subject. Some of the information remains confidential."[157] The description of the organization's establishment and its instigators maintains the ambiguity: "The organization was established as the result of an agreement between groups of young Palestinians who had witnessed the Nakba in their youth and acquired organizational experience in Palestinian student associations and unions, or in Arab national parties. Some had acquired military skills in Fida'iyyun activities emanating from the Gaza Strip in 1953."[158]

Researcher Ziyad Abu 'Amru attempted to clear up some of the obscurity by indicating that four groups were established concurrently.[159] Abu 'Amru describes (1) a Kuwait group, which included Yasir Arafat, Khalil al-Wazir, and Hani al-Qaddumi; (2) a Qatar group, including Kamal 'Idwan, Muhammad Yusuf al-Najjar, Rafiq al-Natsha, and Mahmoud Abbas (Abu Mazen); (3) a Saudi group, including 'Ali al-Sayyid, Sa'id al-Muzayyin, and Mu'iz 'Ubayd; and (4) a Gaza group, which included Fathi Bal'awi, Salim al-Za'nun, and Salah Khalaf.[160] These groups developed mutual communication networks following the founding convention held in Kuwait in October 1957. The Kuwait group, which initiated the first meeting, assumed leadership, and Kuwait became the center of independent Palestinian activity at least until establishment of the PLO was declared in 1964.

The social composition of the group of founders was not much different than that of groups, movements, and political parties active during the British Mandate period. The leaders were from the urban sector. All six senior leaders and seven of the ten "second-rank" leaders were from the cities. Only three of the ten second-rank leaders were rural (Muhammad Yusuf al-Najjar, Kamal 'Idwan, and Walid Nimr). Most became refugees at a young age and grew up amid harsh socioeconomic conditions, nonetheless representing the *a'yan* urban elite (the prominent rank) in public consciousness. Activity patterns of senior leaders indeed remained similar to those of the traditional leadership during the mandate. They, too, nurtured a centralized leadership based on systems of personal loyalty. Genuine institutionalized politics remained as before—a matter of show, rather than a system of substance.

Operational Systems and Recruitment Patterns

Most of the movement's initial activists were functionaries in Gulf state government ministries. The most conspicuous were those involved in attracting teachers, officials, and professionals from the Gaza Strip and West Bank, such as Muhammad Yusuf al-Najjar, Khalil al-Wazir, Salah Khalaf, and Mahmoud Abbas. From this position of power and familiarity they succeeded in persuading immigrants from these circles to join the movement. In addition to recruiting officials and teachers, activists also organized Palestinian student societies, particularly at Egyptian universities. Salah Khalaf had a crucial impact in this field. He would return to the Gaza Strip each summer and meet Palestinian students on vacation. At the same time he also recruited officials, merchants, and remnants of the Fida'iyyun.[161] Khalaf and his friends sought to supplement Fatah with high-status figures from Palestinian communities, such as Munir al-Rayyis, Farouq al-Husayni, and anyone with the potential of serving as a counterbalance to the old leadership.

In the second stage, movement leaders attempted to reach Palestinian communities in other Arab states and even in Europe. Envoys left for Lebanon, Iraq, and Syria. In West Germany, a group of Palestinian students operated under the leadership of Ha'il 'Abd al-Hamid, Amin al-Hindi, 'Abdallah al-Ifranji, and Hani al-Hasan, establishing a society named Path of Return (Tariq al-'Awda). As an independent organization, they cooperated with Fatah until joining the organization in 1965. They formed a significant link between Palestinian activists in Europe and those in Arab countries. They gathered money and donations, bought arms and equipment, and distributed brochures and propaganda. Khalil al-Wazir, who was in charge of contact with these groups, resided in independent Algeria. He transformed the contact with Europe, West Germany in particular, into one of Fatah's basic foundations.[162]

Nida' al-Hayat, Filastinuna *(Call of Life, Our Palestine)*

In early 1959 a decision was made to publish a newspaper expressing the movement's ideas and appealing to a wide Palestinian and Arab audience. Beirut was chosen as the place of publication, a city with relatively free journalist activity and a center of pan-Arab culture. The bureaucratic difficulties involved in publishing a new newspaper were circumvented with the help of a Muslim Brotherhood activist in Lebanon who had a license to publish a journal named *Al-Nida'* (the Call). With his assistance, Fatah representatives published a journal called *Nida' al-Hayat, Filastinuna* (Call of Life, Our Palestine). During 1959–1964, forty issues were published, with Khalil al-Wazir setting the tone. Yasir Arafat wrote only a few articles, which he signed with his initials.[163]

Tawfiq Khouri, Hani Fakhouri, and Isma'il Shammut were members of the editorial board in Beirut. The editorial column Our Opinion was written by Khalil al-Wazir. The paper's primary theme was increasing consciousness of the "Catastrophe of 1948" and instilling the term Nakba. Khalil al-Wazir would sometimes sign his articles Ibn al-Nakba (Son of the Catastrophe) and would appeal to young Palestinians by calling them Shabab al-Nakba (Youth of the Catastrophe). The newspaper's front page regularly carried a photograph stressing the harsh conditions in refugee camps, and the back page displayed a drawing by Isma'il Shammut, conveying messages of suffering and calling for resistance and struggle.[164] The main theme indirectly signified a divergence from the old generation of leaders headed by Haj Amin al-Husayni, who often employed the term *karitha*, "holocaust." At the same time, the editorial offices rapidly evolved into recruitment offices as well. Many young people appealed to the editorial office in Beirut as their link to the movement's activists and leaders.

The Fatah acronym appeared on the front page of the newspaper only from the tenth issue, at first with quotation marks and then without. The movement's identity was gradually revealed in the contents of the first ten issues. The first articles called for "organization, action, resistance, and united struggle."[165] The message was expanded further in the following statement:

> This journal is the exclusive journal of the Palestinian people, a people of valor and struggles. This journal has one main mission

and that is to describe the suffering of the refugees and to forge their perseverance versus those who strive to paralyze the Palestinian cause through partial solutions or fictitious solutions.... This journal was created as the flag that will represent you ... and present your bitterness to the world. [It is intended as] a first shot in the second round of the history of a people that is not used to forgetting injustices, nor to a life devoid of respect and pride. O brothers ... join us and together we will form a thundering voice that will have the imperialists and the Zionists shaking with terror, as well as those who call for reconciliation and partition and surrender and accepting the current state of affairs.[166]

The ninth issue opened with words that became the cornerstone of Fatah's ideological platform: "The sons of Palestine are called upon to bear the flag of liberty to their homeland. They are called upon to carry the pennant of revolt and its weapons in order to put an end to Zionist thievery. All justifications cited by those deterred from acting on behalf of Palestine will be rejected and are the excuses of cowards and defeatists."[167]

The journal *Filastinuna* indeed became a platform influencing the movement's course, and its belligerent yet vague messages enabled a large range of members to join despite their diversity: former members of the Muslim Brotherhood, Marxists, and pan-Arab nationalists, from the left and right wings.

Beginning of the Armed Conflict

In the early 1960s, following initial institutionalization, Fatah began to shape its strategy within Palestinian communities in the West Bank, Gaza Strip, and refugee camps in neighboring countries. These tactics were based on two fundamental principles: (1) Palestinian ability to reach independent decisions, and (2) armed struggle.

Fatah repeatedly claimed that the involvement of the Arab League and of Arab states in the Palestinian cause had resulted in failure, as manifested in 1948: "These countries did not take into consideration Palestinian forces in the field and acted to suspend their armed revolutionary activity. They deprived the Palestinian masses of their ability and will to use force or political pressure. They tore the Palestinian national movement to shreds to ensure their forces safe passage into Palestine."[168] Fatah members repeatedly stated that Arab leaders had taken advantage of Palestinian suffering for personal gain and acted to erase Palestinian identity. They proclaimed the slogan "Above all, Palestine" ("Filastin awwalan"). From their initial activities in 1959, Fatah leaders stressed the term *al-kayan al-Filastini*—the Palestinian entity—and blamed traditional Palestinian leadership headed by the mufti for its neglect.[169] A plan of action, called the "outline of the revolutionary structure," declared the need to establish "a Palestinian Arab entity led by a revolutionary leadership that will assume management of the campaign," and wrested this responsibility from both Arab states and the old Palestinian leadership.[170] The November 1960 issue of *Filastinuna* stated, "Those parts of Palestine remaining under Arab control should institute a revolutionary Palestinian national regime that will operate in cooperation with Arab states to save Palestine from the Jews."

The Fatah doctrine perceived Palestinian ability to reach independent decisions as interrelated with armed struggle. They saw this struggle as the main means of mobilizing the people, stressing their identity, and realizing their national unity. Arab governments would not cede these to the Palestinians of their own free will, and they must be seized by force: "The Palestinian people are in need of a revolutionary revival. The disaster of 1948 afflicted this nation with the most severe infirmities: the inclination to rely on others, internal division, internecine conflicts, and defeatism. Our revival will only come through armed struggle and under the movement's leadership."[171] The correlation between pursuit of independence, preservation of identity, and armed struggle was emphasized by Hani al-Hasan: "The Palestinians have no citizenship and therefore they have no history, rights, obligations, or sense of belonging. Without these they have no value. In order to achieve them it is necessary to return to the homeland, and this will require force."[172]

Using force to achieve political and national goals was a recurring theme in Fatah's endeavors to reinstate the Palestinian people's identity and self-confidence. Historian Yazid Sayigh claims that Fatah theorists were influenced by Frantz Fanon, who wrote about Algeria's War of Independence and preached violence as a way of "purifying" and "cleansing" the souls of the depressed.[173] According to this concept, the principle of armed struggle was aimed at intra-Palestinian needs as well, implying complete rejection of the defeat as a done deal. If the refugees' circumstances were to improve, their standard of living to rise, and their problems to be resolved, they might forget their home and homeland. One Fatah leader wrote, "If the state of mental calm, peace with the enemy, and seeking material comforts will persist, imperialist forces will succeed in crushing the spirit of Palestinian struggle, and the Palestinians will eventually become assimilated in their current environment."[174]

In order to dispel this calm, peace, and well-being, it was necessary to employ resistance, revenge, and use of force, with the goal of returning the Palestinians to their homeland. This was the course espoused by Fatah to erase the Catastrophe of 1948. Nonetheless, the organization recognized that guerrilla combat against Israel would require a sympathetic population and a return to rear bases located in states that would not relinquish their sovereignty and would try to supervise and closely monitor Palestinian guerrilla warfare. Indeed, as long as Fatah operated on the organizational level it did not hasten to proceed to the operative stage. However, when the PLO was founded in 1964 and the Palestine Liberation Army established (subject to the control of Arab governments), planning and propaganda were no longer sufficient. At the beginning of that year, Arafat and his associates transferred their operations base to Damascus, from where they performed secret expeditions to Beirut and Amman. They also intervened in the conflict developing between Ahmad al-Shuqayri, head of the PLO and protégé of Gamal Abdel Nasser, and the traditional Palestinian leadership headed by Mufti Haj Amin al-Husayni. In the debate between depending on Arab patronage, an approach represented by Shuqayri, and the pursuit of independence, represented by the mufti, they chose the latter, although the mufti was perceived as a reactionary who had wrought irreversible damage to the Palestinian cause. In a meeting in Beirut between the mufti and Yasir Arafat, Khalil al-Wazir, and Salah Khalaf, the mufti expressed his support of Fatah and even suggested putting his staff in Lebanese refugee camps at their disposal. His men helped by training Fatah operatives and providing them with guides to Israel and the West Bank.[175]

In addition to opening a line of communication with the mufti, Arafat and his colleagues appended to Fatah other Palestinian groups operating clandestinely in Lebanon. The most significant of these was the Palestinian Revolutionary Organization (al-Munazzamah al-Filastiniyya al-Thawriyya) led by Zakariyya 'Abd al-Rahim. 'Abd al-Rahim was in charge of recruitment to Fatah in Lebanon. At the advice of the mufti, Arafat added Ahmad and Mahmoud al-Atrash, brothers and founders of the Bands of Force (al-Majmou'at al-Darbah), to serve under him. In Jordan, Fatah recruited Palestinian activists from among the Muslim Brotherhood, headed by Muhammad Ghunaym, who had despaired of King Husayn's Western orientation. Members of the Ba'ath movement, such as Samih Abu Kuwayk, and student leaders, such as 'Umar al-Khatib and 'Abbas Zaki, joined as well.[176] As stated, Syria served as Fatah's primary base. Fatah leaders had contacts with several senior government officials: Nur al-Din al-Atasi (future president of Syria), Prime Minister Yusuf Zu'ayyin, Foreign Minister Ibrahim Makhus, Head of Military Intelligence Ahmad Suwaydani, and Commander of the Air Force Hafez al-Assad.[177]

Although the emergence of the PLO in 1964 hastened Fatah's preparations for an armed confrontation, there were those in the organization's higher echelons who sought to postpone the armed struggle in order to be better prepared. Arafat and al-Wazir, however, pressured by the Kuwaitis, Saudis, and Algerians who had provided weapons and ammunition, urged action. The impending decision to initiate combat operations against Israeli targets was announced by *Filastinuna* in November 1964: "The Palestinian people have reached a critical point. This nation believes only in itself and it will courageously raise the wave of revolt that will bring about a complete change in the balance of forces."[178] Toward the beginning of armed operations, the movement founded a network of logistical aides on the Syrian, Jordanian, and Lebanese borders with Israel, and even within Israeli territory. Arafat and other senior commanders performed frequent patrols and prepared the activity centers of the armed Palestinian organizations. The initial operation was unsuccessful. Two bands charged with executing concurrent operations in Israel failed. One was caught on December 31, 1964, by a patrol unit of the Lebanese army, and its members were incarcerated in Beirut. The other band succeeded in crossing the Israeli border on January 1, 1965. They buried a mine by a water pump on the southern bank of the Sea of Galilee, but it did not explode.

Despite the operations' failures, arrogant declarations abounded: "Military Announcement No. 1," from January 2, 1965, detailed the fictitious success of the organization's first military operation. The announcement was published on behalf of the General Command of the al-'Asifa (Storm) Forces, rather than Fatah. The incident became a constitutive myth, and ever since that time, January 1 has denoted the beginning of the armed struggle of the revived Palestinian national movement.

Fatah's Rivals and the Establishment of the Palestine Liberation Army

Fatah's declaration and media coverage of the start of armed combat aroused great interest. Shuqayri's PLO organization hastened to announce that it had no connection with al-'Asifa, and that only the Palestine Liberation Army was authorized to act toward the liberation of Palestine. The head of the United Arab Command, Egyptian general 'Ali 'Ali 'Amer, declared Fatah to be part of the Muslim Brotherhood, and in March 1965 issued instructions to Arab armies to stop members of the organization attempting to cross the Israeli border.[179] Nasser himself asserted that al-'Asifa's actions did not promote the Palestinian cause.[180] The Arab Nationalist Movement, which was associated with Nasser and his government as well, denounced Fatah as a "suspicious movement that has connections with foreign elements and is interested in dragging Nasser into a war that will end with his defeat."[181] The Palestinian group that embraced the Egyptian president's outlook was represented by George Habash, one of the movement's most prominent leaders, who also quoted Nasser as saying that he "believes in armed Palestinian struggle but is sensibly waiting for the proper timing."[182]

In addition to the course taken by Habash, other positions were espoused within the Arab Nationalist Movement as well: Wadi' Haddad, a prominent leader in his own right, had begun planning a military course of action even before Fatah was declared, and he now sought to promote this avenue. In early 1964 he established the Struggle Apparatus (al-Jihaz al-Nidali), with branches in Amman, headed by Abu 'Ali Mustafa al-Zibri, and in Beirut, headed by Ahmad Husayn al-Yamani. Recruits received training at the Egyptian military academy located at the Anshas Base, near Cairo, but attempts to form trained groups in countries opposed to Israel were foiled by those countries' intelligence agencies.[183]

The discord between the two divisions of the Arab Nationalist Movement was discussed at the movement's convention in Beirut in September 1965, at which George Habash triumphed. The convention decided that the movement would conduct itself with restraint and appointed a subcommittee to outline its methods of action. The format agreed upon was summarized by Ghassan Kanafani, a member of the committee: "Activities above zero but with no complications." In other words, the movement would execute intelligence operations in Israeli territory and try to recruit Palestinian Arabs with Israeli citizenship as logistical aides, but would avoid attacking targets.[184] This decision kept the movement's armed and intelligence activities on a slow burner, with fewer than twenty men available as part of Wadi' Haddad's Struggle Apparatus. When a Struggle Apparatus band attempted to enter Israel, it encountered a Jordanian army patrol and one of its men was killed. The Arab Nationalists would later claim that the first *shahid* of the armed conflict came from within their midst and did not belong to Fatah.[185]

In response to Fatah's initiative, the PLO expedited the establishment and arming of the Palestine Liberation Army. This force was initially conceived as a means of quelling the anger and criticism of the Arab public in general and the Palestinian public in particular, following the impotence of Arab governments on the Palestinian issue. Both Gamal Abdel Nasser and General 'Ali 'Ali 'Amer, head of the United Arab Command, were not eager to establish a Palestinian "army" purporting to boast marks of sovereignty. However, Ahmad al-Shuqayri's success in gaining the support of Syria, Iraq, and Saudi Arabia at the Arab League Council convinced Nasser to support establishment of a limited armed force that would be dependent on Egypt. In mid-January 1965, Shuqayri met with the Egyptian Chief of General Staff Muhammad Fawzi for an initial coordination meeting. Fawzi clarified to Shuqayri that Egypt would not object to the establishment of the Palestine Liberation Army, but it would not permit any independent operations in the Gaza Strip, as "a ship with two captains is destined to sink."[186]

In summer 1965, Egyptian authorities in the Gaza Strip announced a recruitment campaign for the Palestine Liberation Army. In late 1965 and early 1966 they announced the founding of two Palestinian National Guard regiments to form the beginning of the Liberation Army. In reality these regiments encompassed no more than 40 percent of the force agreed upon between Shuqayri and the Egyptians. This state of affairs persisted until the War of June 1967, remaining constant because Nasser objected to the establishment of a heavily armed Palestinian army to confront the Israeli army. Nasser preferred the Palestinians to operate as a guerrilla force similar to the Vietnamese model. For this reason, General 'Ali 'Ali 'Amer distanced PLA forces from front posts along the border and announced that even in times of war they would remain in the rear. Thus, establishment of the PLA was more a matter of propaganda than an actual move. To compensate for the restriction of PLO forces and their exclusion from front positions, Nasser gave the PLO authority to operate the Voice of Palestine radio station, broadcasting from Cairo six hours a day. Egyptian authorities imposed a "liberation tax" on residents of the Gaza Strip, and the PLO received all revenues.[187] In a missive sent to the Second Palestinian National Council, Nasser announced that Shuqayri and his men were the exclusive and authorized representatives of the Palestinian people.[188]

The Stages Theory

Fatah had not been expecting such a severe response from Egypt to the initiation of an armed conflict—a response that deterred any further attempts to escalate the military situation. In late January 1965 the organization's spokesman announced that "Fatah's agenda on both the military and political level, does not contradict official Palestinian and Arab policy."[189] A subsequent announcement explained that the movement did not intend to entangle Arab leaders and their governments with Israel, and *Filastinuna* wrote that an Arab lightning war aimed at destroying Israel would not be realistic. Consequently, Fatah theorists began developing the "stages theory." This theory was based on the recognition that Israel could only be defeated by a pan-Arab military effort, preceded by independent actions of popular forces and revolutionary bands. During the first stage, local forces would weaken the enemy, then would proceed to unite Palestinian society until the emergence of pan-Arab military readiness, and finally Arab armies would join the liberating "army of return."[190] Algeria's successful War of Independence served as an inspiration and model for the first stage of Palestinian guerrilla warfare.

Contemporary Fatah theorists display inconsistent views about their organization, due in part to the sharply and frequently changing attitude of Arab governments toward Fatah. The role they assigned to the "revolutionary forces" (i.e., Fatah) was no different than that specified by Nasser and 'Ali 'Ali 'Amer. They added some ideological foundations borrowed from revolutionary fighting doctrines that had evolved in the Algerian, Vietnamese, and Cuban contexts. Thus, for example, Fatah embraced a Cuban theory called "serial bombing." Khaled al-Hasan explains the process:

> Our military operations in the center of the circle will result in an Israeli reaction against our people. They [our people] will respond

by initiating a struggle supported by the Arab masses. Thus the circle will expand, forcing Arab governments to choose between joining our struggle and acting against us. If they act against us, governments will become separated from their people, while the latter will rush to support us and advance from commiseration to action. This gradual process will have an impact on all Arab politics and on the international sphere as well, which will then intervene in the central issue [Palestine].[191]

The expanding circles theory was based on the premise that only the instigating forces, that is, Fatah, would become stronger with the passage of time. It did not consider that maybe the other parties would not respond so predictably and that the strategy of "serial bombing" might not be so conditioned and automatic. Fatah's assumption was that the Arab masses would fully identify with the armed Palestinian struggle and force their governments to join an all-encompassing war focused on Jordan and Lebanon. However, attempts at motivating the people to compel their regimes to do as they wish proved unsuccessful. These were destined to end in bloodshed, refuting the "serial bombing" theory. In strong countries such as Iraq, Egypt, and Syria, the authorities suppressed all independent activities and arrested movement leaders.

Syria and the Suppression of Fatah

Fatah's relationship with Syria was influenced by two major factors: Syria's refusal to support infiltration of Israel from its territory, and the subversion of Arafat-led Fatah by Palestinian Ba'ath members. When the armed struggle was first initiated, Syria allowed Fatah a certain amount of freedom, stipulating, however, that all actions needed to be coordinated in advance with Palestinian officers in the Syrian army. Fatah thought that Syria was unnecessarily interfering with its independence and tried to evade the decree, but Syrian authorities did not yield. Syria applied increasing pressure, and eventually, in early February 1966, Fatah leaders agreed to include two senior Palestinian officers from the Syrian army, 'Ali Bushnaq and Ahmad Jibril, among their higher ranks. Nevertheless, two months later Jibril and Bushnaq angrily abandoned the new organization and proceeded to harass Fatah through their connections in Syrian intelligence. On April 11, 1966, Jibril's men arrested a leader of a Fatah band, Muhammad Hishmi, upon his return from an operation near the

Yarmuk estuary. He was detained for two weeks and was subjected to intensive and humiliating interrogation.[192] A month later Hishmi was involved in an even graver affair: he had an argument with the coordinating Palestinian officer on behalf of Syria, Yusuf 'Urabi, culminating in a shoot-out in which both were killed. The incident led to the arrest of Fatah's eleven senior activists, including Arafat and al-Wazir.[193] They were accused of the murder of 'Urabi and spent two months in solitary confinement. After a lengthy process, the court acquitted ten of the defendants and convicted only the man who shot 'Urabi ('Abd al-Majid Zughamut, who remained incarcerated until his death in 1999). The entire affair continued to haunt relations between the Fatah leadership and the Syrian government.

At the same time, the Palestinian branch of the Ba'ath movement, headed by Kamal Nasser and 'Abd al-Muhsin Abu Mayzar, plotted against the Fatah leaders. They used party and government organs to depict Fatah leaders as heading a reactionary movement amounting to a mere extension of the Muslim Brotherhood, featuring Arafat as an agent of Egyptian Intelligence. Some Palestinian Ba'ath activists were not in favor of this strategy, but the large majority advocated barring Fatah from Syria. In Syria, as in other Arab states prior to the War of 1967, Palestinians were not permitted freedom of action and were unable to implement any part of the "stages" theory. With Arab states (particularly Egypt) controlling Palestinian activity, Palestinian organizations and leaders found it very difficult to act freely. The defeat in the War of June 1967 and the downfall of the regular armies of Israel's neighbors increased the significance of the organizations and further legitimized their actions, as will be elaborated in the following chapter.

Notes

1. Elpeleg, *Grand Mufti*, 109.
2. *Herald Tribune*, October 22, 1948.
3. *'Al-Hamishmar*, December 8, 1948.
4. Elpeleg, *Grand Mufti*, 110–111.
5. Collection of Arabic broadcasts, number 113, December 23, 1948, State Archives.
6. Elpeleg, *Grand Mufti*, 111.
7. The Little Triangle: part of the area called the Large Triangle by the British during the mandate (Nablus, Jenin, Tulkarm). This area is in the shape

of a triangle, and it is located along the border with the West Bank (the Green Line) from Kafr Qasem in the south to Salem in the north, measuring approximately seventy kilometers long and three kilometers wide.

8. Abu al-Nmil, *Qita' Ghazza, 1948–1967: Tatawwurat Iqtisadiyya wa Siyasiyya wa-'Ijtama iyya wa 'Askariyya* [Gaza Strip, 1948–1967], 34–35.

9. Khalusy, *Al-Tanmiya al-Iqtisadiyya fi Qita' Ghazza "Filastin" 1948–1968* [Economic Development in the Gaza Strip], 38.

10. Abu 'Amru, *Usul al-Haraka al-Siyasiyya fi Qita' Ghazza, 1948–1967* [Foundations of the Political Movements in the Gaza Strip], 15.

11. Neuberger, "Hami'ut Ha'arvi: Nikur Vehishtalvut" [Arab Minority], 5.

12. Neuberger, "Hami'ut Ha'arvi: Nikur Vehishtalvut" [Arab Minority], 12.

13. Ian Lustick, *'Aravim Bimdina Yehudit* [Arabs in a Jewish State], 78.

14. Neuberger, "Hami'ut Ha'arvi: Nikur Vehishtalvut" [Arab Minority], 10.

15. Morris, *Milhemet Hagvul Shel Yisra'el, 1949-1956* [Israel's Border War], 587–594.

16. Al-Khalidi, *All That Remains*, 847.

17. Abu Sitta, *Palestinian Right to Return*, 12.

18. On such cases, see Grossman, *Hakfar Ha arvi 'Uvnotav* [Arab Village and Its Offshoots].

19. Al-Hamad et al., *Al-Madkhal ila al-Qadiyya al-Filastiniyya* [Introduction to the Palestinian Problem], 594.

20. Details of the report are cited by al-'Arif, *Nakbat Bayt al-Maqdis wa al-Firdaws al-Mafquod, 1947–1952* [Nakba of Jerusalem and Lost Paradise], 5:1098–1099.

21. UNRWA, the United Nations Relief and Works Agency, was established according to the UN resolution passed on December 8, 1949, and began its activities in May 1950, replacing a special UN agency founded previously. This agency was charged with providing welfare and employment assistance to Palestinian refugees, in coordination with the host governments. At first it was given a mandate to operate for three years, which has been constantly renewed down to the present. Al-Hamad et al., *Al-Madkhal ila al-Qadiyya al-Filastiniyya* [Introduction to the Palestinian Problem], 593n19.

22. Al-Rushdan, *Mustaqbal al-Laj'in al-Filastiniyyin wa Filastiniyyi al-Shatat* [Future of the Palestinian Refugees], 216–217.

23. This term became part of the refugees' way of life. Receiving the card, *al-bitaqa*, was considered a visa to a slightly more secure life. Products distributed by the agency were called *bitaqa* (*Taheen al-bitaqa* [flour of the card] and *sukar bitaqa* [sugar of the card] were distributed on *yawm al-bitaqa* [card day]).

24. As described in the famous novel by Palestinian author Ghassan Kanafani, *Rajal Fi al Shams* [Men in the Sun].

25. On this see Hayat Yaghi, "*Mushkilat al-laji'in fi mukhayyamat al-'Urdon kama yaraha abna'uhom fi ma had tadrib 'amman al-tabi liwakalat*

al-ghawth" [The problem of the refugees in Jordanian refugee camps as seen by their sons in the training institute of the international relief agency] (master's thesis, University of Jordan, 1973).

26. Khammash, "Filistiniyyu al-shatat fi al-'Urdon" [Palestinians of the Diaspora in Jordan], 221–222.

27. On this discourse and its circumstances, see Abu Odeh, *Jordanians, Palestinians, and the Hashemite Kingdom*, 193–236.

28. Abu al-Nmil, *Qita' Ghazza, 1948–1967: Tatawwurat Iqtisadiyya wa Siyasiyya wa-'Ijtama iyya wa 'Askariyya* [Gaza Strip], 44.

29. Abu al-Nmil, *Qita' Ghazza, 1948–1967: Tatawwurat Iqtisadiyya wa Siyasiyya wa-'Ijtama iyya wa 'Askariyya* [Gaza Strip], 45.

30. The term "present absentees" denotes the civil status of Palestinian Arab refugees living in the State of Israel and considered by the Absentees Property Law to be absent from their prewar places of residence; this is to say, they cannot realize their ownership of property in their villages of origin that belonged to them before the War of 1948, although they are citizens currently living in other locations in Israel.

31. H. Cohen, *Hanifqadim Hanokhehim: Haplitim Hafalestinim Beyisra'el Me'az 1948* [Present Absentees: Palestinian Refugees in Israel], 21.

32. H. Cohen, *Hanifqadim Hanokhehim: Haplitim Hafalestinim Beyisra'el Me'az 1948* [Present Absentees: Palestinian Refugees in Israel], 21.

33. Samooha, *Orientation and Politicization of the Arab Minority in Israel*, 79; Rabah, *Al-Laji'un wa al-Nazihun wa mufawadat al-Wadi' al-Da'im* [Refugees and the Displaced and the Negotiations for a Permanent Arrangement], 34.

34. On the role of Yosef Weitz on this issue, see Morris, *Laydata shel Be'ayat Haplitim Hafalestinim 1947–1949* [Birth of the Palestinian Refugee Problem], 47–48, 83–85. Weitz's journals were published under the title *Yomani Ve'igrotai Labanim* [My Diary].

35. Weitz, *Yomani Ve'igrotai Labanim* [My Diary], vol. 3, September 9, 1948, note 35.

36. On this operation, see Central Zionist Archives, JNF Files, 18874/5.

37. H. Cohen, *Hanifqadim Hanokhehim: Haplitim Hafalestinim Beyisra'el Me'az 1948* [Present Absentees: Palestinian Refugees in Israel], 26–27.

38. Morris, *Laydata shel Be'ayat Haplitim Hafalestinim 1947–1949* [Birth of the Palestinian Refugee Problem], 187–188.

39. Morris, *Laydata shel Be'ayat Haplitim Hafalestinim 1947–1949* [Birth of the Palestinian Refugee Problem], 290–291.

40. H. Cohen, *Hanifqadim Hanokhehim: Haplitim Hafalestinim Beyisra'el Me'az 1948* [Present Absentees: Palestinian Refugees in Israel], 38–39.

41. Ayub, *Al-Bina' al-Tabaqi Lilfilastiniyyin* [Class Stratification for Palestinians], 163.

42. Al-Hur, *Al-Filastiniyyun fi Lubnan* [Palestinians in Lebanon], 1:12.

43. *Filastin* (Journal of the Arab Higher Institution) 6, July 25, 1961.

44. Al-Natur, "Al-Laji'un al-Filastiniyyun fi Libnan" [Palestinian Refugees in Lebanon], 342–343.
45. Al-Natur, "Al-Laji'un al-Filastiniyyun fi Libnan" [Palestinian Refugees in Lebanon], 345.
46. Al-Maw'id, "Filastiniyyu al-Shatat fi Surya" [Palestinians of the Diaspora in Syria], 309–312.
47. Al-Maw'id, "Filastiniyyu al-Shatat fi Surya" [Palestinians of the Diaspora in Syria], 309.
48. Al-Maw'id, "Al-Mukhayyam wa al-hawiyya al-Filastiniyya" [Refugee Camp and Palestinian Identity], 3–5.
49. Al-Maw'id, "Filastiniyyu al-Shatat fi Surya" [Palestinians of the Diaspora in Syria], 32n47.
50. On the political integration of Palestinian refugees in Syria, see al-Khadra, *Surya wa al-Laji'un al-Filastiniyyun* [Syria and the Palestinian Refugees], 22–30.
51. Dudin, "Al-Filastiniyyun fi al-'Iraq" [Palestinians in Iraq], 76; Hammuda, *Al-Filastiniyyun fi al-'Iraq: Madkhal Dimughrafi, Ijtama'i wa Iqtisadi* [Palestinians in Iraq], 11; Zu'aytir, *Al-Qadiyya al-Filastiniyya* [Palestinian Problem], 56.
52. Munazzamat al-Tahrir al-Filastiniyya [Palestinian Liberation Organization], *Al-Laji'un al-Filastiniyyun Fi al-'Iraq* [Palestinian Refugees in Iraq], 1.
53. Hammuda, *Al-Filastiniyyun fi al-'Iraq: Madkhal Dimughrafi, Ijtama'i wa Iqtisadi* [Palestinians in Iraq], 9n52.
54. Al-Samara'i, *Al-'Iraq wa al-Qadiyya al-Filastiniyya, 1958–1973* [Iraq and the Palestinian Problem], 138.
55. Nasimah Hasan al-Najjar, "Ittijahat al-Shakhsiyya al-Filastiniyya al-Mu'asira: Dirasah Maydaniyya Lil'usar al-Filastiniyya fi Baghdad" [Directions in Modern Palestinian Identity: A Field Study Among the Palestinian Families in Baghdad] (master's thesis, University of Baghdad, 1986), 53, cited in Mus'ab, *Filastiniyyu al-Shatat fi Baghdad* [Palestinians of the Diaspora], 236–237.
56. Nasimah Hasan al-Najjar, "Ittijahat al-Shakhsiyya al-Filastiniyya al-Mu'asira: Dirasah Maydaniyya Lil'usar al-Filastiniyya fi Baghdad" [Directions in Modern Palestinian Identity: A Field Study Among the Palestinian Families in Baghdad] (master's thesis, University of Baghdad, 1986), 63.
57. Mus'ab, *Filastiniyyu al-Shatat fi Baghdad* [Palestinians of the Diaspora], 253n56.
58. Mus'ab, *Filastiniyyu al-Shatat fi Baghdad* [Palestinians of the Diaspora], 253n56.
59. Shabib, "Muqaddimat al-musadara al-rasmiyya lilshakhsiyya al-Filastiniyya, 1948-1950" [Introduction to the Establishment's Boycott of the Palestinian National Identity], 82–83.
60. *Al-Ahram*, December 21, 1951.

61. Elpeleg, *Grand Mufti*, 113.
62. *Al-Ahram*, February 13, 1951.
63. See, for example, article published by *Al-Ahram* on the topic, October 18, 1955.
64. Elpeleg, *Grand Mufti*, 129.
65. On the unfolding relations between Qasem and Nasser, see Dann, *Iraq Under Qasem*, 69–76.
66. Elpeleg, *Grand Mufti*, 131.
67. On these visits see, for example, the newspaper *Al-Zaman*, published in Iraq, July 5, 1961.
68. On this see, for example, *Al-Ahram*, April 5, 1960.
69. On the summit and its resolutions, see Sela, *Ahdut Betokh Peyrud Hama'arekhet Habeyn-'Arvit* [Unity Within Conflict in the Inter-Arab System], 26–36.
70. On the visit, see *Filastin*, April 14, 1962.
71. *Al-Difa'* (Jordan), February 6, 1964.
72. *Al-Jihad* (Jordan), April 14, 1964.
73. *Al-Jihad* (Jordan), June 3, 1964.
74. A. Cohen, *Miflagot Bagada Hama'aravit Bitqufat Hashilton Hayardeni* [Political Parties in the West Bank], 12.
75. A. Cohen, *Miflagot Bagada Hama'aravit Bitqufat Hashilton Hayardeni* [Political Parties in the West Bank], 12–13.
76. A. Cohen, *Miflagot Bagada Hama'aravit Bitqufat Hashilton Hayardeni* [Political Parties in the West Bank], 20.
77. A. Cohen, *Miflagot Bagada Hama'aravit Bitqufat Hashilton Hayardeni* [Political Parties in the West Bank], 22.
78. Radio Jordan from Ramallah, April 25, 1957, cited by A. Cohen, *Miflagot Bagada Hama'aravit Bitqufat Hashilton Hayardeni* [Political Parties in the West Bank], 23.
79. *Al-Difa'*, August 5, 1957.
80. See, for example, the public statement published by Dr. 'Abd al-Hafiz al-Ashhab on one of the major activities in Hebron and its vicinity, in the newspaper *Al-Difa'*, May 26, 1959.
81. *Al-Jarida* (Lebanon), October 7, 1969.
82. *Al-Sarih*, March 21, 1953.
83. *Filastin*, April 10, 1953.
84. A. Cohen, *Miflagot Bagada Hama'aravit Bitqufat Hashilton Hayardeni* [Political Parties in the West Bank], 105.
85. Barute, *Harakat al-Qawmiyyin al-'Arab al-Nash'ah wa -al-Tatawwur* [Arab Nationalists Movement], 58–59.
86. Barute, *Harakat al-Qawmiyyin al-'Arab al-Nash'ah wa -al-Tatawwur* [Arab Nationalists Movement], 60.

87. Barute, *Harakat al-Qawmiyyin al-'Arab al-Nash'ah wa -al-Tatawwur* [Arab Nationalists Movement], 61–62.

88. For more details, see al-Kubaysi, *Harakat al-Qawmiyun al-'Arab* [Movement of the Arab Nationalists], 82.

89. Barute, *Harakat al-Qawmiyyin al-'Arab al-Nash'ah wa -al-Tatawwur* [Arab Nationalists Movement], 300.

90. Barute, *Harakat al-Qawmiyyin al-'Arab al-Nash'ah wa -al-Tatawwur* [Arab Nationalists Movement], 314.

91. *Filastin* (bulletin published by the Arab Nationalist Movement) 45, July 14, 1966.

92. Abu 'Amru, *Al-Harakah al-Islamiyya fi al-Diffah al-Gharbiyya wa Qita' Ghazza* [Islamic Movement in the West Bank and Gaza Strip], 21.

93. On this see Mitchell, *Society of the Muslim Brothers*, 165.

94. Mitchell, *Society of the Muslim Brothers*, 165.

95. On this see *Al-Difa'*, June 1, 1953; *Filastin*, November 20, 1953.

96. A. Cohen, *Miflagot Bagada Hama'aravit Bitqufat Hashilton Hayardeni* [Political Parties in the West Bank], 134.

97. Interview with Yusuf al-'Azm, cited by Abu 'Amru, *Al-Harakah al-Islamiyya fi al-Diffah al-Gharbiyya wa Qita' Ghazza* [Islamic Movement in the West Bank and Gaza Strip], 23.

98. On the changes in the league's composition and its functioning in light of the new circumstances, see Yasin, *Hizb Shuyu'i zahrurhu Ila al-Ha'it* [Communist Party with Its Back to the Wall], 13.

99. Basisu, *Dafater Filastiniyya* [Palestinian Notebooks], 93.

100. Abu 'Amru, *Al-Harakah al-Islamiyya fi al-Diffah al-Gharbiyya wa Qita' Ghazza* [Islamic Movement in the West Bank and Gaza Strip], 2:53.

101. Abu 'Amru, *Al-Harakah al-Islamiyya fi al-Diffah al-Gharbiyya wa Qita' Ghazza* [Islamic Movement in the West Bank and Gaza Strip], 72–72.

102. Abu 'Amru, *Al-Harakah al-Islamiyya fi al-Diffah al-Gharbiyya wa Qita' Ghazza* [Islamic Movement in the West Bank and Gaza Strip], 71.

103. Abu 'Amru, *Al-Harakah al-Islamiyya fi al-Diffah al-Gharbiyya wa Qita' Ghazza* [Islamic Movement in the West Bank and Gaza Strip], 73.

104. Abu 'Amru, *Al-Harakah al-Islamiyya fi al-Diffah al-Gharbiyya wa Qita' Ghazza* [Islamic Movement in the West Bank and Gaza Strip], 1:113; Yasin, *Shubhat Hawl al-Qadiyya al-Filastiniyya* [Doubts on the Palestinian Issue], 100.

105. Jiryis, *Ha'aravim Beyisra'el* [Arabs in Israel], 110–111.

106. Neuberger, "Hami'ut Ha'arvi: Nikur Vehishtalvut" [Arab Minority], 86.

107. Among the prominent figures elected to the Knesset in such a manner were the mayor of Nazareth, Sif al-Din al-Zu'abi (seven terms); Jabr Dahish Mu'addi (of Yarka, seven terms); Diyab 'Ubayd (of Taybe, three

terms); Ilyas Nakhlah (of Nazareth, three terms); and Faris Hamdan (of Baqa al-Gharbiyya, two terms).

108. Jiryis, *Ha'aravim Beyisra'el* [Arabs in Israel], 111–112.

109. On Mapam's press and on the Arabic press of the period, see Kabha and Caspi, "Miyerushalayim haqdosha ve'ad hama'ayan: Megamot ba'itonut basafa ha'arvit beyisra'el" [From Sacred Jerusalem to the Spring], 50–54.

110. Safran, in Neuberger, "Hami'ut Ha'arvi: Nikur Vehishtalvut" [Arab Minority], 99.

111. Sneh is quoted by Rekhes, "Bayn Qomunizem Lele'umiyut: Raqah Vehami'ut Ha'arvi Beyisra'el, 1965–1973" [Between Communism and Nationalism], 403.

112. Murqus, *Aqwq min al-Nisyan* [Stronger than Forgetting], 240–241.

113. Neuberger, "Hami'ut Ha'arvi: Nikur Vehishtalvut" [Arab Minority], 103.

114. Among the front's founders were Ilyas Kusa from Haifa; Jabbor Jabbor, head of the Shafa'amr local council; and Yanni Yanni, head of the Kfar Yasif local council, who was elected president.

115. For more information on the front, see Qahwaji, *Al-'Arab Tahta al-Ihtilal al-Isra'ili Munzu 'Aam 1948* [The Arabs Under Israeli Occupation], 423–425.

116. On the basic principles of this platform, see Jiryis, *Ha'aravim Beyisra'el* [Arabs in Israel], 117.

117. *Mansour Kardush v. Registrar of Companies*, Supreme Court file 60/241, verdict 15, p. 1151, and *Registrar of Companies v. Mansour Kardush*, supplementary sitting 61/16, verdict 16, p. 1209.

118. Jiryis, *Ha'aravim Beyisra'el* [Arabs in Israel], 118.

119. Neuberger, "Hami'ut Ha'arvi: Nikur Vehishtalvut" [Arab Minority], 110.

120. Sayigh, *Al-Kifah al-Muslah wa al-Bahath 'An al-Dawla: Al-Haraka al-Wataniyya al-Filastiniyya, 1949–1993* [Armed Struggle and the Search for a State], 116.

121. On this see Abu 'Amru, *Usul al-Haraka al-Siyasiyya fi Qita' Ghazza, 1948–1967* [Foundations of the Political Movements in the Gaza Strip], 23–25.

122. Sayigh, *Al-Kifah al-Muslah wa al-Bahath 'An al-Dawla: Al-Haraka al-Wataniyya al-Filastiniyya, 1949–1993* [Armed Struggle and the Search for a State], 119.

123. Sayigh, *Al-Kifah al-Muslah wa al-Bahath 'An al-Dawla: Al-Haraka al-Wataniyya al-Filastiniyya, 1949–1993* [Armed Struggle and the Search for a State], 119.

124. Abu al-Nmil, *Qita' Ghazza Tahta al-Hukm al-Misri* [Gaza Strip Under Egyptian Rule], 114.

125. The monthly wages of an Egyptian soldier in the regular army were eighteen Egyptian pounds, and of a member of the Fida'iyyun, only eight

Egyptian pounds. Sayigh, *Al-Kifah al-Muslah wa al-Bahath 'An al-Dawla: Al-Haraka al-Wataniyya al-Filastiniyya, 1949–1993* [Armed Struggle and the Search for a State], 122.

126. Al-Kitri, *Halaqa Mafqudah min Kifah al-Sha'b al-Filastini: Al-Katiba 141, Fida'iyyun* [Lost Sphere in the Struggle of the Palestinian People], 27–29.

127. Sayigh, *Al-Kifah al-Muslah wa al-Bahath 'An al-Dawla: Al-Haraka al-Wataniyya al-Filastiniyya, 1949–1993* [Armed Struggle and the Search for a State], 123.

128. Sayigh, *Al-Kifah al-Muslah wa al-Bahath 'An al-Dawla: Al-Haraka al-Wataniyya al-Filastiniyya, 1949–1993* [Armed Struggle and the Search for a State], 123.

129. For more details, see Ya'ari, *Misrayim Vehafedayun, 1953–1956* [Egypt and the Fida'iyyun], 27–31.

130. Sayigh, *Al-Kifah al-Muslah wa al-Bahath 'An al-Dawla: Al-Haraka al-Wataniyya al-Filastiniyya, 1949–1993* [Armed Struggle and the Search for a State], 123.

131. Sayigh, *Al-Kifah al-Muslah wa al-Bahath 'An al-Dawla: Al-Haraka al-Wataniyya al-Filastiniyya, 1949–1993* [Armed Struggle and the Search for a State], 123.

132. Sayigh, *Al-Kifah al-Muslah wa al-Bahath 'An al-Dawla: Al-Haraka al-Wataniyya al-Filastiniyya, 1949–1993* [Armed Struggle and the Search for a State], 124; al-Az'ar, *Al-Muqawma fi Qita' Ghazza, 1967–1985* [Resistance in the Gaza Strip], 55.

133. Sayigh, *Al-Kifah al-Muslah wa al-Bahath 'An al-Dawla: Al-Haraka al-Wataniyya al-Filastiniyya, 1949–1993* [Armed Struggle and the Search for a State], 125.

134. On Bart'ah, see Amara and Kabha, *Zehut Hatzuya: Haluka Politit veHishtaqfuyot Politiyot beKfar Hatzui* [Split Personality].

135. Sayigh, *Al-Kifah al-Muslah wa al-Bahath 'An al-Dawla: Al-Haraka al-Wataniyya al-Filastiniyya, 1949–1993* [Armed Struggle and the Search for a State], 116.

136. On this see Glubb, *Soldier with the Arabs*, 306.

137. Sayigh, *Al-Kifah al-Muslah wa al-Bahath 'An al-Dawla: Al-Haraka al-Wataniyya al-Filastiniyya, 1949–1993* [Armed Struggle and the Search for a State], 117.

138. Sayigh, *Al-Kifah al-Muslah wa al-Bahath 'An al-Dawla: Al-Haraka al-Wataniyya al-Filastiniyya, 1949–1993* [Armed Struggle and the Search for a State], 117.

139. Sa'ad and Yasin, *Al-Haraka al-Wataniyya al-Filastiniyya, 1948–1970* [Palestinian National Movement], 69.

140. Sayigh, *Al-Kifah al-Muslah wa al-Bahath 'An al-Dawla: Al-Haraka al-Wataniyya al-Filastiniyya, 1949–1993* [Armed Struggle and the Search for a State], 127.

141. Sayigh, *Al-Kifah al-Muslah wa al-Bahath 'An al-Dawla: Al-Haraka al-Wataniyya al-Filastiniyya, 1949–1993* [Armed Struggle and the Search for a State], 130.

142. Sayigh, *Al-Kifah al-Muslah wa al-Bahath 'An al-Dawla: Al-Haraka al-Wataniyya al-Filastiniyya, 1949–1993* [Armed Struggle and the Search for a State], 131.

143. Al-Kubaysi, *Harakat al-Qawmiyun al-'Arab* [Movement of the Arab Nationalists], 66.

144. Al-Kubaysi, *Harakat al-Qawmiyun al-'Arab* [Movement of the Arab Nationalists], 66.

145. Al-Kubaysi, *Harakat al-Qawmiyun al-'Arab* [Movement of the Arab Nationalists], 89.

146. Sayigh, *Al-Kifah al-Muslah wa al-Bahath 'An al-Dawla: Al-Haraka al-Wataniyya al-Filastiniyya, 1949–1993* [Armed Struggle and the Search for a State], 133.

147. Sayigh, *Al-Kifah al-Muslah wa al-Bahath 'An al-Dawla: Al-Haraka al-Wataniyya al-Filastiniyya, 1949–1993* [Armed Struggle and the Search for a State], 138.

148. On this see al-Kubaysi, *Harakat al-Qawmiyun al-'Arab* [Movement of the Arab Nationalists], 105–106.

149. Hamza, *Abu Jihad Bidayatuhu wa Asbab Ightiyaluhu* [Abu Jihad], 165.

150. Fatah—a reverse acronym of *Harakat Tahrir Filastin*, which otherwise would form the acronym HTF (*hatff*), meaning "death" in Arabic.

151. Sayigh, *Al-Kifah al-Muslah wa al-Bahath 'An al-Dawla: Al-Haraka al-Wataniyya al-Filastiniyya, 1949–1993* [Armed Struggle and the Search for a State], 149.

152. Sayigh, *Al-Kifah al-Muslah wa al-Bahath 'An al-Dawla: Al-Haraka al-Wataniyya al-Filastiniyya, 1949–1993* [Armed Struggle and the Search for a State], 149.

153. Hamza, *Abu Jihad Bidayatuhu wa Asbab Ightiyaluhu* [Abu Jihad], 179.

154. Khalaf, *Filastini Bila Hawiyya* [Palestinian with No Homeland], 61.

155. Khalaf, *Filastini Bila Hawiyya* [Palestinian with No Homeland], 70–71.

156. Abu 'Amru, *Usul al-Haraka al-Siyasiyya fi Qita' Ghazza, 1948–1967* [Foundations of the Political Movements in the Gaza Strip], 93.

157. *The Palestinian Encyclopedia*, vol. 2 (Damascus, 1984), 204.

158. *The Palestinian Encyclopedia*, 205.

159. Abu 'Amru, *Usul al-Haraka al-Siyasiyya fi Qita' Ghazza, 1948–1967* [Foundations of the Political Movements in the Gaza Strip], 94–95.

160. Hani al-Qaddumi was born in the village of Kadum in the Tulkarm District, a wealthy man whose part in the Kuwait cell was aimed at funding the branch's activities.

Kamal 'Idwan (1935–1973) was born in the village of Barbara in the Gaza District. After 1948 he became a refugee in the Gaza camps. In 1961 he joined Fatah and filled senior positions in the organization until appointed in charge of operations in Israeli territory, the West Bank, and the Gaza Strip. He was killed on April 10, 1973, in Operation "Aviv Ne'urim" (Spring of Youth), an Israeli operation targeting senior figures in the PLO.

Rafiq al-Natsha (b. 1934) was born in Hebron, one of the first to join the Fatah, served in senior roles in the movement, and was a member of the Central Committee and PLO representative in Saudi Arabia. In 1989 he was dismissed from the Central Committee due to his objection to the pragmatic attitude that had begun emerging within the PLO.

Mahmoud Abbas (Abu Mazen, b. 1933) was born in Safed, and in 1948 became a refugee and settled in Syria for a while. In the mid-1950s he began working at the Ministry of Education of Qatar and was one of those responsible for recruiting Palestinian teachers to this ministry. After joining Fatah he was a close confidant of Yasir Arafat. He filled important roles in the organization: member of the Fatah Central Committee and secretary of the organization, member of the PLO Central Committee, and member of the Palestinian National Council. Since the late 1970s he has been in charge of the Israel desk and in this capacity had a crucial role in promoting the Oslo Accords and signing the agreement with Israel. In 2003 he became the first Palestinian prime minister of the Palestinian Authority, but resigned after a short time due to disagreements with Chairman Yasir Arafat. After Arafat's death in November 2004 he was elected president of the Palestinian Authority.

Fathi Bal'awi was born in the village of Bal'a in the Tulkarm District. He was a graduate of the al-Azhar University in Cairo and from 1953 worked as a teacher in the Gaza Strip, where he resided. When in Egypt he took part in establishing the Palestinian Student Union in Egypt and was its first secretary. He was affiliated with the Muslim Brotherhood.

161. Abu 'Amru, *Usul al-Haraka al-Siyasiyya fi Qita' Ghazza, 1948–1967* [Foundations of the Political Movements in the Gaza Strip], 98.

162. Abu 'Amru, *Usul al-Haraka al-Siyasiyya fi Qita' Ghazza, 1948–1967* [Foundations of the Political Movements in the Gaza Strip], 98–100.

163. Sayigh, *Al-Kifah al-Muslah wa al-Bahath 'An al-Dawla: Al-Haraka al-Wataniyya al-Filastiniyya, 1949–1993* [Armed Struggle and the Search for a State], 149–150.

164. Hamza, *Abu Jihad Bidayatuhu wa Asbab Ightiyaluhu* [Abu Jihad], 188.

165. Hamza, *Abu Jihad Bidayatuhu wa Asbab Ightiyaluhu* [Abu Jihad], 190.

166. Hamza, *Abu Jihad Bidayatuhu wa Asbab Ightiyaluhu* [Abu Jihad], 188–189.

167. Hamza, *Abu Jihad Bidayatuhu wa Asbab Ightiyaluhu* [Abu Jihad], 192.

168. Fatah, *Fath: Min Muntalaqat al-'Amal al-Thawri* [The Fatah Movement], 35.
169. Al-Wazir, *Harakat Fath Tarikh al-Nash'ah* [Fatah Movement: The Beginning], 4.
170. Fatah, *Fath: Min Muntalaqat al-'Amal al-Thawri* [The Fatah Movement], 113.
171. Fatah, *Fath: Min Muntalaqat al-'Amal al-Thawri* [The Fatah Movement], 158.
172. Fatah, *Fath: Min Muntalaqat al-'Amal al-Thawri* [The Fatah Movement].
173. Fatah, *Fath: Min Muntalaqat al-'Amal al-Thawri* [The Fatah Movement].
174. Fatah, *Fath: Min Muntalaqat al-'Amal al-Thawri* [The Fatah Movement].
175. Sayigh, *Al-Kifah al-Muslah wa al-Bahath 'An al-Dawla: Al-Haraka al-Wataniyya al-Filastiniyya, 1949–1993* [Armed Struggle and the Search for a State], 176.
176. Samih Abu Kuwayk (b. 1940) was born in Lydda. As a student he belonged to the Ba'ath Party and then transferred to Fatah. He was a member of the Central Committee of Fatah and served as head of its Jordanian desk. Abu Kuwayk is an attorney by profession.
177. Sayigh, *Al-Kifah al-Muslah wa al-Bahath 'An al-Dawla: Al-Haraka al-Wataniyya al-Filastiniyya, 1949–1993* [Armed Struggle and the Search for a State], 176.
178. *Filastinuna* 40 (November 1964).
179. The United Arab Command was the joint headquarters of the armies of Arab states that shared a border with Israel.
180. Haykal, *Sanawat al-Ghalayan* [The Years of Boiling], 769. Cairo, 1987.
181. Interviews with some of the movement's activists, cited by Sayigh, *Al-Kifah al-Muslah wa al-Bahath 'An al-Dawla: Al-Haraka al-Wataniyya al-Filastiniyya, 1949–1993* [Armed Struggle and the Search for a State], 180.
182. Fu'ad Matar, *Hakim al-Thawra* [The Wise Man of the Revolution], 93.
183. Interviews with some of those active in these camps are cited by Sayigh, *Al-Kifah al-Muslah wa al-Bahath 'An al-Dawla: Al-Haraka al-Wataniyya al-Filastiniyya, 1949–1993* [Armed Struggle and the Search for a State], 183.
184. Interviews with movement activists are cited by Sayigh, *Al-Kifah al-Muslah wa al-Bahath 'An al-Dawla: Al-Haraka al-Wataniyya al-Filastiniyya, 1949–1993* [Armed Struggle and the Search for a State], 183.
185. On the movement's altercations with Fatah see *Al-Hadaf*, November 1, 1969.

186. Quoted by Sayigh, *Al-Kifah al-Muslah wa al-Bahath 'An al-Dawla: Al-Haraka al-Wataniyya al-Filastiniyya, 1949–1993* [Armed Struggle and the Search for a State], 188.

187. This tax was mainly symbolic. The sum requested was between five and ten Egyptian grush, and the authorities reported weak enforcement of the tax.

188. Sayigh, *Al-Kifah al-Muslah wa al-Bahath 'An al-Dula* [Armed Struggle and the Search for a State], 191.

189. Al-Wazir, *Harakat Fath Tarikh al-Nash'ah* [Fatah Movement: The Beginning], 162.

190. Fatah, *Muntalaqat al-'Amal al-Fida'i* [Beginning of the Fida'iyyun's Guerrilla Activity], 85.

191. Al-Hasan, *Awraq Siyasiyya* [Political Papers], 128–129.

192. Hamza, *Abu Jihad Bidayatuhu wa Asbab Ightiyaluhu* [Abu Jihad], 274.

193. Hamza, *Abu Jihad Bidayatuhu wa Asbab Ightiyaluhu* [Abu Jihad], 275–278. Khalaf, *Filastini Bila Hawiyya* [Palestinian with No Homeland], 79–80, n156.

6

In the Wake of the June 1967 Defeat

The strategy of armed struggle and the stages theory espoused by Palestinian organizations, particularly Fatah, were designed, as mentioned, to lead Arab governments into an all-out war against Israel. Khaled al-Hasan, one of Fatah's founding fathers, concluded, "We subscribed to the 'deliberate entanglement' of Arab armies in the war in confidence that they were in possession of the necessary forces—particularly the Egyptian army, which had a strike force incorporating al-Zafir and al-Qahir missiles."[1] Indeed, it was not only Fatah that endeavored to entangle the Arab governments in a direct conflict; the head of the PLO at the time, Ahmad al-Shuqayri, also did so in contravention of the wishes of his Egyptian patrons. He operated in collaboration with the Arab Nationalists and sought to attach their military branch to the Palestine Liberation Army forces whom he was attempting to prepare for battle. These contacts were formed in Damascus, far from the spying eyes in Cairo, from about two months before the war broke out. The resulting military organization, called Heroes of the Return, was commanded by Rashed al-Madani and Subhi al-Tamimi. 'Abd al-Razzaq al-Yahya, the most senior Palestinian officer in Syria, was in charge of coordination between the PLA and this new force.

Toward the War of June 1967

The Heroes of the Return embarked on their first operation on October 19, 1966. Four guerrilla fighters entered Israel through the Lebanese border and attacked an Israeli force. Three of the attackers were killed and the fourth was taken prisoner.[2] At the same time, Fatah continued its attempts at attacks through the Jordanian border, aimed at escalating the existing state of affairs and embarrassing the Jordanian government, which did its best to avoid such operations. Israel retaliated by raiding the village of al-Samo'a in the Hebron District, resulting in the death of dozens of citizens as well as twenty-one Jordanian soldiers and the demolishing of nearly 120 homes. Following the attack, angry demonstrations broke out in West Bank cities, demanding that the government provide the population with weapons. The Jordanian army firmly suppressed these demonstrations and arrested dozens of Fatah and PLO activists.[3]

Nonetheless, Palestinian organizations did not cease their efforts to embarrass the Jordanian government. Al-Shuqayri intensified his comments and declared that "the Palestinian army would enter Jordan with no consideration for Husayn's government."[4] However, al-Shuqayri's prestige among the younger Palestinian generation gradually declined in light of Fatah's active belligerence. Arafat's men carried out thirty-seven attacks against Israel in the first five months of 1967.

It is possible to discern three different Palestinian approaches in these months: Fatah sought to exacerbate the conflict between Israel and the Arab world in order to cause a wide-ranging regional conflict. The al-Qawmiyyoun al-'Arab Movement believed that Nasser himself would induce such a clash.[5] Only a small group within al-Qawmiyyoun, headed by Munzer 'Anabtawi and Salih Shibl, expressed concern regarding the balance of power and the possible outcome of a confrontation with Israel.[6] Yazid Sayigh summarized the effect of the military activities of Palestinian organizations on the eve of the War of June 1967:

> The Palestinian role in the stages leading up to the war was small, but not completely marginal. According to the Israeli version, Palestinian organizations performed 113 attacks against Israel

beginning from January 1965 (Fatah claimed that it alone performed 300), in which 11 Israelis were killed and 62 injured. The organizations themselves suffered seven casualties (three from friendly fire), and two men were detained during this period. These activities were not a real source of concern for Israel, but they undoubtedly heightened the prevalent sense of threat.[7]

Defeat of the Arab Armies and Rise of Fatah

The defeat of the Arab armies in the War of June 1967 will not be discussed here. From a Palestinian point of view, one of the results of the War of June 1967 held particular significance: the Naksa (Defeat) reunited the entire territory of historical Palestine under Israeli rule. From this point on, Arab world leaders concealed their real views on the conflict and renounced their insistence to return to the partition borders, replacing it with a demand to return to the borders of June 4, 1967. At the Arab League summit conference in Khartoum, Nasser empowered King Husayn to act to ensure the future of the West Bank, as well as that of the Gaza Strip, so long as he did not negotiate directly with Israel. Nasser explained his position and said that in the current circumstances the Arabs were incapable of resolving the conflict by means of force.

Ahmad al-Shuqayri, a Palestinian protégé of the Egyptian president, felt betrayed. In his speech at the conference he attacked Nasser: "No one, be he president, king, or even the PLO, can arrive at a separate resolution of the problems of the West Bank and the Gaza Strip."[8] Subsequently, the PLO and the other Palestinian organizations interpreted the position of the Arab governments as a withdrawal from their commitment to an all-out war against Israel and demanded an "immediate war of liberation." Al-Shuqayri found himself up against increasing opposition within the PLO, and in December 1967 he was forced to resign. His position as temporary chairman was occupied by attorney Yahya Hammuda, a former leader of the armed bands during the 1936–1939 revolt.

Al-Shuqayri's resignation marked a new chapter in the history of the Palestinian national movement. From this point on, the armed organizations began to assume control of PLO institutions and gradually became a dominant element. Sayigh summarized the significance of the change: "The defeat put an end to Palestinian trust in 'progressive' and 'nationalist' Arab governments and encouraged them to openly embrace their unique local nationalism."[9] Palestinian organizations gained prominence in popular consciousness, as Arab states were increasingly less capable of supervising events. As a result of the new state of affairs, the armed organizations managed to develop their bases of operation in Jordan, Syria, and Lebanon and to renew their actions against Israel in March 1968. Fatah increased its stature, particularly after the Battle of Karameh in Jordanian territory on March 21, during which Israeli forces suffered severe losses in a confrontation described by Fatah as "the greatest achievement since 1948" (see below). Arafat gained prominence as the commander of this battle, and in February 1969 the Palestinian National Council appointed him chairman of the PLO.

Fatah's new young leadership managed to invigorate the PLO, instigating a "honeymoon" with several Arab states. Egypt and Syria were busy redeveloping their armies and expressed interest in Palestinian guerrilla warfare as a means of distracting Arab public opinion and harassing Israel. PLO actions also complemented the attrition strategy initiated by Nasser on the banks of the Suez Canal. Iraq became involved as well, by providing armed Palestinian organizations with financial aid.

Fatah and "Guerrilla Warfare Among a Supportive Local Population"

Even before the War of June 1967, Palestinian intellectuals had called for a popular war of liberation modeled on the Vietnamese or Chinese experience; however, Nasserist Arab control of PLO systems and anticipation of a victory by regular Arab armies restricted the impact of their appeals. The June 1967 defeat led to a radical change. Palestinian organizations attempted to use the Naksa as a pretext for disengaging from Arab patronage. When the six-day fighting died down, senior Fatah leaders hurried to convene in Damascus. On June 12–13, 1967, Yasir Arafat, Salah Khalaf, Khalil al-Wazir, Mahmoud Abbas, Khaled al-Hasan, Kamal 'Idwan, and Farouq al-Qaddumi discussed the new circumstances that had been created. Two approaches emerged regarding the organization's possible courses of action. The minority, led by Mahmoud Abbas, advocated waiting until the situation became clearer. The majority, led by Arafat and Khalil al-Wazir, were inclined to promptly renew the armed struggle in the territory occupied by Israel. Although no agreement was reached, Arafat took the initiative. Escorted by a small group, he entered the northern West Bank via the Jordanian border in the area of Jenin-Tulkarm, and Fatah announced that the leadership had moved its military headquarters to the occupied territories.[10] However, Arafat's attempts to replicate the 1936–1939 revolt and construct a stronghold in the mountainous regions of Tulkarm and Ramallah did not prove successful. Arafat barely escaped capture by Israeli security forces, and he returned to Damascus.

The senior leadership met once again, only to be faced with more dissension. Some of the leaders, mainly Khaled al-Hasan and Salah Khalaf, were concerned that the local population would be penalized by Israel for any guerrilla organization operating in their midst. The majority, however, once again supported renewal of guerrilla warfare, both to raise morale and out of fear that Egypt and Jordan might sign peace treaties with Israel and reassume control of the territories. Thus, a decision was made to reorganize the guerrilla forces and establish an information system and a broadcasting station.[11] Arafat was authorized to erect bases of operation in the occupied territories, and his opponents had no choice but to accept his authority.[12] For a short while, it seemed that Syrian leaders would support Arafat and his doctrine. They permitted him to enter the Israeli-controlled Golan Heights from Syria together with his men and to bring back weapons hidden by the Syrian army upon their retreat. The sides reached an understanding that Fatah be permitted to retain the light weapons, while returning the heavy weapons to Syria. However, in a matter of weeks, the Syrian authorities had collected even the light weapons from Fatah.[13] Damascus did not change its policy, and continued to forbid any armed operations against Israel across the Syrian border. In his meeting with Farouq al-Qaddumi and Khalil al-Wazir, Syrian president Nur al-Din al-Atasi left no room for doubt: "If you continue to instigate operations via the Golan we will be forced to put an end to these activities."[14] Under Syrian pressure, Fatah began transferring its bases to Jordan.

In late July 1967, Arafat left again for the West Bank, where he reiterated his message concerning a "popular war of liberation" that would evolve into classic guerrilla warfare.[15] Initial signs of civil resistance, in the form of demonstrations and protest marches, did indeed appear in the territories, and the organization was inundated with youngsters seeking to enlist. Arafat assumed the title of general commander (*al-qa'id al-'aam*) and once again operated from a base located between Nablus and Tulkarm. He wished to begin operations in early August 1967, but the Fatah leadership was in favor of waiting for early September, while al-Qawmiyyoun favored waiting for December.[16] Arafat and al-Wazir held talks with al-Qawmiyyoun, which again resulted in disagreements concerning the appropriate timing for commencing armed operations, and once again Arafat forced a decision by taking matters into his own hands. On August 28, 1967, three days before the summit convention in Khartoum, a Fatah band attacked an Israeli patrol in the Gaza Strip. According to Khalil al-Wazir, this was a message to Arab leaders to choose armed struggle against Israel over negotiations.[17]

Aside from this operation, little more was done, and the outburst of violent acts that Arafat had been expecting, heralding a guerrilla war, did not materialize. Israel's acts of retaliation and the reluctance of the civilian population undermined the concept of "guerrilla warfare among a supportive local population," and Arafat was forced to leave the territories, return to Jordan, and manage the organization's activities from afar. Thus, the Gaza-based Fida'iyyun model of combat operations under the auspices of an Arab country prevailed over the independent guerrilla warfare model of the 1936–1939 revolt. All hopes of establishing some sort of Palestinian entity that would fight Israel while remaining free of Arab political supervision now faded, and Fatah was forced to reshape its plans in accordance with pan-Arab politics.

Fatah and Guerrilla Warfare Replace Arab Armies

In order to meet the challenge of leading the struggle against Israel in place of the Arab armies that had failed, Fatah, under Arafat's command, initiated activities on three levels: recruitment, training, and weapons. The organization's ranks further swelled with the addition of some eight thousand young Palestinians and Arabs who felt let down by the alternatives. Nearly four hundred Arab volunteers from Europe were sent to training camps in Algeria to learn about guerrilla warfare from graduates of the National Liberation Front. Thousands of young people from the Gaza Strip and the West Bank thronged to

Syria to train at the al-Hama Camp near Damascus. Thirty-two Fatah members were sent to the People's Republic of China, where they took part in a five-month officers' course and returned to establish the first operations bases in Jordan. This group was headed by Hani al-Hasan and Mamduh Saydam, and also included Naser Yusuf, Haj Isma'il Jaber, Ha'il 'Abd al-Hamid, Musa Arafat, and al-Tayyib 'Abd al-Rahim, who would later hold key positions in Fatah. In addition to weapons recovered from hiding places in the Golan, four hundred rifles were sent from the People's Republic of China, and the government of Iraq provided weapons from the reserves of its remaining army units in Jordan.[18]

With its newly trained and armed guerrillas, Fatah began a "nesting operation" (*'amaliyyat al-ta'shish*), which included the gradual insertion of bands of ten to fifteen guerrilla fighters into the West Bank and the Gaza Strip. These fighters were carefully merged with the local population, prepared hideouts and escape routes, and waited for orders. In the second half of 1967 there were already a few dozen such units in the Nablus-Jenin-Tulkarm area, and about 150 fighters in the Hebron hills.[19] At this stage, Arafat organized three regional headquarters (again, according to the model of 1936–1939) in the north, center, and south. All were headed by "graduates" of the Algerian and Chinese training camps and the "strike forces" trained in Syria. The plan was for the headquarters also to serve as a type of local government in areas to be liberated once the Israeli authorities were forced out. These governments would then supposedly join forces and form the continuous territory of the Palestinian state. Khalil al-Wazir explained the process:

> We have begun to organize residents and popular groups from all social and religious sectors. We meant to begin by organizing passive resistance, and then move on to active, armed resistance. The passive resistance has been very successful and manifested itself in strikes by merchants, officials, and transportation workers. It included school strikes and the rejection of educational curricula forced upon our people by the authorities of the occupation. Armed resistance has commenced with the operations initiated on August 27, 1967. These operations are being carried out as planned.[20]

However, the plan instigated by Fatah did not materialize. Its outcome was summarized by Sayigh: "Even under optimal conditions such a pretense had no chance. Lack of organization, carelessness in matters of security, Israel's strict responses, and poor civilian involvement, all served to ensure its inevitable failure."[21]

Arafat's strong desire to initiate comprehensive operations led to rapid recruitment of a large number of guerrilla fighters at the expense of quality and training. Information regarding organization of the forces was transmitted carelessly and soon reached the ears of Israeli authorities. This negligence was supplemented by a variety of informants. Israel responded efficiently and decisively: it established two systems of military government in the West Bank and the Gaza Strip, in charge of about 250 officers who served as military governors in Palestinian villages and cities. All banking and commercial activity was stopped for a while and emergency means were employed against any display of resistance. These included arrests, curfews, the demolishing of houses, movement restriction, confiscation of trade licenses, and orders of deportation to Jordan. Israeli intelligence networks utilized Palestinian informants as well as patrols and information-gathering units. From September to December 1967, Israel arrested nearly three hundred Fatah members and abettors in the West Bank.[22]

Al-Qawmiyyoun al-'Arab: From Arab Nationalism to a Marxist Front

Al-Qawmiyyoun was in a state of shock as a result of the June defeat, similar to all Palestinian movements at the time and maybe even more so, as it had strong connections to Nasser's regime and found it hard to cope with the blow. The movement's journal, *al-Huriyya*, ceased appearing for two weeks, and upon resuming publication explained in its headline that "the Arabs had been defeated not by Israel, rather in a comprehensive war with America."[23] The Jordanian branch of the movement was almost completely wiped out. Those of its members who had not been arrested or left in desperation traveled to Beirut to discuss the new situation with the movement's leadership. At the conclusion of feverish discussions, the leadership published a document in late July 1967, in which it stated that "the basic mistake of the Arab revolutionary movement" was that "nationalist and progressive Arab parties and governments had not designed, to begin with, a clear and constant strategy for confronting the new imperialism, a strategy for coping with a general, consistent, and lengthy conflict."²⁴ In this spirit they now expected "another round" planned by Nasser in the form of a war of attrition, while meticulously constructing a new Egyptian army.²⁵

This approach by the veteran leadership no longer received the approval of the younger generation, who had recently developed revolutionary left-wing views, spoke of a popular war of liberation and a guerrilla war, and doubted Nasser's ability to withstand a second round of fighting. Similar to Fatah, they too had despaired of a regular war waged by Arab armies and now turned to the concept of a "popular war of liberation." These new intergenerational tensions hampered the Jordanian branch's attempts at rehabilitation and the leadership decided to focus on rejuvenating the West Bank and the Gaza Strip. Ahmad Khalifa, a veteran al-Qawmiyyoun activist who had entered the West Bank clandestinely, was charged with this task. On October 13, 1967, Khalifa announced the establishment of five bands, organized by Mustafa al-Zibri (better known as Abu 'Ali Mustafa al-Zibri), and the beginning of an "armed revolution for the liberation of Palestine."²⁶

Al-Qawmiyyoun's declaration marked the beginning of a competition with Fatah over military domination. The journal *al-Huriyya* called for unification of the movement with other ideologically affiliated organizations. Contact was made with Heroes of the Return (Abtal al-'Awdah), Ahmad Jibril's Palestinian Liberation Front, and a group of Palestinian Nasserists headed by Ahmad Za'rur, who remained loyal to the Egyptian government. On December 11, 1967, all these organizations announced the establishment of the Popular Front for the Liberation of Palestine (al-Jabha al-Sha'biyya Litahrir Filastin, the PFLP). However the celebratory announcement was meaningless for the bands in the West Bank and Gaza Strip, as their commanders were captured one after another by Israeli security forces. Faisal al-Husayni was arrested first, followed by his assistant, 'Abd Allah al-'Ajrami, as well as Ahmad Khalifa, together with dozens of guerrilla fighters. In early 1968, Fatah's failure to establish itself in the occupied territories was matched by a similar failure by the PFLP. It too was now compelled to run its activities from neighboring Arab countries.

The relationship of the PFLP with the various Arab governments was the main reason for the splits that have marred its record ever since. The first split occurred in April 1968, when Ahmad Jibril left to establish the Popular Front for the Liberation of Palestine–General Command (PFLP-GC), a movement with Islamic leanings to the right of George Habash. The first suicide bombers (*istishhadiyyun*, in the organization's terminology) operating against Israel originated from this movement.[27] This latter organization was the source of another split in July 1977, led by Mahmoud 'Abbas (Abu al-'Abbas, 1948–2003), and resulting in the Palestine Liberation Front, which professed pro-Iraqi and anti-Syrian views. The second split within the PFLP occurred in February 1969 when Nayif Hawatmeh announced his resignation and the establishment of the Popular Democratic Front for the Liberation of Palestine (PDFLP; later known simply as the DFLP). Hawatmeh, formerly a Nasserist Arab nationalist, was now positioned to the left of George Habash and embraced a Leninist orientation, advocating that all Arab governments are reactionary and must be overthrown. His was the only Palestinian organization that tried to establish cooperatives similar to the Soviet kolkhoz, in the northern Jordan Valley.

The Communists and the Armed Conflict

Unlike other parties and political groups that operated in the West Bank and the Gaza Strip, the communists initially objected to the idea of armed conflict. They explained that it was more important to focus on halting the stream of refugees heading for Jordan in a manner reminiscent of the Nakba of 1948.[28] According to data published in the Israeli newspaper the *Jerusalem Post*, about five thousand people a day crossed over to Jordan in June 1967; in mid-July they numbered five hundred, and in August about three hundred a day.[29] The Jordanian Communist Party, represented by Assistant Secretary-General Fahmi al-Salfiti, objected to independent Palestinian action and called for unification of the West and East Banks under Jordanian rule, while waiting for the military recovery of "Arab states that aim to erase all sign of Israeli aggression."[30]

Once the flow of refugees to the East Bank ceased, communist leaders in the West Bank changed their minds. In December 1967 their journal, *al-Muqawama al-Sha'biyya* (Resistance), declared that the military solution is "an inevitable solution" as long as the Palestinians coordinate their actions with the Arab states.[31] This transition to a belligerent outlook was a result of the propaganda disseminated by Fatah and the other organizations as well as the Egyptian declarations regarding rehabilitation of their armed forces. *Al-Muqawama* also took this opportunity to announce the reunification of the party's branches in the East and West Banks. The shift was also a consequence of communist resentment of Israel's security forces. A significant number of communists in the territories found themselves under arrest, together with Fatah and PFLP members, and they could not remain skeptical of the concept of resistance. Even so, the months of self-restraint enforced by the Jordanian branch proved detrimental to the party's prestige among the Palestinian public.

The Palestine Liberation Army and Revival of the Fida'iyyun

The Palestine Liberation Army was, as mentioned, a regular force established by the PLO, under the auspices of Egypt and Syria. On the eve of the War of June 1967, the 'Ayn Jalut Division in the Gaza Strip numbered five thousand troops and the three companies of the Popular Resistance Committees (PLC) numbered nearly thirteen hundred men.[32] The Hittin Division (about fifteen hundred troops) was under Syrian command.[33] However, neither Egypt nor Syria attributed military significance to these forces or specified their actual role in the preparations for war. The Palestine Liberation Army lost 122 soldiers in its defense of the Gaza Strip.[34] The Hittin Division was sent to the Golan Heights, but took almost no part in the fighting. It was used for rear-guard duties and for the construction of military posts. A few of its men crossed over to Jordan during the fighting, fording the Jordan River near Jericho under protection of the Jordanian army. Israeli Air Force planes attacked the force, which suffered major losses. Upon occupation of the West Bank, most of the Liberation Army soldiers, numbering nearly six thousand men, were apprehended by Israel. Of these, one thousand, probably those connected to the Fida'iyyun, were detained in 'Atlit, and the rest were deported to Egypt.[35]

After the war, attempts were made to rehabilitate the Palestine Liberation Army: an agreement between Ahmad al-Shuqayri and Muhammad Fawzi, the new general commander of the Egyptian army, led to the establishment of the Palestinian Storm Units (Wahadat al-Sa'iqa al-Filastiniyya), consisting of about two thousand fighters, who were stationed around the Great Bitter Lake in the Suez Canal, under strict restrictions imposed by Egypt. This arrangement increased the PLO leader's frustration with the Egyptian authorities, who were reluctant to provide him with assistance despite Fatah's rising prestige. Al-Shuqayri then appealed to the Syrian authorities through the commander of the Liberation Army in Syria, 'Abd al-Razzaq al-Yahya, and asked that his men be permitted to infiltrate the Israeli border from Syria. When this request was emphatically denied, al-Shuqayri chose to operate within the territories. However, his man in Gaza, Qusay al-'Abdallah, former head of the PLO military committee, was hounded by the Israeli government and forced to flee the West Bank three months after his appointment.[36] Al-Shuqayri declared the establishment of the Fida'iyyun Company of the Liberation Army, intended to operate in the occupied territories, under the command of Bahjat 'Abd al-Amin and the supervision of Liberation Army Commander Wajih al-Madani and its head of intelligence, Fayiz al-Turk. This company collaborated in the field with a small group called the Palestine Liberation Front–Way of Return, headed by Shafiq al-Hout and Ahmad al-Sa'adi. The inner core thus formed was designed to lead to an extensive course of action: according to the strategic plan created by the PLA command and al-Shuqayri, ten senior Liberation Army officers were supposed to establish clandestine headquarters in the Gaza Strip and the West Bank, which would assume control of the armed struggle and command it.[37]

Al-Shuqayri's declaration proved meaningless. The plan could not be implemented due to the efficiency of Israeli intelligence and because of al-Shuqayri's own conduct. He seemed to be interested mainly in preserving his status as head of the PLO and did not hesitate to make empty statements depicting outstanding but fabricated successes. For example, in mid-1967, he declared that "the *feda'i* activities of the armed struggle are gradually taking the form of an armed popular revolt and are on the way to becoming a popular war of independence. For this purpose I am ready to merge the PLO's efforts within a wider united Arab army."[38] At the height of his empty boasts, on December 9, 1967, following a clandestine conference that supposedly met in Jerusalem, he declared the establishment of the Command Council of the Revolution for the Liberation of Palestine, which would control all military activity of Palestinian organizations operating in the territories. Such fictional declarations only served to arouse the ire of the other organizations, particularly Fatah, which reacted strongly and published an announcement accusing al-Shuqayri of disseminating lies endangering the resistance. Fatah sent a letter in a similar spirit to the Arab League Council with a demand to recall al-Shuqayri. When al-Shuqayri tried to respond in kind by suspending Fatah supporters on the PLO executive committee, he encountered strong opposition and was eventually forced to resign on December 24, 1967.

Fatah Assumes Control of the PLO

Encouraged by the dismissal of Ahmad al-Shuqayri, Fatah invited eleven Palestinian military organizations to take part in a convention in Cairo in mid-January 1968. The convention lasted four days, attended by representatives of five organizations, and it recognized Fatah as the leading element of Palestinian armed resistance.[39] No less important was Gamal Abdel Nasser's recognition of Fatah, whose activity he considered significant as it served to occupy Israel while Nasser attempted to rebuild the Egyptian army. Muhammad Fawzi, general commander of the Egyptian forces after the War of June 1967, wrote, "The activities of the Palestinian organizations held importance for us. Our forces were at a low point, particularly the Air Force. We were in need of action on the Syrian and Jordanian fronts in order to distract the Israeli army and force it to transfer some of its forces to other places while we rebuilt our strength."[40] General Muhammad Ahmad Sadeq, head of military intelligence, was in charge of Egypt's contacts with the Palestinian organizations. He commissioned a Palestinian officer, Ibrahim al-Dakhakhni, to coordinate Egypt's acts of logistic aid to Fatah. In August 1967 the Egyptian army agreed to include fifty Fatah fighters in its Commando Officers' Course.[41] Egyptian transport planes transferred weapons and Palestinian fighters trained in Cairo to Jordan and Syria. The 141st Fida'iyyun Company was reorganized and operated behind the lines in Sinai, in Israeli-controlled territory.[42]

Nonetheless, the Egyptian authorities had limited intentions. They did not intend to let Fatah implicate them in an all-out war, and in fact they did not act to further the liberation of Palestine by means of the same guerrilla warfare they promoted. Muhammad Hasanin Haykal, editor of *Al-Ahram* and confidant of Nasser, wrote, "The guerrilla war and the popular liberation war cannot assume a critical role in the struggle taking place in Israel. The Palestinian struggle for independence bears no resemblance to the Algerian struggle."[43] Indeed, Fatah's wish in early 1968 to transfer most of its operational bases to the territories was only partially successful. Those who spoke on behalf of the organization declared that they had succeeded in recruiting thousands of fellahin and students and that they were executing dozens of operations a day, but in reality the state of affairs was fairly depressing from their perspective.[44] In February 1968 Israeli forces arrested 115 Fatah members in the West Bank and the Gaza Strip, killed thirty-five infiltrators, and stopped another ten on the border. Thus Israel neutralized nearly the entire group of two hundred fighters who by Fatah accounts had entered the country in January.

Notes

1. Interview with Khaled al-Hassan, quoted in Sayigh, *Al-Kifah al-Muslah wa al-Bahath 'An al-Dawla: Al-Haraka al-Wataniyya al-Filastiniyya, 1949–1993* [Armed Struggle and the Search for a State], 243.

2. *Al-Huriyya*, October 31, 1966.

3. Sayigh, *Al-Kifah al-Muslah wa al-Bahath 'An al-Dawla: Al-Haraka al-Wataniyya al-Filastiniyya, 1949–1993* [Armed Struggle and the Search for a State], 220.

4. Center for Palestinian Research, *Al-Kitab al-Sanawi Lilqadiyya al-Filastiniyya 1966* [Yearbook of the Palestinian Problem for 1966], 91.

5. *Al-Huriyya*, January 30, 1967.

6. *Al-Huriyya*, May 15, 1967.

7. Sayigh, *Al-Kifah al-Muslah wa al-Bahath 'An al-Dawla: Al-Haraka al-Wataniyya al-Filastiniyya, 1949–1993* [Armed Struggle and the Search for a State], 224–225.

8. Sayigh, *Al-Kifah al-Muslah wa al-Bahath 'An al-Dawla: Al-Haraka al-Wataniyya al-Filastiniyya, 1949–1993* [Armed Struggle and the Search for a State], 90.

9. Sayigh, *Al-Kifah al-Muslah wa al-Bahath 'An al-Dawla: Al-Haraka al-Wataniyya al-Filastiniyya, 1949–1993* [Armed Struggle and the Search for a State], 234.

10. Research Center of the Arab League, *Al-Watha'iq al-'Arabiyya al-Filastiniyya Lil'am 1968* [The Arab-Palestinian Documents for 1968], 54–56.

11. Al-Wazir, *Harakat Fath Tarikh al-Nash'ah* [Fatah Movement], 106–110.

12. Mahmoud Abbas, *Thawrat al-Mustahil: al-kitaba al-Mustahila* [Impossible Revolution: The Impossible Writing], 20.

13. Sayigh, *Al-Kifah al-Muslah wa al-Bahath 'An al-Dawla: Al-Haraka al-Wataniyya al-Filastiniyya, 1949–1993* [Armed Struggle and the Search for a State], 245.

14. Sayigh, *Al-Kifah al-Muslah wa al-Bahath 'An al-Dawla: Al-Haraka al-Wataniyya al-Filastiniyya, 1949–1993* [Armed Struggle and the Search for a State], 248.

15. Al-Wazir, *Harakat Fath Tarikh al-Nash'ah* [Fatah Movement], 106–110.

16. Sayigh, *Al-Kifah al-Muslah wa al-Bahath 'An al-Dawla: Al-Haraka al-Wataniyya al-Filastiniyya, 1949–1993* [Armed Struggle and the Search for a State], 247.

17. Hamza, *Abu Jihad Bidayatuhu wa Asbab Ightiyaluhu* [Abu Jihad], 343.

18. Al-Wazir, *Harakat Fath Tarikh al-Nash'ah* [Fatah Movement], 82.

19. Sayigh, *Al-Kifah al-Muslah wa al-Bahath 'An al-Dawla: Al-Haraka al-Wataniyya al-Filastiniyya, 1949–1993* [Armed Struggle and the Search for a State], 253.

20. *Al-Mujahid* (Algeria), December 17, 1967, quoted by Hamza, *Abu Jihad Bidayatuhu wa Asbab Ightiyaluhu* [Abu Jihad], 345.

21. *Al-Mujahid* (Algeria), December 17, 1967, quoted by Hamza, *Abu Jihad Bidayatuhu wa Asbab Ightiyaluhu* [Abu Jihad], 345.

22. Hamza, *Abu Jihad Bidayatuhu wa Asbab Ightiyaluhu* [Abu Jihad], 254.

23. *Al-Huriyya*, June 19, 1967.

24. Harakat al-Qawmiyyin al-'Arab [Movement of the Arab Nationalists], "Ba'd al-isti'mar al-Suhyuni: al-thawra al-'Arabiyya amam ma'rakat al-masir" [After the Zionist Colonialism, the Arab Revolution versus the Campaign of Fate], political report published by the expanded gathering of the national executive committee of the Arab Nationalist Movement from late July 1967 (Beirut), p. 14.

25. Muhsen Ibrahim is quoted in Sayigh, *Al-Kifah al-Muslah wa al-Bahath 'An al-Dawla: Al-Haraka al-Wataniyya al-Filastiniyya, 1949–1993* [Armed Struggle and the Search for a State], 250.

26. Center for Palestinian Research, *Al-Kitab al-Sanwi Lilqadiyya al-Filastiniyya Lisnat 1967* [Yearbook of the Palestinian Problem for 1967], 153.

27. Bechor, *Lexicon Ashaf* [Lexicon of the PLO], 129.

28. The refugees of 1967 were called *nazhun*, "displaced."

29. *Jerusalem Post*, June 16, July 11, and August 22, 1967.

30. Sayigh, *Al-Kifah al-Muslah wa al-Bahath 'An al-Dawla: Al-Haraka al-Wataniyya al-Filastiniyya, 1949–1993* [Armed Struggle and the Search for a State], 260.

31. Yasin, *Tajribat al-Jabha al-Wataniyya fi Qita' Ghazza* [Experience of the National Front in the Gaza Strip], 21–30.

32. 'Ayn Jalut was named for the place at which Mameluke Sultan Baybars defeated the Mongols in 1260.

33. Hittin is named for the place (near Tiberias) where Salah al-Din defeated the Crusaders in 1187.

34. Sayigh, *Al-Kifah al-Muslah wa al-Bahath 'An al-Dawla: Al-Haraka al-Wataniyya al-Filastiniyya, 1949–1993* [Armed Struggle and the Search for a State], 262.

35. *Ha'aretz*, April 30, 1968.

36. Sayigh, *Al-Kifah al-Muslah wa al-Bahath 'An al-Dawla: Al-Haraka al-Wataniyya al-Filastiniyya, 1949–1993* [Armed Struggle and the Search for a State], 264.

37. Sayigh, *Al-Kifah al-Muslah wa al-Bahath 'An al-Dawla: Al-Haraka al-Wataniyya al-Filastiniyya, 1949–1993* [Armed Struggle and the Search for a State], 265.

38. *Al-Muharir*, October 14, 1967.

39. The other organizations that attended, aside from Fatah, were the Palestine Popular Liberation Front; Pioneers of the Popular War of Liberation (both affiliated with the Ba'ath Party in Syria); the Sacrificing Pioneers Organization, headed by Subhi Yasin; and the Arab Institution for Support of the Palestinian Revolt, headed by 'Isam Sartawi. It was also attended by representatives of the Liberation Army and of other short-lived organizations.

40. Fawzi, *Harb al-Thalath Sanawat* [Three-Year War], 190–195.

41. Sayigh, *Al-Kifah al-Muslah wa al-Bahath 'An al-Dawla: Al-Haraka al-Wataniyya al-Filastiniyya, 1949–1993* [Armed Struggle and the Search for a State], 271.

42. Al-Kitri, *Halaqa Mafqudah min Kifah al-Sha b al-Filastini: Al-Katiba 141, Fida'iyyun* [Lost Sphere in the Struggle of the Palestinian People: Regiment 141, Fida'iyyun], 59–60, n125.

43. *Al-Ahram*, January 19, 1968.

44. Research Center of the Arab League, *Al-Watha'aq al-'Arabiyya al-Filastiniyya Lil'am 1968* [Arab-Palestinian Documents for 1968], 56.

7

The Confrontation with Jordan

Following the failed attempt to develop a local supportive foundation for guerrilla activities in the occupied territories, Jordan served for two years as operations base of the Palestinian organizations. The weak regime and the presence of a sympathetic Palestinian population seemed to ensure success. Jordan's extensive border with Israel and the Jordanian army's inability to prevent infiltrations added to this assurance. Many Jordanian soldiers identified with the organizations and at times collaborated with them. In the first quarter of 1968 the number of Palestinian fighters in the Jordan Valley reached one thousand: five hundred Fatah men, three hundred men from the various factions of the PFLP, and the rest from a variety of small organizations.

At first the Jordanian authorities hesitated to confront the Palestinian organizations; however, events left them no choice. On February 15, 1968, an Israeli force, chasing Palestinian fighters, clashed with a Jordanian force encamped near the village of Karameh, the largest Palestinian base. The Jordanian army blamed the Palestinians for its losses, surrounded Karameh, and demanded that all fighters surrender their weapons. Only with the intervention of local dignitaries was bloodshed avoided, and the Palestinians promised to operate henceforth only in coordination with the military authorities. King Husayn himself clarified: "Any dedicated and superb action originating from our country must receive our consent and be executed as part of our preparations and plans. From this day on, all who ignore this will not be included among our ranks, and their views are not our views."[1] The minister of the interior was more explicit: "Anyone who causes Jordan to become a target of enemy attacks will not be allowed to leave the country."[2]

Karameh Day

Despite these warnings, the Palestinians increased their infiltrations and attacks in Israel, and on March 18, 1968, Israel reacted by gathering its forces in the Jordan Valley. The PLA guerrilla fighters based in Karameh, headed by Ahmad Za'rur, and those from the PFLP, headed by Ahmad Jibril, wished to retreat from the base, but Fatah insisted on *sumud* (steadfast perseverance).[3] In response to attempts by the Jordanian army commander to convince Arafat to withdraw his forces from Karameh, Arafat declared, "We wish to impress upon the world that there are those in the Arab nation who do not retreat and do not flee. We wish to die under the tank tracks and to change the course of history."[4] About 250 armed men from Fatah and eighty infantrymen from the Popular Liberation Front participated in the battle. If not for the support of the First Jordanian Infantry Regiment and its light tank cannons, which took up positions on the hills surrounding the town, the fighters would have had no chance of withstanding the Israeli force that crossed the Jordan on March 21, 1968. The Israelis took control of Karameh, destroyed it systematically, and retreated several hours later, not without heavy losses to both men and equipment.[5] On the Jordanian side there were 61 fatalities and 108 injured.[6] The Palestinians sustained 116 dead, 100 injured, and an estimated 40–66 were taken prisoner.[7]

Israel's operation at Karameh prevented the formation of a Fatah command and organization base in the vicinity of its borders, but it did not succeed in blocking continued Fatah operations, or the creation of the Karameh Day myth. Fatah leaders and King Husayn invited journalists to the battlefield and were photographed with destroyed and abandoned equipment left by the Israelis. Palestinian opinion shapers noted time and again that Karameh means honor in Arabic, and that this day marked the beginning of the process of reinstating Arab honor, violated in June 1967. Fatah's image as the organization responsible for redeeming Arab honor was revitalized, giving it a supposed advantage over the Jordanian establishment and its army. King Husayn's declaration at Karameh, attempting to establish himself as the "first *fida'i*" while standing next to a burned Israeli tank, was of no avail. Members of the organization proceeded to openly display their weapons and freely roamed Amman, basking in the population's admiration, to the chagrin of the king and the administration.

Fatah enjoyed a place of honor among inter-Arab political circles as well. Its leaders were received in Nasser's offices (through the mediation of journalist Muhammad Hasanin Haykal) and their group photograph was displayed throughout the Arab world. The doors of Arab leaders everywhere were now open to Fatah. The most significant support was that of King Faisal of Saudi Arabia. He gave an audience to Khalil al-Wazir and Salah Khalaf and promised them financial assistance. Nasser announced his intention to begin the second part of his military plan, a transition from defense to deterrence, or from "preventive defense" to "active defense." In this context, Fatah fighters were perceived as an important component of the "eastern front," which Nasser planned to instigate on the borders of Syria, Lebanon, and Jordan, among other actions, as a distraction that would help divert attention from further expansion of his armed forces.

Deterioration of the Relationship with Jordan

Fatah forces in Jordan became overly confident and could be seen promenading and traveling around Jordanian cities adorned with their weapons, despite government directives to avoid traveling in conspicuous military vehicles. They also established recruitment offices, blatantly ignoring all government attempts to restrain them and to close the offices. A confrontation became inevitable. In early October 1968, the Jordanian police shot at a group of Palestinian students who sought to identify with the organization and with its refusal to accept the restrictions imposed by Jordan. The police arrested members of a student cell that called itself the Victory Regiments.[8] The army also attacked Fatah bases at the refugee camps of al-Husayn and al-

Wihdat in Amman, and at the Schneller camp in the city of al-Zarqa. A temporary calm was achieved following a personal appeal by Nasser, but only after thirty Palestinians had been killed.[9]

These events convinced Fatah leaders that the Hashemite regime had declared an all-out war against them. They took steps to arm the Palestinian population in the refugee camps and to establish a popular militia in their defense. The Jordanian authorities toughened their stance as well. King Husayn and his representatives demanded that the organizations notify them of any operations planned against Israel, avoid operating in the vicinity of the Port of Aqaba, and refrain from performing summary executions in Jordanian territory. In practice, the sides did not reach an understanding. The number of operations initiated by Fatah through the Jordanian border doubled in the three months following Karameh Day. In June 1968, 90 operations were recorded; the monthly average in 1969 was 203 operations, and in 1970 it was 231.[10] Israel's harsh retaliatory measures inflicted significant losses on Jordan. The Eastern Valley Canal irrigation project was destroyed, and about one hundred thousand people fled the Jordan Valley for more remote locations. The Port of Aqaba was bombed as well, after Palestinians targeted Eilat with missiles in April 1969.[11] The organizations themselves were also affected by the destruction wrought by Israel: 1,828 Palestinian fighters had been killed by the end of 1970, about two-thirds of the operating groups were paralyzed, and 4,500 combatants and auxiliary forces were arrested and held in Israeli prisons.[12]

In early 1970 the relationship between the Palestinian organizations and the Jordanian government approached its lowest point. The organizations bombed Israeli towns from Jordanian territory without requesting permission, as had been required. In addition, they constructed their own governmental system, erected barricades, performed searches and interrogated Jordanian officials and military personnel, and kidnapped many Jordanian civilians, trying and sentencing them. These actions caused their status among the Jordanian population to deteriorate, with a consequent blow to their image. The Jordanian government decided it was time to confront them.

Beginning of the Conflict

The alleged justification for the Jordanian counterattack was draft evasion by young Palestinians, who refused to enlist in the army on the grounds that they were members of Palestinian resistance organizations. Another reason cited by the government was that left-wing Palestinian organizations were inciting against the Hashemite kingdom and its legitimacy.

The first step was initiated in the summer of 1970, when Jordan's Ministry of Defense published a list of 43,397 security and criminal offenses committed by the organizations from 1968 to 1970.[13] The Jordanian authorities took vigorous measures to strengthen the loyalty of soldiers of Bedouin origin and to increase their identification with the king and the country. They disseminated propaganda depicting the organizations as endangering the kingdom, Arab tradition, and the values of Islam.[14] The king commanded his sympathizers to establish special security systems headed by his close confidants, the army, and intelligence chiefs.[15] Operatives of these organs made efforts to infiltrate the Palestinian organizations, recruit agents from within, and disseminate rumors detrimental to the leadership.[16] In addition, the regime established a militia named the Popular Army, under the direct command of King Husayn.[17]

All the precautionary measures taken by the organizations' leaders, as well as their efforts to become less conspicuous, were of no avail. Four days before the date of the Jordanian army's operation against the Palestinian organizations, set for February 15, 1970, the army attacked a Palestinian political conference in Amman. Thirteen Palestinians and seven Jordanians were killed in the confrontation. Attempts to mediate between the king and Arafat concluded in a *hudna*, a temporary calm, which was not supported by all of the organizations. The Popular Front for the Liberation of Palestine and most of the other factions objected. Leaders of the PFLP called for the prompt establishment of "popular councils everywhere."[18] George Habash declared the calm "a malicious trap" and announced the need for a "national and class struggle."[19] He and his associates in the PFLP now challenged the hegemony of Arafat and Fatah and demanded the establishment of a "progressive revolutionary national front" with equal representation of all organizations. They initiated provocations, apparently designed to lead Fatah and the PLO into a confrontation with Jordan with the aim of overthrowing the monarchy and taking control of the Palestinian leadership. Jordan reacted immediately by taking control of two PFLP bases in the Jordan Valley, an attack that resulted in fatalities. The Palestinian organizations responded by announcing their unification. A proclamation distributed on May 6 on behalf of the eleven Palestinian military organizations operating in Jordan stated, "All Arab lands bordering Israel are legitimate territory for the Palestinian struggle. The Palestinian resistance movement has a legitimate right to arm the Palestinians and all Arabs. . . . Any attempt to exclude Palestinian resistance from an Arab country is a betrayal of the goals of the Palestinian people and of the Arab nation."[20]

On June 7, 1970, in the aftermath of another bloody clash, Arafat and Husayn agreed on a new *hudna*, which also fell apart two days later. A PFLP force attacked two major hotels in Amman and took eighty-eight foreign citizens hostage. The Jordanian army retaliated by bombing a refugee camp that the PFLP and Fatah were using as a base, to which Fatah forces responded by bombing the royal palace in Amman. All restraint was abandoned and hundreds were killed. Order was reestablished on June 12, but the regime became increasingly irritated when Iraq and Egypt informed the king that they would not let him shut down the Palestinian revolution and its organizations.

Encouraged by the various organizations' show of unity under his leadership, Arafat established, side by side with the central committee of the PLO, an "emergency leadership," including George Habash, who was secretary-general of the PFLP; Nayif Hawatmeh, secretary-general of the DFLP; Dafi Jami'ani, secretary-general of al-Sa'iqa (a guerrilla force sponsored by the Syrian government); 'Isam Sartawi, secretary-general of the Institution Acting for the Liberation of Palestine; and PLO spokesman Kamal Nasser.

However, in late July 1970, these organizations encountered an unpleasant surprise. Their strongest ally, Gamal Abdel Nasser, who had supported their battle against the Jordanian government, announced his consent to an initiative of US Secretary of State William Rogers aimed at ending the Egyptian-Israeli war of attrition along the Suez Canal, a truce that was implemented on August 7, 1970. George Habash and Nayif Hawatmeh called for Nasser's resignation. Their broadcasting station, based in Cairo, called the Egyptian president a "traitor."[21] In one of their demonstrations, these organizations depicted the president of Egypt on a donkey. Consequently, 140 of their men were deported from Cairo, and Egypt informed the PLO that it would award the Jordanian army ten thousand rifles as an expression of its outrage.[22] Encouraged by this new and significant support, Husayn began purging his army of soldiers and officers of Palestinian descent who were suspected of having connections to the organizations. Jordanian intelligence services revealed schemes by radical left-wing organizations to overthrow the king and establish a revolutionary regime. These organizations openly advocated taking the offensive, since "Arab regimes are trying to realize plans of capitulation and it is therefore necessary to act quickly."[23] On August 31, after a skirmish involving light weapons, the Jordanian army bombarded the refugee camps in the jurisdiction of its capital, Amman. On September 2, Palestinian fighters attacked the king's entourage on its way to the international airport. Iraq announced that its forces in Jordan would intervene on behalf of the Palestinians if the regime were to provoke an escalation. The first week of clashes resulted in about 150 killed and 500 injured.[24]

On September 6, 1970, the PFLP hijacked three passenger airplanes in an attempt to thwart any possibility of negotiation between Israel and the Arab states. The hijackers, led by Wadi' Haddad and Mustafa al-Zibri, attacked airplanes belonging to Western airlines. A Pan American flight was brought down at the international airport in Cairo, emptied of passengers, and bombed on the runway; TWA and Swissair flights were brought down at Zarqa, deep in the desert of southern Jordan. Three days later the PFLP hijacked a BOAC plane and brought it down at the same site, which was surrounded by Jordanian soldiers.[25] After emptying it of passengers, the hijackers bombed the three planes on September 12, in front of television cameras that broadcast the sight to the entire world.

Arafat and his men hurriedly renounced the acts, announcing the suspension of the PFLP's membership on the central committee of the PLO and asking them to transfer the hostages to a safe place in Amman. However, Fatah quickly found itself drawn into a confrontation with Jordan. Its rivalry with the PFLP did not help its image as a party willing to compromise with the Hashemites or as accepting Husayn's arrogant approach.[26] They also seemed to be overly confident of their own force, as they bragged of having thirty-six thousand fighters "capable of turning Amman's night into day and day into night."[27] Farouq al-Qaddumi, for example, described King Husayn as a "paper tiger who can be overpowered in thirty minutes."[28]

The Arab Domain and the Black September Battles

Jordanian relations with the Palestinians continued to deteriorate. On September 16 the king established a military government headed by

Palestinian Muhammad Dawud al-'Abbasi and appointed those loyal to him to positions such as head of the joint forces and regional governors. Consequently, Fatah and the PLO leadership decided to take outright measures to overthrow the king and establish a "revolutionary national government." A state of emergency was declared in Jordan; military units launched a frontal attack against Palestinian strongholds, and Palestinian forces were commanded to relinquish their weapons.[29]

In the attack that commenced the day the military government was founded, the superiority of Jordanian military manpower and weapons was obvious. About thirty-five thousand soldiers were amassed in the Amman–al-Zarqa area, and their numbers rose throughout the fighting, almost doubling by the end of the month.[30] Confronting this force, which was equipped with heavy weaponry, the Palestinians managed to gather between fifteen thousand and twenty thousand fighters, about half from Fatah and the rest from the PFLP, the Democratic Front, the Democratic Front–General Command, al-Sa'iqa, and the PLA.[31] The Palestinian forces had heavy weaponry as well but these were inferior, both in terms of quantity and quality, to those available to the Jordanian army.[32] The organizations lacked internal coordination and their leaders seem to have counted on the intervention of other Arab states or last-minute Jordanian reluctance. They deluded themselves into believing that there would be no real confrontation and did not truly grasp the king's resolve to prevent the existence of another government in his country. Iraqi assistance, on which the organizations had been relying, was not forthcoming. Iraqi forces, encamped in the vicinity of al-Zarqa, raised no objection to the Jordanian army's attacks on the organizations in the northern sector.

Surprisingly, Syria was the one country that intervened. On September 19, two Syrian tank regiments and one infantry regiment crossed the Jordanian border and advanced toward Irbid. They took control of the al-Ramtha Junction and fought against an armored regiment of the Jordanian army. Their operation enabled two regiments of the PLA to occupy parts of Irbid. Only on September 23 did the Syrian forces retreat, after being bombed by the Jordanian air force and suffering heavy losses.[33] At the same time, the Jordanian army occupied some of the refugee camps and arrested senior PLO leaders, including Salah Khalaf and Farouq al-Qaddumi. On September 20, Nasser intervened; he flew some PLA regiments from Egypt to Syria so that they could enter Jordan, and he initiated an Arab mediation delegation headed by Sudanese president Ja'far al-Numayri. In the meantime, the Jordanian army continued its comprehensive attack and destroyed the organizations' defenses. Syria forbade PLA forces located in its territory to enter Jordan, and Numayri, heading the mediation committee, declared that Jordan was engaged in executing a plan aimed at the total annihilation of Palestinian resistance organizations and of the entire Palestinian presence in Jordan.[34]

Numayri's declaration motivated King Husayn to respond to an urgent invitation by the president of Egypt to participate in an Arab emergency summit in Cairo and to declare his consent to a cease-fire. In Cairo, Husayn submitted to Nasser's pressure. He signed a treaty with Yasir Arafat and agreed to the presence of an observers' force, dispatched by the Arab League and divided between the two sides. This was Nasser's last act before surrendering to a heart attack on September 28. Despite the cease-fire agreement, which was signed on September 26, and in spite of the widespread shock at Nasser's sudden death, the Jordanian army continued its attack until October 1, 1970, when the cease-fire came into effect. After the beginning of the cease-fire, Jordanian authorities and the Palestinians began a series of Arab-mediated talks. The talks continued until October 21 and led to the Amman Treaty.[35] In Palestinian annals, the events of September 1970 have since been known as Black September (Aylul al-Aswad) but various sources disagree as to the extent of their losses. Moderate estimates list between three thousand and five thousand Palestinian casualties and about six hundred Jordanian casualties.[36] During the fighting, Jordanian authorities also detained nearly twenty thousand Palestinians, including both combatants and civilians.

The End of Operations in Jordan

In late September, the entire region underwent transitions that affected Arab involvement in the Jordanian-Palestinian conflict. Egypt and Syria now boasted new leaders who, busy establishing their own positions, no longer supported the PLO as had their predecessors. The organizations' relationships with Iraq and Libya deteriorated, and Iraq even halted its financial assistance and put an end to Voice of Palestine broadcasts from Baghdad. Iraqi rulers explained that they disapproved of the station's political propaganda.

The PLO leadership began a thorough process of self-examination. Yasir Arafat said in an interview in *al-Ahram*, "The Palestinian resistance movement failed to understand Jordan's unique character. It lost the fight when it sought the support of Jordanian army soldiers against the authorities. The organizations also exaggerated their power when presenting themselves as an alternative to the entire Arab nation."[37] Kamal 'Idwan, a senior Fatah leader, said in another interview, "The Palestinian revolutionary movement in Jordan took upon itself responsibilities that were none of its business and portrayed itself as an alternative to the Jordanian national movement."[38] Self-criticism was also voiced within the PFLP, which had been very much in favor of confrontation. In a gathering of the central committee in early November 1970, Wadi' Haddad was attacked for the hijacking that kindled the flames, with its bitter consequences for the Palestinians.[39]

While the Palestinians were busy with their own process of self-scrutiny, the Jordanian authorities were themselves reaching a decisive stage. Thousands of Palestinians were arrested and many thousands dismissed from government positions. In November 1970, the Jordanian army received instructions from the king to gradually put a complete end to Palestinian military presence in the kingdom. The army designed a plan to isolate Amman and take control of the towns and strategic junctions. A first clash occurred in December in the Jarash-Irbid area. The army disarmed Palestinians controlling the 'Asfur Junction and occupied the Suf refugee camp on December 6 in a bloody two-day battle. The battle was the signal for a major attack on all fronts, which began on December 25. By early January the army had taken control of the city of al-Salt, the road leading from Palestinian bases in the Jordan Valley to Amman, and roads from the Syrian border. It surrounded the Palestinian bases in the vicinity of the capital but did not hurry to attack. On March 23, 1971, the Jordanian army occupied the city of al-Mafraq, and two days later invaded Irbid and the adjacent refugee camp. Only in April, when neutralization of Palestinian organizations in all other areas of the country had been completed, did the army concentrate its forces on the battle for Amman. On April 4 the king called upon the organizations to surrender their heavy weapons and the Palestinians had no choice but to do as requested.[40] They were forced to withdraw two thousand fighters from Amman to the area of 'Ajlun, and these were joined by about five hundred fighters from the north. This force was headed by Khalil al-Wazir and his adjutant, Walid Nimr (Abu 'Ali 'Iyad). The army closed all the organization's offices in Amman (aside from two civilian offices), confiscated its weapons caches, and forced most of the leaders to relocate to Beirut or Damascus. In early May the Jordanian army placed the force at 'Ajlun under siege, and on July 12 it was stormed by the most elite army units. About two hundred men on each side were killed in the battle. Some of the Palestinians were killed after surrendering, among them Walid Nimr, who was executed together with a group of Jordanian officers who had defected to the Palestinian side at the beginning of the clashes.[41] Jordanian authorities arrested approximately 2,300 of the organization's men; 500 fled to Syria, and some 100 crossed the Jordan River and surrendered to the IDF.[42]

The battle at 'Ajlun put an end to the Palestinian military presence in Jordan. Thus, the policy of a "safe base" in an Arab country reached its dismal conclusion, as did part of the Popular War of Liberation. At this point the Palestinians began anew in Lebanon, albeit under different circumstances and with a different outcome.

Gaza as an Alternative to Jordan: The Failure

As the siege on Palestinian organizations in Jordan intensified, fighters who had come from Gaza began returning to the Gaza Strip, with the intention of using it as a base for guerrilla operations. Their activities resulted in strict Israeli measures. By mid-1971, about 3,700 men had been arrested, and the Israeli army had cleared wide swaths within the refugee camps, isolating each of the quarters and organizing an efficient network of informants and collaborators. Thousands of houses were destroyed and about one hundred thousand people were forced to find new homes.[43]

The Palestinian organizations tried to prevent the destruction and to act against the collaborators. Palestinians killed seventy-five collaborators in 1970 and sixty-one in the first half of 1971.[44] The PFLP, which was the most active on this issue, spread the slogan "Enemy agents are part of the enemy."[45] In response, the Israeli army, under the command of General Officer of the Southern Command Ari'el Sharon, increased the destruction of houses. Approximately thirty-eight thousand refugees were transferred from the Gaza Strip to the Sinai and to the al-Duhayshe camp in the West Bank. Israel's security forces exposed most of the organizations' weapons stores, hiding places, and routes of escape, and dealt a fatal blow to their operational capacity.[46] In the first half of 1972 the plan to establish an operations base for guerrilla activities in Gaza collapsed.

Husayn's Federation Plan

After the conclusion of fighting at 'Ajlun, pan-Arab pressure on Jordan forced it to reinstate reconciliation negotiations with the PLO; however, neither Jordan nor the PLO were enthused. On the Palestinian side, the Marxist left wing (the PFLP and the DFLP) and the left wing of Fatah (headed by Salah Khalaf and Farouq al-Qaddumi) objected. Arafat, Khaled al-Hasan, and Khalil al-Wazir were more open to the possibility of a solution. In the Jordanian camp, disagreements arose between King Husayn and his prime minister, Wasfi al-Tal, who now urged concessions to the Palestinians. The negotiations, which commenced in Jedda, Saudi Arabia, did not proceed well and ended with no results; however, those who supported continued dialogue were not deterred. Wasfi al-Tal and Khaled al-Hasan met again in the corridors of the Joint Arab Defense Council, held in Cairo in late November 1971. Nonetheless, it was precisely here that the dialogue was destined to come to an end, as Palestinian assassins shot the Jordanian prime minister dead at the entrance to his hotel, and the relationship between the PLO and Jordan reached its end.

On March 15, 1972, King Husayn presented his Plan for a United Arab Kingdom, designed to "reorganize the Jordanian-Palestinian home." The documents spoke of the ideals of the modern state:

> After a lengthy series of consultations held with representatives of the populace in both the East and West Bank, as well as with spiritual leaders and opinion shapers, a consensus has been reached regarding the statehood plan hereby proposed. It is based on the innovative principles of the modern state. It is the embodiment of the best of democracy and its purpose is to construct a new society that will lead us to victory, progress, unity, freedom, and a good life.[47]

By this means the king tried to legitimize Jordan's wish to renew its control of the West Bank. The document did not mention the

"Palestinian people" and it included obvious allusions to the "destructive role" of the PLO leadership. The essential points of the proposal were summarized by the king as follows:

1. The Hashemite Kingdom of Jordan will become the United Arab Kingdom and this will be its name from here on.
2. The United Arab Kingdom will consist of two regions: (1) the Jordan Region (*qutr*), on the East Bank; and (2) the Palestine Region on the West Bank, including all Palestinian territory to be liberated, if such residents wish to join the proposed state.
3. Amman will be the central capital of the kingdom and the capital of the Jordan Region.
4. Jerusalem will be the capital of the Palestine Region.
5. The King will serve as Prime Minister; he will head the main Executive Authority, together with a central council of ministers; the Legislative Authority will consist of the King and a Council of the Nation whose members will be chosen according to the principle of confidential direct elections, with equal representation of both regions.
6. The main Judicial Authority will be headed by a main supreme court.
7. The kingdom will have a united armed force, headed by the King as its supreme commander.
8. The responsibility of the main Executive Authority will be limited to issues related to the international status of the kingdom as a single national entity. It will guarantee the peace, stability, and prosperity of the kingdom.
9. In each region, the responsibilities of Executive Authority will be wielded by a locally appointed general governor, and a local council of ministers will be established.
10. The Legislative Authority of each region will be headed by a People's Council, the members of which will be elected in personal confidential elections. The People's Council will elect the general governor of the region.
11. The Judicial Authority is responsible for the region's courts and it is the highest authority.
12. The Executive Authority of each region will be responsible for current matters, aside from power granted by the constitution to the main Executive Authority.[48]

After the plan was made public, the king began promoting it in meetings with intellectuals and Palestinian businessmen.[49] These efforts, however, were not successful. On March 16, 1972, the central committee of the PLO published its firm objection to the plan, which they depicted as "trying to block the Palestinian revolutionary movement." The announcement said that "only the Palestinian people themselves have a right to determine their national future."[50] Although Israel rejected the plan, the Egyptian newspaper *al-Ahram* described it as a "Jordanian-Israeli plot to sow dissension among the Arabs and put an end to the Palestinian cause."[51] Egypt officially rejected the proposal altogether, and the Palestinian press in the West Bank renounced it almost unanimously.[52]

The objections of the Palestinian organizations also stemmed from their sense that Jordan and Israel were collaborating against them. This impression was created when Israel announced in late 1971 that in April 1972 it would hold municipal elections in the West Bank, followed by King Husayn's announcement of the United Arab Kingdom plan. Reports of confidential talks between the king and Israeli prime minister Golda Meir reached Arafat and his associates, as well as reports of Israelis willing to hold talks with Jordan in order to further a solution in the West Bank based on the Alon Plan. This plan, formed immediately after the conclusion of the War of June 1967, focused on the concept of establishing an Israeli line of defense in the Jordan Valley and returning densely populated Palestinian territory to the Jordanian Kingdom. The Alon Plan aroused extensive public debate in Israel and served as a guide for government actions in the field and for strategically planning settlement locations.

The leadership of the PLO perceived the municipal elections initiated by Israel in the West Bank as an attempt to train an alternate leadership. The PLO chose to detract from the significance of these elections, probably in order to disprove accusations of collaborating with Israel. Only one candidate, Karim Khalaf, who was elected mayor of Ramallah, was indirectly identified with the PLO; however, even among those who were not, not all winning candidates professed support for Jordan.

Notes

1. *Al-Dustur*, February 17, 1968.
2. *Al-Nahar*, February 18, 1968.

3. Shafiq, "Ma'rakat al-Karameh," [Battle of Karameh], 47.

4. H. al-Hasan, "Waqfa 'ind al-zikra al-rabi'ah lima'rakat al-Karameh," [Stating the Arab Memory of the al-Karameh Battle], 56.

5. Michalson et al., *Hama'avaq, Lebithon Yisra'el* [The Struggle for the Security of Israel], 159n61.

6. Dupuy, *Elusive Victory: The Arab-Israeli Wars, 1967-1974*, 351–352.

7. H. al-Hasan, "Waqfa 'ind al-zikra al-rabi'ah lima'rakat al-Karameh," [Stating the Arab Memory of the al-Karameh Battle], 57n4.

8. Center for Palestinian Research, *Al-Kitab al-Sanwi Lilqadiyya al-Filastiniyya Lil'am 1968* [Yearbook of the Palestinian Problem for 1968], 161.

9. Sayigh, *Al-Kifah al-Muslah wa al-Bahath 'An al-Dawla: Al-Haraka al-Wataniyya al-Filastiniyya, 1949–1993* [Armed Struggle and the Search for a State], 282.

10. Sayigh, *Al-Kifah al-Muslah wa al-Bahath 'An al-Dawla: Al-Haraka al-Wataniyya al-Filastiniyya, 1949–1993* [Armed Struggle and the Search for a State], 307.

11. Luttwak and Horowitz, *Israeli Army*, 309–310.

12. Sayigh, *Al-Kifah al-Muslah wa al-Bahath 'An al-Dawla: Al-Haraka al-Wataniyya al-Filastiniyya, 1949–1993* [Armed Struggle and the Search for a State], 308.

13. Sayigh, *Al-Kifah al-Muslah wa al-Bahath 'An al-Dawla: Al-Haraka al-Wataniyya al-Filastiniyya, 1949–1993* [The Armed Struggle and the Search for a State], 390.

14. K. al-Hindi, "Al-Ta'bi'ah al-Urduniyya did al-muqawamah al-Filastiniyya qabl hajmat Siptamber 1970" [Jordanian Effort Against the Palestinian Resistance in Jordan Before the Attack of September 1970], 17.

15. *Al-Hadaf*, May 2, 1970.

16. Sha'th et al., *Al-Muqawamah al-Filastiniyya wa al-Nizam al-Urduni* [Palestinian Resistance and the Jordanian Regime], 472–474, and 139.

17. B. al-Hasan, "Ahdath aylul wa mas'uliyyat al-nizam al-Urduni" [Events of September and the Responsibility of the Jordanian Regime], 49.

18. *Al-Sharara* 6 (April 1970): 7–9.

19. Quoted in Sayigh, *Al-Kifah al-Muslah wa al-Bahath 'An al-Dawla: Al-Haraka al-Wataniyya al-Filastiniyya, 1949–1993* [Armed Struggle and the Search for a State], 369.

20. Sayigh, *Al-Kifah al-Muslah wa al-Bahath 'An al-Dawla: Al-Haraka al-Wataniyya al-Filastiniyya, 1949–1993* [Armed Struggle and the Search for a State], 301.

21. Kabha, *Harb al-Istinzaf Milhemet Hahatasha Bir'i Hameqorot Hamisriyim* [Harb al-Istinzaf: The War of Attrition as Reflected in Egyptian Sources], 129.

22. 'Allush, *Nahwa Thawrah Filastiniyya Jadidah* [In the Direction of a New Palestinian Revolution], 45–46.

23. *Al-Hadaf*, August 8, 1970.

24. Center for Palestinian Research, *Al-Kitab al-Sanwi Lilqadiyya al-Filastiniyya Lisnat* [Yearbook of the Palestinian Problem for 1970], 317n4.
25. *Ha'aretz*, September 14, 1970.
26. Interview with Salah Khalaf, in *Shu'un Filastiniyya* 5 (November 1971): 35.
27. Quoted in Sayigh, *Al-Kifah al-Muslah wa al-Bahath 'An al-Dawla: Al-Haraka al-Wataniyya al-Filastiniyya, 1949–1993* [Armed Struggle and the Search for a State], 384.
28. Sayigh, *Al-Kifah al-Muslah wa al-Bahath 'An al-Dawla: Al-Haraka al-Wataniyya al-Filastiniyya, 1949–1993* [Armed Struggle and the Search for a State], 384.
29. Sayigh, *Al-Kifah al-Muslah wa al-Bahath 'An al-Dawla: Al-Haraka al-Wataniyya al-Filastiniyya, 1949–1993* [Armed Struggle and the Search for a State], 386.
30. International Institute for Strategic Studies, *Military Balance*.
31. PLO Research Center, *Black September*, 59.
32. PLO Research Center, *Black September*, 59.
33. Sayigh, *Al-Kifah al-Muslah wa al-Bahath 'An al-Dawla: Al-Haraka al-Wataniyya al-Filastiniyya, 1949–1993* [Armed Struggle and the Search for a State], 392.
34. Center for Palestinian Research, *Yearbook*, 1970, 391n4.
35. Research Center of the Arab League, *Al-Watha'iq al-Filastiniyya al-'Arabiyya Lisnat 1970* [Arab-Palestinian Documents for 1970], 657–659.
36. On the various estimates, see Center for Palestinian Research, *Yearbook*, 1970, 409n4.
37. *Al-Ahram*, January 2, 1971.
38. *Al-Nahar* (Beirut), January 16, 1971.
39. Sayigh, *Al-Kifah al-Muslah wa al-Bahath 'An al-Dawla: Al-Haraka al-Wataniyya al-Filastiniyya, 1949–1993* [Armed Struggle and the Search for a State], 402.
40. Research Center of the Arab League, *Al-Watha'iq al-Filastiniyya al-'Arabiyya Lisnat 1971* [Arab-Palestinian Documents for 1971], 269–272.
41. Center for Palestinian Research, *Yearbook*, 1971, 112–113n4.
42. Khalaf, *Filastini Bila Hawiyya* [Palestinian with No Homeland], 155n156.
43. *Ma'ariv*, April 1, 1971.
44. *Middle East Record*, 1969–1970, 225.
45. Center for Palestinian Research, *Yearbook*, 1971, 618n4.
46. *Ha'aretz*, October 21, 1971.
47. 'Abd al-Hadi, *Al-Mas'alah al-Filastiniyya wa Mashari' al-Hulul al-Siyasiyya, 1934-1974* [Palestinian Question and Proposed Political Solutions], 409–410.

48. 'Abd al-Hadi, *Al-Mas'alah al-Filastiniyya wa Mashari' al-Hulul al-Siyasiyya, 1934-1974* [Palestinian Question and Proposed Political Solutions], 410–411.

49. *Al-Nahar*, March 16, 1972.

50. The newspaper *Fath*, March 16, 1972.

51. *Al-Ahram*, March 16, 1972.

52. *Al-Ahram*, March 18, 1972; *Al-Fajr* (East Jerusalem), March 17, 1972.

8

Establishing "Fatahland"

Palestinian organizations established an armed military presence in Lebanon following the War of June 1967. After the defeat, hundreds of young volunteers from refugee camps in Lebanon and other countries flocked to an improvised training camp at the village of Kayfun, under the command of PLA officer Muhammad al-Sha'ir. Dozens were referred to camps founded by the Lebanese army, where they received initial weapons training. The surge of volunteers grew following the Battle of Karameh in Jordan and the myths surrounding this battle. Fatah was now the rising force within Lebanese refugee camps and the focal point of local support and identification. In late 1967, Palestinian leaders from Saudi Arabia, Egypt, and Jordan returned to Lebanon to build a civilian infrastructure for Fatah in the "land of cedars." Their efforts were directed mainly at organizing Palestinian students and workers in Lebanon and supporting charity associations operating in the refugee camps—all of which had previously been supervised by Lebanese intelligence forces.[1] Until the arrival of PLO leaders and their military bases in Lebanon, the attitude of the Palestinian leadership toward the refugees in Lebanon had been basically political. Both Shuqayri and Haj Amin had worked to gain the admiration and support of the refugees and to organize them in a way that would prevent permanent assimilation among the Lebanese. However, this state of affairs was disrupted by the arrival of the PLO in Lebanon and its reorganization as the major military arm of the organization.

Syrian restrictions on infiltrating Israel from the Golan Heights, in addition to the persecution of Palestinians in Jordan since mid-1970, hastened Fatah's attempts to become established in Lebanon, particularly in the mountainous southern region of al-Arqub. Supported by local Shiite residents who bore a grudge against the Lebanese government for their discrimination, Fatah established a headquarters in southern Lebanon and extended its authority as far as Bint Jubayl, near the Israeli border. In response, Lebanese authorities distributed approximately seven hundred rifles to locals opposed to the organizations' growing presence.

The Cairo Treaty of 1969

Tensions between the Lebanese establishment and the Palestinian organizations did not focus exclusively on southern Lebanon. The Palestinian issue had become entangled with internal Lebanese rivalries. Many in Lebanese society empathized with the Palestinian struggle and supported its organizations. Others, particularly from Maronite Christian circles, felt alienated by the Palestinian strategies and expressed reservations about the organizations' activities. The population became increasingly polarized, even more so upon the arrival of the organizations' leaders and fighters. When the Lebanese authorities began limiting the newcomers' activities and arresting Fatah activists, the riots known as the Clashes of May 1969 erupted in southern Lebanon, and seven Palestinian guerrilla fighters, as well as two Lebanese soldiers, were killed.

The May Clashes resulted in the intervention of Gamal Abdel Nasser. Egyptian leaders wished to ignite Israel's borders to the east and north and therefore objected to the Lebanese authorities' interference with Palestinian activities originating from their territory. Several days after the May Clashes, Nasser's emissaries succeeded in organizing a meeting between Yasir Arafat and Lebanese president Sharl Hiliw, and the two reached an understanding concerning the activities of Palestinian organizations. A temporary calm ensued, enabling continued efforts at organization in the south. However, the quiet was short-lived. The Lebanese army tried to prevent Palestinian deployment along the Israeli border, and on October 15, 1969, their men surrounded Palestinian units in the western sector, killing sixteen fighters and detaining the remainder.[2] Consequently, an intifada broke out in all fourteen Lebanese refugee camps. Lebanese police forces were thrown out of the camps with the help of thousands of Lebanese who sympathized with the Palestinians. The Lebanese opposition called for a general strike on October 24 and a strike was indeed declared in most parts of the country, aside from the Maronite areas. The strike was accompanied by demonstrations and riots and fifteen demonstrators were killed. The Palestinian organizations retaliated with an attack on the Lebanese border patrol, apprehending fourteen of their men and taking control of the roads and main junctions in the south and of two major towns—Hasbayya and Rashiyya al-Wadi.

At the same time, however, Lebanon's status in the Arab world was in a state of decline. Syria closed its joint border with Lebanon; Libya, Algeria, and the Sudan declared their support of the Palestinian organizations. Feeling threatened, Sharl Hiliw appealed to Nasser and asked for his immediate intervention. Hiliw sent the supreme commander of the Lebanese army, Emil al-Bustani, to Cairo to meet with the Palestinian leadership, with Egyptian mediation. Arafat arrived in Cairo on October 31, and after exhausting negotiations with the Lebanese delegation in the presence of the Egyptians, the parties signed the Cairo Treaty of 1969 on November 3, 1969. This treaty, although often breached, became the foundation of Palestinian-Lebanese relations. It ensured Palestinian refugees the right to live, work, and travel in Lebanon. The PLO was awarded the responsibility of managing the refugee camps by means of popular committees. The organizations received permission to attack Israel from Lebanon, subject to coordination with the Lebanese army. The PLO was required to provide the Lebanese government with reports on operating forces and its men were subject to Lebanese laws.

The Cairo Treaty enabled the PLO and the other organizations to build an alternative base of operations in Lebanon, in place of that lost in Jordan. The PLO assumed complete control of southern Lebanon and the area became known as "Fatahland." In the vicinity of Beirut and in the north, the PLO established a "supreme political coordination committee" headed by Muhammad Yusuf al-Najjar, a Fatah operative, to supervise the refugee camps and coordinate operations with the government. However, the pattern established in Jordan emerged here as well. Once government supervision of the camps was removed, bands of fighters rapidly appeared and weapons were widely distributed. As had occurred in Jordan, young refugees sought to take their revenge on the Lebanese for many years of humiliation and subservience. Carrying their weapons, they repeatedly harassed officers of the Lebanese government, the police, mail carriers, and tax collectors. They organized military training within the camps and openly displayed their weapons in densely populated areas, roads, and major junctions, and even at Beirut's international airport.[3]

The Maronites, who had objected to the Cairo Treaty to begin with, were particularly vexed by the Palestinian conduct. Even some Palestinian allies, such as Druze leader Kamal Junbalat, were angered by the blow to Lebanese sovereignty. In March 1970 members of the right-wing Phalanges organization ambushed a Palestinian funeral procession and killed ten armed men.[4] Kamal Junbalat calmed matters for a while, but the relationship between the Palestinians and the Christian Phalange organization continued to spiral out of control.[5]

Expanding the Circle of Violence: Black September and Munich

Once the ten thousand Palestinian fighters had left Jordan and arrived in Lebanon, where they were not overly welcomed, two camps were formed within Fatah's revolutionary committee, based on disagreements over their future strategy. One was led by Yasir Arafat, together with Khalil al-Wazir, Muhammad Yusuf al-Najjar, and Kamal 'Idwan. The other group was led by Salah Khalaf and his second in command, 'Ali Hasan Salameh. The first camp criticized the organization's attitude toward the host countries and called for a conciliatory approach, while the second camp justified resistance toward their host countries' sovereignty. The high command of the PLO ruled in favor of the orientation represented by Arafat, but this did not stop Salah Khalaf from instructing 'Ali Hasan Salameh to found an organization named Black September that would concentrate on revenge. Members of this organization murdered Jordanian prime minister Wasfi al-Tal in Cairo in November 1971. The organization also attempted to target economic elements and firms maintaining business relationships with Israel, such as a Dutch gas company and a German electronics company. On

May 8, 1972, two Fatah men, together with 'Ali Taha, from the Special Unit of the PFLP headed by Wadi' Haddad, hijacked a Belgian Sabena plane carrying one hundred passengers and brought it down at Israel's International Airport in Lydda. The operation was carried out by the Black September group. Israeli commandos liberated the airplane and freed the hostages. Despite the fact that the plan ultimately failed, and even though the involvement of Fatah in the operation was marginal, several Fatah men still hastened to take responsibility and to declare their pride in its outcome.[6] On May 30, 1972, three terrorists from the Japanese Red Army organization attacked passengers in the Lydda Airport passenger lounge, murdering thirty-one people. Kamal 'Idwan, the PLO spokesman, was quick to take credit for the operation: "We were forced to leave Jordan, but operations such as this prove that nonetheless our operational capabilities remain strong."[7]

Black September's activities motivated Israel's security forces to initiate a global comprehensive war against the PLO. On July 8, 1972, Israeli agents killed writer and journalist Ghassan Kanafani, spokesman of the PFLP and editor of its journal. In another attempt against PLO leaders, eleven days later, Anis Sayigh, director of the PLO research center in Beirut, and Bassam Abu Sharif, editor of the newspaper *al-Hadaf*, were seriously injured. On September 5, 1972, a Black September group entered the Israeli dormitories in the Munich Olympics athletes' village and murdered eleven Israeli athletes. Five of the attackers and one German soldier were killed in the failed attempt to free the athletes.[8] In retaliation for the murder of the athletes in Munich, Israeli agents initiated acts of revenge against PLO representatives in Europe. From October 1972 to January 1973 Israel targeted Fatah representatives, including Wa'il Zu'aytir in Rome, Mahmoud al-Hamshari in Paris, and Husayn Abu al-Khayr, in Nicosia.

The operation in Munich, the global reactions it aroused, and the Israeli response resulted in a deep crisis among PLO decisionmakers. Some of those in favor of expanding the struggle, who had also advocated its intensification and expansion from the Middle East arena, led by 'Ali Hasan Salameh and Muhammad Yusuf al-Najjar, quickly relinquished this strategy and began emphasizing the need to refocus on the Israeli domain.[9] PLO leaders, particularly Khalil al-Wazir and Kamal 'Idwan, blamed Salah Khalaf for inciting global public opinion against the PLO and prompting Israel's harsh reactions. Khalaf's situation worsened with the failure of an operation in Amman in February 1973 that he had planned on behalf of Black September. Jordanian authorities arrested seventeen Fatah operatives who had planned to kidnap the prime minister and the US ambassador, and a swift military tribunal sentenced them to death. At the same time, nearly 1,200 soldiers and officers of Palestinian origin were dismissed from the Jordanian army. On February 21, 1973, Israeli forces attacked Palestinian bases near Tripoli in northern Lebanon and killed forty Palestinians, mostly from the PFLP.[10] On April 10, 1973, Israel raided the offices and residences of PLO leaders in Beirut, killing Muhammad Yusuf al-Najjar, Kamal 'Idwan, and Kamal Naser.[11] Subsequently, Arafat reorganized the leadership of his organization. He also reconciled with Salah Khalaf, whom he appointed in charge of PLO intelligence and of coordination with the other Palestinian factions. Arafat charged 'Ali Hasan Salameh with founding his personal guard, known since as Force 17. Finally, during the years 1970–1973, the military efficacy of the Palestinian organizations diminished and their ability to perform operations within Israeli territory was reduced: In 1971 they performed 670 operations, in 1972 these dropped to 351, and in 1973 there were only 271 operations.[12]

Return to Lebanon

In the meantime, tensions rose between the Lebanese establishment, particularly its Maronite sector, and Palestinian organizations, which behaved as though they owned southern Lebanon. In mid-September 1972, the Israelis raided southern Lebanon and killed thirty of the organizations' men and eighteen Lebanese soldiers, causing the Lebanese army to take action.[13] It declared an emergency situation and demanded that the PLO vacate all noncivil offices in the south. Left-wing Christians demanded that the government cancel the Cairo Treaty of 1969 and act to remove all five thousand members of the armed organizations from the country. In light of these pressures, Arafat agreed to evacuate some of the bases in the vicinity of Qana and Bint Jubayl and began a series of reconciliation visits focusing on the Christians; however, these visits resulted in only a temporary and partial calm. In December 1972, the clashes between the army and the organizations resumed and became routine. In the initial months of 1973 the radical organizations once again caused a deterioration of the Lebanese-Palestinian relationship—as they had previously in Jordan—and renewed their deployment along the Israeli border. Now the rift among Lebanese society deepened as well: most of the Christian leaders called for removal of the Palestinian organizations, while many of the Muslims empathized with the organizations and supported them. The Christians became infuriated when a quarter of a million people took part in the funeral of the three PLO leaders murdered in April 1973. Muslim leaders accused the army of fomenting tensions with the Palestinians. Following the events in April, the Sunni Muslim prime minister, Sa'ib Salam, tendered his resignation to the Christian president, Sulayman Franjiyya.[14]

On April 30, 1973, Lebanese security forces arrested three members of the PFLP at Beirut International Airport, and the PFLP responded by kidnapping two Lebanese soldiers. Lebanon reacted decisively. Its army surrounded the five refugee camps in Beirut and gave the kidnappers an ultimatum whereby they would release the two kidnapped soldiers. When the time set elapsed, on the morning of May 2, the army attacked the organizations' forces in the camps and the air force initiated operations. On May 5, PLO leaders announced that they wished to avoid a conflict but would not forego the Cairo Treaty.[15] Pressure applied by Egypt and Syria forced President Franjiyya to agree to a cease-fire on May 8, 1973. The PLO announced that the status quo would be maintained, thus declaring their undisputed victory and continued armed presence in Lebanese territory. A total of seventy-seven fighters were killed throughout this crisis—forty Palestinians and thirty-seven Lebanese—as well as almost seventy civilians on both sides.[16]

Notes

1. Sayigh, *Al-Kifah al-Muslah wa al-Bahath 'An al-Dula: Al-Haraka al-Wataniyya al-Filastiniyya, 1949–1993* [Armed Struggle and the Search for a State], 288–289.

2. *Al-Nahar*, October 23, 1969.

3. Sayigh, *Al-Kifah al-Muslah wa al-Bahath 'An al-Dula: Al-Haraka al-Wataniyya al-Filastiniyya, 1949–1993* [Armed Struggle and the Search for a State], 296.

4. The Phalanges (al-Kata'eb): a Christian right-wing party founded by Pierre Jemayel in the 1930s.

5. *Al-Nahar*, March 18, 1970.
6. *Fath*, May 17, 1972.
7. Research Center of the Arab League, *Al-Witha'iq al-Filastiniyya al-'Arabiyya Lil'am 1972* [Arab-Palestinian Documents for 1972], 306.
8. Sayigh, *Al-Kifah al-Muslah wa al-Bahath 'An al-Dula: Al-Haraka al-Wataniyya al-Filastiniyya, 1949–1993* [Armed Struggle and the Search for a State], 451.
9. 'Umar, "Ru'iya al-mustaqbal" [Story of the Future], 61.
10. Center for Palestinian Research, *Yearbook* 1972, 141n4.
11. Shalhat, "Sir al-haqibatayn al-da'i'tayn" [Secret of the Two Lost Files], 26–27.
12. The data is from the Center for Palestinian Research, *Yearbook* 1972, 219n4.
13. Center for Palestinian Research, *Yearbook* 1972, 219n4.
14. Center for Palestinian Research, *Yearbook* 1972, 219n4.
15. *Al-Nahar*, April 13, 1973.
16. *Filastin al-Thawra*, May 23, 1973.

9

The PLO at Home and Abroad

While Syria and Egypt secretly prepared for the War of October 1973, they refrained from sharing their plans with other Arab countries. Even Fatah was only aware of certain aspects. President Hafez al-Assad of Syria, whose relationship with Fatah had soured, insisted on excluding the organization. Even when Egyptian president Anwar Sadat asked that the PLO be updated, al-Assad insisted that only his allies, Khalid al-Fahum, head of the Palestinian National Council, and Zuhir Muhsin, leader of al-Sa'iqa, be informed. Only in late September 1973 did Sadat appeal to Yasir Arafat and ask that PLO fighters and units of the PLA take part in the war effort. Syria submitted this request to the commanders of the PLA and not to PLO leaders. In early October Fatah informed the other organizations of the anticipated combined Arab attack against Israel, but even its leaders were not aware of the exact timing.[1]

The Palestinians and the War of October 1973

Palestinian forces took part in the war on both fronts. The PLA 'Ayn Jaloud Company fought on the Egyptian front in the vicinity of the Great Bitter Lake and in the defense of the city of Suez, and a Fatah company took part in patrol assignments. These Palestinian forces sustained forty-eight casualties, seventy wounded, and forty-five prisoners of war.² On the Syrian front they played a more substantial role. The PLA Hittin Regiment took part in the Syrian offensive on October 6, while the al-Qadisiyya Regiment took part in the holding action later on. Al-Sa'iqa units took part in the battles for Mount Hermon, and Fatah's al-Jalil Company took part in the fighting in the southern sector.³ These forces and other Palestinian units on the Syrian front sustained 121 casualties.⁴ As the fighting progressed, Palestinian organizations attempted to open a "third front" on the Lebanese border, and executed about 140 sorties and offensive initiatives, which continued for five days after the general cease-fire. On this front the Palestinian units sustained forty-four casualties.⁵

Arab Recognition and Political Dilemma

PLO forces had a marginal military role in the war, but subsequently won an important political advantage. Yazid Sayigh explained:

> The October War created a historical opportunity for the PLO, but a challenge as well. Now it could, on the one hand, use the advantage created by the recent show of Arab military and financial power to become part of the political process and reach accomplishments in Palestinian territory. On the other hand, taking part in regional negotiations with Israel was a crucial deviation from the historical goals of the Palestinian national movement since 1948 and from its declarations.⁶

Many in the Palestinian national movement did not find it easy to accept this transition. The slogan "Liberation of all Palestinian land" had become entrenched in the masses' political consciousness and was an integral part of the platform of all Palestinian political movements and groups. Total rejection of UN Resolution 242, which included recognition of Israel's right to exist, was an essential foundation of the national rhetoric in all its nuances. However, following the War of October 1973, pragmatic voices began emerging in almost all the organizations, and these espoused a realistic reading of the political map and of the balance of powers in the Middle East and in the world. Two individuals were most emblematic of this new trend: Salah Khalaf (Abu 'Iyad) of Fatah and Zuhir Muhsin of al-Sa'iqa. At gatherings and internal meetings Khalaf spoke of the need to prevent the Arab states from resuming their dominance of the Palestinian cause as in the days of the Government of All Palestine. He believed that for this purpose "the PLO must translate its principles into a new working plan, relevant and suited to current developments."[7] Zuhir Muhsin claimed that the war had changed the understanding and awareness of many Palestinians: "Before the war we yearned for it to prove to ourselves that we can fight. The war was more important to us than the actual cause. After the war our sense of helplessness disappeared. Now the Arab nation and the Palestinian national movement could no longer allow themselves to remain bound to romantic ways of thinking. They were required to define their goals in a practical and realistic manner."[8]

In contrast to the pragmatic voices, there were those who objected to any participation of the PLO in a political process with Israel. The most vocal were Ahmad Jibril's PFLP-GC. They claimed that any involvement in peace talks would imply recognition of Israel and that its final outcome would be the establishment of a tiny Palestinian state in the West Bank and the Gaza Strip. They warned of the emergence of a group striving to put an end to the "Palestinian struggle" by resolving the conflict with Israel. They summarized their position in the slogan "No to solutions that put an end to the struggle, no to a small Palestinian state, yes to a struggle against back-stabbing opportunists."[9] The PFLP joined those who objected to the pragmatic outlook. They stated that the War of October 1973 had opened a new window of opportunity and created a relative strategic balance between Israel and the Arabs, enabling "a basis for increasing the struggle and causing the enemy to completely withdraw from occupied Arab and Palestinian lands, consequently achieving national independence for the Palestinian people in a sovereign national state."[10] In the words of George Habash, "It does befit us to put an end to the outcome of the aggression of 1967 by complying with the outcome of the aggression of 1948."[11]

PLO decisionmakers therefore found themselves in a dilemma. On the one hand, they did not want to completely reject the possibility of indirect or even direct involvement in the political process; on the other hand, many found it difficult to publicly proclaim the annulment of the campaign for "Liberation of all Palestinian land." However, a decisive element in their deliberations was the strict veto against relinquishing territories vacated by Israel to Jordan. An editorial in the Fatah journal *Filastin al-Thawra* expressed this well:

> The October War has forced the PLO to discuss the issue of the future of liberated Palestinian lands [as an outcome of the political process]. We must stress our objection to return any Palestinian territory to Jordan. Homeland territory liberated from the occupation must be restored to the Palestinian people in order to realize their full national sovereignty and construct an independent national entity.[12]

This approach by the PLO—albeit stating no express intention of directly negotiating with Israel—was countered by the Rejection Front (Jabhat al-Rafd), which objected to any political process. It consisted of the PFLP, the PFLP-GC, and the DPFLP. The Rejection Front sought to revive the principle of armed struggle and to shame supporters of the political process. Since their military capabilities were limited compared to Fatah, Rejection Front organizations chose to launch demonstrations. The first such operation occurred on April 11, 1974, in Kiryat Shmona. Three members of Ahmad Jibril's organization seized a local youth hostel, took dozens of teenagers hostage, and demanded the release of one hundred Palestinian prisoners imprisoned in Israel. An Israeli force broke in and released the hostages, but nineteen Israeli hostages and soldiers were killed, in addition to the three kidnappers. Ahmad Jibril thereby announced that the murderous incident proved his organization's ability to "block any negotiations for peace, any negotiations with Israel, and the establishment of a negligible Palestinian state."[13] The operation enhanced the organization's prestige and led to renewed Iraqi and Libyan financial aid. Jibril's men assaulted Kibbutz Shamir as well, where four of their own and three Israelis were killed. Israel reacted with airstrikes of refugee camps in southern Lebanon. Twenty-seven Palestinians were killed, and 105 injured.[14]

The DFLP, led by Nayif Hawatmeh, initiated similar operations. On May 15, 1974, three of its men broke into a school in Ma'alot, took 100 schoolchildren hostage, and demanded the release of Palestinian prisoners. After hours of unsuccessful negotiations, Israeli commandos broke into the building and released some of the hostages. The three members of the DFLP were killed, as well as twenty-three Israeli children and soldiers. Israel retaliated with air strikes of 'Ayn al-Hilwe and al-Nabatiyyeh refugee camps. In these assaults sixty Palestinians were killed and 140 were injured.[15]

From Arab to International Recognition

The raids instigated by the Rejection Front did not prevent the PLO from taking part in the political process and establishing its status as the exclusive, legitimate representative of the Palestinian people. On October 29, 1974, the Arab summit, convened in Rabat, Morocco, recognized the PLO as the exclusive, legitimate representative of the Palestinians. Jordan was not happy with this decision, but it was forced to go along with the other Arab countries. The PLO's new status received international recognition two weeks later, on November 14, 1974, when Yasir Arafat spoke before the UN Assembly in New York. In his speech Arafat summarized his organization's achievements:

> The PLO has achieved legitimacy due to its pioneering efforts in promoting all aspects of the Palestinian struggle. It has been recognized first and foremost by the Palestinian masses, who gave it the right to lead and adhered to its counsel. It has been recognized since all armed bands, societies, and groups were represented in its national council and popular institutions. Its legitimacy was further strengthened by the support of the entire Arab nation, as confirmed at the recent Arab summit, which reiterated the PLO's right to establish an independent authority on all liberated Palestinian territory. It intensified thanks to the support of the liberation movements and of the friendly states that supported the organization's efforts to realize the rights of the Palestinian people.[16]

This turn of events was challenged by a coalition accusing Arafat of treachery and of "eliminating the Palestinian national struggle," headed by George Habash, who withdrew his organization from the executive committee of the PLO, as well as its central committee. Ahmad Jibril's organization and the Arab Liberation Front, supported by Iraq, joined this move, and together they founded an organization named the Front of Palestinian Forces Objecting to Defeatist Solutions.

Return to the West Bank and the Gaza Strip

Since the failure of the Popular War of Liberation in the West Bank and Gaza Strip after the 1967 June War, these territories had been, in effect, neglected by the Palestinian organizations. In contrast, Israel operated an "open bridges" policy with Jordan, opened its economy to workers from the territories, and succeeded in bringing the population to a state of peaceful routine. Palestinian attempts to revitalize the organizations in the West Bank after 1973 and to establish a united front were only partially successful. Israeli security forces arrested many of those who pursued this course, and some were even deported.[17]

The PLO's efforts to revive its former status in the West Bank and the Gaza Strip were obstructed by the efficient control exercised by Israeli authorities and by Jordanian operations. The military government established by Israel maintained direct and uncontested control and became involved in events in the territories and in residents' lives. Israeli security forces recruited an extensive intelligence network, whereby collaborators were promised special benefits. Strict Israeli administration and daily dependence on the Israeli economy nearly silenced the PLO's appeals for national mobilization and *sumud* (steadfast perseverance), which called for a determined struggle, stressing the boycotting of Israel, and avoiding all mutual contact. Jordan continued to pay salaries to officials and teachers whom it had employed prior to 1967. Tens of thousands of families subsisted on these payments, and the PLO found it difficult to undermine this reliance and the ensuing loyalty it garnered.

The PLO and the Mayors

Nonetheless, the PLO succeeded in forming a support base for its movement. In the 1976 municipal elections, PLO candidates won 40 percent of the votes, and a similar proportion voted for independent candidates affiliated with nationalist circles. Only 20 percent voted for candidates identified with traditional forces or recognized as associates of the Israelis or the Jordanians.[18] An analysis performed by Yazid Sayigh shows that election results indicated a weakening of the traditional wealthy elements and the elite affiliated with Jordan, probably because Israel had transferred part of their authority to the mayors. Some of this elite eventually lost faith in Jordan and embraced the concept of Palestinian singularity. Sayigh states that this trend was evident as early as 1970–1972, when Muhammad 'Ali al-Ja'bari, the mayor of Hebron; Hamdi al-Taji al-Farouqi, a Jerusalem physician; and Muhammad Abu Shilbaya, an *al-Quds* reporter, were already demanding the establishment of a Palestinian state.[19] A more deep-rooted reason for the rising impact of the PLO may have been its increasing pragmatism, as well as the hope that if the PLO embarked on a political course it would lead to a change in the current state of affairs. These factors were compounded by the rising recognition that Arab states, led by Jordan, were incapable of putting an end to the occupation. The establishment of three West Bank universities during 1972–1975—the University of Bir Zayt, the University of Bethlehem, and the al-Najah University in Nablus—also contributed significantly to nurturing an independent Palestinian identity and the reluctance to once again be subjected to Jordanian rule. These campuses were home to a new generation that was not dependent on Jordan for its subsistence and was sustained by the spirit of national struggle with its strong objection to Israeli occupation. The University of Bir Zayt required its students to devote 120 hours to volunteer work in the community, including paving roads in the villages, gathering crops, and fighting illiteracy; the University of Bethlehem required national service in the field of civil medicine; and the al-Najah University established a center for development of the rural sector.[20]

The new mayors elected in 1976, who were affiliated with the PLO, focused on the political sphere. They made noticeable efforts to reinstate the PLO as the major force active in determining and shaping the future of the territories, under any potential arrangement, and attained significant success. They objected to the influence of both Jordan and Israel and raised money in oil-producing states to compensate those adversely affected by the struggle.[21] Mayor Bassam al-Shak'ah of Nablus traveled to Libya, where he raised donations to ease the suffering of "the Palestinians true to their homeland."[22] Mayor Karim Khalaf of Ramallah embarked on a similar journey to Algeria and other countries, where he claimed to have collected over ten million dollars.[23] These mayors could not ask the population to become completely detached from the Hashemite Kingdom, which remained their official and physical bridge to the Arab and international world, but they acted to undermine its influence. They supported the PLO to the best of their ability and helped block the Israeli strategy of removing the organization from the territories. The peace initiative of Egyptian president, Anwar Sadat, his historic visit to Israel in November 1977, and the Egypt-Israel peace treaty signed in 1979, which alluded only to negotiations for Palestinian autonomy, increased the mayors' identification with the exiled Palestinian leadership led by the PLO and with its demand for full Israeli withdrawal from the territories occupied in 1967.

Fatah and Its Rivals in the Territories

The Israeli authorities, meanwhile, acted to prevent the mayors from pursuing this path. The steps taken against them grew gradually stricter, beginning with warnings and proceeding to dismissal, detention, and deportation of the heads of municipal and rural councils, their members and activists. Bassam al-Shak'ah, the mayor of Nablus and a prominent figure on the contemporary national scene, arranged a gathering of mayors identified with the PLO at the Nablus town hall on May 2, 1978. The next day he was summoned to the Israeli military governor of Nablus and warned.[24] In early July of that year the military governor of Jericho decided to dismiss two members of the municipal council due to similar activities.[25] The mayors responded by establishing a National Guidance Committee at a convention in Bayt Hanina in October, at which speakers renounced the Camp David Accords and the concept of autonomy. Due to their disregard of the military governors' warnings, the mayors of Nablus and Bayt Jala, as well as several other local council members, received dismissal and deportation orders.[26]

It was not long before three different opinions emerged within the National Guidance Committee. The first pragmatic view was held by the mayors of Gaza and Bethlehem, who had previously been considered supporters of Jordan. They now displayed rather nationalist inclinations, albeit constantly stressing that preference must be given to fulfilling current needs of the municipalities and allowing multiple political opinions and freedom of organization. The second opinion was held by the mayors of Hebron and Tulkarm, who acted in coordination with Fatah leaders. They preferred to protest the "occupation" without creating a confrontation with the military government. The third view was held by the mayors of Ramallah and Nablus, who were affiliated with Palestinian left-wing forces. They called for complete nonparticipation with Israeli authorities and led the campaign against Egypt's peace initiative and attempts to hold discussions with the United States.

Another issue occupying these leaders was how to use "steadfast perseverance" funds provided to the West Bank and the Gaza Strip by Arab sources, mainly oil-producing states, to the tune of 100 million dollars a year. At first, Palestinian organizations and associations reached understandings with the Jordanian government concerning distribution of the funds, and they were used to begin building a parallel health care and welfare system, particularly for the unemployed who refused to work in Israel. From 1981 the committee in charge of these funds also began giving loans and mortgages to the self-employed and the urban middle class; however, soon after, mutual accusations of political bias and corruption abounded.[27] Local leaders accused Jordan of favoring its sympathizers with excessive generosity, particularly those in the Bethlehem region, as well as agricultural concerns owned by rural families, particularly in the vicinity of Jenin. They also accused PLO affiliates of distributing money among their supporters in the trade unions, on university campuses, and in the refugee camps. These accusations did not prevent the PLO from continuing with this course of action, or from forming a support base among significant social groups, thereby gradually creating a small nationalist bourgeoisie that empathized with its goals and supported its activities.

Leaders of the radical left wing in the territories, headed by Bassam al-Shak'ah, objected to the strengthening of Fatah and of the PLO leadership. Al-Shak'ah enjoyed an enhanced reputation as a result of a deportation order issued against him by the Israeli authorities in early December 1979. When the order was cancelled a short while later, al-Shak'ah resumed his efforts at chastising rivals on the National Guidance Committee. He and members of the PFLP announced the establishment of a new entity named the Palestinian National Front and attacked Fatah, "which perceives the struggle of the Palestinian people in the territories as no more than an instrument of its diplomatic capers on the Arab and international sphere."[28]

The strong leftist criticism gradually infiltrated some Fatah groups as well. This criticism intensified, particularly upon the introduction of two plans for resolving the Arab-Israeli conflict by prominent Arab leaders: In September 1979, King Husayn called for an international convention that would "act to reach a total solution to the Palestinian issue and the Arab-Israeli conflict."[29] In early January 1980, Sadat announced that it was necessary to examine the option of beginning to implement the autonomy plan in the Gaza Strip, and only later in the West Bank. In response to these two initiatives, a wide Palestinian coalition began forming around Fatah, advocating rejection of what was perceived to be an attempt to reinstate Arab patronage of the Palestinian cause.[30]

Israeli authorities tried to block the rising influence of the PLO in two ways: by encouraging a new Islamic orientation opposed to the PLO and the nationalist-secular left wing, and by attempts to nurture a collaborative local leadership (similar to the "peace bands" established by the British in 1936–1939). Experts advising the Israeli military government believed that a controlled surge of Islamic orientation would counterbalance the nationalist-secular orientation and that the authorities would benefit from the ensuing tensions. The authorities turned a blind eye to rising Islamic trends, demonstrated in early January 1980, when members of this group attacked a cinema in Gaza, a cultural club, and cafés that sold alcoholic beverages, but were not rebuffed. The rioters also attacked the headquarters of the Palestinian Red Crescent, as well as the home of its director, Hayder 'Abd al-Shafi.[31]

The idea of encouraging an alternate rural leadership in order to curb the influence of the PLO-supporting mayors was proposed in the spring of 1978 by the adviser to the military government, Middle East scholar Menahem Milson, who since September 1981 also served as an adviser to Israeli defense minister Ari'el Sharon. The civil administration founded by Israel began the establishment of "village societies," which reached the height of their power in 1981. These societies had their governmental center in the Hebron hills. Their members, who received a budget of three million Jordanian dinars from the Israeli authorities, were trained and equipped to use light weapons.[32] The power awarded by the authorities to these societies and to village heads resembled that of city councils. Regulations forbade displays of "empathy or support for organizations defined as terrorist organizations, by means of flags, symbols, or slogans. Such action [would] be considered a criminal offense carrying a maximal sentence of three years in prison."[33]

Although these steps succeeded in curbing the rise of nationalist groups, these groups nonetheless gradually became recognized as the primary representatives of the West Bank populace. The establishment's deliberate inattention to intensifying religious trends did not have the anticipated effect and instead resulted in the opposite, as these groups would later prove to be the core of a no less significant threat to the Israeli authorities' continued hold on the territories.

Palestinian Arabs in Israel: Connecting with Their People

Until Israel's occupation of the West Bank and Gaza Strip, Palestinian Arabs residing in Israel were almost completely severed from their brethren across the Jordanian border and in Arab countries. Throughout the period leading up to the 1967 War, they had tried to keep a low profile, maintained low levels of political activity, and tended to adhere to the laws of the military government. After the War of 1967, nineteen years of separation came to an end, and martial law was lifted.

Enhancing the Palestinian-Arab Identity

The new situation enabled families to be reunited, marriage ties to be restored, and connections to global Arab culture to be revived through personal contacts, newspapers, literature, and other types of cultural activities. The Arabs of Israel resumed their connections with two circles of identity with which they had been associated for generations—local Palestinian nationalism and pan-Arab nationalism. Binyamin Neuberger summarized the transition:

> During 1967–1977 a significant change occurred in the views of the Arab public in Israel. Before the Six-Day War most of the Arabs identified themselves as Israelis or Israeli Arabs, but the 1970s saw a significant increase in the proportion of Israel's Arabs who identified themselves as Palestinians, Arab Palestinians, or Israeli Palestinians.... There was a gradual rise in the number of votes given to communist and nationalist lists, lists featuring prominent figures from the elite constantly diminished and even disappeared, the proportion of abstainers rose, and nationalist and Islamic lists were formed and competed successfully in municipal elections.[34]

The stormy events that agitated the Palestinian-Arab world in the 1970s, from the War of October 1973 to Sadat's visit to Israel in November 1977, may have further enhanced Palestinian national identity and intensified dilemmas among Israel's Arab population. Some of these changes may be attributed to a sustained sense of foreignness and estrangement resulting from many years of discrimination. The discrimination changed form with the end of military rule, but it remained evident in all spheres of life: fewer allocations to Arab versus Jewish local authorities, disparate distribution of resources, continued land expropriation, minimal investment in the educational system and infrastructure, and so on. A concrete indication of the growing Palestinian-nationalist identity of Israel's Arabs was evident in the changes that occurred in the Israeli Communist Party. Before Israel's Arabs resumed their ties with the Arab world, this was nearly the only forum in which they could express their protest, although during Israel's initial years most of the party's supporters were Jewish. Now the number of Arab members rose, the number of Jews diminished, and the party's formerly militant ideology with its focus on class issues was replaced with Palestinian-nationalist concepts. A glance at the writings of some of the party's leaders during this period, including Arab authors Emil Habibi, Tawfiq Zayyad, and Salem Jubran, will confirm the difficulty of discerning between their own work and that written as part of what may be called the general trend of Arab literature with a Palestinian agenda. This process of transition from a workers' party to a Palestinian-Arab nationalist party reached its apex in 1975 with the founding of Hadash (the Hebrew acronym for the Democratic Front for Peace and Equality), which encompassed the Israeli Communist Party and other Jewish and Arab groups.

The feelings of alienation and discrimination experienced by Arab citizens of Israel were accompanied by a sense of helplessness upon encountering social, cultural, and professional barriers that precluded any hope of reducing the disparity and becoming truly integrated. Arab intellectuals, frustrated with the absence of social mobility, chose to establish organizations representing the desire of the Arab populace to enjoy full equality within Israeli society. The examples cited below are only a sample of the most significant. The National Association of Arab Academics was established in 1971 in Nazareth at the initiative of communist and nationalist intellectuals. That same year, intellectuals with nationalist inclinations founded the Academics of Nazareth. The National Committee of Heads of Arab Local Councils was founded in Shafa'amr in 1974. The Committee for the Defense of Arab Lands, the National Committee of Arab High School Pupils, and the National Committee of Arab Students were founded in Nazareth in 1975 at the joint initiative of communist and nationalist groups. The High Follow-up Committee for Arab Citizens of Israel is composed of mayors, Arab members of the Knesset, and public figures and representatives, and was founded in Shafa'amr in 1982. Although most of these associations and organizations were not officially recognized by Israel, they had occasional unofficial contact with state agencies (the Committee of Heads of Council and the High Follow-up Committee in particular). This type of relationship resembled that of the British toward the Executive Arab Committee and the Arab Higher Committee during the British mandate.

The Role of Land Day in Shaping Palestinian Identity

The incident most indicative of the changes occurring in the political behavior of Arab citizens of Israel, and of the conduct of the new organizations and societies, has become known as Land Day. At its heart was an episode in which land in the vicinity of the villages of Sakhnin, 'Arrabeh, and Dayr Hanna, in an area marked "firing range number 9," was expropriated as part of a plan called Development of the Galilee. The Committee for the Defense of Arab Lands and the Committee of Heads of Arab Local Councils protested the plan and demanded that it be cancelled as it was based, in part, on the expropriation of lands owned by Arabs. When their demand met with refusal, they decided to call for a strike in all Arab towns on March 30, 1976.

Severe riots broke out, resulting in clashes between police forces and demonstrators. The Committee for the Defense of Arab Lands and the Committee of Heads of Arab Local Councils convened in the Shafa'amr town hall and disagreements emerged: Mayors associated with the authorities applied pressure to cancel the strike or moderate its manifestations. Council heads and mayors with communist and nationalist orientations objected to this approach. Large police forces were deployed near the building, surrounded by hundreds of youth, who urged the leaders not to give in to the moderates. At the same time, reports were coming in of casualties in clashes between police and demonstrators in 'Arrabeh and Sakhnin and the atmosphere in Shafa'amr became stormy. The next day the clashes spread. In Kfar Kanna and Taybeh two demonstrators were killed by police, three were killed in Sakhnin, and one in 'Arrabeh. In addition to the six casualties, dozens of policemen were injured. March 30 has since become a prominent date on the Palestinian calendar and it is commemorated throughout the diaspora. Those killed are remembered as *shahid* (martyrs), and a central memorial was established at the entrance to Sakhnin. More modest memorials were erected in the other villages that sustained casualties. The day is devoted to marches and a central assembly. Those engaged in forging the Palestinian national memory are conflicted as to the processes that led up to Land Day and to the identity of its leaders. The communists emphasize their leading role (and particularly that of Tawfiq Zayyad).[35] Spokesmen for the nationalist camp emphasize the preeminence of the Committee for Defense of Arab Lands (headed by Muhammad Mi'ari and Bishop Riyah Abu al-'Asal).[36] The events of this day have become a bone of contention among these groups.

The Village Sons Movement and Student Activism

Another manifestation of the heightened local Palestinian identity was the emergence of the Village Sons Movement on Israeli university campuses as a counterbalance to Hadash. The movement was founded in 1972 by Muhammad Kaywan, an attorney and former member of the al-Ard movement and chairman of the Arab Students' Association at Tel Aviv University. Unlike al-Ard, which emphasized pan-Arab nationalism, the new movement stressed local Palestinian nationalism and called for the establishment of a democratic secular state on the entire territory of historical Palestine. The movement denounced the participation of Arab citizens in elections for the Israeli parliament, but took part in local elections and even attained modest success.[37]

An important shift in Arab engagement in Israeli politics was evident upon the transfer of power between the two main political blocs in the 1977 national elections in Israel. The defeat of the Labor Party (which had merged with the left-wing Mapai Party in 1968) marked the culmination of affiliated Arab satellite parties active since 1948 and the end of traditional patronage by prominent families. The Labor Party opened its ranks to full membership of Arab citizens and began to reserve specific slots on its Knesset list for Muslims, Christians, and Druze. The right-wing Likud Party reserved a slot for a Druze candidate.

Notes

1. Sayigh, *Al-Kifah al-Muslah wa al-Bahath 'An al-Dula: Al-Haraka al-Wataniyya al-Filastiniyya, 1949–1993* [Armed Struggle and the Search for a State], 497.

2. 'Abd al-Rahman, *Al-Harb al-'Arabiyya al-'Isra'iliyya al-Rabi'ah, Waqai' wa Tafa'ulat* [Fourth Arab-Israeli War], 163.

3. Mahmoud Abbas, *Thawrat al-Mustahil: al-kitaba al-Mustahila* [The Impossible Revolution: The Impossible Writing], 44.

4. 'Abd al-Rahman, *Al-Harb al-'Arabiyya al-'Isra'iliyya al-Rabi'ah, Waqai' wa Tafa'ulat* [Fourth Arab-Israeli War], 157n2.

5. "Al-Nashat al-feda'i hasab a'itrafat al-nateq al-Isra'ili" [The Activity of the Fida'iyyun as Announced by the Israeli Spokesman].

6. Sayigh, *Al-Kifah al-Muslah wa al-Bahath 'An al-Dula: Al-Haraka al-Wataniyya al-Filastiniyya, 1949–1993* [Armed Struggle and the Search for a State], 482.

7. "Al-Muqawama al-Filastiniyya amam al-tahddiyat al-jadida" [The Palestinian Resistance versus the New Challenges] *Shu'un Filastiniyya* 30 (February 1974): 25.

8. "Al-Muqawama al-Filastiniyya amam al-tahddiyat al-jadida" [The Palestinian Resistance versus the New Challenges] *Shu'un Filastiniyya* 30 (February 1974): 11.

9. *Ila al-Amam*, November 9, 1973.

10. *Al-Hadaf*, December 9, 1973.

11. Habash, *Al-Nahaj al-Thawri fi Mawajhat al-Tahdiyat* [Revolutionary Course], 41.

12. *Filastin al-Thawra*, January 29, 1974.

13. *Al-Safir*, March 2, 1976.

14. Sayigh, *Al-Kifah al-Muslah wa al-Bahath 'An al-Dula: Al-Haraka al-Wataniyya al-Filastiniyya, 1949–1993* [Armed Struggle and the Search for a State], 492.

15. *Al-Safir*, May 19, 1974.

16. 'Abd al-Hadi, *Al-Mas'alah al-Filastiniyya wa Mashari' al-Hulul al-Siyasiyya, 1934-1974* [Palestinian Question and Proposed Political Solutions], 572.

17. Sayigh, *Al-Kifah al-Muslah wa al-Bahath 'An al-Dula: Al-Haraka al-Wataniyya al-Filastiniyya, 1949–1993* [Armed Struggle and the Search for a State], 501.

18. Sahliyeh, *In Search of Leadership*, 22–23.

19. Sayigh, *Al-Kifah al-Muslah wa al-Bahath 'An al-Dula: Al-Haraka al-Wataniyya al-Filastiniyya, 1949–1993* [Armed Struggle and the Search for a State], 658–659.

20. Graham-Brown, *Education, Repression, and Liberation: Palestinians*, 83–85.

21. *Al-Sha'b*, May 8, 1978.

22. *Al-Fajr*, April 9, 1978.

23. *Al-Fajr*, May 7, 1978.

24. *Al-Sha'b*, May 4, 1978.

25. *Al-Fajr*, July 3, 1978.
26. *Al-Quds*, January 3, 1979.
27. Tamari, "Al-Dinamiyat al-ijtama'iyya wa-'ydiolojiyyat al-muqawama fi al-diffa al-gharbiyya" [Social and Ideological Dynamics of the Resistance in the West Bank], 256–257.
28. Sayigh, *Al-Kifah al-Muslah wa al-Bahath 'An al-Dula: Al-Haraka al-Wataniyya al-Filastiniyya, 1949–1993* [Armed Struggle and the Search for a State], 679.
29. *Journal of Palestine Studies* 9, no. 2 (Winter 1980), 170.
30. *Filastin al-Thawra*, January 20, 1980.
31. Sayigh, *Al-Kifah al-Muslah wa al-Bahath 'An al-Dula: Al-Haraka al-Wataniyya al-Filastiniyya, 1949–1993* [Armed Struggle and the Search for a State], 680.
32. 'Abd al-Jawad, *Al-Awamir al-'Askariyya al-Isra'iliyya* [Israeli Military Orders], 19.
33. Kretzmer, *Legal Status of the Arabs in Israel*, 140.
34. Neuberger, "Hami'ut Ha'arvi: Nikur Vehishtalvut" [Arab Minority], 66.
35. For an example of this narrative, see Murqus, *Aqwq min al-Nisyan* [Stronger than Forgetting], 291–293.
36. For an example of this narrative, see Jarbuni, *Sira' 'Ala al-Ard* [Struggle for the Land], 48–61.
37. Neuberger, "Hami'ut Ha'arvi: Nikur Vehishtalvut" [Arab Minority], 110.

10

In the Lebanese Maelstrom: Arafat Loses Ground

In Lebanon, PLO-Lebanese relations remained volatile following the 1973 impasse. Incidents between Lebanese army and police units and Palestinian organizations occurred time and again, albeit at a moderate-enough level as to be controlled under the 1969 Cairo Treaty. Nevertheless, it needed only a spark to ignite the ultimate confrontation.

War Erupts

On April 13, 1975, shots were fired at a Maronite church in the Christian suburb of 'Ayn al-Rummana, where Phalange leader Pierre al-Jumayyil was praying. One person was killed, and the Phalangists, certain that the shooters were Palestinian, retaliated by ambushing a bus carrying Lebanese and Palestinians to the Tal al-Za'tar refugee camp in east Beirut. In the ambush, twenty-seven passengers were killed and nineteen were injured. This massacre was the opening salvo of the civil war. Several members of Palestinian organizations and their allies in Lebanese left-wing and Muslim organizations demanded the dismissal of Phalange ministers from the government and the dismantling of their militia.[1] Yasir Arafat was careful not to be perceived as intervening in Lebanese matters and tried to talk to President Sulayman Franjiyya, but to no avail. The Lebanese army received orders to assist the Phalange in its clashes with Lebanese left-wing forces and their Palestinian allies. A Maronite coalition of Phalange members, army commanders, and the president joined forces to overthrow Sunni prime minister Rashid al-Salah on May 15, 1975. The alliance opposed to the Maronites was now united in the demand for general structural reform of the regime and for "reexamination of the Citizenship and Immigration Act, with unreserved support of the Palestinian resistance movement."[2]

The Phalange and army commanders focused their wrath on the Tal al-Za'tar refugee camp, located in a Christian-populated area, and demanded that it be transferred elsewhere.[3] Arafat declared that "the PLO will be obliged to defend the Palestinian refugee camps in Lebanon."[4] He tried to hold talks with the Phalange command but was deterred by internal Palestinian pressures. Meanwhile the other Palestinian organizations, together with Muslim forces and the Lebanese left wing, attacked Christian neighborhoods in east Beirut. Arafat initially attempted to declare Palestinian neutrality in the internecine Lebanese conflict on May 25, but it became impossible to avoid Palestinian involvement in the maelstrom of Lebanese civil war.[5] As in Jordan, here too Arafat's leadership was insufficient to prevent entanglement in a course of events that was to exact an incredibly heavy price. Although he attempted to talk to the Maronites through confidential channels, radicals on both sides dictated the eventual escalation.[6]

The PLO's situation was further aggravated once the Maronites drew closer to Damascus in late 1975. The reconciliation of Syrian rulers with the Christian camp disrupted Arafat's plans, however, and rampant rumors surrounded the Syrians' intention of taking control of the PLO and replacing Arafat with their trusted ally, al-Sa'iqa leader Zuhir Muhsin.[7] Phalange leader Pierre Jumayyil was summoned to Damascus on December 6, 1975, for discussions on the future of the Lebanese regime, while his son Bashir was busy slaughtering Lebanese Muslims and Palestinians.[8] Consequently, the Christians imposed a siege on the Palestinian refugee camps of Tal al-Za'tar, Jiser al-Basha, and Dbayeh, the Muslim slums, and in fact all of west Beirut.

The PLO Is Drawn into War

By January 1976, the "joint forces" coalition had formed, made up of left-wing movements and Palestinian organizations that objected to the Lebanese forces. On January 6, Arafat gathered the representatives of this coalition for a meeting in his office in west Beirut. Those present planned a combined attack on the junctions and strongholds of east Beirut with the aim of opening the routes to the refugee camps and the besieged neighborhoods. The attack occurred the same day but failed, due to lack of coordination between the various forces, as well as problems with obedience. The Maronites launched a counterattack, taking over the Dbayeh refugee camp and expelling its residents to west Beirut. In response, Fatah forces surrounded the towns of Damour, Jiyeh, Zahleh, and al-Sa'diyyat, thus involving the Lebanese army in the vicious sectarian fighting. Up to this point, despite military orders to fight the Palestinians, some officers and soldiers had tried to remain neutral. Now, though air force and army units attacked the Palestinians, groups of Muslim soldiers and officers deserted and joined the "joint forces." A detailed description of the civil war is not within the purview of the current work, however.

While Lebanon was, for all intents and purposes, breaking up into sectarian districts embroiled in internecine rivalries, it was also under increased danger of foreign intervention. Two unofficial alliances gradually formed, between Israel and the Maronites on the one hand and between Egypt and Fatah on the other. At this point, Syria was called into action to defend its exclusive authority in Lebanon. On February 14, 1976, Damascus succeeded in forcing leaders of the rival parties to accept a compromise in which the Palestinians were mentioned only as part of Lebanon's Muslim left-wing camp. Syrian leaders tried to force the agreement on the PLO through al-Sa'iqa, using threats and executions. The rift between Syria and the PLO deepened, as can be seen from the words of Salah Khalaf: "The Palestinian revolution is not a number that can be added to the number of Muslims in this country. . . . We of Fatah will not let any Arab regime become the guardian of our concerns."[9] Mustafa Tlas, the Syrian minister of defense, responded: "Syria will strike any party attempting to object to the arrangement reached in Lebanon."[10]

Syrian-PLO relations became even more complicated following the Palestinian initiative, advanced by Khalil al-Wazir, to encourage Muslim defection from the Lebanese army and to organize the defectors into an Arab Lebanese army commanded by allies of the PLO. Commanders of this force opened Lebanese army weapons stores to the Palestinians, allowing them to steal heavy weapons. Once again, Arafat tried to prevent the rift from intensifying, and on March 27,

1976, he left for Damascus, where his talks with Assad led to a cease-fire. However, Lebanese and Palestinian left-wing forces continued their attacks on the Maronites and supporters of President Franjiyya and called for disengagement from Syria. The Journal of the Popular Front for the Liberation of Palestine, *al-Hadaf*, welcomed Arafat upon his return from Damascus with the headline, "No to the cease-fire, no to the Syrian initiative, yes to further fighting."[11] The PFLP was joined by leaders of Fatah's left-wing division, headed by Nimr Salah. They renewed the fighting and threatened the port of Junya, the Maronites' primary outlet to the sea.

The military actions of the Lebanese left wing and Palestinian coalition were a source of concern for Syrian rulers. On April 2, 1976, they sent the PLO an ultimatum to hold its fire. To underscore their intentions, Syrian authorities also immediately initiated an extensive operation to arrest Fatah members in Syria. While the PLO headquarters was overcome by uncertainty and torn between its factions, in Damascus a decision was made to directly intervene in Lebanon.

Syria, Israel, and the End of the Civil War

The Syrian authorities presented their plan as an attempt to save the Maronites, thus ensuring that Israel, the United States, and others would not prevent them from invading Lebanon. They began by instructing al-Sa'iqa to conquer key locations, and the next day, April 9, their forces crossed the border. Arafat was surprised by Syria's strong reaction; he instructed his men to avoid any contact with Syrian forces and asked Damascus for a further discussion of the cease-fire. Another round of talks in Syria produced an additional Damascus Treaty, in which Assad promised Arafat that he would withdraw the Syrian army and permit free elections, and Arafat promised to recognize Syria's status in Lebanon. The document listed the terms of Syria's relationship with the Palestinians in Lebanon.[12] Arafat, however, did not represent all Palestinian forces operating in Lebanon. The other forces did not consider themselves bound by his agreements with Assad and consequently a cease-fire was not reached. Moreover, the PLO and the Syrian regime did not reach a state of mutual trust, and Syrian forces continued to pour into Lebanon.

Syria succeeded in convincing elements in the coalition comprising the PLO and the left to publish an announcement on May 31, 1976, supporting the presence of its forces in Lebanon. Syrian rulers sought to use this strategy to end all resistance to their involvement. They promised to support Maronite forces, in return for instigating a comprehensive attack on the strongholds of the PLO and their allies in west Beirut. The Syrians also encouraged PLA units in west Beirut and al-Sa'iqa fighters to attack PLO headquarters in the Fakhani neighborhood and PLO strongholds in the refugee camps. This integrated attack failed and PLO forces seized some of their Palestinian brethren who had been operating under Syrian instructions. The head of al-Sa'iqa, Zuhir Muhsin, succeeded in fleeing to east Beirut and from there to the clusters of Syrian forces situated in the Beqa' Valley of Lebanon. A reconciliation initiative by the Arab League did nothing to calm this bloody turn of events and the Palestinians, with all their organizations and refugees, continued to be buffeted by the raging currents.

On June 20, Christian forces attacked the besieged refugee camps of Tal al-Za'tar and Jisr al-Basha in east Beirut. About thirty thousand Palestinians and locals were living in the two camps, defended by some twelve hundred militia and seventy PLA soldiers. Jisr al-Basha succumbed first, as the attackers broke into the camp, murdering dozens of men, raping women, and looting whatever they could take.[13] In the first week of August 1976, Tal al-Za'tar surrendered as well, and similar atrocities were committed. This time the assaulters were accompanied by tanks and bulldozers, which destroyed all buildings to prevent the residents from returning. Estimates indicate that one thousand to two thousand people were killed after the camp surrendered, while total casualties from the beginning of the siege on both camps are estimated at 4,280.[14]

The surrender of the refugee camps in east Beirut, and Syria's part in these events, led to increased cooperation between Fatah and Egypt on the one hand, and the left-wing organizations and Iraq on the other. Egypt sent supplies, ammunition, and about two thousand Palestinian volunteers who convened in Cairo. Iraq sent its allies weapons and some five thousand volunteers. Saudi Arabia sent the PLO and its allies assistance as well.[15] Arafat initiated meetings between his envoys and Pierre al-Jumayyil's men and the latter displayed willingness to accept a compromise between the Maronites and the Palestinians; however, once again radicals from both camps prevented any chance of compromise. On September 28, the Syrians launched a comprehensive attack and by mid-October had dislodged the Muslim-Palestinian coalition from most strategic locations. Only after the conquest of Mount Lebanon did Syria respond positively to an inter-Arab initiative promoting a total cease-fire in Lebanon. The cease-fire agreement was signed on October 21, stating that the Lebanese government would once again control all essential government facilities and the PLO would reorganize its presence in Lebanon according to the Cairo Treaty of 1969.[16] This marked the end of eighteen months of civil war, clearing the field for further mutual harassment with no territorial conquests.

These turbulent episodes formed the setting for the secret treaty gradually materializing between Israel and the Maronite forces. A Lebanese army force commanded by Major Sa'd Haddad established the Army of Free Lebanon, in cooperation with Christian militiamen, which deployed along the Lebanese border with Israel. This force maintained a strong relationship with Israel and its spokesmen called for removal of the Palestinians and Syrians from Lebanon. It also took control of a strip of land that prevented contact between PLO bases in eastern and western Lebanon.[17]

The PLO's situation in Lebanon had now significantly worsened. Its "safe base" in the south, for which it had worked so hard, ceased to exist. The area in which it had enjoyed freedom of action before the civil war was now occupied by four rivals: Syrian forces, Maronite forces, Sa'ad Haddad's militia, and the Israeli army. In other parts of Lebanon it was no better off. Two Palestinian camps in east Beirut had been completely destroyed, and the others were partially ruined. The militant forces had suffered harsh losses and the option of armed struggle against Israel now seemed more remote than ever.

A Diplomatic Opportunity

Other options presented themselves to the Palestinians in early 1977. President Anwar Sadat of Egypt and King Husayn of Jordan issued a joint call to renew peace talks with Israel, initiated in Geneva after the War of October 1973. The joint declaration stressed their continued recognition of the PLO as the exclusive legitimate representative of the Palestinian people and included a demand that the PLO be invited to the talks as a full partner, with the same status as the other parties.[18]

Encouraged by this declaration, Arafat instructed several of his assistants, primarily Mahmoud Abbas (Abu Mazen), to hold initial talks with Israelis lacking official status who were known for supporting contacts with the PLO, led by Major General (res.) Matityahu Peled and journalist Uri Avneri. Arafat himself met with UN Secretary-General Kurt Waldheim in Damascus in early February 1977 and subsequently opened diplomatic missions in many capitals. Farouq al-Qaddumi declared on behalf of the PLO that they would be willing to take part in the peace conference in Geneva in order to establish a Palestinian state.[19] However, these appeals to the diplomatic world did not produce the anticipated results. Israeli prime minister Yitzhak Rabin declared that his country objected both to the establishment of a Palestinian state and to negotiations with the PLO, which he called a terrorist organization.[20] The Army of Free Lebanon launched an attack against PLO forces, and southern Lebanon was once again engulfed in conflict. Soon the conflagration reached other parts of the country as well, following the March 1977 murder, most likely by Syrian agents, of Kamal Junbalat, a Druze leader and close ally of Arafat.

Sadat's Initiative and the Rejection Front

While the PLO was fortifying its position as the exclusive representative of the Palestinian people, and the United States was gradually beginning to accept the organization as a possible partner for reaching a general settlement in the Middle East, Sadat announced his own peace initiative with Israel. His historic visit to Jerusalem and his declarations of the end of hostilities between Egypt and Israel met with unwavering and sweeping objections throughout the Arab world. Finding himself in the midst of a split between his Egyptian ally and every other Arab country, particularly his sworn rival Hafez al-Assad, Arafat decided to join the majority of the Arab world. He took part in a summit meeting convened in Libya in early December 1977 and calling itself the Summit of Resistance and Steadfast Perseverance, where a Rejection Front was subsequently formed. He also signed the conclusive announcement declaring Sadat a "traitor to the Arab cause."

Nonetheless, Arafat wished to maintain open channels with the United States, whose president, Jimmy Carter, was the first US president to declare the Palestinians' right of self-determination. For this purpose he continued to maintain official Fatah and PLO delegates in Cairo. But the PLO's boisterous and public objection to Sadat's peace endeavors significantly reduced this option, resulting in a decrease in US support of the PLO and eroding the confidential contacts between them. At this stage, Arafat chose to enhance his Soviet ties, and in early March 1978, he headed a Palestinian delegation to Moscow, where he gave a speech on the Soviet Union's assistance to national liberation movements in general and in the Arab world in particular. He also asked for, and received, military aid intended to provide compensation for losses accrued during the Lebanese civil war.

The Confrontation with Israel and Moving Out of Lebanon

Arafat's decision to side with the Rejection Front and the Soviet Union coincided with an unfolding military confrontation with Israel. Khalil al-Wazir received Yasir Arafat's approval to stage a demonstration. On March 11, 1978, a large Fatah force landed on an Israeli beach and hijacked a bus traveling to Tel-Aviv. In the operation to free the hostages, thirty-six Israelis were killed, mostly civilians, as well as nine Fatah men. In an interview in *Shu'un Filastiniyya*, al-Wazir said, "This operation has proven that our people can reach any location we wish."[21]

Operation Litani

The Israeli response to the attack on the Coastal Road was not late in coming. A large Israeli force crossed the Lebanese border and occupied a seven- to eight-kilometer-wide "security zone," in effect creating a buffer between the Palestinian organizations and the border. Operation Litani ended in a cease-fire declared by the UN Security Council on March 20, 1978. Israel lost twenty-one soldiers in the fighting, and the Palestinian organizations sixty-five. The estimated number of local civilians killed was in the hundreds. Tens of thousands left their homes in panic and fled northward, unable to return to the area occupied by Israel. PLO forces were pushed north of the Litani River and the Army of Free Lebanon deployed in the security zone. UN forces stationed themselves between the two, and the PLO's capacity to strike Israel at its border seemed to have come to an end.

Operation Litani disproved the assumption by PLO command that Israel would demonstrate restraint as long as it was engaged in peace talks with Egypt, and that operations such as hijacking a bus within Israeli territory would not lead to strict retaliation. Consequently, it led to a torrent of self-criticism regarding the type of judgment employed, combined with criticism of the Arab states that had remained on the sidelines during the invasion of Lebanon. The PLO was rife with controversy as well. The faction headed by Arafat expressed distrust of the Rejection Front's ability to operate efficiently on behalf of the Palestinian people and asserted that it was necessary to embrace a pragmatic orientation and strive for the establishment of a Palestinian state or entity in any territory vacated by Israel as part of negotiations with Egypt. Leaders of the radical fronts, as well as Fatah leftists, objected to any compromise and sought to continue applying the concept of armed struggle. Although the majority supported Arafat's view, he did not publicly come out in support of Sadat's course of action, not even when Sadat's confidants suggested that he join in negotiations for the autonomy plan proposed by Israel. Whether concerned about a split in the PLO, or in capitulation to pressures brought to bear by Hafez al-Assad, Arafat rejected all opportunities to join the peace process.

Reorganization in Lebanon

After Operation Litani, and in light of the relative quiet along the cease-fire line with the Phalange and its allies, Arafat resumed his attempts to build the PLO a virtual state within Lebanon. The primary bases of his new system were in west Beirut and in the southern cities of Sidon and Tyre, as well as in the towns of Nabatiyyeh and Damour. The main offices and headquarters were in west Beirut, and the "state" they controlled was named the Republic of Fakhani, after the neighborhood in which they resided. Sayigh summarized: "The PLO became more than a state within a state in Lebanon. It became a state in exile that enjoyed independence by virtue of its control of Lebanese territory and thanks to financial resources originating from inter-Arab assistance and international recognition."[22] The revitalized PLO "state" in Lebanon rapidly achieved control of both military and civil systems. It deployed its forces along extensive territories in the south and shared control of west Beirut and the Beqa' Valley with other forces. It exercised exclusive control over several neighborhoods and refugee camps in the cities of Tyre, Sidon, and Tripoli. All these were directly supervised by a military organization assisted by a civil-service apparatus.

On the municipal-civil level, the PLO declared that it was transferring primary authority to the Lebanese government, but in reality its men ran a parallel, and sometimes alternate, system to that operated by the government. The bureaucratic structures produced new leaders interested in exercising authority and competing for positions, power, and proximity to decisionmakers. In these circumstances, Arafat proved himself an expert at the art of "divide and rule." He forcibly controlled all rivalries, took care that all those capable of independent initiatives neutralized each other, and succeeded in controlling all processes of decisionmaking, money distribution, and nominations. In retrospect, it seems that it was in the Republic of Fakhani that Arafat assumed leadership of both the military and political systems. He would later implement the lessons he learned there in the Palestinian Authority when it was established in 1994.

This PLO government was a cause of concern for many, including Syria, Israel, the Maronites, and the central Lebanese government. Each made efforts to overthrow it, sometimes in coordination with each other. From early 1979, Israel and the Army of Free Lebanon initiated daily bombardments in the south, causing tens of thousands of villagers to abandon the area and move north, mainly to Beirut, where they became a burden on the Lebanese authorities as well as on the organizations and the Palestinians. Israel also occasionally bombed refugee camps and other places controlled by the PLO in Beirut and Tripoli. In July 1979 the commander in chief of the IDF concluded that over the past year the Israeli army had performed 1,020 "preventive operations in Lebanon against PLO targets."

Israel's continuous military pressure and the stream of Lebanese refugees created friction between the PLO and the Lebanese population in PLO-controlled territory. Representatives of the population repeatedly complained of the arrogant conduct of Palestinian operatives, theft, and damage to property, as well as the imposition of special taxes and collection of protection money. PLO leaders responded to these accusations by expressing their regret, promising to move the organization's offices out of residential neighborhoods, and announcing the payment of compensation to anyone damaged by Israeli or Shiite Amal organization operations. The latter, led by Nabih Berri, now headed the list of those criticizing the Palestinians and their conduct. The deep disapproval intensified, eventually resulting in an armed conflict with the Palestinian left wing in March and April 1980.

Israel's Invasion of Lebanon and the Departure of the PLO

The PLO control of Lebanon was challenged by Israel. Routine hostility toward the Army of Free Lebanon and Israel, its patron, worsened in July 1981, when Israel systematically bombed PLO targets in southern Lebanon. IDF Commander in Chief Refa'el Eytan said that the purpose of the bombing was to prevent the PLO from becoming established and organized, a development that would put Israel at risk. The PLO retaliated with barrages of Katyusha rockets aimed at towns in northern Israel. The UN Security Council intervened to no avail and the Israeli air force destroyed six bridges on the Zaharani and Litani Rivers, cutting off PLO forces in the south. Even these bombings did not put an end to PLO attacks against Israeli towns. In response to the death of three Israelis, the Israeli government approved a massive bombardment of Fatah headquarters in the Fakhani neighborhood, in which nearly thirty PLO operatives were killed. In addition, some one hundred and fifty civilians were killed and six hundred injured. The PLO continued to shoot Katyusha rockets at Israeli towns. On July 24 a cease-fire agreement went into effect, mediated by Phillip Habib, an American diplomat of Lebanese descent. However, Israel was unwilling to put up with the existence of a PLO state enforcing the concept of armed struggle from a safe haven in Lebanon. Israeli forces prepared an extensive military operation and waited for the right opportunity, which arose ten months after the cease-fire was initiated.

PLO leaders were aware of Israel's military preparations and made an effort to avoid providing an excuse for putting them into effect. They tried to maintain the cease-fire even at the expense of confrontations with other Palestinian forces. However, Sabri al-Banna's group (Abu Nidal) refused to cooperate with PLO leaders, and on June 3, 1982, they attempted to assassinate Shlomo Argov, the Israeli ambassador to London. The next day Israel embarked on the First Lebanon War by aiming concentrated aerial bombardments at PLO headquarters in Beirut and at bases located up to forty kilometers from the border. The PLO was astonished at the military might wielded by Israel and at the scope of its invasion of Lebanon, which resembled a major modern war. It was unable to handle this show of force and promptly succumbed all the way to Beirut. Nabatiyyeh surrendered on the first day of the war, followed by the Beaufort Castle. The next day saw the surrender of the city of Tyre, and in a matter of two to three days the refugee camps in its vicinity followed suit. Two days later the largest refugee camp, al-Rashidiyyeh, succumbed as well. Israeli forces surrounded Sidon and the refugee camps encircling it and managed to destroy the PLO forces by June 13. At the same time, they attacked Syria's forces in the Jezzin sector, destroying its aerial defense in the Beqa' Valley. Syria withdrew its forces to the Beirut-Damascus Road and thus enabled the Israeli forces to meet up with the Maronites in east Beirut and lay siege to the PLO base in west Beirut. Massive Israeli bombardments were aimed at crushing the Palestinian and Lebanese defense forces entrenched in the western part of the city.

The PLO leadership had planned to hold on for a lengthy period of time, in which international and inter-Arab political pressure would be put to bear on Israel, but to its dismay no such pressure was formed. Instead, many Lebanese elements, wishing to save Beirut from complete destruction, began pressuring the PLO to leave Lebanon. About a month after the war began, on July 2, 1982, Arafat submitted a document signed by the PLO leadership to Lebanese prime minister Shafiq al-Wazzan, expressing the Palestinians' willingness to withdraw from Lebanon. Al-Wazzan presented the document to the American mediator, Phillip Habib, who passed it on to the American secretary of state, George Schultz. The American government accepted the proposal and submitted it to Israel for its approval. However, the hawks in the Israeli government, led by Minister of Defense Ari'el Sharon and supported by Commander in Chief Refa'el Eytan, were determined to bring the Palestinians to their knees. On July 6, Israel began heavy artillery shelling of the PLO forces besieged in west Beirut. When the destruction intensified with no surrender in sight, the United States succeeded in facilitating an agreement for the withdrawal of PLO forces from west Beirut, backed by Arab and European guarantees organized by Egypt and France, to ensure the safety of the Palestinian leadership.

On August 21, most of the Palestinian leadership and four hundred special forces men were evacuated through the Port of Beirut. Throughout the next eleven days nearly fourteen thousand Palestinian fighters and Arab volunteers were evacuated to eight Arab countries: Algeria, Tunisia, South Yemen, North Yemen, Jordan, Sudan, Syria, and Iraq. The last to leave was Yasir Arafat himself. He chose to depart for Athens, maybe as an expression of his disappointment at the conduct of his Arab brethren. From Athens he traveled to Tunisia, where he remained with many of the organization's elite until the Oslo Accords with Israel were signed on September 13, 1993. He returned to Gaza in May 1994.

This was the end of the PLO's second attempt to establish a safe base of operations from which to launch its armed struggle. In Tunisia, two thousand kilometers from Palestine, with its fighters dispersed among eight countries, it would reach the decision that there was no recourse but to recognize the existence of Israel, and that the way to its ultimate goal of Palestinian sovereignty must take a political path involving compromises and concessions.

Notes

1. *Al-Safir*, April 16, 1975.
2. *Al-Nahar*, May 16, 1975.
3. *Al-Nahar*, May 22, 1975.
4. Center for Palestinian Research, *Al-Kitab al-Sanwi Lilqadiyya al-Filastiniyya Lisnat 1975* [Yearbook of the Palestinian Problem for 1975], 544n4.
5. *Filastin al-Thawra*, May 25, 1975.
6. *Filastin al-Thawra*, December 5, 1975.
7. Center for Palestinian Research, *Al-Kitab al-Sanwi Lilqadiyya al-Filastiniyya Lisnat 1975* [Yearbook of the Palestinian Problem for 1975], 544n4.
8. Research Center of the Arab League, *Al-Watha'iq al-'Arabiyya al-Filastiniyya Lisnat 1975* [Arab-Palestinian Documents for 1975], 738.
9. *Al-Safir*, February 16, 1976.
10. *Al-Hayat*, February 28, 1976.

11. *Al-Hadaf*, March 27, 1976.

12. *Tishrin*, April 16, 1976.

13. Center for Palestinian Research, *Al-Kitab al-Sanwi Lilqadiyya al-Filastiniyya Lisnat 1975* [Yearbook of the Palestinian Problem for 1975], 565.

14. *Al-Huriyya*, August 30, 1976.

15. *Al-Safir*, August 22, 1976.

16. Research Center of the Arab League, *Al-Watha'iq al-'Arabiyya Lisnat 1976* [Arab-Palestinian Documents for 1976], 741–744.

17. *Al-Nahar*, October 11, 1976.

18. Research Center of the Arab League, *Al-Watha'iq al-'Arabiyya al-Filastiniyya Lisnat 1977* [Arab-Palestinian Documents for 1977], 5.

19. *Al-Ahram*, February 26, 1977.

20. *New York Times*, January 20, 1977.

21. *Shu'un Filastiniyya* 77 (April 1978): 27.

22. Sayigh, *Al-Kifah al-Muslah wa al-Bahath 'An al-Dula: Al-Haraka al-Wataniyya al-Filastiniyya, 1949–1993* [Armed Struggle and the Search for a State], 604–605.

11

The Move to Tunisia

The move to Tunisia after the elimination of the state-within-a-state administered by the PLO in Lebanon was certainly not easy for Arafat or the PLO. It meant that they were located farther away from the lands of Palestine, which had been visible from the areas they controlled in Jordan and Lebanon. It also meant losing their almost complete domination of an extensive area, comprising a significant part of the Palestinian populace, and management of quasi-governmental institutions. The departure from Beirut can probably be considered a turning point in the history of the PLO, the Palestinian national movement in general, and the armed struggle in particular.

Following a visit to Yasir Arafat's headquarters in Tunis, Palestinian historian Samih Shabib wrote, "In the neighborhood of Solimar in Tunis there is a hotel, home of the head of the PLO and most of its commanders and activists. It is hard to believe that the PLO consists of no more than a hotel defended by Tunisian armored personnel carriers, bearing the title 'Riot Restraint Forces.'"[1]

The PLO Reaches an Impasse

After evacuating his headquarters in the Fakhani neighborhood of west Beirut, Arafat tried to return to Lebanon and reestablish himself in the refugee camps near the city of Tripoli in the north. This time, however, Syria's forces were tenacious; they surrounded the refugee camps of Nahr al-Bared and al-Baddawi, bombed them, and forced Arafat to leave with the remainder of his forces. Thus the military dominance of the PLO and its entire infrastructure, established over the years as part of a strategy of armed struggle, were lost forever. Now it was no longer possible to envision the revival of this strategy using similar methods. In addition, the Syrians infiltrated various Palestinian organizations, including Arafat's own, to undermine his status and his position as the exclusive leader of the Palestinian cause. This policy succeeded in arousing an internal revolt among Fatah during the first half of 1983, which continued until the end of the year.

The rebellion within Fatah emerged in response to Arafat's delay in carrying out a thorough investigation into the relatively easy collapse of the PLO's defense lines during the Israeli invasion of Lebanon in June 1982. After the PLO forces left Beirut, senior military commanders in the PLO were promptly accused of deserting their posts and fleeing northward toward Tripoli. Most of the accusations were directed at the commander of the al-Qastal forces, Haj Isma'il Jaber, and the commander of the al-Karama forces, Ghazi 'Atallah. Some say that the demand for a committee of inquiry was made by General Sa'd Sayil, a senior PLO military commander and a member of the organization's supreme military council, during the boat trip from Beirut to Tunisia. It seems that Arafat gave his consent to establishing committees of inquiry in each unit. Sayil even composed an investigation questionnaire, which began circulating among members of the units immediately after arriving in Tunisia. But the assassination of Sayil on September 27, 1982, put an end to the investigative process in this format.[2]

However, the pressure on Arafat to hold a strict internal probe did not cease, leading him to appoint an official committee of inquiry in late 1982, led by the head of the Fatah Revolutionary Justice Department, Muhammad al-Rusan, and the head of military intelligence, 'Atallah 'Atallah. Some 100 Palestinian officers appeared before this committee, but it failed to produce an official report of its conclusions, while the protocols of the discussions were shelved, apparently at the direction of Yasir Arafat himself.[3]

Arafat's reluctance to engage in self-criticism was a transparent attempt to conceal the trauma of leaving Beirut and to turn his back on the central sphere of events in the Middle East. It also indicated an attempt to rehabilitate the reputation of the PLO and its status as exclusive leader of the Palestinian cause. Arafat's first real test was in mid-February 1982, at the sixteenth convention of the Palestinian National Council, held in Algiers. The atmosphere at this convention was described by Shafiq al-Hout, the PLO's most senior representative remaining in Lebanon:

> This convention was not a "historic" convention in the scientific sense of the word . . . because what happened to the Palestinian revolution in Lebanon was an important strategic event, and this event should have been accorded the same degree of importance in its analysis, evaluation, and conclusions. This did not happen at the convention and it may have happened only marginally in a way that did not manage to impact the general atmosphere of the convention, which appeared to be very festive, emphasizing stories of bravery and fierce resistance. . . . Those who followed the convention were surprised to see that none of the Palestinian leaders made any attempt to criticize the course of the Palestinian revolution in Lebanon. They all made do with praise for the bravery and fierce resistance of the people and of the Palestinian fighters in Lebanon without indicating who was responsible for the fiascos there.[4]

A strong impression persisted that nothing had changed and that the lessons of what had happened in Lebanon had not been learned. This led some senior Palestinian officers and PLO activists, from Fatah and other organizations—those who had special ties with Syria—to begin acting against Arafat's domination. These included Salih Abu Salih and Samih Abu Kuwayk, who were members of Fatah's Central Committee, as well as Colonel Musa Maragha, better known as Abu Musa. These actions were supported by Libya and Syria, as manifested in generous financial aid by Muammar Qaddafi and permits facilitating movement within Lebanon provided by the Syrians. Both the senior group of rebels and their followers came from two major factions: members of the left-wing branch of Fatah, and former officers and soldiers of the Jordanian army who had deserted to the ranks of Palestinian organizations following the 1970–1971 confrontation between PLO forces and the Jordanian army.

These two groups were the last to join Fatah and for this reason had never managed to worm their way into the higher echelons, crowded as they were with members of the "old guard" who were loyal supporters of Arafat. These people took advantage of Arafat's moves in the political arena to begin planning a revolt. Operative preparations probably began in early April 1983, with the reorganization of Palestinian units that had been massively damaged during the Israeli invasion of Lebanon in summer 1982. In addition, military cooperation with forces of the "rejection organizations" (organizations that had rejected any political arrangement with Israel) in Lebanon increased, making it easier for the rebels to receive supplies and armaments on a regular and effective basis.

The next step was taken in early May of that year, when rebel leaders resolved to establish a central military command. This was composed of the rebel Fatah officers and representatives of the other organizations who objected to Arafat. Included in this group were members of the PFLP, the DFLP, Ahmad Jibril's people, and the al-Sa'iqa organization, plus three combat sectors in the al-Beqa` area. It was declared that the purpose of these steps was to correct the "deviation from the course of the Palestinian revolution."[5] Obviously, the decision to publicly oppose Arafat could not have been reached without Syrian logistical support, including the delivery of sixty tons of weapons and ammunition, and the financial support of the Libyan ruler, who promised, during a clandestine visit to Libya with Ahmad Jibril, a delegation of rebels plus generous support in the form of five million dollars a month.[6]

Meanwhile Arafat, at his location in Tunis, found out about the rebels' plans and decided to take preventive measures to repress the revolt while it was still in its initial stages. He issued an order to relocate forty PLO officers (including Abu Musa and the remainder of his senior officers) from Lebanon to PLO headquarters in Tunisia, and at the same time appointed Ghazi 'Atallah and al-Haj Isma'il Jaber as military commanders of the Palestinian forces in the al-Beqa' area. The rebels responded immediately upon learning of Arafat's moves. On May 9, 1983, Abu Musa and his friends took over the headquarters for which Jaber and 'Atallah had been destined, and from there announced the initiation of the Movement for the Reform of Fatah. Other senior officers, such as Wasef 'Ariqat, Mahmoud 'Issa, and Ziyad al-Saghyyer, joined this movement, while Abu Salih and Abu Kuwayk announced from Damascus that they were joining as well.[7]

In a declaration issued by the rebels on May 13, they explained the motivation for the uprising, linking it to the actions of the leadership, which had refused to listen to demands for a thorough investigation of the PLO's conduct during and after the war. In addition, they expressed their objection to reinstating those officers who had been accused of negligence and of the oversights that led to the downfall. Arafat's ineffective actions were used by the rebels to explain their drastic step. They described Arafat's moves as an "organizational revolt" within Fatah, which perpetuated the rule of the "perverts, the defeated, and those sought for trial."[8] They also contended that these moves were a clear sign that the leadership had chosen to go along with an American-style political arrangement. In order to prevent this, they demanded that PLO forces remain in Lebanon, that Palestinian relations with Arab countries and the Soviet Union be reinforced, and that the PLO voice its objection to the plans proposed by US president Ronald Reagan, by the Arab summit in Fez, and to the federal plan with Jordan.[9]

The response of the PLO leadership ranged from outright contempt for the scope of the revolt to almost total denial of its existence. At the same time, the propaganda branches of the organization launched an extensive slander campaign against the leaders of the revolt and against Syria and Libya, accused of supporting them.[10] In order to get a closer view of events and to try and put out the fire, Arafat visited Lebanon clandestinely on May 21, 1983, and conducted a tour of PLO bases in Lebanon. Salah Khalaf, Farouq al-Qaddumi, and Ha'il 'Abd al-Hamid accompanied him on this visit. It was important for Arafat to have these three people standing by him in order to dissipate tensions between them, as the three had previously been inclined to support the rebels' demands. During this five-day visit, Arafat made a short trip to Damascus and even met with President Hafez al-Assad, who proclaimed Syria's neutrality toward the revolt and asserted that it had no wish to intrude on internal Palestinian affairs. This attitude was, of course, incompatible with Syrian operations in Lebanon and its unreserved support of the rebels.

Matters with Syria became even more complicated when Arafat was asked by a junior Syrian official, on June 24, 1983, to leave Syrian territory on the first plane departing from Damascus. Moreover, Syria declared Abu Jihad unwelcome both in Syria and in territory controlled by Syria (i.e., Lebanon). Arafat indeed returned to Tunis but ordered his forces in Lebanon to resist the Syrian-backed rebel forces, who had meanwhile continued to improve their positions, taking over control from Fatah forces throughout the summer months. Arafat's forces were also involved in battles on other fronts in Lebanon, both against the Maronites and against Shiite Amal forces. The situation became even more complicated when Israel announced its retreat from western Beirut and the al-Shouf Mountains. Lebanese forces were once again fighting among themselves for control, leading some PLO leaders to pressure Arafat anew to reopen dialogue with Syria.[11] A dialogue indeed took place, but its chances of success were meager to begin with. This fact became clearer when armed clashes with Syria resumed, this time with the direct personal involvement of Arafat, in the vicinity of the two Palestinian refugee camps near Tripoli, al-Baddawi and Nahr al-Bared. What led Arafat to return to Lebanon and to become embroiled in a direct and hopeless confrontation with Syria is a question that Shafiq al-Hout, who represented the PLO in Lebanon at the time and was a close acquaintance of Arafat, attempts to answer:

> At that time Arafat showed clear signs of impatience and mental distress due to his "exile" in Tunisia, his many frequent travels, and his visits to members of the Palestinian forces in Algeria, Yemen, and Sudan, which could not compensate him for what he had lost in Lebanon. Abu 'Amar suffered doubly: both as a leader and as a "person," with no private life, no wife, no family, and no children; and he loved the children, even as friends. The nature of this relationship was for him political and general, with no opportunity for heart-to-heart conversations to let out some personal steam.[12]

Al-Hout also testifies that Arafat did not tell anyone of his decision to join his militia in Tripoli. Some think, however, that one of the senior leaders, Abu Jihad, who was already in Lebanon fighting the rebels, did know of this plan.[13]

It is possible to surmise that during Arafat's stay in Tunis he came to a realization of the extent of the PLO's loss after the departure from Beirut and thus sought to rebuild its presence there. It is also feasible that his frustration with Syria's involvement in the revolt against him led him to seek direct ways of fighting against Syria. There may also have been a certain component in Arafat's personality that caused him to flourish and become energized in times of siege.

Arafat spent the entire fall of 1983 and early 1984 leading his militia, who were under siege by Syria and the Palestinian rebels within the city of Tripoli and in the two refugee camps. The Palestinian forces departed on January 20, 1984. Arafat left from Tripoli's port in northern Lebanon on Greek ships flying UN flags, accompanied by French warships, with American assurances that Israel would not attack the convoy of evacuees, among them Yasir Arafat and senior commanders of his militias.[14]

The losses and damage to Tripoli and the two refugee camps in the aftermath of the fighting were particularly severe. The camps and several quarters in Tripoli were almost completely demolished, with 438 people killed and 2,100 injured, including fighters and civilians.[15] However, from a political point of view, Arafat achieved some successes that made it possible for him to return to center stage and not be ignored. For instance, while under siege in Tripoli, his men negotiated the release of 5,900 Lebanese and Palestinian prisoners held at the Ansar detention center, established by Israel in southern Lebanon, in return for the release of six Israeli soldiers captured by PLO guerrilla fighters in the War of 1982. These negotiations were concluded in early December, raising Arafat's popularity immeasurably, at exactly the point in time when Syria was trying to subdue him, with Israeli help in the form of military operations from the sea against his forces in the Tripoli complex. This unwritten alliance between Syria and Israel bolstered his reputation as well. In addition, during the siege he used his contacts among Arab leaders and among the unallied countries and the Eastern Bloc to pressure Syria to desist.

While the ship from Tripoli was passing through the Suez Canal, Arafat surprised everyone by stopping for a short talk with Egyptian president Hosni Mubarak, for the first time since Egypt was boycotted by Arab countries following its peace treaty with Israel. The mood with which the news of the Mubarak-Arafat meeting was received can be sensed in al-Hout's description:

> Upon arriving at the Tunisian capital I felt a buzz among Palestinian circles there; I felt that the Day of Judgment had arrived. What had happened? What was the matter? The answer

was in an item placed centrally on the first page of newspapers all over the world, on the meeting between Mubarak and Arafat. I had no need for fortune tellers to tell me what would happen next—problems and disputes that could keep us busy for an entire year, problems that could put an end to all that was left of the history of the Palestinian revolution.[16]

Al-Hout's words were not without criticism of Arafat's last move, one that was hard to interpret in light of the state of the Palestinian cause at the time. Egypt was no longer the political capital of the Arab world; the offices of the Arab League were closer to him in Tunisia, but he sought to take advantage of Mubarak's wish to return to the center of the political inter-Arab stage and he certainly knew that the Palestinian cause was the best way to do this. Historian Yazid Sayigh interprets Arafat's move as an answer to his deepest wishes for Egypt to be a historical ally of the Palestinian cause:

> Arafat's surprising visit to Cairo proved that the loss of the territorial base in Lebanon had led the leaders of the main Palestinian stream to take controversial moves in regard to its diplomatic strategy. In addition, this visit showed to what degree Arafat had managed to strengthen his position both in Fatah and in the PLO. Both these results are indicated by the ease with which Arafat managed to assuage the anger of his friends in Fatah's Central Committee.[17]

Arafat indeed managed to silence his opponents within Fatah, although some of them did not conceal their anger and objection to the rapprochement with Egypt, but he did not find it easy to harness the other factions within the PLO to the process. These groups (the PFLP, the DFLP, the Palestinian Liberation Front, and the Palestinian Communist Party) declared the establishment of a Democratic National Alliance on March 27, 1984: "In their first official announcement, they objected to the PLO's dialogue with Egypt and to the idea of a joint Jordanian-Palestinian delegation. They also called for stronger relations with Syria and the Soviet Union, and at the same time they called upon Fatah to hold a dialogue on the most urgent issues."[18] The dialogue between Fatah and the left-wing fronts took place for about three months, during April through July 1984, and ended with the signing of an accord between the two sides: the Aden-Algiers Agreement, in which Arafat made a commitment to give in to the demands of the coalition by ceasing all dialogue with Egypt and rejecting the idea of the joint delegation with Jordan, as well as rejecting the Reagan plan for solving the conflict in the Middle East.[19] In addition, Arafat agreed to recognize the Palestinian Communist Party as an official member of the Palestinian National Council and to award this party and the Arab Liberation Front (supported by Iraq) seats on the Executive Committee of the PLO.[20]

These understandings were not to the liking of the Palestinian organizations associated with Syria, and particularly the Fatah rebels, al-Sa'iqa, and Ahmad Jibril's organization, the PFLP–GC. These organizations also declared a coalition, called the National Coalition, and in the first pamphlet that appeared on its behalf they expressed their objection to agreements between Fatah and the Democratic National Alliance and to the plan for the PLO Executive Committee to hold the Palestinian National Convention.[21]

Holding a convention of the Palestinian National Council also became a bone of contention between members of the National Coalition and the Democratic National Alliance. Things became even more complicated when the PFLP quit the Democratic National Alliance and joined forces with those who claimed that the convention should not be held while the organization was in a state of disarray. President Assad backed the objectors by pressuring President al-Shazili Ben Jadid of Algeria not to hold the convention in his country. When these pressures proved successful, Arafat had no choice but to accept the Jordanian offer to host the convention, but not before his assistant, Salah Khalaf, threatened to hold it on the deck of a Greek ship in the territorial waters of Greece, in a show of frustration at the Arab countries' refusal to hold the convention on their territory.[22]

Once Arafat's people managed to gather the necessary legal quorum, the convention finally opened in Amman on November 22. Of the National Council's 374 members, 257 attended. Some of the organizations and fronts were divided over the controversy regarding convention attendance. Arafat and his assistant, Abu 'Iyad, gave speeches accusing Syria of wishing to take control of the PLO and its autonomy. King Husayn spoke as well, asking the Palestinians to accept Resolution 242 of the UN Security Council, on the basis of "land for peace." The Jordanian king also demanded that an international convention be held, as well as direct negotiations involving the PLO. Husayn intentionally did not mention the joint Jordanian-Palestinian delegation. He did stress the fact that world opinion supported the Jordanian-Palestinian plan for receiving the occupied territories, but acknowledged that if the Palestinians preferred a separate solution, he would honor their wishes, as the decision would be ultimately up to them.[23]

The convention concluded its debates in late November. The final announcement emphasized the need for constant coordination and dialogue with Jordan. In addition, Egypt's sympathetic and supportive attitude toward the PLO during the internal revolt received positive mention. In this announcement the PLO expressed its acceptance of all UN resolutions pertaining to the Palestinian cause without specifically referring to Resolution 242. Despite the praise of Egypt for its role during that period, the convention once again stressed the PLO's complete objection to the Camp David Accords.[24]

This announcement and the many views expressed in it deepened the rift between Arafat and his Palestinian opponents and their Syrian ally. The latter held a well-publicized campaign throughout the entire convention in Amman and in its aftermath, aiming heavy accusations at Arafat and at his leadership of the Palestinian cause.[25]

Particularly harsh was the criticism voiced by George Habash, who had been among those heading the Democratic National Alliance but quit following the strategic course chosen by Arafat. Habash summarized: "Arafat resolved to ally himself with the Egyptian regime of Camp David and the Jordanian regime and at the same time to develop antagonism toward Syria."[26]

Later on, and from a lengthier historical perspective, Habash summarized his disputes with Arafat:

> After the Lebanon War, two trends were evident on the Arab and Palestinian stage: one wished to continue with the resistance while the other thought that the time for resistance had passed and strived to reach achievements after twenty years of struggle, on a political foundation. But the latter did not manage to enlist in its support the previously accumulated experience and expertise. Moreover, they were inclined to sever all connections with that experience in favor of a rapid and traumatic transition to gambling on what the enemy is willing to give us.[27]

The rift referred to by Habash was indeed deep and very hard to bridge, particularly once it deteriorated to acts of violence and assassinations. On the day the Amman convention ended, unknown assassins attacked and killed Fahd al-Qawasmi, the former mayor of Hebron and a member of Fatah's Executive Committee. Inquiries led to PLO rebels and some even accused President Assad of personally ordering the assassination.[28]

This act and other failed attempts to assassinate those close to Arafat increased his determination to gamble on new allies in the Arab world. Once the PLO systems in Lebanon had collapsed with no option of rehabilitation, and in light of the internal challenge posed to Arafat's leadership and the decisive hostility manifested by the Ba'ath regime in Damascus, the PLO leader went in search of other Arab allies, namely Egypt and Jordan. Arafat had always perceived Egypt as the Arab ally of choice, even after Sadat's peace initiative with Israel and even after Egypt was renounced and shunned by most Arab states. No less significant was the transformation of his relationship with Jordan. Shifts and changes in inter-Arab relationships in the early half of the 1980s managed to turn the formidable, recalcitrant Hashemite rival of yesteryear into a potential ally. This may have stemmed from the common rivalry with Syria and the Iran-Iraq War.

When the Iran-Iraq War broke out, a pro-Iraqi Arab camp was formed, consisting of Egypt, Jordan, the Gulf states, and to a great degree the PLO as well. These were countered by Syria and Libya, who supported Iran. The PLO was financially crippled by this war, as Saudi Arabia and the Gulf states chose to devote most of their external aid to Saddam Hussein. This extensive campaign, as well as efforts by the Saudis and their allies to counter Iran's threat of spreading political Islam throughout the region, removed the Palestinian issue from its prime place on the pan-Arab agenda. Thus, Arafat now developed a strategy consisting of two combined courses of action: first, to place the goal of establishing an independent Palestinian state on the global political and diplomatic agenda, and second, to ensure participation of the PLO in any political or diplomatic negotiations for the rights of the Palestinian people. He was aware of the fact that any political process would depend on the goodwill of the United States and that he himself could not initiate direct contact with its government. For this purpose he was now all the more in need of alliances with Egypt and Jordan.

A closer relationship with the king of Jordan ensued once the king became concerned at the rise of the Israeli right wing and the proposals of some of its leaders (particularly Ari'el Sharon) to solve the Palestinian problem by recognizing Jordan as Palestine. Some time ago, King Husayn had reached the conclusion that there was no chance of resolving the Palestinian issue without including the PLO. Now that the organization had weakened, Husayn could finally accept this fact. Egypt, under Mubarak's lead, was happy to cooperate as well. Reinstating its patronage of the PLO seemed a reasonable way of eliminating pan-Arab ostracism, a legacy of Sadat's peace policy.

The PLO and Jordan slowly examined ways of cooperating, and in February 1985 they reached an agreement to create a mechanism that would facilitate US consent to include the PLO in the peace talks. However, this collaboration encountered difficulties when Arafat proved unwilling to explicitly recognize UN Resolution 242 as the basis for negotiations. Consequently, Husayn gravitated toward Syria and closed the PLO offices in Amman.[29] Syrian authorities continued to obstruct Arafat's attempts to reinstate the status of his sympathizers in Lebanese refugee camps.[30]

The PLO's predicaments increased, as evident during the 1987 Arab summit in Amman, which proceeded to disregard all topics advanced by the Palestinians. Even the peace initiative proposed by US secretary of state George Schultz made no mention of the PLO. The organization had reached its lowest point since the first glorious days of the Rabat summit and Arafat's rousing speech at the United Nations in 1974.

The Palestinians in Lebanon

The first to pay the price for the rift between the PLO and Syria and its allies in Lebanon were the Palestinian refugees in Lebanon and Syria. Their financial situation worsened, and they were shunned and harassed by any groups at odds with the PLO and Yasir Arafat. The fighting within the refugee camps and their encirclement by the Syrian army and its allies greatly eroded the refugees' sense of security.

The differences in the quality of life of Palestinians living in Lebanon versus other Palestinians, including those who had moved to Tunisia, were expressed by al-Hout on the eve of one of his frequent visits to Arafat's headquarters in Tunisia: "I often became depressed whenever I would arrive in Tunisia from Beirut, burdened by the concerns of the Palestinians in Lebanon. No one would ask me about the problems and hardships, while paradoxically, I would receive dozens of invitations to meals and entertainment."[31] Further on, al-Hout describes the lives of the Palestinians who had moved to Tunisia with Arafat:

> The Palestinians during their years in Tunisia lived like tourists. They constituted a not inconsiderable source of income, in addition to the assets they brought with them. They enjoyed general life in the capital Tunis, particularly in the diplomatic and media context. Just as Beirut was the capital of the Palestinian revolution, Tunis became so too, with one important and fundamental difference—the absence of all military spectacles, with the exception of Abu 'Amar's pistol.[32]

In the absence of the PLO senior leadership, al-Hout became the major leader of the Palestinians in Lebanon and was responsible for managing their affairs among the Lebanese authorities and other local forces. This was complicated considering the many bitter residual feelings, with some Lebanese elements even professing open hatred for the Palestinians. This is clear from a conversation that al-Hout held with Zahi al-Bustani, Lebanon's director of internal security. Al-Hout described the conversation:

> The activity was definitely not easy, particularly since I was not among the supporters of any organization or regime. I can say, almost certainly, that I was alone, and I had only my reputation and the few dedicated men who surrounded me. I tried to begin from points where contact had been renewed, following my conversation with the General Director of the Lebanese Internal Security Office, Zahi al-Bustani, appointed by President Bashir Jumayyel before his death. This was not a heartfelt conversation, and it even aroused many concerns. I remember what he said to me in that conversation, that although he had gone to a Catholic school and he does not like the Jews, he feels toward us (we, the Palestinians) a deeper hatred than he feels toward the Jews. He even took this opportunity to list some of the issues that aroused in him these feelings toward us. My response to these words was that despite the emotions that govern us at such a time, in our position the only option is to act to heal the injuries in order to ease the great suffering we feel, thus preventing him from becoming ensnared in new mistakes and inequities. . . . I ended the conversation with my advice to him, which he could either take or reject, to gamble on a serious and positive relationship with the Palestinians, as the Israelis cannot be trusted, considering that the occupation is temporary and will not continue forever.[33]

In time it became evident that al-Bustani did not take al-Hout's advice and the Lebanese army and its security forces continued to repress all attempts by Fatah to reoccupy influential positions in Lebanon, particularly in the refugee camps. The Lebanese army was not deterred from helping the Shiite Amal organization, which held bloody battles within the refugee camps against the limited Fatah forces remaining there.[34]

The Palestinians in Jordan

After the Palestinian National Convention was held in Amman in December 1984, many hoped for a new start to the precarious relationship between Arafat and King Husayn, one that held promise for improving the situation of Palestinians in Jordan. But it was soon clear that these hopes had no real justification. Arafat did not manage to convince the major group in the Palestinian national movement and his allies in the Arab world and elsewhere to accept the alliance with Jordan as a done deal, and when King Husayn realized that Arafat did not have this ability he set out to punish him, by strengthening his relationship with the West Bank and setting his sights on Syria, Arafat's greatest enemy at the time.

Relations with the West Bank were strengthened through a series of moves by the Jordanian authorities, manifested in a new law on elections to parliament, enacted on March 25, 1986, whereby the number of members of parliament was increased from 60 to 142 members, equally divided between the West and East Bank. In early April of that year, Jordanian actions became even more radical, with a decision to close the offices of Fatah in Amman. On April 8, 1986, Jordan backed a new revolt within Fatah, led by Colonel 'Atallah 'Atallah.[35]

At the same time, Jordanian authorities began an extensive campaign to resume their dominance and leadership in the West Bank. In late August 1986, a plan for economic development of the West Bank was announced, involving generous financial support for large municipalities, Gaza included. The Jordanian government resumed payment of salaries to Palestinian officials in the West Bank and even awarded a license to renew operations of the Bank of Amman in Nablus.[36]

The Palestinian response to Jordanian attempts, voiced in King Husayn's speech on February 19, 1986, and in subsequent declarations by senior officials, was not late in coming: on March 8, 1986, the PLO made a forceful announcement on the moves taken by Jordan, which it saw as aiming to "separate the organization from its people."[37] The PLO firmly stated their objections:

> From the very beginning, the PLO's representation of the Palestinian people would have never become a legitimate recognized political reality if the organization had not been a manifestation of the Palestinian national entity, in all its dimensions and forms, and an expression of Palestinian national ambitions and causes. Moreover, the Palestinian people in its entirety has constantly emphasized in all means at its disposal that the organization is the combative national identity that represents each and every individual within it. This fact has never contradicted and will never contradict the pan-Arab national dimension of the Palestinian people in the struggle for its national cause and the definition of its fate.[38]

This response did not make do with a general statement, and instead referred directly to Jordanian-Palestinian relations:

> After the Israeli invasion of Lebanon in 1982 the PLO's approach acknowledged the significance of forming a relationship with Jordan based on their joint fate leading to a course of joint action predicated on the Arab peace plan . . . but the conflict between the attitudes of Jordan and the PLO to the Reagan plan resulted in the conclusion of this chapter in the relationship without reaching a joint agreement.[39]

In fact, King Husayn wanted the PLO to declare its acceptance of the Reagan plan and of Resolution 242 of the Security Council, something that Yasir Arafat could not accept or pass in the PLO. Husayn saw the attitude of the PLO as a return to previous views from before the Jordanian-Palestinian alliance and the strategic shift of the PLO after the departure from Beirut. Based on this perception, he intensified the actions taken against the organization's activities in Jordan and the West Bank, which reached their climax in his support of the rebels and the deportation of Abu Jihad from the Jordanian capital in July 1986.

The lives of Palestinians living in Jordan were obviously affected by this vacillating relationship, as they were throughout the very complex history of the PLO and the Jordanian regime.

The Palestinians in Israel

The Palestinian population in Israel experienced many transformations during this period. Paradoxically, the Lebanon War in 1982 made it possible for a significant number of internal refugee families to see members of their family who had been living in Lebanon and who now received special permission to visit their relatives in Israel. At the same time, Jewish-Arab discord within Israel became more acute under Israel's right-wing governments and with the rightward move of Israeli public opinion. Issues of integration and disintegration reemerged, particularly involving the discourse concerning Hadash and the Progressive List for Peace, established in the early 1980s as a counterweight to Hadash among the non-Zionist parties.[40]

This movement emerged locally in Nazareth and even took part in the municipal elections in 1983, reaching quite significant achievements, despite its failure to wrest the mayorship of Nazareth from Hadash. In 1984 the movement decided to become a national organization and even to run for elections to the Knesset in a joint Arab-Jewish list founded by attorney Muhammad Mi'ari and Major General (res.) Matityahu Peled.[41] The list was approved despite a right-wing Israeli appeal to the Supreme Court to ban it from the elections. The appeal was rejected and the list took part in the elections and even won two seats in the Knesset. Although it was a joint Arab-Jewish list, it did not conceal its nationalist goals, even symbolically. It chose the letter *P* (for Palestine) as its election symbol. In addition, its campaign conspicuously made use of the four colors (white, black, green, and red) of the flag of Palestine and of the Arab flag. Nonetheless, the list stressed in its platform that both peoples—the Jews and the Arabs—should have equal political and social rights in Israel.[42]

Despite a good showing in the elections (in the 1988 elections the list received about 18 percent of all Arab votes), the list did not persevere for long and it suffered from divisions at important historical junctions (the Gulf War in 1991, for example). In particular, it could not compete among the Arab population with Hadash, with its lengthier history. However, it may be credited with arousing a deeper awareness among the Arab population in two major spheres: civic activities and Palestinian and Arab national identity. Notably, the list generated changes within Hadash as well as new trends, particularly increasing the dominance of the concept of Palestinian and Arab identity. Relations with the PLO intensified (leaders of the list were among the first to visit Yasir Arafat's headquarters in Tunisia as early as 1985) and the affiliation with the pan-Arab cultural expanse increased immeasurably, transforming this affiliation into a clear and lucid reality.

Along with the strengthening of national identity on all levels, an important shift was also apparent in the enhancement of Islamic identity. This shift became a factor to be reckoned with upon the reestablishment of political Islam in the form of the Islamic Movement in Israel. It began operating in the late 1970s and became entrenched in the mid-1980s, at first under various names such as Harakat al-Shabab al-Muslim (the Young Muslims Movement), or 'Usrat al-Jihad (the Family of Jihad), and later under the name al-Haraka al-Islamiyya (the Islamic Movement). The initial emergence of this movement was described by Uri Shtendel: "Within the mosaics of the political orientations in the Arab sector, the Young Muslims are forging their way as a major movement with a special nature, neither party nor 'list,' neither ideological circle, operational organization, or 'entity,' rather a multifaceted phenomenon that may embrace within it all these definitions in a complex combination."[43]

These descriptions by Shtendel are true of the first stages of development of the Islamic Movement. In 1988, after a decade of engaging in philanthropy, it first took part in municipal elections and attained notable successes, coming in first in several key towns, the most conspicuous of which was the city of Umm al-Fahm, which passed from the control of Hadash to the Islamic Movement, in time becoming its main stronghold.[44] In 1996 there was a heated controversy within the movement concerning the possibility of taking part in elections for the Knesset. This dispute did not lead to a decision agreed upon by all members of the movement, and caused it to split in two: the southern group, headed by founder Shaikh 'Abdallah Nimr Darwish from the village of Kafr Qasem, which ran for the

Knesset, and the northern group, headed by Shaikh Ra'id Salah from Umm al-Fahm, which objected to running for the Knesset.

Concurrently with the emergence of new political streams, attempts were made to organize groups operating among the Arab population in a nonpolitical national framework. This was the basis for the establishment of the National Committee of Arab Mayors, which had indeed begun operating within a smaller format in the 1970s, but became more established in the 1980s as a national organization encompassing almost all Arab mayors in Israel. The first chairman of the committee was Hanna Muways, mayor of Rama in the Galilee and a member of Hadash. When Muways resigned in 1981, Ibrahim Nimr Husayn, the mayor of Shafa'amr, who had run as an independent candidate, was chosen for this position. Of Ibrahim Nimr Husayn (Abu Hatim), the mythical head of the committee, Shtendel wrote, "He spared no effort to create a bridge between the many political forces within it. At his initiative, negotiations began for the establishment of a joint list for the Histadrut, with a platform focusing on equal rights for the Arab public, two states for two nations, recognition of the PLO as representing the Palestinian people, and fighting for the rights of Palestinian workers."[45] In addition to heading the Committee of Mayors, Abu Hatim was also the first president of the High Follow-up Committee for the Arab Citizens of Israel.[46]

This organization was established in late October 1982, in response to increasing acts of protest by the Arab population, both against Israeli policies toward the Arab population of Israel and toward the Israeli-Palestinian conflict. The founding convention was held in Shafa'amr and Ibrahim Nimr Husayn was elected chairman of the committee, thus holding the double title of chairman of the Committee of Mayors and of the High Follow-up Committee. The mayors became part of the High Follow-up Committee and they were joined by current members of the Knesset and in time by representatives of nonparliamentary parties and movements as well. The High Follow-up Committee existed to document government treatment of the Arab population in different spheres, with an attempt to influence decisionmaking processes in regard to this population, although the Israeli government never officially acknowledged it as an organization representing the Arab population.[47] The Israeli government, on its part, did not recognize these committees, but neither did it reject all dialogue with them, particularly in times of tension, protest, and demonstrations. By holding such a dialogue, representatives of the government managed to ensure a reasonable level of quiet and public order.

Notes

1. Samih Shabib, "Al-Zakera al-dai'a" [Lost Memory], *Al-Ayyam*, November 6, 2005.

2. Sayigh, *Al-Kifah al-Muslah wa al-Bahath 'An al-Dawla: Al-Haraka al-Wataniyya al-Filastiniyya, 1949–1993* [Armed Struggle and the Search for a State], 760.

3. Sayigh, *Al-Kifah al-Muslah wa al-Bahath 'An al-Dawla: Al-Haraka al-Wataniyya al-Filastiniyya, 1949–1993* [Armed Struggle and the Search for a State], 760.

4. S. al-Hout, *Bayn al-Watan wa al-Manfa, min Yafa Bada al-Mishwar* [Between the Homeland and the Exile], 298.

5. Sayigh, *Al-Kifah al-Muslah wa al-Bahath 'An al-Dawla: Al-Haraka al-Wataniyya al-Filastiniyya, 1949–1993* [Armed Struggle and the Search for a State], 787.

6. Sayigh, *Al-Kifah al-Muslah wa al-Bahath 'An al-Dawla: Al-Haraka al-Wataniyya al-Filastiniyya, 1949–1993* [Armed Struggle and the Search for a State], 787.

7. Yasin, *Azmat Fatah* [Crisis of Fatah], 45–47.

8. 'Ali, *Al-Intifada, thawra hatta al-Naser* [Intifada], 88–89.

9. 'Ali, *Al-Intifada, thawra hatta al-Naser* [Intifada], 88–89.

10. About this campaign, see Sayigh, *Al-Kifah al-Muslah wa al-Bahath 'An al-Dawla: Al-Haraka al-Wataniyya al-Filastiniyya, 1949–1993* [Armed Struggle and the Search for a State], 788.

11. For more information, see S. al-Hout, *Bayn al-Watan wa al-Manfa, min Yafa Bada al-Mishwar* [Between the Homeland and the Exile], 333–343.

12. S. al-Hout, *Bayn al-Watan wa al-Manfa, min Yafa Bada al-Mishwar* [Between the Homeland and the Exile], 345.

13. S. al-Hout, *Bayn al-Watan wa al-Manfa, min Yafa Bada al-Mishwar* [Between the Homeland and the Exile], 348.

14. S. al-Hout, *Bayn al-Watan wa al-Manfa, min Yafa Bada al-Mishwar* [Between the Homeland and the Exile], 355.

15. Sayigh, *Al-Kifah al-Muslah wa al-Bahath 'An al-Dawla: Al-Haraka al-Wataniyya al-Filastiniyya, 1949–1993* [Armed Struggle and the Search for a State], 803.

16. S. al-Hout, *Bayn al-Watan wa al-Manfa, min Yafa Bada al-Mishwar* [Between the Homeland and the Exile], 356.

17. S. al-Hout, *Bayn al-Watan wa al-Manfa, min Yafa Bada al-Mishwar* [Between the Homeland and the Exile], 805.
18. S. al-Hout, *Bayn al-Watan wa al-Manfa, min Yafa Bada al-Mishwar* [Between the Homeland and the Exile], 805.
19. *Al-Hurriya*, July 15, 1984.
20. *Al-Hurriya*, July 15, 1984.
21. The full version.
22. *Shu'un Filastiniyya* (double issue) 142–143 (January–February 1985): 132.
23. Cited by Sayigh, *Al-Kifah al-Muslah wa al-Bahath 'An al-Dawla: Al-Haraka al-Wataniyya al-Filastiniyya, 1949–1993* [Armed Struggle and the Search for a State], 808.
24. *Shu'un Filastiniyya* (double issue) 140–141 (November–December 1984): 167.
25. For examples, see *Al-Safir*, December 5, 1984.
26. *Al-Hadaf*, December 12, 1984.
27. Suwayyid, *Al-tajriba al-nidaliyya al-Filastiniyya, hiwar shamel ma' George Habash* [Experience of the Palestinian Struggle: Extensive Interview with George Habash], 63.
28. *Al-Nahar*, December 31, 1984.
29. *Jerusalem Post*, April 14, 1986.
30. On this attack, see *Al-Safir*, May 21–22, 1985.
31. S. al-Hout, *Bayn al-Watan wa al-Manfa, min Yafa Bada al-Mishwar* [Between the Homeland and the Exile], 381–382.
32. S. al-Hout, *Bayn al-Watan wa al-Manfa, min Yafa Bada al-Mishwar* [Between the Homeland and the Exile], 381.
33. S. al-Hout, *Bayn al-Watan wa al-Manfa, min Yafa Bada al-Mishwar* [Between the Homeland and the Exile]. 378.
34. On Amal's efforts in this respect, see Sayigh, *Al-Kifah al-Muslah wa al-Bahath 'An al-Dawla: Al-Haraka al-Wataniyya al-Filastiniyya, 1949–1993* [Armed Struggle and the Search for a State], 812–820.
35. Sayigh, *Al-Kifah al-Muslah wa al-Bahath 'An al-Dawla: Al-Haraka al-Wataniyya al-Filastiniyya, 1949–1993* [Armed Struggle and the Search for a State], 823.
36. For more information on the Jordanian plan, see Hilal, "Al-khitta al-aurduniyya al-khumasiyya litanmiyat al-Diffa wa al-Qita'" [Jordanian Five-Year Plan for Development of the West Bank and the Gaza Strip], 85–95.
37. For the full response, see *Shu'un Filastiniyya* (double issue) 156–157 (March–April, 1986): 56–63.
38. *Shu'un Filastiniyya* (double issue) 156–157 (March–April): 57.
39. *Shu'un Filastiniyya* (double issue) 156–157 (March–April): 57.
40. On this discourse see, Kabha and Caspi, *Palestinian Arab In/Outsiders*, 153–180.

41. Muhammad Mi'ari (b. 1939) was born in the village of Birwa in the Galilee. He became a refugee when the village was occupied by Israeli forces in July 1948. He received his law degree from the Hebrew University Faculty of Law, was active in the al-Ard group and later served as chairman of the Committee for Defense of Arab Lands. Mi'ari also served as a member of Knesset during 1984–1992.

Matityahu Peled (1923–1995) was a graduate of the Faculty of Law at the University of London and held a doctorate in Arabic literature from the Hebrew University. He had a rich military past and was discharged from the Israeli army in 1969 with the rank of major general. He served as professor of Arabic Literature at Tel Aviv University and was a member of the Knesset during 1984–1988.

42. *Ha'aretz*, October 18, 1985.

43. Shtendel, *Arviyei Yisra'el, Bayn Patish Lasadan* [Israel's Arabs], 270.

44. In October 2012 the movement's leaders announced that they would not take part in the municipal elections in Umm al-Fahm in 2013 and that they would have no candidates running for mayor. If this has come about it will have brought to its end a lengthy twenty-five-year period of domination.

45. Shtendel, *Arviyei Yisra'el, Bayn Patish Lasadan* [Israel's Arabs], 297.

46. Ibrahim Nimr Husayn was succeeded in this position by Muhammad Zaydan, mayor of Kafr Manda (two terms: 1998–2001 and 2008–present) and Shawqi Khatib, mayor of Yafi'a, 2001–2008.

47. R. Cohen, *Zarim Bevetam, 'Aravim, Yehudim, Medina* [Strangers in Their Homeland], 103.

12

The First Intifada and Advancing Toward Oslo

The intifada was the means by which the PLO lifted itself out of the depths into which it had fallen while based in Tunisia, in both the inter-Arab and the international spheres. It also rehabilitated itself via regular contact with most of the Palestinian groups, including those who had remained in their land or were currently in the diaspora.

Shafiq al-Hout, the PLO representative in Beirut at that time, best described the positive implications of the intifada for the PLO:

> It is not surprising that 1988 is called "the year of the intifada." This word, which has inveigled its way into foreign languages, appears to describe an unprecedented event. It was only the intifada that managed to considerably reduce the level of the Syrian-Palestinian conflict. It silenced their war cannons. It restored a little of the "Palestinian national unity" and reinstated the Palestinian cause. It reestablished the status of the PLO, on Palestinian lands, as the only legitimate representative of the Palestinian people.[1]

The first grassroots intifada erupted spontaneously on December 9, 1987. The previous day, four Palestinian workers had died in a traffic accident in the vicinity of the Jabalya refugee camp in the Gaza Strip, and a rumor began circulating that an Israeli truck driver had intentionally rammed Palestinian vehicles. Raging demonstrations broke out all over the Gaza Strip, and the next day they crossed over into the West Bank and did not subside. Both the Israeli government and the PLO leadership in Tunis did not initially grasp the wide popular nature of the revolt. Only when Arafat and his associates in the PLO leadership became aware that the uprising was indeed widespread did they hurry to join in and attempt to assume command, reminiscent of the mufti and his associates following the strike of April 1936.

The incident in Jabalya was the spark that ignited the rage that had been accumulating for some time. Israel's derogatory system of government following the initial occupation created among the Palestinian population a sense of frustration and insult that increased in direct proportion to growing Jewish construction in the occupied territories and the policy of land expropriation. Feelings of rage, insult, and degradation had been accumulating since Israel occupied the territories. During the period of 1967–1985 Israel had arrested nearly 250,000 people, 40 percent of whom were detained for longer than one night.[2] At the same time, the Palestinian economy and standard of living suffered a decline. The number of production workers in the territories had diminished significantly since the early 1980s. Employment at small-scale local industries dropped from 15 to 10.4 percent of the potential workforce. Agricultural jobs in the territories dropped from 34.3 to 15.9 percent of the workforce, construction from 11.7 to 7.3 percent, and services from 38.6 to 30.1 percent.[3] In contrast, the number of Palestinian workers employed in Israel rose and reached 125,000 in 1987, encompassing about 40 percent of the entire Palestinian workforce. Consequently, the Palestinian economy became almost completely dependent on the Israeli economy. As a result, and in light of Israel's economic difficulties and soaring inflation, Israel deliberately avoided investing in the Palestinian economy. Jordan also played a part in weakening the economy of the territories and increasing its dependence on Israel: The Amman government cut back its payments to Palestinian officials and teachers whom it had been employing prior to the occupation. It also cancelled the Jordanian-Palestinian committee that transferred "steadfast perseverance funds" from wealthy Arab countries. At the same time, income accruing from transfers by Palestinians working outside Israel and the territories also declined significantly. The number of Palestinian workers in the Gulf sharply dropped in the years prior to the intifada, from about eighteen thousand workers in the mid-1970s to five thousand in the mid-1980s.[4]

Two other processes contributed to the widespread frustration. In the 1980s, the educational system in the territories had significantly expanded, with a corresponding rise in the number of graduates of higher education. However, with a lack of jobs, unemployment rates rose as well. During the 1984–1985 academic year, for example, there were 13,500 Palestinian students studying at West Bank and Gaza Strip universities, in addition to thousands of students at vocational institutions and colleges and nearly 10,000 students studying abroad. The impoverished Palestinian economy was able to absorb only 20 percent of the graduates.[5] The rest joined the thousands of Palestinian workers who traveled daily to work at unskilled and odd jobs in the Israeli economy. Research has shown a correlation between the rise in demonstrations of active resistance to the occupation and the educational level of the instigators. A sample of five hundred young Palestinians convicted of security offenses in Israeli courts during those years has shown that 87 percent were younger than thirty, while 82 percent had a secondary or tertiary education.[6] The number of incidents defined by Israel as "acts of disorderly conduct," primarily demonstrations and stone throwing, rose from 953 in 1985 to 1,358 in 1986 and 2,982 in 1987. The number of armed attacks against Israeli targets rose from 351 in 1983 to 780 in 1986.

The Intifada: The PLO Regains Its Strength

The PLO's weakened state following its evacuation from Lebanon, as well as the measures taken by Israel and Jordan to cripple the organization, led it to appeal to the educated bourgeoisie in the territories. Academics and university graduates received financial support from the PLO through organizations such as trade unions, institutes of higher education, public relations bureaus, and research centers. Most of these organizations operated in the Jerusalem, Ramallah, Bethlehem, and Hebron regions, and they were most often controlled by Fatah. Nonetheless, they were also influenced by the Communist Party, the PFLP, and the DFLP. These social institutions were seriously affected in the mid-1980s when Israel began instituting emergency regulations: closing institutions and associations, enforcing administrative detentions, and employing means such as house arrests and "removal" of undesirable elements.[7] During 1985–1986, thirty-six senior Palestinian leaders were deported. Examples of these prominent figures are Akram Haniyyah from Fatah (editor of *al-Sha'b*, at the time the unofficial journal of Fatah in the occupied territories); Abu 'Ali Shahin, a senior Fatah activist in the territories; and 'Azmi al-Shu'aybi and 'Ali Abu Hilal, senior activists in the DFLP. These measures had the effect of slightly diminishing overt activities by various Palestinian organizations and movements, but they did nothing to prevent continued efforts by nationalist activists to assume control of political life in the territories. Jordanian attempts to promote their own people (including the establishment of a journal called *Al-Nahar* in favor of Jordanian rule) had no effect.

The ranks of national leadership expanded in May 1985 with the release of 1,125 Palestinian prisoners, experienced in political activity, in a prisoner exchange known as the Jibril Deal. Young Palestinians incarcerated in Israeli prisons, mostly high school and college students, often took the opportunity to learn firsthand about political and underground leadership. Most intifada leaders were undoubtedly a product of this young leadership cadre, trained in the prisons.

PLO leaders in the diaspora quickly overcame their initial surprise at the intensity of the revolt in the territories and the nature of its organization. They were quick to take control of the situation and to put their own people in charge. Particular urgency arose from the emergence of a new force in the field—the Islamic element, primarily the Hamas and Islamic Jihad movements.[8] In his declarations, Arafat began praising the "stone-throwing kids," who continued the rage and exploits of the former "RPG kids," known for their use of rocket-propelled grenades.[9] When Khalil al-Wazir was asked how several weeks of grassroots revolt managed to achieve more than years of armed struggle, he answered that the two were inseparable and that the intifada was a result of the stubborn struggle maintained by the PLO in the past and present.[10]

An analysis of events shows a slightly different picture. As early as December 10, 1987, Islamic movements published announcements describing the incidents as a "popular uprising" and praising the masses' role in their success. A similar announcement was then published by the Communist Party.[11] The first announcement on behalf of Fatah only appeared on January 8, 1988, about one month after the intifada began. Two days later announcements were published on behalf of the PFLP and the DFLP. Fatah and the fronts established a "unified national leadership" (*al-qiyadah al-wataniyya al muwh-*

hadah) on January 16, 1988, which published announcements side by side with those of Hamas and Islamic Jihad. This split between the nationalist and Islamic blocs created a new reality in the history of the Palestinian national movement. From now on it consisted of two distinct and separate sections: those who continued to pursue a secular-oriented nationalist agenda, and an emerging group with religious convictions, that perceived Palestine in its entirety as Islamic holy land destined to be the site of a Muslim state governed by religious law.

Diplomacy in the World, Protest in the Territories

Once the PLO recovered from its initial shock, it began acting to recover from its downfall and to draw new energy from the revolt in the territories. In early January 1988, Arafat outlined the PLO's new strategy, which centered on three goals: return, realizing national sovereignty, and establishing a free independent state with Jerusalem as its capital.[12] From now on he did not resume the policy of armed struggle, preferring to emphasize the political course instead. The road to achieving our goals, declared the chairman of the PLO, is through an international conference backed by the United Nations and attended by the five members of the Security Council as well as all parties to the conflict, with the PLO receiving equal status. He stated that the conference's discussions must be based on UN resolutions and on the decisions of Arab summit conferences, and particularly on the Fez summit of 1982, in which the PLO was recognized as the exclusive representative of the Palestinian people.[13]

At the same time, elements in the PLO suggested founding a government in exile to prepare the ground for a declaration of independence and for receiving the occupied territories. This proposal turned into a bone of contention. Fatah partners in the Unified National Leadership and senior members of the Executive Committee, such as Salah Khalaf, Khalil al-Wazir, and Khaled al-Hasan, perceived the establishment of such a government as an empty gesture.[14] Mahmoud Abbas (Abu Mazen) believed that a government in exile would create a wider framework than could the leadership of a liberation organization and would facilitate real political achievements.[15] Arafat was apparently dissuaded by the objectors, as he allowed a suspension of discussions on the topic and stated that "any revolution on the threshold of victory must call for the establishment of a temporary government. We will declare the establishment of such a government when appropriate."[16]

Abu Jihad

Although it is unclear whether the intensity of the intifada had caught the exiled PLO leadership by surprise, there is almost no doubt that the main figure leading its initial stages was Khalil al-Wazir, also known as Abu Jihad. This man had been subjected to intensive attempts at exclusion and dissociation by Arafat immediately before the intifada broke out and particularly after his deportation from Jordan. Arafat took advantage of this to try to pressure Abu Jihad's followers and associates to withdraw their support for him, by relocating them to places over which al-Wazir had no control. Arafat also took over the *Sawt al-Balad* newspaper, which was part of Abu Jihad's responsibility.[17] Nevertheless, al-Wazir played an important role in rehabilitating the PLO's relationship with the Soviet Union and the Eastern Bloc, as well as with Algeria and Libya. He also acted to reconcile the Palestinian opposition and to draw some of it back under PLO authority. At the same time, al-Wazir and his assistants developed and increased their contacts with Palestinian institutions and activists in the occupied territories. Thus, al-Wazir's men were not far from the truth when they boasted, immediately prior to the intifada, that they could incite demonstrations anywhere in the occupied territories whenever they wished.[18]

A month after the beginning of the intifada, the PLO's Central Council convened and was presented with a detailed report written by Khalil al-Wazir on the events of the past month. In this report, al-Wazir tried to downplay the surprise factor, rather portraying the intifada as yet another link in the continuous struggle of the Palestinian people. He claimed it was a response to the charged situation in the territories, in light of Israeli forces' adherence to British emergency laws. In al-Wazir's opinion, these laws were used as justification for administrative arrest without trial, demolition of houses, and deportation of people. The intifada aimed to change this "insufferable situation."[19] Al-Wazir concluded his report by saying, "No voice is above the voice of the intifada. The intifada is not a temporary emotional uprising, it is a new page in history and a new state of affairs carrying within it the horizons of a new future, stressing the uniformity of Palestinians within their country and outside it."[20]

Al-Wazir, considered by many to be the active force behind the uprising in the territories, now enjoyed a growing reputation. Armed with the slogan "No voice is above the voice of the intifada," he prevailed against Arafat and against the call for a diplomatic course of action. As commander of the western sector and responsible on behalf of the PLO for those operating in the field, he both promoted the popular struggle and facilitated military operations instigated by select guerrilla fighters of various organizations. He defined the concept of government in exile as "a hasty attempt to pick a rotten fruit," and called for a conflagration in the territories, even pushing for the involvement of Palestinian Arabs in Israel, in the hope that these would serve as the bridgehead of an all-encompassing revolt. Yazid Sayigh explained that al-Wazir sought three forms of confrontation: "popular means," such as throwing rocks and Molotov cocktails; military actions by groups of commandos; and the invasion of Israel by guerrilla fighters. Once he grasped the enormous symbolic effect of the Palestinians as "stone throwers" versus Israel's might, he decided to refrain from implementing his plan for armed guerrilla warfare. Al-Wazir planned to activate the PLO's fighting units at a later stage of the intifada, but set no date.[21] The guerrilla operations he planned, which included an attack on a bus transporting workers employed at Israel's nuclear reactor in Dimona, motivated Israeli plans to assassinate him. On April 16, 1988, an Israeli commando unit attacked al-Wazir's villa in Tunis, killing him along with several bodyguards.

The death of al-Wazir, who had been orchestrating the intifada from afar, hampered coordination among the various organizations and among the external and local leadership; but it had no effect on the determination of the lower ranks, who continued their activities. Popular committees organized by town, sector (youth, women, schoolchildren, and college students), or trade union, were in charge of operations. Israeli sources estimated the hard core and popular base of the Palestinian struggle at ten thousand to twenty thousand people.[22] A Fatah activist estimated the number of activists from his movement alone at forty thousand.[23] This number included, aside from demonstrators and fighters, local guards, fundraisers, and food collectors, as well as those active in organizations providing mutual aid, boycotting Israeli goods, and other manifestations of the revolt.

Israel made an effort to contain the operational capacity of the Unified National Leadership by arresting thousands of activists, deporting some of them to Lebanon and Jordan, imposing "closures," and bearing down on the population; in particular, preventing tens of thousands of workers from entering Israel, thus cutting off their families' primary, and sometimes only, source of income. During the first eighteen months of the intifada, Israel arrested nearly 40,000 Palestinians for varied durations. This included 2,600 administrative detainees (held without trial).[24]

The Islamic Alternative: Hamas and Jihad

The legacy of Islamic-oriented political movements had become a fixture of Palestinian history during the British Mandate. Signs of this trend were evident in the activities of the Young Muslim Society, the doctrine of Shaikh 'Izz al-Din al-Qassam, and to a great degree, the doctrine and conduct of Haj Amin al-Husayni, as well as many of the leaders of the 1936–1939 revolt and the warrior bands whose actions were typical of its final years. After the Nakba of 1948, the Muslim Brotherhood was the first to recover and to engage in resistance to the new reality in the West Bank and the Gaza Strip. Many Fatah leaders, primarily Arafat, had originated from the Muslim Brotherhood. The political Islam now reviving among the Palestinians was represented by two main groups—Hamas and Islamic Jihad.

The Hamas Movement

The roots of the Islamic Resistance Movement, or Hamas, may be found in the Muslim Brotherhood established in Egypt in 1928, which eventually also opened branches and cells in other Arab countries. From 1948 to 1967 the Palestinian cells acted in opposition to the Egyptian authorities in the Gaza Strip and to the Jordanian authorities in the West Bank. Nonetheless, for short periods, the movement was willing to cooperate with these regimes for tactical reasons. When Israel occupied the territories, the remaining Muslim Brotherhood members did not rush to take part in acts of resistance.

Some of its leaders explained their passivity as "emotional separation" from society in general, with its secular and ignorant orientation (*jahiliyya*). They claimed that they would rather focus on social-religious reform and on restoring Islamic values among the masses. In contrast, some Islamic leaders, such as Ya'qub Qarrash and Muhammad Abu Tir, disagreed with the policy of "separation," and instead joined Fatah cadres and took part in the resistance.

In the first half of the 1980s, Islamic movements embraced a new approach, espousing involvement in the political Palestinian cause and in secular concerns occupying society. This approach was manifested in the establishment of the "Islamic complex" (*al-mujamma' al-Islami*) as a social endeavor, which led to the emergence of Hamas. The driving force behind this outlook was Shaikh Ahmad Yassin (1934–2004), born in the village of Jura (near Ashqelon) and crippled in an accident in the early 1950s. Despite his disability and his family's poverty, Yassin persevered at his studies, graduated from a teachers' seminary, and worked as a teacher at UNRWA schools. At first, Israeli authorities had no problem with Shaikh Yassin's social-religious project, perceived as a counterbalance to the nationalist-secular orientation of Palestinian belligerence. It seems that they saw no reason to suspect his intentions due to his former "separatist" views. However, in 1983, Shaikh Yassin founded the first military cell of al-Mujahidun al-Filastiniyyun (the Palestinian Mujahidin) and was consequently imprisoned for two years. When the intifada began, he and his movement were already part of its foundations.

In one of the movement's announcements at the beginning of the intifada's second year, Shaikh Yassin explained how he perceived the popular struggle: "What is happening today on this blessed land is a reforging of the Islamic nation and of the current Muslim generation as the flag bearers of Islam."[25] In an interview in 1989 he explained the movement's transition to active resistance: "Advancing from stage to stage is a natural development in the life course of all movements. The decision to do so is up to the leaders. Current events forced the Islamic movement to progress to a stage of confrontation with the occupying forces. The scope of resistance and its forms always correspond with the movement's actual capacity."[26] In this interview Shaikh Yassin did not reject the possibility of progressing to a stage of armed resistance: "Jihad is the responsibility of all Muslims whose land has been a target of degradation. Their response should be consistent with their capabilities."[27]

'Abd al-'Aziz al-Rantisi (1948–2004), one of the movement's leaders, emphasized the intifada's Islamic roots in a February 1988 interview with *al-Sirat al-Mustaqim* (the journal of the Islamic movement in Israel):

> The intifada began with one enduring slogan: Allah Akbar. It issued forth from the mosques where the Quran was read and Islamic songs memorized to guide the people. The prisons were filled with young Muslims and eventually became mosques. The streets and mosques were filled with Hamas announcements until these resounded among the people. All who follow political and journalist declarations will notice that these reports clearly indicate the role of the Islamic forces as the driving force behind the intifada.[28]

Shaikh Yassin explained the concept of collaboration with the PLO and with the secular division of the nationalist movement:

> It is necessary to have a common ground, based on a commitment to Islamic values and principles and their promotion in times of struggle and resistance. Prior consent must be reached concerning the Islamic nature of any future government established after liberation. We object to the Palestinian National Charter. Recognition of the principle of the secular state, set forth in this charter, would constitute a deviation from the way of Islam. The Palestinian organizations were founded in order to realize political and national goals; the Muslim Brothers have such goals as well but they are defined by an Islamic platform.[29]

Hamas published its charter in August 1988. Despite tensions with the Muslim Brotherhood, due to Hamas's preference to operate independently, the charter specifically defined the movement as a chapter of the Muslim Brotherhood. It declared the movement's objection to the establishment of a democratic secular state and its desire to establish "an Islamic state throughout Palestine"; however, it provided no details as to the future state's social, political, and economic nature. Regarding cooperation with the PLO, the charter objected to any peace negotiations that "will leave parts of the Islamic land in non-Muslim hands." However, it did not completely reject dialogue with Fatah and the other Palestinian organizations. On the issue of the conflict with Israel, the charter employed an inconclusive tone. It did not specifically mention the policy of armed struggle, but stated that "there is no recourse but to call for jihad. Such a task requires the assimilation of an Islamic consciousness among the masses, on a local, Arab, and Islamic level."[30]

The ambiguous platform was supplemented by thousands of leaflets distributed from time to time by local Hamas leaders in the West Bank and the Gaza Strip. The movement gradually grew, becoming a large popular faction, second only to Fatah. In time, Israel assumed a stricter approach toward Hamas. In August 1989, Israeli authorities arrested 'Abd al-'Aziz al-Rantisi, and in September they arrested Shaikh Yassin and some 250 major activists. These arrests enabled Arafat to regain control of the intifada.

The Islamic Jihad Movement

The Islamic Jihad Movement was established in 1980 by Dr. Fathi Shaqaqi and 'Abd al-'Aziz 'Awda. Shaqaqi was born in 1953 to a family of refugees originally from the village of Zarnuqa and completed his graduate studies in pharmacology at the University of Cairo. As a young man he tended toward Nasserist nationalism, but joined the Muslim Brotherhood in the early 1970s, and toward the end of that decade drew closer to the teachings of Ayatollah Khomeini, even writing a book on the topic. 'Abd al-'Aziz 'Awda, a refugee from the vicinity of Beer Sheva, was born in 1948 and joined the Muslim Brotherhood at an early age. He worked as a preacher and lecturer at the Islamic University of Gaza. When the movement was founded, the two published an underground journal named *Al-Talai' al-Islamiyya* (Pioneers of Islam). Israeli authorities arrested them several times before deporting them to Lebanon. Shaqaqi was arrested for the first time in 1983, accused of hostile activities, and sentenced to eleven months in prison. He was arrested again in 1986, sentenced to four years in prison, and deported from the country on August 1, 1988. 'Awda was imprisoned several times as well, before being deported to Lebanon in November 1987.[31]

From an ideological perspective, the movement was influenced by three prominent, modern Islamic figures: Hasan al-Banna, 'Izz al-Din al-Qassam, and Sayyid Qutb. Qutb's book, *Ma'alim al-Tariq* (Guidelines), is still used as a type of entrance exam for new members and recruits.[32]

Arafat Resumes the Political Option: From Madrid to Oslo

After the death of Khalil al-Wazir, whose orchestration of the intifada showed an independent streak, and once the Islamic organizations had been weakened by Israeli arrests, Arafat and his associates in Tunis resumed their key positions. Arafat's representatives were now in control of the uprising. He himself declared the establishment of a government in exile in November 1988, appointing himself "president of the Palestinian State." Thus Arafat took over leadership of the Palestinian representative institutions almost uncontested and enhanced his position in every possible way.

At first, several leaders of the Unified National Leadership tried to object to Arafat's absolute powers, but they were undermined by repeated Israeli attempts to suppress the local leadership. However, by early 1990, the strategy of leading by remote control, as well as increasing acts of revenge and the elimination of those suspected of collaborating with Israel, brought the intifada to a dead end. Even Arafat himself yearned for a period of calm to promote the "Palestinian Peace Attack" that he had initiated in the spring of that year. He traveled to Arab and European capitals to foster US recognition of his status. His efforts were futile and in August 1990, when Iraq took control of Kuwait, Arafat found himself in a tough spot. He was one of the few Arab leaders who openly supported Saddam Hussein, and he even visited Baghdad in January 1991 when the forces of the international coalition staged their attack. This angered the United States and the Gulf states, who stopped the flow of "steadfast perseverance funds" to the PLO. Tens of thousands of Palestinians who had been working in Kuwait and other Gulf states lost their jobs and some were even deported. However, the sanctions against the PLO, enforced by halting Gulf state support, did not apply to Hamas, which declared that Iraq must withdraw from Kuwait. The funds filling Hamas coffers sustained the expedited process of building institutions, founding a political bureau, and establishing a military branch called Regiments of 'Izz al-Din al-Qassam.

Under pressure from these developments, Arafat chose to gamble once again on a political course of action as a way of drawing closer to Washington. Aware of the damage inflicted by his support of Saddam Hussein, Arafat agreed to join peace talks held at the initiative of the United States in Madrid in late October 1991. A Palestinian contingent headed by Faisal al-Husayni and Hayder 'Abd al-Shafi took part in the discussions as part of the Jordanian delegation. Arafat's consent to participate in the talks aroused considerable criticism, mainly by the Islamic organizations, headed by Hamas. This step was described as a futile act that would be of no avail and would even lead to erosion of the intifada's achievements and to its end.[33] Members of the Islamic group managed to assemble a wide opposition, which included both left-wing organizations and some secular forces, totaling some ten groups and movements. They declared their objection to holding the talks in Madrid and called themselves the Alliance of the Ten. Arafat responded to the criticism of this group and said, expressing both ridicule and bitterness, "I was surprised that members of Hamas allied themselves with left-wing elements, which were the very reason they had refused to join the united party—these ten organizations, Hamas and the Popular Front and half of the Democratic and the other little organizations. I, for example, do not recognize Fathi Shaqaqi, because I see his as an Iranian organization rather than a Palestinian one."[34]

In contrast, Yazzid Sayigh maintains that the new reality created by the intifada is what prompted Arafat to take part in the Madrid talks:

> The intifada forced Arafat, by giving voice to the changes and transformations in the mechanisms and methods of the national struggle, to accept the fact that the national struggle had become an internal Palestinian struggle. This means recognition that the entire axis of political action had moved from the diaspora to the occupied territories. This fact was very visible and well established in the Oslo Accords.[35]

From an international perspective, Palestinian participation in the Madrid conference under a joint Jordanian-Palestinian flag (interpreted as reducing the status of the PLO as the exclusive legitimate representative of the Palestinian people) was indicative of the problems encountered by Arafat in his attempt to receive US recognition of the PLO as a legitimate partner in the peace talks. US recognition was important for him, due to his reading of the new international situation formed after the collapse of the Soviet Union, previously the PLO's most important strategic ally in the international sphere. He also saw it as a means of creating a single international axis.

Holding the talks in Madrid also invited a comparison between the fate of Palestine and that of Arab Andalusia. Writer Ragheb al-Serjany believes that the decision to hold the talks in Madrid was no coincidence:

> The Palestinian issue is very similar to the issue of Andalusia. The question is why were the Israeli-Palestinian talks held in Madrid, of all cities, one of Andalusia's ancient cities? The answer is that these talks were held exactly on the fifth centennial of the fall of Andalusia. At the time massive celebrations were held in the streets of Madrid to commemorate the defeat of the Muslims and the victory of the Crusaders five hundred years earlier. The organizers of the talks must have planned their message well: History repeats itself and the events in Andalusia are repeating themselves in Palestine. The intifada in Palestine is approaching its end just as the intifada of Mousa Ibn Abi Ghassan in Granada was brought to an end. History repeats itself, there is no need for war and there is no need for much argument, as the fate of the Palestinians will be identical to the fate of the people of Andalusia.[36]

Notes

1. S. al-Hout, *Bayn al-Watan wa al-Manfa, min Yafa Bada al-Mishwar* [Between the Homeland and the Exile], 395.
2. These statistics were obtained from the book by al-Jayyusi, ed., *Filastin al-Muhtalla 1985–1987: Al-Sumud wa al-Tahaddi* [Occupied Palestine].
3. On this see 'Aliyyan, "Al-Iqtisad al-Filastini bayna al-tabai'yya wa al-istiqlal" [The Palestinian Economy Between Belonging and Independence], 39.
4. Abu Shkur, "Al-Hijra al-kharijiyya lil 'amalah fi al-aradi al-Filastiniyya al-muhtallah: hajmuha, khasa'isuha wa dawafi'uha" [Outward Immigration for Workers in the Occupied Palestinian Territories], 65.
5. Khalil al-Sawahiri, *Al-Filastiniyyun al-Tahjir al-Qasri wa al-ri'aya al-Ijtima'iyya* [Palestinians and the Displacement and Social Treatment of the Refugees], 34.
6. On this see, for example, Ben Rafael, *Israel-Palestine*, 109–110.
7. Those "removed" were usually transferred to a neighboring Arab country, most often Lebanon or Jordan.
8. The name Hamas in Arabic is an acronym for *Harakat al-Muqawama al-Islamiyya*—the Islamic Resistance Movement. The name itself is significant, meaning enthusiasm, bravery, and zealotry.
9. Arafat was quoted in *Filastin al-Thawra*, January 14, 1988.

10. Proclaimed by Khalil al-Wazir in an interview in the Lebanese newspaper *Al-Safir* on January 27, 1988.

11. Al-Salihi, *Al-Za'amah al-Siyasiyya wa al-Diniyya fi al-Aradi al-Muhtalla* [Political and Religious Leadership in the Occupied Lands], 121–122.

12. Arafat was quoted in Fatah's journal, *Filastin al-Thawra*, January 7, 1988.

13. *Filastin al-Thawra*, January 7, 1988.

14. Shabib, "Al-Muqawamah al-Filastiniyya: Siyasiyyan" [Palestinian Resistance], 99.

15. Shabib, "Al-Muqawamah al-Filastiniyya: Siyasiyyan" [Palestinian Resistance], 98.

16. *Al-Yawm al-Sabi'*, January 18, 1988.

17. Sayigh, *Al-Kifah al-Muslah wa al-Bahath 'An al-Dawla: Al-Haraka al-Wataniyya al-Filastiniyya, 1949–1993* [Armed Struggle and the Search for a State], 845.

18. Sayigh, *Al-Kifah al-Muslah wa al-Bahath 'An al-Dawla: Al-Haraka al-Wataniyya al-Filastiniyya, 1949–1993* [Armed Struggle and the Search for a State], 858.

19. Parts of the report are cited by S. al-Hout, *Bayn al-Watan wa al-Manfa, min Yafa Bada al-Mishwar* [Between the Homeland and the Exile], 396.

20. S. al-Hout, *Bayn al-Watan wa al-Manfa, min Yafa Bada al-Mishwar* [Between the Homeland and the Exile], 396.

21. Sayigh, *Al-Kifah al-Muslah wa al-Bahath 'An al-Dawla: Al-Haraka al-Wataniyya al-Filastiniyya, 1949–1993* [Armed Struggle and the Search for a State], 864.

22. This number is cited by Litvak, "West Bank and the Gaza Strip," 236.

23. This number was cited by a Fatah activist removed from the country due to his activity in the intifada, Lu'ay 'Abdu, in an interview in *Filastin al-Thawra*, November 12, 1988.

24. Litvak, "West Bank and the Gaza Strip," 236.

25. Islamic Resistance Movement (Hamas), announcement no. 36, February 25, 1989.

26. Abu 'Amru, *Usul al-Haraka al-Siyasiyya fi Qita' Ghazza, 1948–1967* [Foundations of the Political Movements in the Gaza Strip], 87.

27. Abu 'Amru, *Usul al-Haraka al-Siyasiyya fi Qita' Ghazza, 1948–1967* [Foundations of the Political Movements in the Gaza Strip], 87.

28. Al-Tayyib al-Mahdi, "Muqabalah ma' 'Abd al-'Aziz al-Rantisi," interview with 'Abd al-'Aziz al-Rantisi, in *Al-Sirat* 10 (February 1988): 25.

29. Abu 'Amru, *Usul al-Haraka al-Siyasiyya fi Qita' Ghazza, 1948–1967* [Foundations of the Political Movements in the Gaza Strip], 95–96.

30. The charter is quoted in the book by Yasin, *Hamas, Harakat al-Maqawama al-Islamiyya fi Filastin* [Hamas], 96–101.

31. Abu 'Amru, *Usul al-Haraka al-Siyasiyya fi Qita' Ghazza, 1948–1967* [Foundations of the Political Movements in the Gaza Strip], 116–117.

32. Abu 'Amru, *Usul al-Haraka al-Siyasiyya fi Qita' Ghazza, 1948–1967* [Foundations of the Political Movements in the Gaza Strip], 119.

33. On this see, for example, Zelikovich, *Tnu'at HaFath, Islam, Le'umiyut Vepolitika Shel Ma'avak Mezuyan* [Fatah Movement], 86.

34. Cited by Zelikovich, *Tnu'at HaFath, Islam, Le'umiyut Vepolitika Shel Ma'avak Mezuyan* [Fatah Movement], 86.

35. Sayigh, *Al-Kifah al-Muslah wa al-Bahath 'An al-Dawla: Al-Haraka al-Wataniyya al-Filastiniyya, 1949–1993* [Armed Struggle and the Search for a State], 960.

36. Ragheb al-Serjany, "Qissat al-Andalus Min al-Fath Ila al-Suqout" [The Story of Andalusia, from the Arab Occupation until the Fall], *Mawsu'at 'Iqra'* [The Encyclopedia of 'Iqra'] (2011), 728–730.

13

The Oslo Accords: Leading Where?

In the summer of 1992, Yasir Arafat consented to an initiative by Israeli academics to hold confidential talks between Israelis and Palestinians in Oslo. This initiative overshadowed the Madrid talks and led to the signing of a declaration of principles between the two nations in September 1993 on the White House lawn, with the ultimate goal of reaching peace and reconciliation treaties. The Oslo Accords paved the way for mutual PLO-Israel recognition and for the establishment of the Palestinian National Authority in the spring of 1994. It was not easy for Arafat to promote acceptance of the Oslo Accords on the internal Palestinian front. These accords were considered by many, in essence, as a worse version of the autonomy offered to the Palestinians at Camp David, which was firmly rejected by Arafat and the PLO leadership. Criticism was voiced, both from within Fatah and by Arafat's partners in the PLO, and even among Palestinian intellectuals who, in the past, had been ardent supporters of Arafat.

Within the PLO a bitter argument was waged with opponents of the agreement, who perceived it as a retreat from the original guidelines of the Palestinian national movement. The most prominent of the opponents within Fatah was Shafiq al-Hout, a member of the PLO Central Committee and its representative in Beirut. Al-Hout relates in his memoirs that he was surprised, as were most members of the Central Committee, by the Oslo Accords with Israel, and once these were officially announced he resigned all his responsibilities in the PLO, seeing that all his attempts to prevent Arafat from signing the agreement had been to no avail. As a result of the persuasion campaign held in Tunisia, Arafat agreed to an emergency meeting of Fatah's Central Committee, in which, to Yasir Arafat's chagrin, al-Hout voiced his opinions most clearly. In his speech before the Central Committee, during which he was repeatedly interrupted by Arafat, al-Hout objected to the narrow scope of the declaration of principles:

> In format, this agreement is called a declaration of principles concerning arrangements for a transitional government of the autonomy. But it should have been a declaration of principles concerning the entire Palestinian cause, including all its aspects, followed by arrangements for the intermediate stage as part of a full and detailed agreement between the two sides. When we read this agreement thoroughly we discover that there are no clear principles in this declaration of principles, and all we find is a collection of vague signals that have no source of authority aside from the decision of 242, which lost its role as a legal source of authority and became an appendix of the possible consequences of negotiations for the permanent arrangements. . . . And in the context of our reading of other sections we find that we have admitted, to begin with, [the fact] that our lands are no longer occupied lands.[1]

As al-Hout relates in his memoirs, he constantly sparred with Arafat throughout the speech. According to al-Hout, Arafat spared no snide comment and even came close to insulting the speaker. Nonetheless, he says that he subjected himself to self-examination once the results of the vote on his reservations concerning the agreement and on the call to annul it became known. From among the 120 people present, only eight voted in favor of his proposal and the rest voted in support of Arafat's proposal to confirm the agreement.[2] What was surprising about this vote was the conduct of some of the Fatah old guard, such as Khaled al-Hasan, who had previously expressed in public their bitterness at their exclusion by Arafat from the secret negotiations held in Oslo and had sharply criticized Arafat's conduct and the excessive concentration of power in his hands. Among Fatah's partners in the PLO, one notable response was that of George Habash, Arafat's rival for many years, who had aligned himself with Arafat's policy at the conference of the National Council held in Algiers in November 1988, after the deep conflict between them following the departure from Beirut in 1982. Habash saw Arafat's signing of the declaration of principles in 1993 as the unforgivable crossing of a red line. In a lengthy interview given to the Palestine Research Institute, and published in a pamphlet in 1998, Habash tried to judge the Oslo Accords by profit-and-loss criteria and reached the conclusion that Israel's profit was much greater than any to be gained by the Palestinians:

> A quick reading of the events and their results shows that our losses are much greater than our achievements. Our losses are of course a net profit for Israel. In contrast, Israel's profits are much greater than its losses. This can explain the entanglement in which we have become embroiled following the Oslo Accords and the extreme hardships of the Palestinian people living in the occupied homeland and in the diaspora.[3]

Habash's opinions did not prevent his men, who were currently outside the country, from taking the opportunity to return to the West Bank and the Gaza Strip per the Oslo Accords and from establishing the Palestinian Authority (PA) in 1994, including his assistant and successor as head of the PFLP, Abu 'Ali Mustafa al-Zibri, whom the Israeli forces attempted to assassinate at the beginning of the Second Intifada.

Palestinian intellectuals operating in the United States and the West also criticized the Oslo Accords, including Edward Sa'id and Rashid Khalidi. In his book *The Iron Cage* Rashid Khalidi described the Oslo Accords as a "regretful error of faulty agreements" and elsewhere as a "disastrous error."[4]

Some would allege that Khalidi was one of the consultants of the Palestinian delegation for the peace talks in Madrid, and that he was one of the academics associated with the PLO leadership, and as such should have voiced these opinions at the time, rather than a decade or more later. In contrast, Edward Sa'id began attacking the accords publicly a short time after the establishment of the PA. He published a series of articles in the newspaper *Al-Hayat*, in which he described the disadvantages of the accords for the Palestinians. Later on all these articles were collected and published in a book entitled *The End of the Peace Process: The Oslo Accords and Their After-*

math.⁵ In an article written in late May 1995, he summarized the damages inflicted on the Palestinians as a result of the Oslo Accords:

> The Oslo Accords and their outcome led to a rise in unemployment and poverty among the Palestinians. The worst aspects of the Israeli occupation—the worst military occupation in the twentieth century—persisted, the process of land expropriation and expansion of the settlements continued. The lives of Palestinians living in areas of "limited autonomy" under virtual control of the Palestinian Authority became tougher: Liberties were reduced and horizons restricted.⁶

Two years later, Sa'id wrote an article in the same paper, reflecting an even firmer attitude toward the accords and the oversight of the Palestinian leadership in this matter:

> It took four years for the Oslo peace process to disintegrate and for the shiny mask to come off, and now these accords are shown for what they are: not a peace treaty, rather a treaty to perpetuate Israeli control of Palestinian lands through nice words on one hand and military might on the other. Most of these things harken back, as I have been saying for a long time, to the regretful Palestinian failure to read Israeli intentions—particularly those of the Labor Party, when it was in control—and to take the necessary safety measures against them. Based on all the above, we entered a dilemma of loss and subjugation, after the United States and the various media gave us the false feeling that we had finally achieved a certain degree of respect and acceptance, while Israel forced us, through its continuous blows against us, to accept its gangland understanding of the terms "security" and "dialogue," eventually leading our people to a bottomless pit of poverty and misery.⁷

It is notable that Sa'id wrote this after the murder of Yitzhak Rabin and after the change in government six months later, with the rise of the Likud, headed by Prime Minister Benjamin Netanyahu, and particularly after the relationship between Israel and the PA was compromised following the tunnel clashes in September 1996.

The Palestinian Arabs in Israel also voiced their criticism of the signing of these accords. The main parties and movements (aside from the Islamic Movement) did not object to them outwardly, but some of the speakers and writers did not forgive the PLO leadership for completely disregarding them and their position in the final form of the accords. The internal refugees, for example, who had seen themselves as part of any possible solution to the Palestinian cause, expressed bitterness at the lack of regard for them, and they consequently formed an independent organization and established the Association for the Defense of the Rights of Internally Displaced Persons in Israel. Since 1998 this association has been organizing an annual procession in one of the destroyed villages, stressing their right of return to their villages.[8]

On the nineteenth anniversary of the accords, journalist Zuhayr Andreus wrote an article on the subject: "The Oslo Accords were a type of 'bribe' given to the Palestinian people or to those negotiating on their behalf. For twenty-five billion dollars the Palestinian leadership conceded the third side of the triangle, that is, the Arabs of '48. In other words, the distorted entity—the Oslo Authority—gave the Hebrew state a gift of the Arabs of 1948 and left them orphaned at a table of mean people."[9] Nevertheless, the leaders of the Arab population made sure to appear in Arafat's chambers during his last days in Tunisia and upon his return to Gaza after the founding of the PA. Arafat also had connections with this population, both in the sphere of political organization and in the activities of civil institutions and associations. He even appointed Dr. Ahmad Tibi to be his personal adviser on Israeli matters, before Tibi was elected to the Knesset. The relationship between Arafat and the PA became an issue in the local elections and candidates hung pictures of themselves taken with Arafat in his chambers as a promotional instrument to increase their chances of being elected.[10]

Notes

1. S. al-Hout, *Bayn al-Watan wa al-Manfa, min Yafa Bada al-Mishwar* [Between the Homeland and the Exile], 472–473.
2. S. al-Hout, *Bayn al-Watan wa al-Manfa, min Yafa Bada al-Mishwar* [Between the Homeland and the Exile], 478.
3. Suwayyid, *Al-tajriba al-nidaliyya al-Filastiniyya, hiwar shamel ma` George Habash* [Experience of the Palestinian Struggle], 66.
4. Khalidi, *Iron Cage*.
5. Sa'id, *Nihayat 'amaliyyat al-salam, Oslo wauma ba'adha* [End of the Peace Process].
6. *Al-Hayat*, May 30, 1995.
7. *Al-Hayat*, August 19, 1997.

8. The website of this committee is http://www.ror.org.

9. Zuhayr Andreus, "Oslo min al-hilm hatta al-kabus" [Oslo: From the Dream to the Trauma]. http://www.tarshiha.co.il, accessed December 2012.

10. On this see, for example, newspapers *Kul al-'Arab* and *Al-Sinnara* from the period prior to the municipal elections of 1998.

14

The Struggle Between Fatah and Hamas

Even before his return to the Palestinian Authority–administered territories in July 1994, Arafat was aware of the challenges that Hamas-led Islamic opposition would pose to his control of Palestinian Authority territories and to his leadership of the Palestinian fight for full independence. His associates insisted that Islamic terminology be emphasized more prominently in announcements and street slogans on walls and buildings. These slogans included distinctly Islamic symbols and verses from the Quran and even stressed the nonsecularism of Fatah.[1] Arafat himself repeatedly dipped into the Islamic lexicon. In a visit to South Africa on May 10, 1994, he compared the Oslo Accords that he had signed with Israel to the Treaty of Hudaybiyah that Prophet Muhammad had signed with the Quraysh who drove him out of Mecca and refused to accept Islam. In Arafat's declaration, which attracted much criticism, particularly from Israel, he sought to convey a message to opponents of the accords and to those who harbored reservations, that reaching agreements with your enemies is permitted by Islam and that even Prophet Muhammad himself engaged in this practice.[2] After the uproar caused by Arafat's words, his men silenced the critics and denied that Arafat had reached the agreement with the express intention of breaching it.[3] Moreover, Arafat chose to make his statement in South Africa, where the agreement that put an end to the lengthy rule of apartheid was signed during that period. Thus, he was addressing the weak who, despite many years of victimization, had accepted the principle of compromise, notwithstanding all the suffering and hardships involved.

The use of Islamic motifs by Fatah members was detected by Israeli elements in the West Bank already in the first years of the intifada:

> The integration of religious motifs in proclamations by PLO elements derives, in our opinion, not only from the ideological proximity between Fatah and Islam, but also from the concern of Fatah elements that Islamic elements will take over control of the population. Thus, by using religious motifs, PLO-Fatah elements are attempting to halt the effect of Islamic proclamations and to attract religious elements to them and to their ranks, while creating an image of united ranks.[4]

The Islamic threat posed by Hamas and other Islamic organizations was not the only problem facing Arafat in his attempts to manage the affairs of the Palestinian Authority. Arafat also confronted internal challenges within the PLO and within Fatah. First of all, the constant vicissitudes of Fatah in its transition from a national liberation movement to a ruling party were evident in the organization's conduct beginning from the establishment of the PA until the Second Intifada (1994–2000) and even later on.[5] This transition required a merging of two active groups within the organization: the more veteran activists who had come from Tunisia with Arafat and the newer activists who ran the intifada from within. The differences between the two generations were significant, as manifested in their behavior, concepts of government, dealings with the people, and mainly their attitude toward the practical role of religion within the social fabric and daily life.[6] The intergenerational struggle was also evident in the fight for control of PA apparatuses that arose immediately upon arrival of the old guard from Tunisia. Arafat was obliged to maneuver between the young leaders of the intifada, exemplified by Muhammad Dahlan and Marwan al-Barghouti, and more veteran leaders who came from Tunisia, such as Mahmoud Abbas (Abu Mazen), Nasser Yousef, and others. Arafat managed to perform these maneuvers quite deftly, but upon his death, many fissures appeared in the delicate construct of the Palestinian Authority, undermining internal solidarity within Fatah.

In addition to these factors, PA leaders suffered from the general identification of Fatah with the Palestinian Authority. The problem encountered by the authority was voiced by ex-minister Hisham 'Abd al-Raziq: "If we were to say that the Palestinian Authority is Fatah we would be greatly mistaken, but if we were to claim that Fatah has no connection with the authority we would be even more mistaken, as Fatah is leading the political work and implementing the first Palestinian political program on Palestinian territory and it is the very foundation of the authority."[7]

Fatah was also a target of criticism from the left side of the Palestinian political map. Mustafa al-Barghouti, head of the Palestinian left wing, remarked on the subject of Fatah's Islamic messages and its conduct as a ruling party:

> Fatah should not be perceived as a homogeneous movement, as it is composed of many elements, from the radical right wing to the far side of the center. In the past it had a left-wing section, but this was gradually decimated, particularly following establishment of the Palestinian Authority. Since then Fatah has become identified with the Palestinian Authority, once it became the ruling party. Perhaps this is the reason for the dual discourse, as it is impossible to be both a national liberation movement and a government authority under occupation at one and the same time. It creates many unsolvable and complex problems. I myself do not see any inclination of Fatah toward Hamas; rather I would say that it embraced the methods of Hamas because it felt threatened.[8]

In addition to the constraints and difficulties listed above, and considering the murder of Israeli prime minister Yitzhak Rabin, on November 4, 1995, and the rise to power of the right wing, headed by Benjamin Netanyahu, six months later, Arafat's situation became even tougher. The change in identity and ideology of the Israeli partner to the peace process reduced or even eliminated his chances of completing implementation of the process. This was the setting for the outbreak of the Second Intifada in late September 2000, despite the change in the Israeli government in 1999 and the rise to power of Ehud Barak from Yitzhak Rabin's camp.

The peace talks held by Barak and Arafat at Camp David in the United States in the summer of 2000 did not manage to bridge the differences concerning restarting the peace process and it was not long before the intifada erupted, redirecting the conflict to a new course of struggle: one that was complex, charged, and bloody. The catalyst for this intifada was a visit by member of the Knesset Ari'el Sharon to the complex encompassing the al-Aqsa Mosque and holy sites, but this was only the last straw. The major reasons were more complex and they had to do, first and foremost, with the failure of the Camp David talks, increasing agitation in the field among the Palestinian population due to nonimplementation of the Oslo draft program, and continued activities involving the construction and expansion of Israeli settlements in PA-administered territories and territories so intended. Within its first two weeks, the intifada had trickled over to the Palestinian population of Israel, and following bloody clashes between Arab demonstrators and Israeli security forces, thirteen young Arabs were killed, intensifying the Jewish-Arab schism within Israel. In Palestinian terminology, these events were designated the October Uprising (Habbat Oktober), commemorated every year by this community in early October as an important memorial day.[9]

In PA-administered territories, the intifada developed from a popular uprising by Palestinian demonstrators against the Israeli forces, similar to that of the First Intifada, to more violent confrontations, at first with young demonstrators and later on with armed young men and guerrilla fighters. This transition, which involved Fatah's al-Tanzim youth, who answered directly to Arafat, led to what we can call the "militarization of the intifada," with its disastrous results for the structure and functioning of the PA.[10] This failure was brought about by the transition to suicide operations within densely populated areas and buses in Israeli city centers. These operations eventually led to a massive Israeli response in the form of a major military operation in April 2002, designated Operation Defensive Shield, in which Palestinian cities were reoccupied, including the city of Ramallah, the political center of the Palestinian Authority and one of Arafat's two places of residence. The chairman of the Palestinian Authority was placed under siege at the Muqata'ah until contracting a mysterious illness that led to his evacuation to Paris for medical treatment, where he subsequently died on November 11, 2004.[11]

* * *

Following the establishment of the Palestinian Authority as a result of the Oslo Accords in the fall of 1993, the Palestinian national struggle for independence and for a state of their own can be characterized as progressing along two main axes. The first was that of the PLO, and particularly Fatah, which tried to develop the idea of an independent national identity that would eventually lead to an independent state founded after negotiations with Israel and backed by an international formula determined by other parties (mainly the United States and other international and Arab supporting players).[12] According to this axis, the crucial decisions necessary to solve the conflict would be made by Palestinian representative bodies under the umbrella of Palestinian national unity. The other axis, which adhered to Hamas and the other Islamic movements, tried to solve the conflict through uncompromising confrontations, linked to a wide pan-Islamic view of the historic land of Palestine as holy *waqf* land that is not open to negotiations.[13]

This was the basis for Hamas's refusal to recognize and accept the PLO's political plan, which also had implications for the Palestinian political map, causing it to split into two streams. These two paths were eventually designated the "national stream" and the "Islamist stream." The ideological, political, and social dimensions of the split have made it very difficult to form a uniformly accepted position in the face of the challenges encountered by the Palestinian people and all its communities. The two streams are divided over their interpretation of "Palestinian nationalism" and over the character of the future Palestinian state.

Hamas was in the opposition when the Oslo process was first implemented and it found itself in a serious dilemma: to be part of the Palestinian establishment and participate in the process of founding its institutions, or to carry the flag of resistance to Israel. For some reason, the movement chose a route of two parallel, concurrent courses of action. Israel could not accept this and the leadership of the Palestinian Authority found it very difficult to conduct itself in this process. At first Hamas was committed to the second course, as manifested in suicide operations executed by fighters of the organization within Israel. At the same time, it refused to be subsumed under the political umbrella of the Palestinian Authority, despite public declarations by some of its leaders who spoke of their longing and commitment to national unity. For example, they refused to join the joint field leadership of the intifada or to join the PLO.

In time, the leaders of Hamas found it necessary to reach a clear position on the Palestinian Authority's political actions and to accept it as an inevitable circumstance, despite their reservations. The turning point was the decision of Hamas to take part in elections for the legislative council, which in fact meant that it was entering into a political partnership with the other components of the Palestinian national movement. Winning the majority of the seats on this council in the elections held in January 2006 made things even more complicated, as now Hamas was required to provide an answer to the constraints and complications ensuing from the principles that had served as the foundation of the Palestinian Authority.[14]

Anyone examining the shifts in the views of Hamas leaders on this issue will see that as long as Arafat was head of the Palestinian Authority they had avoided openly opposing him, but also hesitated to take part in processes under his leadership. However, when Arafat died in the fall of 2004 and Mahmoud Abbas (Abu Mazen) became head of the authority, Hamas began to harbor thoughts of taking over PA institutions and its leadership. This started with the organization's signing of the Cairo Agreement in 2005 and continued with its participation in elections for the legislative council, which it won, culminating in the Hamas takeover of the Gaza Strip and the expulsion of PLO and Fatah loyalists in 2007.

A surprising development in the constant struggle between Fatah and Hamas were the strong differences in approach that culminated in bloody clashes between the two organizations in Gaza, eventually leading to the removal of Fatah members and total separation between the West Bank and the Gaza Strip. In June 2007 two Palestinian governments were established—one in Gaza, headed by Ismaʻil Haniyeh of Hamas, and one in the West Bank, headed by Salam Fayyad of Fatah. In terms of depth of hatred, this rift was reminiscent of the last stage of the 1936–1939 revolt, when civil war broke out between the bands of the revolt and the peace bands established by the British.[15] These events resulted in deep wounds within Palestinian society, particularly in the domain of national solidarity. Some of these wounds continued to fester for a long time and had an extremely detrimental effect on the Palestinian people's endurance in the War of 1948.

The total control of Hamas over the Gaza Strip and the establishment of a type of independent entity there resulted in an array of consequences and complications that aroused several complex questions about the future of the Palestinian national enterprise and particularly the chances of establishing an independent Palestinian state in the West Bank and Gaza Strip. This complexity has two dimensions: an internal Palestinian dimension and an external dimension. On the internal Palestinian scene, there are serious questions regarding the political structure of the Palestinian Authority and of the more independent political entity that will allegedly replace it in the future. Questions also remain as to its political participants and their ability to shape the essence of Palestinian national unity, as well as their many views of democratization, which must form the basis of a future independent state.[16] Externally, there are questions about the Israeli plan for contact with the factious Palestinian reality, as well as the response of Arab and other international parties.

The deep rift between Fatah and Hamas has significantly changed the priorities of the Palestinian people. The goal of national reconciliation has become a major part of its priorities. The leaders of both streams constantly emphasize their commitment to attaining this main goal, which is crucial for all Palestinians. They also have met many times and signed several agreements (the Damascus Understandings, the Cairo Agreement, and the Mecca Agreement) but the hoped-for reconciliation has not materialized and a new reality of two competing Palestinian entities, that of Fatah in the West Bank and Hamas in the Gaza Strip, has emerged. The feelings of distrust and mutual accusation have led to an almost complete separation of the two sides, so much so that Hamas accused the Palestinian Authority and Fatah of coordinating their positions on the eve of the comprehensive Israeli operation in the Gaza Strip (entitled Operation Cast Lead) in late 2008 and early 2009. They also accused the Palestinian Authority of inaction in the face of the Israeli siege on the Gaza Strip and even of rejoicing at the suffering of their brethren in the Gaza Strip.[17]

In light of these hard feelings, a Palestinian reconciliation is not imminent, and neither is the reunification of the Gaza Strip and the West Bank under a single authority. Moreover, the possibility of national unity that would enable a uniform representative leadership that could negotiate on behalf of the Palestinians does not seem feasible. Each of the current leaders of the two blocs has resolved to be victorious, each pulling in their own direction, and therefore it may be assumed that only the emergence of a new leadership, free of the residues of violent struggle characteristic of the relationship between the two movements to date will be able to lead the Palestinian people toward the light at the end of the tunnel.

Notes

1. For more detail see Muhammad and Muhammad, *Shi'arat al-Intifada* [Slogans of the Intifada], 365–367.
2. See for example: Karsh, *Arafat: Ha'ish Umilhamto Beyisra'el* [Arafat], 74.
3. For the full version of Arafat's speech in Johannesburg and the criticism it aroused see "PLO Chairman Yasir Arafat's Speech on Jerusalem to South African Muslims, Johannesburg, 10 May 1994," *Journal of Palestine Studies* 93 (Autumn 1994): 131.
4. "Report of the Civil Administration for Judea and Samaria, Department of Arab Affairs," April 1988, p. 4. Cited by Zelikovich, *Tnu'at HaFath, Islam, Le'umiyut Vepolitika Shel Ma'avak Mezuyan* [Fatah Movement], 82.
5. On Fatah's radical transition from a national liberation movement to a ruling party in a demilitarized authority, see Abu Fakhr, *Al-Haraka al-Wattaniyya al-Filastiniyya Min al-Nidal al-Muslah ila Dawla Manzo'at al-Silah* [Palestinian National Movement].
6. On this see Rema Hamami, "From Immodesty to Collaboration: Hamas, the Women's Movement, and National Identity in the Intifada," 194–210.
7. *Fath al-Thawra*, January 1, 1995, p. 5.
8. From an interview of Mustafa al-Barghouti with Eric Hazan on the website http://kibosh.co.il, December 15, 2011.
9. On all these events and their effect on the relationship between Israel and its Palestinian-Arab minority, see the report of the Or Commission, appointed by the Israeli government to investigate the events. The document and the background for the commission's work are available on the website of the Adalah organization, at http://www.old-adalah.org.
10. On the discourse that developed as a result of this term, see Nidal Fathi al-'Arabid, *Ma' 'askarat al-intifada um didha* [With the Militarization of the Intifada or Against It], http://www.Arabtimes.com, September 2012.
11. On the last chapter of Arafat's life in the Muqata'ah, his illness and death, and accusations that he was poisoned, see al–Hsan, *Qira'at fi al-Mashhad al-Filastini,'an 'Arafat wa-Oslo wahaq al-'awda* [A Reading of the Palestinian Political Scene].
12. On this see Hilal, *Al-Nizam al-Siyasi al-Filastini ba'd Oslo* [Political Regime in Palestine after Oslo], 125.

13. For more details, see al-Harub, *Hamas: Al-Fikr wa al-Mumarsa al-Siyasiyya* [Hamas].

14. On this see al-Hamad, *Dirasa fi al-Fikr al-Siyasi Lilharaka al-Islamiyya (Hamas)* [A Study on the Political Thought of the Islamic Resistance Movement (Hamas)].

15. For more details on this stage, see al-Hamad, *Dirasa fi al-Fikr al-Siyasi Lilharaka al-Islamiyya (Hamas)* [A Study on the Political Thought of the Islamic Resistance Movement (Hamas)], the chapter on the Revolt of 1936–1939.

16. The views of Hamas on these issues are evident from the white paper issued by the movement after it took control of the Gaza Strip and in which it explains its political views. For more details see Harakat al-Muqawma al-Islamiyya (Hamas), Al-Maktab al-I'lami. Al-Kitab al-Abid, 'Amaliyyat al-Hasm fi Qita' Ghazza, Idtiraran la Ikhtiyaran [Hamas Media Bureau, the White Paper, the Resolution in the Gaza Strip: An Act of Necessity and Not of Choice], November 2007.

17. On this see, for example, an article published on behalf of the Hamas movement on the Amgad al-'Arab website, entitled "Hamas Will Reveal Who Devised the Plot Against Gaza," at http://www.amgadalarab.com.

15

The Palestinians in the Whirlwind of the Arab Spring

In a post on the online Palestine's Dialogue Forum, under the heading "Why are the Palestinians enduring a hot scorching summer in the midst of the Arab Spring?" a surfer who called himself "Hunter of the Truth," apparently Islamist oriented, wrote the following:

> While the Arab nations are living in the shade of a blooming spring, the Palestinians are enduring an endless broiling summer. In Gaza the legitimate government is under siege, while in the West Bank a collaborator government is at the beck and call of the enemy; in Jordan Palestinians are being stripped of their Jordanian citizenship, although liberally awarded to Syrians, Chechens, Iraqis, and Egyptians. The Palestinians in Syria will shortly meet a similar fate to that of Palestinians in Iraq, victims both of the uprising with its faulty solidarity and of the tyrannical regime. The situation of the Palestinians in Lebanon is one of humiliation and subjugation, as is evident even toward those buried in the cemeteries. The Palestinians in Iraq are among those who have been slain or imprisoned, while the rest were thrown into exile in Chile or Brazil. All Arab nations are enjoying the Arab Spring and becoming liberated with a view to progress and prosperity, while the Palestinians are deteriorating in almost every aspect. Why? Have we been cursed by Heaven? Or is there some other reason? I don't know why everyone is experiencing the spring while only we are in the midst of a tough, blistering desert summer.[1]

These were the thoughts of a young Palestinian, fifteen months after the onset of events that have been termed the "Arab Spring," probably inspired by the European "Spring of Nations" denoting the events of 1848 in Europe. His words voice common sentiments among the Palestinian population, particularly young people who had hoped that these events would have positive implications for the Palestinian cause, or at least some improvement, however slight, in the Palestinian course of life. Obviously, advocates of this outlook would have preferred these events to include the Palestinians and would have liked to have seen young Palestinians taking part in the "age of rage," as some called these events. In contrast, others are mainly concerned with making sure that these events will pass over the Palestinians and not harm their cause. This group primarily includes Palestinian Authority personnel and representatives of the "old guard" of Fatah and its branches in the West Bank and in the diaspora.

It is clear that the Palestinian case is unique among the Arab nations. The Palestinian nation has not yet realized its national aspirations for an independent sovereign state and it is split between communities in different locations, living in different circumstances. This situation is even more glaring, since for many years young Palestinians were considered a model of revolutionary and combative action. Now that Arab nations have rebelled and revolted against their corrupt dictatorial regimes, it remains unclear as to who should be the target of the Palestinian revolt. Who should they be striving to topple? This dilemma was described by Hani 'Awda, a lecturer at the Al-Quds Open University of Jerusalem:

> The question among young Palestinians was not whether to rebel, but who should be the target of their revolt and rage? Young people in the Arab world have rebelled against undemocratic corrupt regimes and forcefully demanded the demise of these regimes. While young Palestinians had prior experience in resisting the Zionist occupation, at present the territory of the Palestinian Authority is under occupation but the leadership is also split into two authorities and two governments, forming an obstacle that prevents them from rising up against the occupation. As a consequence, young Palestinians decided to decry the internal division, resulting in mass demonstrations on March 15, 2011, in the Gaza Strip and the West Bank, under one united slogan protesting the

split and calling for unity. This angered the two splintered authorities, and although they were forced to give in to the will of the Palestinian masses and declare the end of the internal split and unity, their unity was manifested in taking all measures to repress the Palestinian popular movement, weaken its resolve, and shatter all hope of real Palestinian national unity.[2]

'Awda's last words may have been intended as an answer to the question discussed throughout the period since the start of the Arab Spring demonstrations: Why has Palestinian involvement remained passive, and why, on the few occasions in which it was more active, did this burst of action not continue, instead resuming its prior state of inactivity after a day or two? Why have the demonstrations and processions been limited to the anniversaries of important historical events in Palestinian collective memory, such as the 1948 Nakba Day or the 1967 Naksa Day?

Researcher Nabil al-Sahli contends that the crux of the matter is the rift between Fatah and Hamas, which are both interested in furthering the "new political geography," as he calls it. Al-Sahli refers to the possibility that a Palestinian spring will indeed "blossom":

> The many challenges encountered by the Palestinian national project must help facilitate Palestinian national reconciliation, such that the division into two entities in the West Bank and the Gaza Strip shall come to an end and a joint political plan be embraced, in order to develop future political options and manners of struggle capable of eroding the dangers of the Israeli settlement policy with its destructive effect on Palestinian territory and its transformation of the demographic state of affairs. Only when all these are effected will we be able to speak of a Palestinian Spring that will blossom in the aftermath of the Arab Spring.[3]

In an editorial entitled "So that the Palestinians will not become victims of the Arab Spring," *Al-Quds*, an East Jerusalem newspaper, and in recent years a supporter of the Palestinian Authority, summarized events a year and a half after the outbreak of the Arab Spring, saying that "although the Palestinian issue was one of the catalysts of the Arab Spring, it has been excluded and marginalized following these events, enabling the Israelis to increase their pressure on the Palestinians, now that the Arab world is no longer asserting its clear and decisive support."[4] Reading between the lines of the article, it is evident that the Palestinians did not manage to join the tide of the Arab Spring due to increasing Israeli pressure as a consequence of Arab neglect of the Palestinian cause by countries occupied with their own affairs or with those of other Arab countries. To ensure that the Palestinians will not be the only ones to pay the price of recent events, the editorial makes the following proposal:

> Although the Palestinian people know that Arab neglect of the Palestinian cause shall not persevere, firm and effective Arab initiatives and declarations are necessary, in order to show Israel that the Arab and Islamic nation support the joint cause [the Palestinian cause], such that it will understand that its acts against the Palestinians cannot continue, and if they do they will lead to severe retaliation in the not too distant future, particularly once the new Arab regimes have established themselves.[5]

Researcher Tariq Hammoud claims that more dramatic actions in the Palestinian camp were indeed expected in response to the Arab Spring events but that such an outcome was stymied due to the minimal attention accorded to the Palestinian cause by the Arab uprisings. Even the historic prisoners' strike did not manage to renew interest in the Palestinian issue.[6] Hammoud offers an explanation:

> The longing for a popular Palestinian movement capable of changing the balance of powers that has existed for the past several decades, particularly in regard to political accords and their implications, seems impracticable at the moment, for a list of reasons that begin with the occupation and conclude with the internal division. This, although the Palestinian people are living in historic times of which they should have made the best if there had only been elements facilitating internal insurgence. In my opinion, the social-local nature of the uprisings in Arab countries is not compatible with the popular Palestinian longing for upheaval, which must be a political upheaval closely associated with the regional and global context, that is, not one with limited local demands. The Palestinian interior cannot contain social-local demands for rebellion while overshadowed by the occupation.[7]

Significantly, a group organized by young Palestinians, called Young Palestinians for Change on Facebook, was established, inspired by events in the Arab world. An article was posted on the website by 'Abir Zayyad:

> When I try to understand young Palestinians, of whom I am one, I promptly arrive at the conclusion that young Palestinians, when referring to the various uprisings in the Arab world, perceive any insurgence that does not involve the Palestinian cause as suspicious and questionable. I don't mean, of course, that Arab nations should relinquish their rights and liberty or their local national interests for the sake of the Palestinian cause, but I mean that we have always seen the inability of Arab regimes to support the Palestinian cause as a surrender to Western forces, with their support of the Zionist movement since its inception. Even if some governments tried to object to this orientation or to be antagonistic, as long as they do not try to effect an essential change in the reality of the occupation experienced by the Palestinian people they shall be considered lackeys of the West, notwithstanding the premise whereby all Arab nations are affected and motivated by sweeping popular support for the Palestinian cause. My conclusion in this matter is that any government that does not support the Palestinian cause in actual fact as a just cause based on a legitimate demand for liberty is a government that does not represent the will of its people, but rather follows the Western desire to facilitate the demands of a certain group or party or movement and give jobs to leaders of their choice.[8]

According to Zayyad, the Palestinian cause should have been among the major catalysts of the Arab Spring uprisings, and any uprising that did not emphasize this dimension was not a true expression of the will of the people. Still, the question is, why did young Palestinians not emulate those uprisings that did make room for this cause?

The Palestinians had high hopes and expressed strong support for the relatively smooth victories achieved in Tunisia and Egypt. They hoped for positive consequences for their own situation, particularly as a result of the Egyptian upheaval. For example, three days after the fall of Hosni Mubarak, Muhannad 'Abd al-Hamid had this to say on the left-wing secular-oriented website al-Hiwar al-Mutmaddin (Progressive Dialogue) under the title "The revolution in Egypt and the anticipated Palestinian transformation":

> Today Egypt is free by all standards and criteria, free thanks to the great revolution which broke its chains and fetters, free because it

refused to further endure the tyranny and the corruption. Today Egypt is in devoted hands that delivered it from darkness to light. The Egyptian people are now bringing about change and rebuilding, while struggling with thievery and corruption. . . . When the nations resume their place on stage, their conduct will be radically changed. The Egyptian people have returned to the stage, preceded by the Tunisian people, while the Palestinian people, not long absent, will probably return in full force as well. If only young Palestinians have learned their lesson. The international forces sided with the Tunisian regime against the Tunisian people until its last moments. This was also true in the Egyptian case, and they have been acting similarly over the past few decades by siding with Israel while it violated international law and all its agreements on the Palestinian issue. This state of affairs will continue as long as the Palestinian people do not intervene and do not put the issue of the occupation on the international agenda, under the clear and firm slogan "The people want to end the occupation immediately."[9]

The waning enthusiasm for developments in Egypt following the ascent of Islamic elements did not result in a decline in the sweeping Palestinian support for the transformation in Egypt, and it can almost be said that no Palestinian was sad to see the end of Mubarak's regime. But the optimism voiced by Muhannad 'Abd al-Hamid and others writing not long after the fall of Mubarak's regime seems to be misplaced, if not unfounded. Popular activity showed no increase and the quiet on the Palestinian front was surprising. Nonetheless, there were those who stressed the positive implications of events in Egypt for the Palestinian cause, particularly for the Palestinian internal conflict, including Egyptian-initiated attempts at reconciliation between Fatah and Hamas. Khaled Mash'al, the political bureau head of Hamas, concurred with these sentiments in a television interview with the Egyptian satellite channel:

> I personally, and my friends in Hamas, have managed to smooth over quite a few points of contention for the sake of our people, with the goal of returning the smile to Palestinian faces. We did not wish to reject the Egyptian initiative nor to cause any embarrassment to Egypt after the blessed revolution that occurred there. The spirit of the Egyptian revolution has caused the change, as the word Egypt means a lot to the Palestinian public and to the Arab and Islamic public. For many years the Palestinian people have seen in Egypt a savior and a supporter. Even under the former regime, the

Egyptian public served as a type of sensor of the sentiments of the entire Arab nation.[10]

The reconciliation to which Mash'al is referring had few practical consequences, but the upheavals in Egypt can be credited with attracting the almost uniform support of both Palestinian camps, to such a degree that the Egyptian revolution can be said, with almost complete certainty, to be one of the only subjects on which they are in agreement. Marwan al-Barghouti, in his reply from prison to questions addressed to him clandestinely by the popular Egyptian newspaper *Al-Ahram*, expressed similar sentiments and strong empathy for the revolution in Egypt and Tunisia and said that the Palestinian reconciliation in May 2011 was the first positive outcome of the Egyptian revolution.[11]

With regard to events in Syria, at first, most Palestinian speakers supported the demands for change voiced by the demonstrators, as did, for example, Budur Hasan, in an article entitled "The Syrian uprising through Palestinian eyes":

> Palestinians chanted "Yallah Irhal Ya Bashshar" [Bashshar, leave!] in Nazareth, Haifa, Jaffa, Baqa, Jerusalem, Bil'in, and Nabi Saleh. Many of us will continue to do so since it's our duty to stand on the side of those who sing for freedom, dance, and even make jokes through the horror visited by bullets and mortar shells. A victory for the brave Syrian people over Assad's tyranny will be a triumph for every oppressed community in the world.[12]

But in time, some also expressed support for the government, explaining that it is "the last bastion of resistance to Israeli and American dominance in the region" or that it is "the strategic depth of resistance." This was also the view of Joseph Mas'ad of Columbia University in the United States:

> Those who see the Syrian popular struggle for democracy as having already been hijacked by these imperial and pro-imperial forces inside and outside Syria understand that a continuation of the revolt will only bring about one outcome, and it is not a democratic one—namely, a US-imposed pliant and repressive regime à la Iraq and Libya. If this is what the Syrian demonstrators are struggling for, then they should continue their uprising; if this is not their goal, then they must face up to the very difficult conclusion that they

have been effectively defeated, not by the horrifying repression of their own dictatorial regime, which they have valiantly resisted, but rather by the international forces that are as committed as the Syrian regime itself to denying Syrians the democracy they so deserve. In light of the new move by the Arab League, the United States, and Europe, the struggle to overthrow Assad may very well succeed, but the struggle to bring about a democratic regime in Syria has been thoroughly defeated.[13]

The range of Palestinian views includes quite a few surprises. While the spokesmen of the Palestinian Authority and of Hamas did not often express decisive views on happenings in Syria, some groups changed their traditional attitudes toward the regime. The Islamic movements, considered in the past to be allies of the government, crossed sides and began to censure the government and its symbols. This was also true of representatives of the Israeli Tajammu' Party (the National Democratic Assembly, or NDA)—and particularly of its leader, Azmi Bishara, residing in Qatar—who before the Arab Spring were considered ardent supporters of the Ba'ath regime in Syria. Bishara, who left Israel in 2007, often appeared on the popular Al-Jazeera television channel and did not conceal his sympathy for the views of Assad and his regime. In contrast, the NDA's political rivals, particularly the Democratic Front for Peace and Equality (Hadash), which had criticized the NDA in the past for its alliance with the "dictatorial regime that suppresses its people," expressed sympathetic views toward the current regime and described the popular uprising as a "tool wielded by the imperial powers, headed by the United States and its allies." The only ones who supported the regime before the events and remained constant in support of them were the Democratic Front for the Liberation of Palestine, headed by Nayif Hawatmeh, and the PFLP–General Command, headed by Ahmad Jibril, both Palestinian left-wing fronts.

In an article titled "With Syria or Against Syria," 'Abd al-Sattar Qasem, a lecturer at the Bir Zayt University, explains the Palestinians' dilemma concerning events in Syria:

> When there is a struggle between the regime and the people, we support the people, and when it is between a country and external forces we support the country. This is a rule that can be applied to Syria and to other Arab countries. The explanation is simple.

> Obviously, the people are not objecting to the government or the political regime for no reason or for their entertainment. Their resistance stems from significant reasons such as growing tyranny. It is also obvious that external forces are not fighting for the sake of a people suffering from tyranny but to serve their own interests while exploiting the state of the masses. Therefore, it was important to side with the Syrian people or with those of them who demonstrated against the regime at the beginning of events in Syria, as the regime was a tyrannical regime and it left the masses no choice but to demand its rights. But when the Syrian regime or people or land or country become the target of external aggression, any attempts at excuse are political demagoguery and even disloyalty to the nation and the homeland.[14]

After listing the forces operating against Syria, Qasem reaches the conclusion that there is no room for penalizing the regime for its mistakes and crimes; rather it is first necessary to act against the forces seeking to destroy Syria, and the solution as he sees it is as follows:

> It is undoubtedly necessary to change the political formula in Syria, but not to the American-Israeli formula. The current task is to defend Syria, but while maintaining the right to change, such that the unity of the people, the army, and the land, is preserved, and complete disintegration and division prevented. The conduct of any group or Islamic or national movement that joins a coalition with the United States or Israel is unacceptable. Hatred toward Arab elements is permissible, as well as resistance and even conflict, but we shall not fight them with American and Israeli arms or bombs or guns. Here I would like to remind everyone of the Zionist siege on Arafat. At the time no Palestinian or Arab chose to side with Israel simply because they hated Arafat or objected to the Oslo Accords, rather everyone sided with him against Israel. We did not agree with Arafat on the issue of Oslo when he was under siege, but not for a moment did we contemplate siding with Israel against a Palestinian. And now, will we side with Israel and America against a Syrian?[15]

This question, with which 'Abd al-Sattar Qasem concludes, summarizes the views of those who support Assad's regime; not because they think that Assad's regime is good and not because they are ignorant of his faults, but due to their wish to avoid being in the same camp as the United States and Israel, who have oppressed the Palestinians for many years.

Then again, there are those who have supported Assad's regime continuously, at first silently and later on openly. The best example are the members of Hadash, formerly part of the opposition to the Ba'ath regime in Syria during the era of Assad the father and Assad the son. They were hesitant at first, but in time their hesitation was transformed into clear support of the regime, maybe out of concern that Islamic groups would dominate the wave of protest in the Arab world and in Syria as well. In an article titled "Syria, the Safety Valve of Arab Nationalism," published on the Hadash website in early August 2012, Tamim Mansur (a senior NDA activist until leaving NDA in the summer of 2011) discusses the central and primary role of Syria in shaping and developing the concept of Arab unity in modern times.[16] After a detailed, and at times generalized and inaccurate, historical overview, Mansur refers to occurrences in Syria during the Arab Spring:

> This is only one of Syria's many radiant pages in history, but because of this pioneering role, Syria's enemies have made constant attempts against the people of Syria, with the goal of discouraging their strong views on the subject. The plots being hatched today against Syria, aimed at destroying its unity and economy and boycotting the Arabism of its people, are some of the most dangerous encountered by Syria to date, as its enemies believe that they are engaged in a fateful campaign due to Syria's role as the safety valve that prevents them from realizing their plots. We are certain that these plots are doomed to fail, as the Syrian army has been trained for a tougher struggle than this. Every day it eliminates hundreds of soldiers-for-hire employed by al-Hariri, Arduan, and the leaders of Jordan, Saudi Arabia, Qatar, and Bahrain.[17]

The views voiced by these Palestinians in their varied locations probably took into consideration the fact that some half a million Palestinian refugees reside at refugee camps in Syria. Journalist Anahid Hardan wrote of the practical implications of local events for this population:

> What these latest rounds of events tell us is that the fictitious boundaries between Palestinians in Syria and the unrest are just

that, becoming increasingly more difficult to maintain. As the situation on the ground continues to change, the fate of the Palestinians in the country, like the fate of Syrians and the country as a whole, remains uncertain. However, unlike their Syrian counterparts, Palestinians are refugees with nowhere to go in the event of further deterioration of the turmoil in Syria.[18]

In contrast, researcher Majid al-Kayyali tries to portray a fairly balanced picture and presents the problems encountered by Palestinian residents of the camps in Syria, who mostly supported the opposition forces, with some differences between the camps:

> The fact that the Palestinian camps have not become one of the focuses of the Syrian uprising does not mean that they sought to remain uninvolved in the issue from a passive point of view. These camps voiced their support of the Syrian revolution in various ways, among other things by giving refuge to residents of the beleaguered cities and suburbs and providing them with basic supplies, medical aid, housing, and even communications, when Palestinian activists spoke on behalf of the revolution on Facebook and helped win over public opinion. Moreover, some Palestinians took an active part in revolutionary activities, whether in demonstrations or by helping coordinate, transferring the injured, and giving refuge to activists. Some were killed, tortured, or arrested and persecuted, and some have completely disappeared.[19]

Al-Kayyali also says that the Palestinians in Syria, wherever they lived, responded in a manner similar to that of their Syrian neighbors. While in Homs, Ladikiyya, and Hamat, they found themselves embroiled and caught up in the upheavals, in Haleb and Damascus the process was slower, as these two cities were slower to respond.[20]

In summary, much has been said, and will be said, of the emotional and practical Palestinian involvement in the events of the Arab Spring. At present, more than eighteen months after these events erupted, it is obvious that the Palestinians did not have the sense to join the tide, or at least to reap benefits for the Palestinian cause from the wave of changes that swept regimes often accused by the Palestinians of helplessly neglecting their cause and doing the will of the West and of Israel. This state of affairs will probably not change unless a deep transformation takes place, redesigning the Palestinian political regime. This means a fundamental change in the forms and systems of Palestinian political activity and even in the movements and groups that set the tone of the Palestinian national movement. Such change should occur, not as a consequence of events in various Arab countries, but as a real solution to a national Palestinian need, one not maintained or achieved by current methods. Such a solution will not be possible so long as the Palestinian national movement lacks a single strong leadership, united operations, and first-rate forces in the field.

In order to succeed in redesigning the Palestinian political regime, it is necessary to identify the weaknesses of the existing regime and deal with them thoroughly, even if this involves a painful process. This process needs to begin with the selection of experienced groups not infested by sectarianism or guided by personal interests. The inability of the Palestinian political regime in its current format to work through its weaknesses is proof of the need for change, change that will prevent the existing system from replicating itself. The solution may well be the liberal formula of a civil state, one that recognizes the natural development of civil society, independent of official institutions and their affiliates and without being subjected to the will of external international aid. As long as civil society is an active, initiating, and independent society, the prospect of far-reaching change is a plausible and promising way of advancing toward a modern, healthy, and strong society.

Notes

1. These words appeared on the website of the Palestine's Dialogue Forum, http://www.paldf.net, accessed September 2012.

2. Hani 'Awda, "Al-Laji'un al-Filastiniyun fi al-diwal al-'Arabiyya wa al-rabi' al-'Arabi" [The Palestinian Refugees in the Arab Countries and the Arab Spring], http://www.thabit-lb.org, accessed September 2012.

3. Nabil al-Sahli, "Al-musalaha al-Filastiniyya fi ikhtibar al-rabi' al-'Arabi" [The Issue of Palestinian Reconciliation in the Test of the Arab Spring], *Al-Hayat* (London), June 27, 2012.

4. *Al-Quds* (East Jerusalem), June 29, 2012.

5. *Al-Quds* (East Jerusalem), June 29, 2012.

6. Tariq Hammoud, "Al-rabi' al-Filastini, hal yasna'ahu al-laji'un?" [The Palestinian Spring: Was It Created by the Refugees?], May 21, 2012, http://www.aljazeera.net.

7. Tariq Hammoud, "Al-rabi' al-Filastini, hal yasna'ahu al-laji'un?" [The Palestinian Spring: Was It Created by the Refugees?], May 21, 2012, http://www.aljazeera.net.

8. 'Abir Zayyad, "Filastin bayn al-rabi' wa al-sayf al-Isra'ili" [Palestine Between the Arab Spring and the Israeli Summer], http://gazatalkent.com, accessed September 2012.

9. Muhannad 'Abd al-Hamid, "Al-thawra al-misriyya wa al-taghayyur al-Filastini al-Ma'mul" [The Egyptian Revolution and the Hoped-for Palestinian Change], *Al-Hiwar al-Mutmaddin*, February 15, 2011.

10. The interview was held on May 5, 2011, and quoted in http://www.gate.ahram.org.

11. *Al-Ahram*, May 18, 2011.

12. Budur Hasan, "The Syrian Uprising Through Palestinian Eyes," April 11, 2011, http://www.electronicintifada.net.

13. Joseph Massad, "The Struggle for Syria," November 11, 2011, http://www.aljazeera.com.

14. 'Abd al-Sattar Qasem, "Ma' Surya au did Surya" [With Syria or Against Syria], August 1, 2012, palestin1@googlegroups.com.

15. 'Abd al-Sattar Qasem, "Ma' Surya au did Surya" [With Syria or Against Syria], August 1, 2012, palestin1@googlegroups.com.

16. Tamim Mansur, "Surya sammam al-aman lilqawmiya al-'Arabiyya" [Syria, the Safety Valve of Arab Nationalism], August 4, 2012, http://www.aljabha.org.

17. Tamim Mansur, "Surya sammam al-aman lilqawmiya al-'Arabiyya" [Syria, the Safety Valve of Arab Nationalism], August 4, 2012, http://www.aljabha.org.

18. "Uncertain Fate for Palestinians in Syria," July 12, 2012, www.electronicintifada.net, July 12, 2012.

19. Majid al-Kayyali, "Al-Filastiniyun fi al-thawra al-Surya" [The Palestinians in the Syrian Revolution], July 25, 2012, http://www.middle-east-online.com.

20. Majid al-Kayyali, "Al-Filastiniyun fi al-thawra al-Surya" [The Palestinians in the Syrian Revolution], July 25, 2012, http://www.middle-east-online.com.

Afterword

In the introduction to this book I presented three triangles within and around which Palestinian history has been shaped. One is the external triangle: the superpowers, the Arab countries, and the state of Israel. It seems that in the early twenty-first century this external triangle has gradually lost its significance. The superpowers have ceased their direct intervention in Palestinian matters. After direct British rule until the end of the 1940s and unambiguously aggressive Soviet influence until the end of the 1980s, all that was left were US and European declarations in support of a Palestinian state based on territorial compromise. The Arab world has changed the extent of its involvement as well. The Palestinians are no longer a pawn in the hands of Arab states, and they are no longer under Jordanian or Egyptian rule. The Arab world no longer doubts Palestinian self-governing capabilities. However, Israel's significance has not diminished. The Israeli occupation has changed form but remains potent. All chances for peace and rehabilitation, or, more ominously, the risk of resuming a course of confrontation and destruction, depend on Palestinian-Israeli relations. It seems that the history of the two nations will continue to intermingle for many generations to come.

The second triangle is related to national identity: the pan-regional Arab dimension, the national-Palestinian dimension, and the political-Islamic dimension. Significant changes have occurred in this context as well. The pan-regional revolutionary Arab outlook, with its secular, social, and political core, reached the height of its drive in the 1960s and 1970s and was nurtured by movements and organizations that had a significant effect on the upheavals of those years. However, this outlook, and the movements and organizations that promoted it, have since been pushed aside. The national struggle and its leadership were led, even then, by revolutionaries who preferred the Palestinian to the pan-Arab dimension. Fatah, headed by Arafat, rehabilitated and promoted the national-secular Arab-Palestinian identity, combining contrasting strategies of belligerence and maximalism with pragmatism and statesmanship. This identity and this course of action produced the most achievements and the most failures discussed in the current volume. They also overshadowed the Palestinian-Islamic identity, which began its process of construction in the 1930s but left no conspicuous mark. However in the last two decades, political Islam returned once again with a vengeance to the very heart of Palestinian existence. As these words are being written, Palestinian identity seems to be wavering between Fatah's Palestinian-Arab secular legacy and the course suggested by Hamas, with its religious-political ideology and goals.

Many changes are evident in the third, internal, social triangle as well. The traditional elite are currently no longer active. Representatives of the leading families, who had a significant impact in the years prior to the defeat of 1948, remained an influential factor in subsequent years. Mufti Haj Amin al-Husayni, an important representative of this political culture, had a crucial role in the events described in the first chapters of this volume. However, the rise of Fatah signaled the victory of the middle class over the elite. Over the next few decades there was no real sign of the return of notable families to leadership positions, aside from Faisal al-Husayni, who is clearly an exception. It is possible to generalize and say that Palestinian-Arab nationalism with its secular-revolutionary essence and its organizations and fronts was led by intellectuals and liberal professionals. However, the First and Second Intifadas added the working classes, both rural and urban, as well as the youth, in schools and in the streets, to the cycle of political action.

The tensions emerging between the middle class, with its institutions and mechanisms, and the working class, with its tribulations and political culture, seem to intermesh with the tensions between the national-secular and religious elements of the Palestinian identity. Together, they continue to revolve around, and to influence, the fateful conflict with Israel, much as the conflict itself influences all the components and elements of the Palestinian identity.

Acronyms

AH	Archives of the Haganah
DFLP	Democratic Front for the Liberation of Palestine
Fatah	Movement for the Liberation of Palestine
HHA	Hashomer Hatza'ir Archives
IDF	Israel Defense Forces
Lehi	Fighters for the Freedom of Israel
NDA	National Democratic Assembly
PA	Palestinian Authority
PCP	Palestinian Communist Party
PDFLP	Popular Democratic Front for the Liberation of Palestine
PFLP	Popular Front for the Liberation of Palestine
PFLP-GC	Popular Front for the Liberation of Palestine–General Command
PLA	Palestine Liberation Army
PLC	Popular Resistance Committees
PLO	Palestine Liberation Organization
UAR	United Arab Republic
UN	United Nations
UNRWA	UN Relief and Works Agency
UNSCOP	United Nations Special Committee on Palestine

Bibliography

'Abbas, Ihsan. *Ghurbat al-Ra'i, Sira Zatiyya* [The Foreignness of a Shepherd: An Autobiography]. Amman, 1996.
Abbas, Mahmoud. *Thawrat al-Mustahil: Al-kitaba al-Mustahila* [The Impossible Revolution: The Impossible Writing]. Unpublished manuscript, May 1990.
'Abd al-Hadi, Mahdi. *Al-Mas'alah al-Filastiniyya wa Mashari' al-Hulul al-Siyasiyya, 1934–1974* [The Palestinian Question and Proposed Political Solutions, 1934–1974]. 4th ed. Beirut, 1992.
'Abd al-Jawad, Salih, ed. *Al-Awamir al-'Askariyya al-Isra'iliyya* [Israeli Military Orders]. Amman, 1986.
———. "Tatawwur al-nidal al-watani al-Filastini munzu bidayat al-istitan al-Suhuoni wahatta al-taqsim" [Development of the Palestinian National Struggle from the Beginning of Zionist Settlement Until the Partition Resolution]. In *Al-Mujtama' al-Filastini, Arba'un 'Aman 'Ala al-Nakba wa-Wahid wa-'Ishrun 'Aaman 'ala Ihtilal al-Daffa wal-Qita'* [Palestinian Society: Forty Years Since the Nakba and Twenty-One Years Since the Occupation of the West Bank and Gaza Strip]. Taybeh, 1990.
'Abd al-Rahman, As'ad. *Al-Harb al-'Arabiyya al-'Isra'iliyya al-Rabi'ah, Waqai' wa Tafa'ulat* [The Fourth Arab-Israeli War: Course and Consequences]. Beirut, 1974.
Abdullah, Ibn al-Husayn. *Muzakkirat Sahib al-Jalalah al-Hashimiyya* [Memoirs of His Majesty the Hashemite King]. Amman, 1970.
Abed, George. *The Palestinian Economy: Studies in Development Under Prolonged Occupation*. London: Routledge, 1988.
Abu 'Amru, Ziyad. *Al-Harakah al-Islamiyya fi al-Diffah al-Gharbiyya wa Qita' Ghazza* [The Islamic Movement in the West Bank and the Gaza Strip]. Acre, 1989.

———. *Usul al-Haraka al-Siyasiyya fi Qita' Ghazza, 1948–1967* [Foundations of the Political Movements in the Gaza Strip, 1948–1967]. Acre, 1987.
Abu Fakhr, Saqr. *Al-Haraka al-Wattaniyya al-Filastiniyya Min al-Nidal al-Muslah ila Dawla Manzo'at al-Silah* [The Palestinian National Movement: From Armed Struggle to a Demilitarized State]. Beirut, 2003.
Abu Gharbiyya, Bahjat. *Fi Khidam al-Nidal al-'Arabi al-Filastini, Muzakkarat al-Munadil Bahjat Abu Gharbiyya* [In the Whirlwind of the Palestinian Arab Struggle: Memoirs of Fighter Bahjat Abu Garbiyya]. Beirut, 1993.
Abu al-Nmil, Husayn. *Qita' Ghazza, 1948–1967: Tatawwurat Iqtisadiyya wa Siyasiyya wa-'Ijtama'iyya wa 'Askariyya* [The Gaza Strip, 1948–1967: Economic, Political, Social, and Military Developments]. Beirut, 1979.
———. *Qita' Ghazza Tahta al-Hukm al-Misri* [The Gaza Strip Under Egyptian Rule]. Beirut, 1987.
Abu Odeh, Adnan. *Jordanians, Palestinians, and the Hashemite Kingdom in the Middle East*. Washington, DC: United States Institute of Peace Press, 1999.
Abu al-Shabab, Wasif. "Al-Qissa wa al-riwaya al-masrahiyya fi Filastin, 1900–1948" [The Theatrical Story and Novel in Palestine, 1900–1948]. In *The Palestinian Encyclopedia*. Beirut, 1990.
Abu Shaqra, Ibrahim. *Al-Haj Amin al-Husayni wa-Thawrat 1936–1939* [Al-Haj Amin al-Husayni and the Revolt of 1936–1939]. Damascus, 1999.
Abu Shkur, 'Abd al-Fattah. "Al-Hijra al-kharijiyya lil 'amalah fi al-aradi al-Filastiniyya al-muhtallah: hajmuha, khasa'isuha wa dawafi'uha" [Outward Immigration for Workers in the Occupied Palestinian Territories]. *Samid al-Iqtisadi* 11, no. 75 (January–March 1989).
Abu Sitta, Salman. *Palestinian Right to Return: Sacred, Legal, and Possible*. London: Palestine Return Centre, 1999.
'Ali, Muhsen Hashem. *Al-Intifada, thawra hatta al-Naser* [The Intifada: Revolution to Victory]. Damascus, 1983.
'Aliyyan, Nafiz. "Al-Iqtisad al-Filastini bayna al-tabai'yya wa al-istiqlal" [The Palestinian Economy Between Belonging and Independence]. *Shu'un Filastiniyya* 188 (November 1988).
'Allush, Naji. *Nahwa Thawrah Filastiniyya Jadidah* [In the Direction of a New Palestinian Revolution]. Beirut, 1972.
Amara, Muhammad, and Sufyan Kabha. *Zehut Hatzuya: Haluka Politit ve-Hishtaqfuyot Politiyot beKfar Hatzui* [Split Personality: Political Partition and Political Manifestations in a Divided Village]. Givat Haviva: HaMachon LeHeker HaShalom, 1999.
Amin al-Husayni, Muhammad. *Haqa'iq 'an Qadiyyat Filastin* [Truth About the Issue of Palestine]. Cairo, 1957. Published in Hebrew with commentary by Zvi Elpeleg (Tel Aviv, 1995). The annotated version was later translated into English as *Through the Eyes of the Mufti: The Essays of Haj Amin Translated and Annotated* (London: Vallentine Mitchell, 2009).

Amitay, Yosi. *Ahvat 'Amim Bemivhan: Mapam 1948–1954—'Amadot Be-sugyat 'Arviyei Yisra'el* [Fraternity Among Nations Brought to the Test: Mapam 1948–1954—Views on the Issue of the Arabs of Israel]. Tel Aviv, 1988.
al-'Arif, 'Arif. *Nakbat Bayt al-Maqdis wa al-Firdaws al-Mafquod, 1947–1952* [The Nakba of Jerusalem and Lost Paradise, 1947–1952]. Beirut, 1956.
Ayub, Samir. *Al-Bina' al-Tabaqi Lilfilastiniyyin* [The Class Stratification for Palestinians]. Beirut, n.d.
al-Az'ar, Muhammad Khalid. *Al-Muqawma fi Qita' Ghazza, 1967–1985* [The Resistance in the Gaza Strip, 1967–1985]. Cairo, 1987.
al-Badiri, Musa. *Tatawwur al-Haraka al-'Ummaliyya al-'Arabiyya Fi Filastin, 1919–1948* [Development of the Arab Workers' Movement in Palestine, 1919–1948]. Beirut, 1981.
al-Barghuti, 'Umar al-Salih, and Khalil Tawtah. *Tarih Filastin* [History of Palestine]. Jerusalem, 1926.
Barute, Muhammad Jamal. *Harakat al-Qawmiyyin al-'Arab al-Nash'ah wa-al-Tatawwur* [The Arab Nationalists Movement: The Beginning and the Development]. Beirut, 1998.
Basisu, Mu'in. *Dafater Filastiniyya* [Palestinian Notebooks]. Beirut, 1978.
Bechor, Guy. *Lexicon Ashaf* [Lexicon of the PLO]. Tel Aviv, 1991.
Ben Rafael, Eliezer. *Israel-Palestine: A Guerrilla Conflict in International Politics*. New York: Greenwood Press, 1987.
Benziman, Uzi, and 'Atallah Mansour. *Dayarey Mishne* [Subletters]. Jerusalem, 1992.
Boimel, Yair. "Hamimshal Hasva'i Vetahalich Bitulo, 1958–1968" [The Military Government and the Process of Its Abolition, 1958–1968]. *Hamizrah Hahadash* 43 (2002): 133–156.
Center for Palestinian Research. *Al-Kitab al-Sanawi Lilqadiyya al-Filastiniyya* [Yearbook of the Palestinian Problem]. Various years from 1966. Published in Beirut.
Cohen, Amnon. *Miflagot Bagada Hama'aravit Bitqufat Hashilton Hayardeni* [Political Parties in the West Bank in the Period of Jordanian Rule]. Jerusalem, 1981.
Cohen, Hillel. *'Aravim Tovim—Hamodi'in Hayisre'eli Veha'arvim Beyisra'el: Sochnim Umaf'ilim, Mashtapim, Matarot Veshitot* [Good Arabs—Israeli Intelligence and the Arabs in Israel: Agents and Controllers, Collaborators, Goals, and Methods]. Jerusalem, 2006.
———. *Hanifqadim Hanokhehim: Haplitim Hafalestinim Beyisra'el Me'az 1948* [Present Absentees: Palestinian Refugees in Israel Since 1948]. Jerusalem: Institute for Israeli Arab Studies, 2000.
Cohen, Ra'anan. *Zarim Bevetam, 'Aravim, Yehudim, Medina* [Strangers in Their Homeland: Arabs, Jews, and the State]. Tel Aviv: Tel Aviv University, 2006.
Dann, Uriel. *Iraq Under Qasem: A Political History, 1958–1963*. Jerusalem: Israel Universities Press, 1969.
Darwaza, Muhammad 'Izzat. *Hawl al-Haraka al-'Arabiyya al-Haditha* [About the New Arab Movement]. Sidon, 1951.

---. *Muzakkarat* [Memoirs]. 6 vols. Damascus, 1994.
Dudin, Yunis Tahir. "Al-Filastiniyyun fi al-'Iraq" [The Palestinians in Iraq]. *Majallat Markiz al-Dirasat al-Filastiniyya* [Journal of the Center for Palestinian Research] 31 (1978).
Dupuy, T. N. *Elusive Victory: The Arab-Israeli Wars, 1967–1974*. London: Kendall Hunt, 1978.
Elpeleg, Zvi. *The Grand Mufti*. London: Frank Cass, 1993. Also published in Hebrew (Tel Aviv, 1989).
Eyal, Yigal. *Ha'Intifada Harishona, Dikuy Hamered Ha'arvi 'al Yedey Hasava Habriti Be'eretz Yisra'el, 1936–1939* [The First Intifada: Quelling of the Arab Revolt by the British Army in the Land of Israel, 1936–1939]. Tel Aviv, 1998.
Farah, Boulos. *Al-Haraka al-'Ummaliyya al-'Arabiyya al-Filastiniyya, Jadaliyyat Ba'thuha wa Suqutuha* [The Arab Palestinian Workers' Movement: The Paradox of Its Rise and Fall]. Haifa, 1987.
---. *Min Tarikh al-Kifah al-Filastini al-Musallah, Idrab wa-Thawrat 1936–1939* [A Sample of the Armed Palestinian Struggle: The Strike and Revolt of 1936–1939]. Haifa, 1991.
Fatah. *Fath: Min Muntalaqat al-'Amal al-Thawri* [The Fatah Movement: From the Beginnings of the Revolutionary Activity]. Kuwait, n.d.
Fawzi, Muhammad. *Harb al-Thalath Sanawat* [The Three-Year War]. Cairo, 1986.
Fleischmann, Ellen. *The Nation and Its "New" Women: The Palestinian Women's Movement 1920–1948*. Berkeley: University of California Press, 2003.
al-Gabha al-'Arabiyya, Yafa. *Al-Qanoun al-Asasi wa al-Nizam al-Dakhili* [The Arab Front, the Basic Constitution, and the Internal Regulations]. Jaffa, 1945.
Gavish, Dov. *A Survey of Palestine Under the British Mandate, 1920–1948*. London, 2005.
Ghanayim, Mahmoud. *Al-Madar al-Sa'b, Rihlat al-Qissa al-Filastiniyya fi Isra'il* [The Tough Journey: The Journey of Palestinian Short Stories in Israel]. Kafr Qara', 1995.
al-Ghoul, Omar Hilmi. *'Usbat al-Taharrur al-Watani fi Filastin, Nash'atuha wa Tatawwuruha wa Dawruha, 1943–1948* [The National Liberation League in Palestine: Its Growth, Development, and Role, 1943–1948]. Beirut, 1987.
Gilbert, Gad. *Megamot Bahitpathut Hademografit Shel Hafalestinim, 1870–1987* [Trends in the Demographic Development of the Palestinians, 1870–1987]. Tel Aviv: Tel Aviv University, 1989.
Glubb, John Bagot. *A Soldier with the Arabs*. London: Hodder and Stoughton, 1957.
Gorny, Yosef. *Hashe'ela Ha'arvit Vehabe'aya Hayehudit* [The Arab Question and the Jewish Problem]. Tel Aviv, 1985.
Graham-Brown, Sara. *Education, Repression, and Liberation: Palestinians*. London: World University Service, 1984.
Grossman, David. *Hakfar Ha'arvi 'Uvnotav* [The Arab Village and Its Offshoots]. Jerusalem, 1994.

Habash, George. *Al-Nahaj al-Thawri fi Mawajhat al-Tahdiyat* [The Revolutionary Course versus the Challenges]. Beirut, 1974.
Hakim, Sami. *Tariq al-Nakba* [Way of the Nakba]. Cairo, 1969.
al-Hamad, Jawad, et al. *Dirasa fi al-Fikr al-Siyasi Lilharaka al-Islamiyya (Hamas)* [A Study on the Political Thought of the Islamic Resistance Movement (Hamas)]. Ramallah, 2010.
———. *Al-Madkhal ila al-Qadiyya al-Filastiniyya* [Introduction to the Palestinian Problem]. Amman, 1997.
Hamami, Rema. "From Immodesty to Collaboration: Hamas, the Women's Movement, and National Identity in the Intifada." In *Political Islam: Essays from the Middle East Report*, edited by Joel Beinin and Joe Stork. Berkeley and Los Angeles: University of California Press, 1997.
Hammuda, Huda. *Al-Filastiniyyun fi al-'Iraq: Madkhal Dimughrafi, Ijtama'i wa Iqtisadi* [The Palestinians in Iraq: Demographic, Social, and Economic Introduction]. Baghdad, 1987.
Hamza, Muhammad. *Abu Jihad Bidayatuhu wa Asbab Ightiyaluhu* [Abu Jihad: His Beginnings and the Reasons for his Assassination]. Safakes, 1989.
al-Harub, Khaled. *Hamas: Al-Fikr wa al-Mumarsa al-Siyasiyya* [Hamas: The Idea and Its Political Application]. Beirut, 1997.
al-Hasan, Bila. "Ahdath aylul wa mas'uliyyat al-nizam al-Urduni" [The Events of September and the Responsibility of the Jordanian Regime]. *Shu'un Filastiniyya* 1 (March 1971).
al-Hasan, Hani. "Waqfa 'ind al-zikra al-rabi'ah lima'rakat al-Karameh" [Stating the Arab Memory of the al-Karameh Battle]. *Shu'un Filastiniyya* (April 8, 1972).
al-Hasan, Khaled. *Awraq Siyasiyya* [Political Papers]. No. 10. Amman, 1987.
al-Hawari, Muhammad Nimr. *Sir al-Nakba* [Secret of the Nakba]. Nazareth, 1955.
Haykal, Muhammad Hasanin. *Sanawat al-Ghalayan* [The Years of Boiling]. Cairo, 1987.
———. *Al-'Urush wa al-Juyush, Kazalika infajara al-Sira' fi Filastin* [The Chairs of Kings and Armies: This Is How the Struggle in Palestine Imploded]. 2 vols. Cairo, 1998.
Hilal, Jamil. "Al-khitta al-aurduniyya al-khumasiyya litanmiyat al-Diffa wa al-Qita'" [The Jordanian Five-Year Plan for Development of the West Bank and the Gaza Strip]. *Al-Aurdun al-Jadida* 8–9 (Fall–Winter 1986).
———. *Al-Nizam al-Siyasi al-Filastini ba'd Oslo* [The Political Regime in Palestine after Oslo]. Beirut, 1998.
al-Hindi, Hani. *Jaysh al-Inqaz* [The Army of Salvation]. Beirut, 1974.
al-Hindi, Khalil. "Al-Ta'bi'ah al-Urduniyya did al-muqawamah al-Filastiniyya qabl hajmat Siptamber 1970" [The Jordanian Effort Against the Palestinian Resistance in Jordan Before the Attack of September 1970]. *Shu'un Filastiniyya* 4 (September 1971).
Hizb al-Ba'th al-'Arabi [Arab Ba'ath Party]. *Al-Ba'th wa Qadiyyat Filastin, 1944–1948* [Al-Ba'ath and the Question of Palestine, 1944–1948]. Beirut, 1973.

al-Hout, Bayan Nuwayhid. *Al-Qiyadat wa al-Mu'ssasat al-Siyasiyya Fi Filastin, 1917–1948* [Leadership and Political Institutions in Palestine, 1917–1948]. Acre, 1984.

al-Hout, Shafiq. *Bayn al-Watan wa al-Manfa, min Yafa Bada al-Mishwar* [Between the Homeland and the Exile: From Jaffa Began the Course]. Beirut, 2007.

al–Hsan, Bila. *Qira'at fi al-Mashhad al-Filastini,'an 'Arafat wa-Oslo wahaq al-'awda* [A Reading of the Palestinian Political Scene: On Arafat, Oslo, and the Right of Return]. Beirut, 2008.

al-Hur, Layla. *Al-Filastiniyyun fi Lubnan* [The Palestinians in Lebanon]. Beirut, 1970.

al-Husayni, Ishaq Mousa. *Al-'Ikhwan al-Muslimun* [The Muslim Brothers]. Beirut, 1952.

International Institute for Strategic Studies. *The Military Balance*. London, 1971.

Jarbuni, Ahmad Salih. *Sira' 'Ala al-Ard* [Struggle for the Land]. Arrabeh, 1998.

Jarrar, Husni Adham. *Al-Haj Amin al-Husayni, Ra'id Jihad wa-Batal Qadiyya* [Al-Haj Amin al-Husayni: Pioneer of the Jihad and Hero of the National Cause]. Amman: Dar Al-Dia, 1987.

al-Jayyusi, 'Abd al-Fattah, ed. *Filastin al-Muhtalla 1985–1987: Al-Sumud wa al-Tahaddi* [Occupied Palestine, 1985–1987: The Strong Stance and the Provocation]. Amman, 1988.

Jbara, Taysir. *Palestinian Leader Haj Amin al-Husayni*. Princeton, NJ: Kingston Press, 1985.

Jiryis, Sabri. *Ha'aravim Beyisra'el* [The Arabs in Israel]. Haifa, 1966.

John, Robert, and Sami Hadawi. *The Palestine Diary*. 2 vols. Beirut, 1970.

Kabha, Mustafa. "Batey hadin shel hamered ha'arvi-falestini" [The Courts of the Palestinian-Arab Revolt]. *Zemanim* 92 (2005): 26–35.

———. *Harb al-Istinzaf, Milhemet Hahatasha Bir'i Hameqorot Hamisriyim* [Harb al-Istinzaf: The War of Attrition as Reflected in Egyptian Sources]. Tel Aviv University and Yad Tabenkin, 1995.

———, ed. *Nahwa Siaghat Riwaya Tarihiyya Lilnakba, Ishkaliyyat Watahdiyyat* [Toward Designing a Narrative History of the Nakba: Complexities and Challenges]. Haifa, 2006.

———. "'Oyev oyvi haveri': Hatenu'ah hale'umit hafalestinit veyahasa el hafashizem vehanazizem, 1925–1945" ["My Enemy's Enemy Is My Friend": The Palestinian National Movement and Its Attitude Toward Fascism and Nazism, 1925–1945]. *Zemanim* 69 (1999): 79–86.

———. *The Palestinian Press as Shaper of Public Opinion: Writing Up a Storm*. London, 2007. Also published in Hebrew as *'Itonut Be'ayn Hase'ara* [The Press in the Eye of the Storm] (Jerusalem, 2004).

———."Tafkida shel ha'itonut ha'arvit hafalestinit be'irgun hashvita hafalestinit haklalit, April–October 1936" [The Role of the Palestinian Arab Press in Organizing the General Palestinian Strike, April–October 1936]. *'Iyunim Bitkumat Yisra'el* 11 (2001): 212–229.

Kabha, Mustafa, and Dan Caspi. "Miyerushalayim haqdosha ve'ad hama'ayan: Megamot ba'itonut basafa ha'arvit beyisra'el" [From Sacred Jerusalem to the Spring: Themes in the Arabic Press in Israel]. *Panim* 16 (March 2001): 50–54.

———. *The Palestinian Arab In/Outsiders: Media and Conflict in Israel.* London: Vallentine Mitchell, 2011.

Kabha, Mustafa, and Sara Osatzky-Lazar. "Irgun hahagana be'aynay ha'aravim, hiquy shelo hisliah" [The Hagana Organization as Seen by the Arabs: An Emulation That Did Not Work Out]. *'Aley Zayit* (Spring 2002).

Kabha, Mustafa, and Nimr Sirhan. *'Abd al-Rahim al-Haj Muhammad, al-Qa'id al-'Aam Lethawrat 1936–1939* ['Abd al-Rahim al-Haj Muhammad, General Commander of the 1936–1939 Revolt]. Ramallah, 2000.

Kanafani, Ghassan. *Rajal Fi al Shams* [Men in the Sun]. Beirut, 1964.

al-Karmi, 'Abd al-Karim. *Diwan* [Poetry]. Beirut, 1989.

Karsh, Efrayim. *Arafat: Ha'ish Umilhamto Beyisra'el* [Arafat: The Man and His Fight Against Israel]. Tel Aviv: Sifriyat Ma'ariv, 2004.

al-Kayali, 'Abd al-Wahab. *Tarikh Filastin al-Hadith* [The Modern History of Palestine]. Beirut, 1985.

al-Khadra, Zafir. *Surya wa al-Laji'un al-Filastiniyyun* [Syria and the Palestinian Refugees]. Damascus, 1999.

al-Khafsh, Husni Salih. *Muzakkarat Hawl Tarikh al-Haraka al-'Ummaliyya al-Filastiniyya* [Memories of the History of the Palestinian Workers' Movement]. Beirut, 1973.

Khalaf, Salah. *Filastini Bila Hawiyya* [Palestinian with No Homeland]. Kuwait, n.d.

Khalidi, Rashid. *The Iron Cage: The Story of the Palestinian Struggle for Statehood.* Boston: Beacon Press, 2007.

———. *Palestinian Identity: The Construction of Modern National Consciousness.* New York: Columbia University Press, 1997.

al-Khalidi, Walid. *All That Remains: The Palestinian Villages Occupied and Depopulated by Israel in 1948.* Washington, DC: Institute for Palestine Studies, 1992.

———. *Dayr Yasin, al-Jum'a 9 bi'april 1948* [Dayr Yasin: Friday April 9, 1948]. Beirut, 1999.

———, ed. *From Haven to Conquest: Readings in Zionism and the Palestine Problem Until 1948.* 2nd ed. Washington, DC: Institute for Palestine Studies, 1987.

al- Khalili, 'Ali. *Al-Waratha al-Ruwah, Min al-Nakbah ila al-Dawla* [The Generation of Heirs of History Relaters: From the Nakba to the Establishment of Israel]. Acre, 2001.

Khallah, Kamel. *Filastin wa al-Intidab al-Britani 1922–1939* [Palestine and the British Mandate, 1922–1939]. Tripoli, 1982.

Khalusy, Muhammad 'Ali. *Al-Tanmiya al-Iqtisadiyya fi Qita' Ghazza "Filastin" 1948–1968* [Economic Development in the Gaza Strip, 1948–1968]. Cairo, 1968.

Khammash, Majd al-Din. "Filistiniyyu al-shatat fi al-'Urdon" [The Palestinians of the Diaspora in Jordan]. In *Mustaqbal al-Laj'in al-Filastiniyyin wa Filastiniyyu al-Shatat* [The Future of the Palestinian Refugees and the Refugees of the Diaspora], edited by 'Abd al-Fattah al-Rushdan et al. Amman, 2002.

al-Khoury, Yusef. *Al-Sihafah al-'Arabiyya fi Filastin 1948–1876* [The Arabic Press in Palestine, 1876–1948]. Beirut, 1976.
Kimmerling, Baruch, and Joel Shmuel Migdal. *Palestinim, 'Am Behivazruto* [Palestinians: The Making of a People]. Jerusalem: Keter, 1999.
al-Kitri, Yunis. *Halaqa Mafqudah min Kifah al-Sha'b al-Filastini: Al-Katiba 141, Fida'iyyun* [The Lost Sphere in the Struggle of the Palestinian People: Regiment 141, Fida'iyyun]. Cairo, 1987.
Kretzmer, David. *Legal Status of the Arabs in Israel.* Boulder, CO: Westview Press, 1990.
al-Kubaysi, Basil. *Harakat al-Qawmiyun al-'Arab* [Movement of the Arab Nationalists]. Beirut, 1982.
Litvak, Meir. "The West Bank and the Gaza Strip." *Middle East Contemporary Survey* 12 (1989).
Lustick, Ian. *'Aravim Bimdina Yehudit* [Arabs in a Jewish State]. Haifa, 1985.
Luttwak, Edward, and Dan Horowitz. *The Israeli Army.* London: Allen Lane, 1975.
Mansour, Kamil, ed. *Al-Sha'b al-Filastini fi al-Dakhl* [The Palestinian People in the Homeland]. Beirut, 1990.
Marlowe, John. *Rebellion in Palestine.* London: Cresset Press, 1946.
Matar, Fu'ad. *Hakim al-Thawra* [The Wise Man of the Revolution]. Beirut, 2008.
al-Maw'id, Hamad. "Filastiniyyu al-Shatat fi Surya" [Palestinians of the Diaspora in Syria]. In *Mustaqbal al-Laj'in al-Filastiniyyin wa Filastiniyyu al-Shatat* [The Future of the Palestinian Refugees and the Refugees of the Diaspora], edited by 'Abd al-Fattah al-Rushdan et al. Amman, 2002.
———. "Al-Mukhayyam wa al-hawiyya al-Filastiniyya" [The Refugee Camp and Palestinian Identity]. *Samid al-Iqtisadi* (Summer 1998).
Michalson, Benny, et al. *Hama'avaq Lebithon Yisra'el* [The Struggle for the Security of Israel]. Tel Aviv: 1999.
Mitchell, Richard. *The Society of the Muslim Brothers.* London: Oxford University Press, 1969.
Moghannam, Metiel. *The Arab Woman and the Palestinian Problem.* London, 1937.
Morris, Benny. "Hahistoriografya hahadasha: Yisra'el pogeshet et 'avarah" [The New Historiography: Israel Meets Its Past]. In *Tikun Ta'ut, Yehudim Ve'aravim Be'erez Yisrae'el 1936–1956* [Correcting a Mistake: Jews and Arabs in the Land of Israel 1936–1956], edited by Benny Morris. Tel Aviv, 2000.
———. *Laydata shel Be'ayat Haplitim Hafalestinim 1947–1949* [The Birth of the Palestinian Refugee Problem 1947–1949]. Tel Aviv, 1991.
———. *Milhemet Hagvul Shel Yisra'el, 1949–1956* [Israel's Border War, 1949–1956]. Tel Aviv, 1996.
Muhammad, 'Abd al-Rahim. *Diwan 'Abd al-Rahim Muhammad* [The Poetry Collection of 'Abd al-Rahim Muhammad]. Jerusalem, 1995.
Muhammad, Tariq, and Ibrahim Muhammad. *Shi'arat al-Intifada* [Slogans of the Intifada]. London, 1994.

Munazzamat al-Tahrir al-Filastiniyya [The Palestinian Liberation Organization]. *Al-Laji'un al-Filastiniyyun Fi al-'Iraq* [The Palestinian Refugees in Iraq]. Baghdad, 1999.

Al-Munjid Fi al-Lugha wa al-'Alam [Dictionary of Language and Biographies]. Vol. 27. Beirut, 1984.

"Al-Muqawama al-Filastiniyya amam al-tahddiyat al-Jadida" [The Palestinian Resistance Versus the New Challenges]. *Shu'un Filastiniyya* 30 (February 1974).

Murqus, Nimr. *Aqwq min al-Nisyan* [Stronger than Forgetting]. Kfar Yassif, 1999.

Mus'ab, Jamil. *Filastiniyyu al-Shatat fi Baghdad* [The Palestinians of the Diaspora]. In *Mustaqbal al-Laj'in al-Filastiniyyin wa Filastiniyyu al-Shatat* [The Future of the Palestinian Refugees and the Refugees of the Diaspora], edited by 'Abd al-Fattah al-Rushdan et al. Amman, 2002.

Nakhla, Muhammad 'Urabi. *Tatwwur al-Mujtama' fi Filastin* [Development of Society in Palestine]. Kuwait, 1982.

al-Naqib, Khuldun Hasan. *Al-Fikr al-Ta'amuri 'End al-'Arab* [The Conspiracy Idea Among the Arabs]. Damascus, 1997.

"Al-Nashat al-feda'i hasab a'itrafat al-nateq al-Isra'ili" [The Activity of the Fida'iyyun as Announced by the Israeli Spokesman]. *Shu'un Filastiniyya* 27 (November 1973): 200–224.

Nasser, Gamal Abdel. *Falsafat al-Thawra* [Philosophy of the Revolution]. Cairo, 1966.

al-Natur, Suhayl. "Al-Laji'un al-Filastiniyun fi Libnan" [The Palestinian Refugees in Lebanon]. In *Mustaqbal al-Laj'in al-Filastiniyyin wa Filastinitti al-Shatat* [The Future of the Palestinian Refugees and the Refugees of the Diaspora], edited by 'Abd al-Fattah al-Rushdan et al. Amman, 2002.

Nawfal, Sayyed. *Al-'Amal al-'Arabi al-Mushtarak: Madihi wa-Mustaqbaluhu* [Joint Arab Activity: Its Past and Future]. Cairo, 1986.

Neuberger, Binyamin. "Hami'ut Ha'arvi: Nikur Vehishtalvut" [The Arab Minority: Estrangement and Integration]. In *Mimshal Vepolitiqa Bimdinat Yisra'el* [Governance and Politics in the State of Israel]. Unit 11. Tel Aviv: Open University, 1998.

Nevo, Joseph. *King Abdullah and Palestine: A Territorial Ambition*. London: Macmillan, 1996.

al-Nimr, Ihsan. *Tarikh Jabal Nablus wa al-Balqaa* [The History of the Nablus Hills and the Area of al-Balqaa]. Nablus: Matba'at al-Naser al-Tajariya, 1961.

Ohana, Yuval Arnon. *Herev Mibayit: Hama'avak Hapnimi Batnu'ah Hale'umit Hafalestinit* [A Sword at Home: The Internal Struggle in the Palestinian National Movement]. Tel Aviv: Tel Aviv University, 1981.

Palestine Liberation Organization Research Center. *Black September*. Beirut: PLO Research Center, 1971.

The Palestinian Encyclopedia. Vol. 2. Damascus, 1984.

Porat, Yehoshua. *Mimehumot Limrida, Hatnu'ah Hale'umit Ha'arvit Hafalestinit, 1929–1939* [From Unrest to Uprising: The Palestinian Arab National Movement, 1929–1939]. Tel Aviv, 1978.

Qahwaji, Habib. *Al-'Arab Tahta al-Ihtilal al-Isra'ili Munzu 'Aam 1948* [The Arabs Under Israeli Occupation Since 1948]. Beirut, 1972.
Qanazi', Gourge. "Qira'a Jadida Likitab Muzakkarat Dajaja" [A New Reading of the Book *Memoirs of a Chicken*]. *Al-Karmil* 3 (1981): 117–120.
Qasmiyya, Khayriyya. *'Awni 'Abd al-Hadi, Awraq Khassa* ['Awni 'Abd al-Hadi: Personal Documents]. Beirut, 1974.
———. *Al-Hukowmah al-'Arabiyya fi Dimashq Bayn 1918–1920* [The Arab Government in Damascus, 1918–1920]. Cairo, 1971.
Rabah, Ramzi. *Al-Laji'un wa al-Nazihun wa mufawadat al-Wadi' al-Da'im* [The Refugees and the Displaced and the Negotiations for a Permanent Arrangement]. Beirut, 1996.
Radwan, Arwa. *Al-Lajna al-Siyasiyya lijami'at al-Diwal al-'Arabiyya* [The Political Committee of the Arab League]. Beirut, 1973.
Rawhi, Husayn. *Al-Mukhtasar fi Gughrafiyyat Filastin* [Concise Geography of Palestine]. Jerusalem, 1923.
Rekhes, Eli. "Bayn Qomunizem Lele'umiyut: Raqah Vehami'ut Ha'arvi Beyisra'el, 1965–1973" [Between Communism and Nationalism: Rakach and the Arab Minority in Israel, 1965–1973]. PhD diss., Tel Aviv University, 1986.
Research Center of the Arab League. *Al-Watha'iq al-'Arabiyya al-Filastiniyya Lil'am* [The Arab-Palestinian Documents]. Cairo, various years from 1968.
al-Rushdan, 'Abd al-Fattah et al. *Mustaqbal al-Laj'in al-Filastiniyyin wa Filastiniyyu al-Shatat* [The Future of the Palestinian Refugees and the Refugees of the Diaspora]. Amman, 2002.
Sa'ad, Ahmad, and 'Abd al-Qader Yasin. *Al-Haraka al-Wataniyya al-Filastiniyya, 1948–1970* [The Palestinian National Movement, 1948–1970]. Jerusalem, 1970.
Sa'ada, Anton. *Marahil al-Mas'ala al-Filastiniyya, 1921–1949* [Stages of the Palestinian Question, 1921–1949]. Beirut, 1949.
al-Safri, 'Issa. *Filastin al-'Arabiyya Bayn al-Intidab wa al-Suhyuniyya* [Arab Palestine Between Mandate and Zionism]. Jaffa, 1937.
Sahliyeh, Emile. *In Search of Leadership: West Bank Politics Since 1967*. Washington, DC: Brookings Institution, 1988.
Sa'id, Edward. *Nihayat 'amaliyyat al-salam, Oslo wauma ba'adha* [The End of the Peace Process: Oslo and Its Aftermath]. Beirut, 2002.
al-Sakakini, Khalil. *Filastin Ba'd al-Harb al-'Uthma* [Palestine After the Great War]. Jerusalem, 1925.
———. *Kaza Ana Ya Donya* [That's Me, People]. Jerusalem, 1990.
al-Salihi, Bassam. *Al-Za'amah al-Siyasiyya wa al-Diniyya fi al-Aradi al-Muhtalla* [Political and Religious Leadership in the Occupied Lands]. Jerusalem, 1993.
al-Samara'i, Younes Hamad. *Al-'Iraq wa al-Qadiyya al-Filastiniyya, 1958–1973* [Iraq and the Palestinian Problem, 1958–1973]. Baghdad, 1999.
Samooha, Sami. *The Orientation and Politicization of the Arab Minority in Israel*. Haifa: University of Haifa, 1984.

al-Sawahiri, Khalil. *Al-Filastiniyyun al-Tahjir al-Qasri wa al-ri'aya al-Ijtima'iyya* [The Palestinians and the Displacement and Social Treatment of the Refugees]. Amman, 1986.

Sayigh, Yazid. *Al-Kifah al-Muslah wa al-Bahath 'An al-Dawla: Al-Haraka al-Wataniyya al-Filastiniyya, 1949–1993* [The Armed Struggle and the Search for a State: The Palestinian National Movement, 1949–1993]. Beirut, 2002.

Sayqali, May. *Hayfa al-'Arabiyya, 1918–1939, al-Tatawwur al-Ijtima'i wal-Iqtisadi* [Arab Haifa, 1918–1939: Social and Economic Development]. Beirut, 1997.

Sela, Avraham. *Ahdut Betokh Peyrud Hama'arekhet Habeyn-'Arvit* [Unity Within Conflict in the Inter-Arab System]. Jerusalem: Magnes, 1983.

Shabib, Samih. "Muqaddimat al-musadara al-rasmiyya lilshakhsiyya al-Filastiniyya, 1948–1950" [Introduction to the Establishment's Boycott of the Palestinian National Identity, 1948–1950]. *Shu'un Filastiniyya* 129–131 (August–October 1982): 82–83.

———. "Al-Muqawamah al-Filastiniyya: Siyasiyyan" [The Palestinian Resistance: From a Political Perspective]. *Shu'un Filastiniyya* 179 (February 1988).

Shafiq, Munir. "Ma'rakat al-Karameh" [The Battle of Karameh]. *Shu'un Filastiniyya* 19 (March 1973).

Shahin, 'Ali. *Sawt Min Qubur Filastin al-'Arabiyya, Zulm al-'Arabi Leakhihi al-'Arabi* [Voice from the Cemeteries of Arab Palestine: The Arab's Tyranny Toward Arab Brethren]. Cairo, 1939.

Shalhat, Antwan. "Sir al-haqibatayn al-da'i'tayn" [Secret of the Two Lost Files]. *Filastin al-Thawra* 553 (April 13, 1985).

Sha'th, Nabil, et al. *Al-Muqawamah al-Filastiniyya wa al-Nizam al-Urduni* [The Palestinian Resistance and the Jordanian Regime]. Beirut, 1971.

Shemesh, Moshe. *Mehanakba Lanaksa: Hasichsuch Ha'arvi Yisre'eli Vehaba'aya Hafalistinit 1957–1967* [From the Nakba to the Naksa: The Arab-Israeli Conflict and the Palestinian National Problem 1957–1967]. Beer Sheva: Ben-Gurion University, 2004.

Shimoni, Yaakov. *'Arviyei Eretz Yisrael* [The Arabs of Palestine]. Tel Aviv: Am Oved, 1947.

Shlaim, Avi. *Collusion Across the Jordan: King Abdullah, The Zionist Movement, and the Partition of Palestine*. New York: Columbia University Press, 1988.

———. "The Rise and Fall of the All Palestine Government in Gaza." *Journal of Palestine Studies* 20, no. 1 (Autumn 1990).

Shtendel, Uri. *Arviyei Yisra'el, Bayn Patish Lasadan* [Israel's Arabs: Between the Hammer and the Anvil]. Jerusalem: Akademon, 1992.

Shufani, Elias. *Al-Mujaz fi Tarikh Filastin al-Sayasi* [Summary of the Political History of Palestine]. Beirut, 1998.

al-Shuqayri, Ahmad. *Arba'oun 'Aman fi al-Hayat al'Arabiyya wa al-Dawliyya* [Forty Years in Arab and International Life]. Beirut, 1973.

Steinberg, Mati. *'Omdim Legoralam: Hatoda'ah Hale'umit Hapalestinit 1967–2007* [Standing to Their Fate: The Palestinian National Consciousness 1967–2007]. Tel Aviv, 2008.

Suwayyid, Mahmoud. *Al-tajriba al-nidaliyya al-Filastiniyya, hiwar shamel ma' George Habash* [The Experience of the Palestinian Struggle: Extensive Interview with George Habash]. Beirut: Muwassat al-Dirasat al-Filastiniyya [Institute for Palestinian Research], 1998.

Swedenburg, Ted. *Memories of Revolt: The 1936–1939 Rebellion and the Palestinian National Past*. Minneapolis: University of Minnesota Press, 1995.

Sykes, Christopher. *Cross Roads to Israel: Palestine from Balfour to Bevin*. London: Collins, 1965.

al-Tal, 'Abdullah. *Karithat Filastin* [The Disaster of Palestine]. Cairo, 1959.

Tamari, Salim. "Al-Dinamiyat al-ijtama'iyya wa-'ydiolojiyyat al-muqawama fi al-diffa al-gharbiyya" [The Social and Ideological Dynamics of the Resistance in the West Bank]. In *Al-Sha'b al-Filastini fi al-Dakhl* [The Palestinian People in the Homeland], edited by Kamil Mansour. Beirut, 1990.

Tuqan, Ibrahim. *Diwan Ibrahim* [Ibrahim's Poetry Collection]. Ramallah, 1992.

al-'Umar, 'Abd al-Karim. *Muzakkarat al-Haj Muhhamad Amin al-Husayni* [Memoirs of Haj Amin al-Husayni]. Damascus, 1999.

'Umar, Mahjub. "Ru'iya al-mustaqbal" [Story of the Future]. *Shu'un Filastiniyya* 17 (January 1973).

al-Wazir, Khalil. *Harakat Fath Tarikh al-Nash'ah* [Fatah Movement: The Beginning]. N.p., n.d.

Weitz, Yosef. *Yomani Ve'igrotai Labanim* [My Diary and Letters to the Children]. 4 vols. Tel Aviv: Massada, 1965.

Ya'ari, Ehud. *Misrayim Vehafedayun, 1953–1956* [Egypt and the Feda'iyyun, 1953–1956]. Givat Haviva, 1975.

Yaghi, 'Abd al-Rahman. *Hayat al-Adab al-Filastini al-Hadith* [History of Modern Palestinian Literature]. Beirut, 1986.

Yasin, 'Abd al-Qader. *Azmat Fatah* [The Crisis of Fatah]. Beirut, 1985.

———. *Hamas, Harakat al-Maqawama al-Islamiyya fi Filastin* [Hamas: The Islamic Resistance Movement in Palestine]. Cairo, 1990.

———. "Al-Hizb al-Shuyu'i al-Filastini wa al-qadiyya al-wataniyya" [The Palestinian Communist Party and the National Issue]. *Al-Katib* 121 (April 1971): 114.

———. *Hizb Shuyu'i zahrurhu Ila al-Ha'it* [A Communist Party with Its Back to the Wall]. Beirut, 1978.

———. *Shubhat Hawl al-Qadiyya al-Filastiniyya* [Doubts on the Palestinian Issue]. Cairo, 1977.

———. *Tajribat al-Jabha al-Wataniyya fi Qita' Ghazza* [The Experience of the National Front in the Gaza Strip]. Beirut, 1980.

Yusuf, 'Abd al-Qader. *Mustaqbal al-Tarbiya fi al-'Alam al-'Arabi fi Dou' al-Tajriba al-Filastiniyya* [The Future of Education in the Arab World in Light of the Palestinian Experience]. Cairo, 1962.

Zelikovich, 'Ido. *Tnu'at HaFath, Islam, Le'umiyut Vepolitika Shel Ma'avak Mezuyan* [The Fatah Movement: Islam, Nationalism, and Politics of an Armed Struggle]. Tel Aviv: Riesling, 2011.

Zohar, Michael Bar. *Ben Guryon: Biografya* [Ben-Gurion: A Biography]. 2 vols. Tel Aviv: 'Am Oved, 1975.

Zu'aytir, Akram. *Bawakir al-Nidal* [The First Fruit of the Struggle]. Amman, 1994.

———."Min ajl ummati" [For My Nation]. In *Min Muzakkarat Akram Zu'aytir, 1939–1946* [From the Memoirs of Akram Zu'aytir]. Amman, 1994.

———. *Al-Qadiyya al-Filastiniyya* [The Palestinian Problem]. Cairo, 1955.

———. *Watha'iq al-Haraka al-Wataniyya al-Filastiniyya, Min Awraq Akram Zu'aytir* [Documents of the Palestinian National Movement: From the Papers of Akram Zu'aytir]. Beirut: Institute for Palestine Studies, 1979.

———. *Yawmiyyat Akram Zu'aytir, 1935–1939* [From the Diary of Akram Zu'aytir, 1935–1939]. Beirut: Institute for Palestine Studies, 1980.

Index

al-'Abbasi, Muhammad Dawud, 244
'Abbas, Madlul, 100
'Abbas, Mahmoud, 197, 198, 216n160, 224, 230, 285, 319, 338, 342
'Abd al-Amin, Bahjat, 232
'Abd al-Baqi, Ahmad Hilmi, 40, 44, 66, 67, 125, 161
'Abd al-Hadi, 'Awni, 32, 40, 63, 66, 126, 140n87
'Abd al-Hadi, Fakhri, 14
'Abd al-Hadi, Salim, 13
'Abd al-Hadi, Tarab, 63
'Abd al-Hamid, Ha'il, 227, 297
'Abd al-Hamid, Muhannad, 351, 352
'Abd al-Karim, 'Adel, 196
'Abd al-Khaliq, Mutlaq, 76
al-'Abdallah, Qusay, 232
'Abd al-Qadir, Ibrahim, 58
'Abd al-Rahim, al-Tayyib, 227
'Abd al-Rahim, Zakariyya, 202
'Abd al-Rahman, Salim, 66
'Abd al-Ra'ouf, 'Abd al-Mun'im, 188
'Abd al-Raziq, Hisham, 339
'Abd al-Raziq, 'Arif, 13, 14, 81n15
'Abd al-Shafi, Hayder, 179, 272, 327
'Abd al-Wahab, Muhammad, 58
Abdullah (King of Transjordan), 11, 12, 32, 99, 111, 113, 114; accusations against Haj Amin, 126, 127, 128; anger at formation of Government of All Palestine, 126, 127, 128; aspirations for expansion, 141, 142; assassination of, 144, 163; blocks Haj Amin's establishment of Government of All Palestine, 142; conflict with Haj Amin, 142, 161, 162; denounced for annexation of Palestine, 143; Greater Syria Plan by, 32, 33; promotes cease-fire in War of 1948, 118; secret agreements with Jews and British, 112, 113; self-serving attempts during World War II, 32, 33; tries to annex Arab territories to Jordan, 122, 125; tries to annex Palestine, 142
Abkarius, Mishal, 125, 140n87
Abu al-'Asal, Bishop Riyah, 276
Abu al-Huda, Huda, 63
Abu 'Ali Shahin, 318
Abu al-Khayr, Husayn, 259
Abu al-Khayr, Mahmoud, 107
Abu al-Niml, Husayn, 188
'Abu 'Ammar. *See* Arafat, Yasir
Abu 'Amru, Ziyad, 179, 197
Abu Diyya, Ibrahim, 104, 107
Abu Durra, Yusuf, 13, 14, 81n15
Abu Gharbiyya, Bahjat, 104, 105, 107
Abu Hatim, 310
Abu Hilal, 'Ali, 318
Abu 'Iyad, 194–195, 264, 301

Index

Abu Jihad, 194–195, 297, 298, 307, 320–322. *See also* al-Wazir, Khalil
Abu Khadra, Kan'an, 48
Abu Kuwayk, Samih, 203, 218n176, 295, 296
Abu Mayzar, 'Abd al-Muhsin, 208
Abu Mazen, 197, 216n160, 285, 319, 338, 342
Abu Musa, 295, 296
Abu Qawwara, 'Abd al-Latif, 176
Abu Salih, Salih, 295, 296
Abu Salma, 76, 77
Abu Sharif, Bassam, 259
Abu Shilbaya, Muhammad, 269
Abu Tir, Muhammad, 323
Abu Warda, Farid, 179
Abu Yusuf, 194–195
Academics of Nazareth, 274
Academy of Arabic Language, 78
Aden-Algiers Agreement (1984), 300
'Aflaq, Meshel, 52
al-'Ajrami, 'Abd Allah, 229
Al-Ahram (newspaper), 233, 250, 353
Al-Akhbar (newspaper), 74
al-'Alami, Musa, 32, 42, 48, 62, 68, 69, 86
Al-Aqsa Mosque, 340
Al-Ard Group, 185–186, 313n41
Al-Ba'th (journal), 52
Al-Difa (newspaper), 49, 55, 74, 75
Alef Baa (newspaper), 74
Al-Fajr (journal), 183
Algeria: support for Palestinian organizations, 257; war for independence as role for Palestinians, 194, 201, 206, 234
Al-Ghad (newspaper), 45, 75
Al-Hadaf (journal), 259, 282
Al-Huriyya (journal), 75, 228, 229
'Ali, Taha Muhammad, 156
al-Istiqlal (Independence) party, 5, 26, 28, 34, 48, 51, 66, 67, 68; activity in revolt of 1936-1939, 9, 11; in Arab national movement, 48; conflict with Husayni-led group, 41; membership, 21n2; post-revolt recovery of, 40, 41; reaches agreement with Haj Amin, 94
Al-Ittihad (journal), 45, 46, 47, 75
Al-Karmil (newspaper), 2, 73
Alliance of the Ten, 327
All That Remains (al-Khalidi), 134
Al-Mihmaz (newspaper), 75

Al-Misri (newspaper), 132
Al-Mustaqbal (newspaper), 75
Al-Nafa'is (newspaper), 73, 77
Al-Nafir (newspaper), 74
Al-Nahar (journal), 318
al-Najjada organization, 53–55, 132
Alon, Yigal, 138n64
Alon Plan, 250
Al-Qawmiyyoun al-'Arab Movement, 169, 173–175, 222, 226, 228–230, 235n24
Al-Ra'i (journal), 173, 174
Al-Sha'b (newspaper), 48, 49, 75, 318
Al-Shura (newspaper), 74
Al-Sirat al-Mustaqim (newspaper), 75, 322
Al-Th'ar (journal), 173, 174
Al-Wihda (newspaper), 55, 75
'Amer, 'Abd al-Hakim, 189
'Amer, 'Ali 'Ali, 204, 205
'Amira, Khaled, 196
Amman Meeting (1954), 174
Amman Treaty (1970), 245
'Amr, Mukhlis, 45, 46, 60
'Anabtawi, Munzer, 222
Andrews, Lewis, 12, 16
Anglo-American Committee of Inquiry, 85
al-'Ani, Mahdi Salah, 100
'Anabtawi, Wasfi, 79
Antonius, George, 42
'Aql, Amin, 53, 126, 140n87
'Ara, Wadi, 13
Arab Club, 58, 174
Arab Executive Committee, 59
Arab Higher Committee (AHC), 10, 32; absence during World War II, 40; attempts to reinstate, 42; banned by Great Britain, 16; control by Haj Amin, 12; dissolution of, 12, 15; rejection of White Paper (1939), 25; withdrawal of National Defense Party from, 11, 12
Arab Higher Institution (AHI), 55, 134, 167; activity during partition period, 92–94; Arab League and, 86; attacks on partition plans, 47; attacks on unions by, 62, 63; calls for boycott of International Commission of Inquiry, 62; claim to represent Palestinian interests, 86; declares day of mourning over partition, 90; in fight

against partition, 96; founding, 44, 45; funding for Holy Jihad Army by, 104; moves to Lebanon, 165; partition and, 87; recognized Council of Trade Unions, 61; rivalry with Arab League, 92–94

Arabic press, 73–75; complaints about British discrimination in, 74; dissemination of information by, 73; hostility towards Jewish settlement by, 74; inter-Arab issues, 73; Istiqlali oriented, 75; leftist, 75; post–World War II revitalization of, 75; publicizing demands of national movement, 74; relations with Britain and, 74; shaping public opinion, 73; sports/leisure, 75

Arab Institution for Support of the Palestinian Revolt, 236n39

Arab League: approves management of Gaza Strip by Egypt, 144; assumes administration of Palestinian political and civil affairs, 93; attempts to send Palestinian delegate to, 41–43; awareness of balance of power issues, 95; calls for cooperation with UNSCOP, 88; cancels ministries of Government of All Palestine, 128; decision to implement military course of action against partition, 95, 96; desire to dominance in Palestine, 86; establishment of, 35; establishment of military committee during partition, 94; internal dissent over partition plans, 46, 47; involvement in Palestinian cause, 35–36; Military Committee, 108; objections to annexation of Palestine by Jordan, 143; organization of pan-Arab unions by, 65; as patron of Palestinians, 36; as platform for activism for Palestinian national movement, 35, 36; proposes independent state with equal status for Palestinians and Jews, 88, 89, 111; reaction to Resolution 181, 90; relations with Husayni-led group, 46; rivalry with Arab Higher Institution, 92–94; warns UN against establishment of Jewish state, 88; War of 1948 and, 47; widens rifts within national movement, 36

Arab League Council, 44, 205, 233; demands right to choose Palestinian representative, 86

Arab Legion, 133, 142

Arab Liberation Front, 267, 301

Arab Nationalist Movement, 173–175, 192; discord within, 204

Arab Nationalist Party, 47–49

Arab national movement, 47–49; Arab Nationalist Party in, 47, 48, 49; communists in, 47, 48, 134; founding of *Al-Sha'b* (newspaper) in, 48, 49

Arab National Republic, 194

Arab News Agency, 75

Arab Palestinian General Congress, 3

Arab Revival Party. *See* Ba'ath Party

Arab Revolt. *See* Revolt of 1936–1939

Arabs and Arab countries: avoidance of confrontation with Britain and UN, 111; beginning of fight for Palestine, 91–110; clamp down on irregular Palestinian fighters, 187; collaboration with Great Britain to prevent establishment of Palestinian state, 192, 193; criticized by Fatah, 200–203; desire to be seen as nonaggressive in global public opinion, 111; donation of arms in fight against partition, 97; doubts about establishment of independent Palestine, 125; identity, 1, 2; interest-based involvement in Palestine by, 6; internal rivalries in, 163–168; lack of unified effort in War of 1948, 111; leaves Lebanon, 293, 294; limited fighting by in War of 1948, 110; needed by Palestine for support, 2; Palestinian independence and, 124–129; paternalistic interest in Palestine by, 6; "perseverance" funds provided by, 271; unity concept, 35–36; in War of 1948, 110–124; in World War II, 29–32

Arab Scouts, 56, 57; nurturing of nationalism by, 56, 57

Arab Spring, 8, 347–358; action in Palestinian camp expected in, 350; marginalization of Palestinian issue in, 349, 350

Arab Students Association, 276

Arab Summit (Morocco, 1974), 267

Arab Workers' Congress, 60, 61

Arab Workers' Union, 59, 60, 61, 61tab
'Arafa, Rashad, 53
Arafat, Yasir, 167, 180, 202, 216n160; agrees to recognition of Palestinian Communist Party, 301; attacks on Israel by forces of, 222; attempts at recognition from United States, 326, 327, 328; attempts to build PLO state in Lebanon, 287–289; calls for renewal of armed struggle after defeat, 224, 225; as chairman of Palestine Liberation Organization, 224; criticisms of, 302; death of, 7, 340, 342; declares self as President of Palestinian State, 326; delays investigation of collapse of PLO defense under Israeli attack, 294, 295; develops political and diplomatic agenda, 303, 304; drawn into Lebanon civil war, 280–282; enlists Soviet aid, 286; evacuates Lebanon, 291; founding of Fatah and, 196, 197; hegemony in Jordan challenged, 241; in Lebanon, 258, 279–291; at Madrid peace talks, 326, 327; meets with Waldheim, 285; organizes regional headquarters for Fatah, 227; reaches rapprochement with Egypt, 300; reaches temporary understanding with Lebanon, 256; rebellion of PLO elements against, 293–304; relations with other Arab countries, 293–311; return to Gaza Strip, 291; signs Cairo Treaty, 257; speaks at UN, 267; support for Saddam Hussein, 7, 326; suspends PFLP from PLO, 243; takes part in Sadat peace initiative, 285, 286; takes preventive measures against internal rebellion in PLO, 296, 297; in talks with Al-Qawmiyyoun al-'Arab Movement, 226; tries to assume command of first intifada, 316; in Tunisia, 291, 293–311
al-Ard Movement, 276
Argov, Shlomo, 290
al-'Arif, 'Arif, 3, 96, 130, 131, 132
'Ariqat, Kamel, 106
'Ariqat, Wasef, 296
Army of Free Lebanon, 284, 285, 287, 288
al-Asbah, 'Abdallah, 13
'Asfur, Hanna, 60
'Ashour, 'Ali, 178

al-Assad, Hafez, 203, 282, 285, 287, 297, 301, 303
Association for Helping Needy Druze, 59
Association of Arab Women, 63
Association of Observers of Virtues, 58
Association of Sons of Palestine, 159
'Atallah, 'Atallah, 306
'Atallah, Ghazi, 296
al-Atasi, Nur al-Din, 203, 225
al-Atrash, Ahmad, 202
al-Atrash, Farid, 58
al-Atrash, Mahmoud, 202
Authority for Rehabilitation of Refugees in Israel, 153–156
Avneri, Uri, 285
'Awad, 'Atiyya, 13
'Awda, Abd al-'Aziz, 325
al-'Azm, Yusuf, 177
al-'Azma, 'Adel, 26
al-'Azma, Nabih, 26
'Azzam, 'Abd al-Rahman, 92, 118, 125, 143

Ba'ath Party, 52, 159, 169, 181, 236n39, 354, 356
Baghdad Alliance, 164, 173
Bal'awi, Fathi, 180, 197, 216n160
Balfour Declaration (1917), 1, 29, 133; objections to, 3
Bands of Force, 202
al-Banna, Hasan, 50, 128, 325; founds Muslim Brotherhood, 49
al-Banna, Sabri, 290
Barak, Ehud, 339
Baransi, Salih, 186
al-Barghouti, Marwan, 338, 353
al-Barghouti, Mustafa, 339
al-Barghuti, 'Umar al-Salih, 4, 79
Basisu, Mu'in, 178, 179
Bastuni, Rustom, 155, 183
Battalion of the Truth, 194–195
Battalions of Arab Sacrifice, 192–194
Battle of Karameh, 224
Battle of the Ten Days, 119
Baydas, Khalil, 77
Ben-Gurion, David, 138n64, 146
Bernadotte, Count Folke, 118, 119, 121, 122, 124, 139n69
Berri, Nabih, 289
Bishara, Azmi, 354
al-Bitar, 'Omar, 66
Black September, 243–245, 258–260
"Black Tuesday" (Tuqan), 76

Blue Book Plan, 32, 34–35
Boys of Muhammad Association, 58
British Council: establishes Anglo-Arab cultural clubs, 57; support for women's organizations, 63
British Mandate (1920), 3, 14; call for termination of, 45; demands for termination of, 60; recognition of Arab unions, 60; scouting during, 56, 57
al-Budayri, Hasan, 3
al-Budayri, Musa, 46
Bunche, Ralph, 122
Bushnaq, 'Ali, 207
al-Bustani, Emil, 257
al-Bustani, Zahi, 305

Cairo Agreement (2005), 342, 343
Cairo Treaty (1969), 256–258, 284
Call of Life, Our Palestine (newspaper), 199–200
Camp David Accords, 302, 339, 340
Carter, Jimmy, 286
Casey, R. G., 34
Catastrophe of 1948, 199, 202
Christians: alienation by Palestinian strategies, 256; Arabic-speaking, 2; call for removal of Palestinian organizations from Lebanon, 261; in Lebanon, 156; left-wing, 260; Maronite, 34, 256, 258, 260, 279, 280, 281, 282, 283, 284; objections to Cairo Treaty, 258, 260
Clapp, Gordon, 147
Clashes of May 1969, 256
Class: intellectual, 5, 6, 21n2; middle, 5, 17, 54; struggle, 179; urban, 17, 47; working, 6, 17
Clayton, General Charles, 86, 105
Clubs and organizations, 58; Arab, 57, 58; Christian, 58; cultural, 57–59; family-centered, 59; nationally oriented, 58; for organizing popular protests, 58; religious-ethnic, 58; as spy centers, 57; Unity, 57; women's, 63–64
Committee for the Defense of Arab Lands, 274, 275, 276, 313n41
Communists, 17, 45, 47, 48, 77, 134, 171; in armed conflict, 230–231; collaboration with Muslim Brotherhood in Gaza Strip, 179–180

Consciousness: Arab-Palestinian, 2; national, 2
Constructive Enterprise project, 62, 68–70
Council of Trade Unions, 61, 62
Custodian for Absentees' Property, 153

al-Dabbagh, Rashad, 53
Dahlan, Muhammad, 338
al-Dajani, Hasan Sidqi, 11
al-Dajani, Sa'id, 181
al-Dakhakhni, Ibrahim, 233
Damascus Treaty, 282
Damascus Understandings, 343
Danin, 'Ezra, 155
al-Dannan, 'Abd Allah, 196
Darwaza, Muhammad 'Izzat, 11, 13, 18, 28, 40, 42, 79, 81n15, 132
Darwish, 'Abdallah Nimr, 309
Darwish, Ishaq, 13
Democratic Front for Peace and Equality. *See* Hadash
Democratic Front for the Liberation of Palestine (DFLP), 230, 242, 248, 296, 300, 317, 318
Democratic National Alliance, 300, 301
Development of the Galilee project, 275
al-Din, 'Aadil Najm, 100
al-Din, 'Ali Naser, 174
al-Din, Farid Zayn, 47
al-Din, Sa'id Zayn, 53
Dizdar, Shahinda, 63

Education, 70–73; Arab schools, 71, 72; in British Mandate period, 70, 71, 72; demand for, 70, 71; government schools, 71, 72; private vs. public, 71; secondary, 72; teacher training colleges, 72, 73
Egypt: annexes Gaza Strip, 110, 144; approval of infiltration of Israeli borders by Fida'iyyun, 188; Arabic press in, 74; armistice with Israel, 129, 144; capitulation to King Abdullah on Palestinian issue, 162; conflict with Israel, 190; control of Gaza Strip, 177–181; demands withdrawal of British army, 49; Free Officers revolt in, 163, 180; internal war against Muslim Brotherhood in, 187, 188; intervention in Lebanon, 256; logistic aid to Fatah, 233; Muslim Brotherhood in, 49;

opposition forces in, 162; organizes guerrilla warfare against Israel, 188; plans to incorporate territory from War of 1948, 110; replaces Haj Amin with al-Shuqayri, 166; resentment over Haj Amin demand that aid be given to Government of All Palestine and Arab Higher Institution., 162; rivalry with Jordan, 112; secret preparations for War of October, 263; warns Jordan not to shut down Palestinian revolution, 242; in War of 1948, 112, 113, 114, 115tab, 116, 117, 118

Egyptian Club, 58

Emergency Defense Regulations (1945), 146

Executive Arab Committee (EAC), 4, 104

Eytan, Refa'el, 289, 290

Faisal II (King of Iraq), 111
Faisal (King of Saudi Arabia), 239
Fakhouri, Hani, 199
Family of Jihad, 309
Family of the Earth, 185
Fanon, Frantz, 201
Farah, Boulos, 20, 45, 46, 60, 134, 183
al-Farhan, Hamad, 173
al-Farouqi, Hamdi al-Taji, 268
Farouq (King of Egypt), 111, 112, 113
Farraj, Ya'qub, 42
Fatah, 167; advocates rejection of reinstatement of Arab patronage of Palestinian cause, 272; aid from Egypt to, 233; al-Tanzim youth in, 340; ambiguity over beginnings of, 196–198; armed conflict by, 200–203; assumes control of PLO, 233–234; attacks on Israel, 226, 286–291; attempts to reconstruct independent nation, 6; Central Committee, 295; civilian infrastructure for, 255; critical of Arab League and Arab states, 200; design on entangling Arab countries in all-out war against Israel, 221; deterioration of relations with Jordan, 239–245; early failure, 203; establishment of, 195–208; establishment of Palestine Liberation Army and, 204–206; Executive Committee, 303; guerrilla warfare among supportive local population and, 224–226; guerrilla warfare replaces Arab armies by, 226–228; hegemony in Jordan challenged, 241; identification with Palestinian Authority, 339; increase in stature of, 224; infiltrates Israeli borders, 222; intergenerational tensions in, 229; inundated with young people enlisting, 226, 227; Islamic messages from, 339; as leading element of armed resistance, 233; leftist criticism of, 271; military presence in Lebanon, 255–261; nesting operations by, 227; obstructed by Arab countries, 204; operational systems, 198; plans for attacks on Israel fail, 227, 228; rebellion within, 296; recruitment patterns, 198; relations with Palestine Liberation Organization, 203; rise of during War of 1967, 223–224; rivals in occupied territories, 270–272; rivals of, 204–206; serial bombing theory and, 206, 207; stages theory and, 206–207; struggle with Hamas, 337–344; suppression of, 207–208; transfers bases to Jordan, 225; transition from national liberation movement to ruling party, 338; transition to belligerent outlook, 230, 231; tries to overthrow King Husayn, 244; turns to popular war of liberation, 229; use of Islamic motifs, 338; West Germany and, 198, 199

"Fatahland," 255–261
Fatat al-'Arab Society, 64
Fawzi, Muhammad, 205, 231, 233
Fayyad, Salam, 342
Fez Summit (1982), 319
Fida'iyyun: in Gaza Strip, 187–190; model of combat operations, 226; revival of, 231–233; salaries of, 214n125
Fighters for the Freedom of Israel, 122
Filastin (newspaper), 2, 3, 49, 73, 75
Filastinuna (newspaper), 199, 200, 201, 206
Flag of the Youth (bulletin), 178
Franjiyya, Sulayman, 261, 279, 282
Free French Forces, 32, 33
Free Officers revolt, 163, 164, 180
Furayj, Futi, 125, 140n87

Gaza Strip: annexed by Egypt, 110, 144; Ba'ath Party in, 181; as base for

guerrilla operations, 247, 248; control by Hamas, 342; dissolution of National Liberation League, 178; under Egyptian control, 177–181; Fida'iyyun and, 187–190; Hamas control of, 7; liberation tax on residents in, 206, 219n187; Muslim Brotherhood in, 179–181; occupation by Israel, 165, 179, 181, 189; Palestinian Communist Party in, 178–179; Palestinian refugees in, 148, 151–152; PLO efforts to revive status in, 268; refugees in, 177–181
General Syrian Congress, 8n10
Germany: Palestinians in, 198, 199
Ghanayim, Mahmoud, 78
al-Ghazali, Shaikh Muhammad, 180
al-Ghouri, Emil, 44, 87
Ghunaym, Muhammad, 203
al-Ghusayn, Ya'qub, 40, 66
Ghusha, D. Subhi, 173
Glubb, General John, 191
Golan Heights, 225, 255
Government of All Palestine, 125–126; Arab disregard for, 167; doubt about legality of, 143; Holy Jihad Army and, 186; King Abdullah blocks establishment of, 142; marginalization of, 126–129; recognition from all Arab countries except Jordan, 128; unrepresented in Arab League, 161
Great Britain: attempts more positive relations with Arab countries, 32; challenged to bring Palestinian issue to UN Security Council, 49, 87; demands by Egypt for withdrawal of armies of, 49; desire to make Haj Amin pay for collaboration with Axis powers, 105; encouragement of traditional factionalism in Palestine by, 4; expresses support for Jewish homeland, 29; imposes restrictions on immigration of Jews to Palestine, 16; invasion of Iraq, 27; occupation of Palestine by, 133; policy on Arab unity, 35; in revolt of 1936-1939, 10; sanctions against Palestinians, 29, 30; support for Jews in partition, 91; tries to neutralize Haj Amin, 35; use of sanctions in revolt of 1936-1939, 14; vacillates in support of Jewish national homeland, 16
Greater Syria, 3, 8n10, 32, 33, 99

Greater Syria Plan, 32, 33
Great Palestinian Revolt. *See* Revolt of 1936–1939
Great Strike (1936), 9–10, 57
Green Shirt Organization of Young Egypt, 193
Gromyko, Andrei, 90

Habash, George, 173, 174, 192, 193, 194, 204, 230, 241, 242, 265, 267, 302
Habib, Phillip, 289, 290
Habibi, Emil, 45, 47, 134, 274
Haboqer (newspaper), 74
Hadash, 274, 276, 308, 309, 310, 354, 356
Haddad, Sa'd, 284
Haddad, Wadi', 204, 205, 243, 259
al-Haddad, Mansour, 178
Hafiz, Mustafa, 188, 189
Haganah, 54, 107; Palmach force, 103
Hajjawi, Sulafa, 160
Hamas, 319, 322–325; call for jihad against Israel, 325; charter, 324; commitment to Islamic values, 322, 323, 324; concept of collaboration with PLO, 324; control of Gaza Strip by, 342; electoral victory of, 7; Islamic threat posed by, 338; refusal to accept PLO political plan, 341; rise to position of influence, 7; roots in Muslim Brotherhood, 322, 324; struggle with Fatah, 337–344; war with Palestine Liberation Organization, 7
Hamdan, Faris, 214n107
Hammoud, Tariq, 350
Hammuda, Yahya, 223
al-Hamshari, Mahmoud, 259
Haniyeh, Isma'il, 342
Haniyyah, Akram, 318
Harb, Muhammad Salah, 128
al-Hasan, Hani, 227
al-Hasan, Khaled, 196, 221, 224, 225, 319
al-Hashemi, Taha, 94, 96, 98
Hasna, 'Ali, 126, 140n87
Hassunah, 'Abd al-Khaliq, 167
Hawatmeh, Nayif, 194, 230, 242
al-Hawwari, Muhammad Nimr, 53, 55, 82n43, 132
Hawwash, Yahya, 104
Haykal, Muhammad Hasanin, 111, 112, 233, 239

Haykal, Yusuf, 48
Haymour, 'Abd al-Hamid, 59, 60
The Heir (Baydas), 77
Heroes of the Return, 221, 229
Higher Arab Front, 42, 44; Arab League and, 86; claim to represent Palestinian interests, 86
High Follow-Up Committee for the Arab Citizens of Israel, 274, 310
Hijackings, 243, 259, 286
Hiliw, Sharl, 256, 257
al-Hiliw, Radwan, 45, 169, 170
al-Hindi, Amin, 192, 193
al-Hindi, Mahmoud, 94
Hishmi, Muhammad, 207, 208
Histadrut, 310
Hitler, Adolf, 28
Holocaust of Palestine (al-Tal), 133
Holy Jerusalem (newspaper), 73
Holy Jihad Army, 79; arena of operation, 107; declared illegal by Jordan, 186; enlistment by young Palestinians in, 104; in fight against partition, 97, 98, 106–110; formation of, 105; founding, 137n40; guerrilla warfare and, 104, 106–110; inability to defend Arab population, 109; local support for, 104; pre-resolution preparations for war, 105; shock at death of commander, 108
al-Hout, Bayan Nuwayhid, 20, 31, 39, 44, 88, 110, 133, 304, 305
al-Hout, Shafiq, 232
Husayn, Ahmad, 128
Husayn, Ibrahim Nimr, 310, 313n46
al-Husayni, 'Abd al-Qadir, 13, 97, 98, 99, 104, 105, 106, 107, 108
al-Husayni, Faisal, 229, 327
al-Husayni, Farouq, 198
al-Husayni, Hamdi, 179
al-Husayni, Ishaq Musa, 78
al-Husayni, Jamal, 13, 42, 44, 55, 78, 125, 142; in Arab Higher Institution, 44; imprisonment, 40; at Nation's Bank, 66; in Palestinian Arab Party, 49; support for Great Britain in World War II, 32
al-Husayni, Khaled, 108, 109
al-Husayni, Mousa Kathim, 4, 53, 104
al-Husayni, Mufti Haj Amin, 11; account of Revolt by, 18; accusations against by King Abdullah, 126, 127, 128; accuses Jews of conspiracy against Arabs, 165; alleges British treachery, 32; alliance with Muslim Brotherhood, 162, 164; approaches King Husayn, 166, 167; in Arab Higher Institution, 45; attempts to exonerate self from blame for various failures, 19, 27, 36; attempts to neutralize influence of, 35; in Berlin, 25, 28, 29, 40, 46, 67; blamed for failure of Revolt, 20; blamed for The Nakba, 165, 166; collaboration with Axis powers, 27, 28, 29; concern over rise of al-Najjada organization, 54; conflict with King Abdullah, 142, 161, 162; control of Arab Higher Committee by, 12, 42; criticism against, 126; deserted by political allies, 160, 161; desire to employ violence against opponents, 16; in Egypt, 44, 126, 127, 164; escape to Lebanon, 12, 15, 25; establishes al-Futuwwa alternative organization without autonomy, 55; failed leadership in revolt of 1936-1939, 15–16; focus on thwarting reorganization of national movement toward new leadership, 36, 42; founds Holy Jihad Army, 104; Government of All Palestine and, 125–126; head of Muslim Higher Council, 5; incites riots in West Bank, 163, 164; in Iraq, 25, 26–28; leadership ambitions, 26, 36, 42; leadership from afar, 25–29; loss of status and authority, 87; as mufti of Jerusalem, 5; objections to support of Axis powers by, 46; opposition to, 26, 36; organizes Pan-Islamic Conference, 162; poor relations with Great Britain, 35; presents self as pan-Arab leader, 36; prevented from return to Palestine, 44; pursuit of Arab countries for assistance, 163–168; reactionary leadership of, 48; refusal to accept authority of Arab League in partition, 92; reinstatement of former status in Palestine, 93, 94; rejection of all solutions to Palestinian issues, 26; rejection of White Paper by, 16; relations with Arab League, 46; relations with Egypt, 162; relations

with Hasan al-Banna, 49, 50; relations with Islamic world, 162, 163; return to Palestine, 87; self-interest of, 15; tries to incite opposition in Egypt to government activities in Gaza Strip, 162; unrealistic goals of, 15, 16; work detrimental to Palestinian relations with Egypt and Saudi Arabia, 36
al-Husayni, Munif, 75, 166
al-Husayni, Raja'i, 87, 125, 140n87
al-Husayni, Tawfiq Salih, 42, 44
Husayni Arab Party, 143
Husayni-led group, 5; antipathy to alliances precluding Haj Amin, 41; apprehension over armed youth movement, 54; Arab League proposals and, 42; exile after Revolt, 17; obstruction of alternate leadership by, 40–45, 54, 55; relations with Arab League, 46; resistance to Arab front, 43; in revolt of 1936-1939, 10, 13
Husayn (King of Jordan), 163, 166, 167, 238–239, 240, 284; army purge by, 242; ask Palestinians to accept UN resolutions, 301; attempts to solve Arab-Israeli conflict, 271, 272; backs revolt within Fatah, 306, 307; clashes with Palestinians, 240–245; clash with Nasser, 174; concludes necessity of including PLO in resolution of Palestinian issue, 304; conflict with PLO, 175; dissolves political parties in Jordan, 171; establishes military government, 243, 244; Federation Plan, 248–250; plans United Arab Kingdom, 248, 249, 250; support for Palestinian national movement, 167–168; support for US intervention in Middle East, 172, 173
al-Husri, Hamed, 178
al-Husri, Sati', 26

Ibn al-Husayn, Faisal, 3
Ibn Sa'ud, 'Abd al-'Aziz (King of Saudi Arabia), 32, 35, 111
Ibrahim, General Husayn Fawzi, 96
Ibrahim, Rashid al-Haj, 40, 41, 66
al-Ibrahim, Tawfiq (Abu Ibrahim al-Saghir), 13, 104, 107, 191
Identity: Arab, 1, 2, 71; Arab-Palestinian, 3, 4, 273–276; attempts to erase Palestinian by Jordan, 151; Eastern sense of, 3; Islamic, 2, 309; modern, 2, 3; national, 4, 6, 309; Palestinian, 1, 2, 174; pan-regional, 2, 6
'Idwan, Kamal, 197, 216n160, 224, 246, 258, 259, 260
al-Imam, Raghib, 18
Institution Acting for the Liberation of Palestine, 242
Institution for Objection to Reconciliation with Israel, 174
Intifada, First, 15, 315–328; decline in standard of living and, 316; ignited by sense of rage over Jewish construction in occupied territories, 316; introduction from below, 7; lack of opportunity for educated Palestinian youth, 317; land expropriation and, 316; PLO strength in, 317–320; reintroduction of civil disobedience in, 6; spontaneous beginning, 315; unemployment and, 316, 317
Intifada, Second, 15, 338; development from popular uprising against Israel, 340; militarization of, 340; outbreak of, 339; Sharon and, 340
Intifada of March 1955, 187
Iran-Iraq War, 303
Iraq: Association of Sons of Palestine in, 159; British invasion, 27; as center of Palestinian political operations, 26; failure of coup in, 27, 30; financial aid to Palestinian organizations, 266; Haj Amin in, 25, 26–28; lack of assistance in PLO conflict with Jordan, 244; Palestine Liberation Organization in, 159; Palestinian refugees in, 148, 158–160; provision of financial aid to armed Palestinian organizations, 224; split with Palestinian national movement, 27; struggle against Great Britain, 26; in War of 1948, 114, 115tab, 116, 117; war with United States, 7
Iraqi al-Muthanna Club, 26
Irshid, Mustafa, 11
Islamic: identity, 309; movement s, 318; trends, 272; values, 323
Islamic Jihad Movement, 309, 318, 325
Islamic Liberation Party, 169, 171–173
Islamic Resistance Movement. *See* Hamas

Islamic Sports Club, 53
Israel: annexations of territory by, 145; armistice agreements with Arab countries after War of 1948, 129; armistice with Egypt, 144; armistice with Jordan, 143; attacks of retaliation on Palestinians, 226; attacks on Lebanon, 260; attacks on Palestinian military bases, 260; attempts to curb influence of PLO, 272; Authority for Rehabilitation of Refugees in, 153–156; Committee of Displaced in, 153; Communist Party in, 183–185; conflict with Egypt, 190; counterattacks in War of 1948, 119; Custodian for Absentees' Property in, 153; development of state of, 6; discrimination experienced by Arab citizens in, 273–275; elections in, 308, 309; Emergency Defense Regulations in, 146; enhancement of forces during ceasefire in War of 1948, 119, 121; establishes global comprehensive war against PLO, 259, 260; establishment of state of, 47, 110–113; evacuates Arab populations from occupied areas, 120, 121; in First Lebanon War, 289–291; in Gaza Strip, 247; infiltrated through Syria, 191, 192; initiation of retaliatory acts after Olympic massacre, 259; intervention in Palestinian organizations' actions by, 266; invasion of Lebanon by, 289–291; Labor Party, 276; Mapai Party, 276; military rule in, 146; murder of Bernadotte as political burden for, 122; neutralization of Fatah fighters by, 234; occupation of Gaza Strip, 165, 179, 181, 189; "open bridges" policy with Jordan, 268; operation at Karameh, 238–239; Palestinians in, 144–147, 148, 152–156, 181–186, 273–276, 308–311; promises of special benefits to Palestinian collaborators, 268; proposes establishment of village societies in occupied territories, 272; recognition of, 7; relations with Palestine Liberation Organization, 7; retaliates against Black September, 259, 260; retaliation for attacks on, 187, 188, 240, 266, 267, 286–291; strict approach toward Hamas, 325; targets Fatah representatives for assassination, 259; unwritten alliance with Syria, 299; in War of 1967, 221–234; in West Bank, 190
Israeli Communist Party (Maki), 45, 47, 183–185, 274
'Issa, Mahmoud, 296
al-'Issa, Issa Daoud, 2, 3
al-'Issa, Khalil (Abu Ibrahim al-Kabir), 13, 104
al-'Issa, Mechel, 100
al-'Issa, Yusuf Hanna, 2

al-Ja'bari, Husayni, 143
al-Ja'bari, Muhammad 'Ali, 142, 268
Jaber, Haj Isma'il, 227, 294, 296
Jaber, Salah, 92, 96
Jabbor, Jabbor, 214n114
Jabra, Jabra Ibrahim, 160
Jaffa Front, 43
Jami'ani, Dafi, 242
al-Jammali, Muhammad Fadhel, 174
Jarallah, Shaikh Husam al-Din, 128
Jarrar, Fawzi, 18, 107
al-Jawad, Salih 'Abd, 20, 21
Jericho Conference (1948), 143
The Jerusalem Post (newspaper), 230
Jewish Agency, 4; Arab Division, 30, 56, 155; representatives to partition resolution conference, 87; support for partition plan, 89
Jewish National Fund, 153, 155
Jewish National Home, 35
Jewish national movement: Blue Book Plan and, 34; efforts to construct homeland in Palestine, 1; evolvement of organizations aspiring to assist in recovery from Revolt of 1936–1939, 40–80; Greater Syria Plan and, 34; post–World War II strength, 39
Jewish settlement: in Arabic press, 74; attacks on, 102; easing of restrictions on, 85; efforts at, 1; fortification by immigrants, 5; "international conspiracy" toward, 86; land sales by Arabs, 60, 65–68; support from Great Britain for, 29; sympathy for, 85
Jews: calls for ban on sale of land to, 60, 65–68; demand for ban on immigration of, 60; immigration to

Palestine by, 2; restrictions on autonomy of, 34; during World War II, 28, 29
Jibril, Ahmad, 207, 238, 265, 266, 267, 296, 301
Jibril Deal, 318
Jiryis, Sabri, 186
Joint Arab Defense Council, 248
Jordan: annexes West Bank, 110, 141–144, 169, 170; armistice with Israel, 129, 143; arrests Fatah operatives, 260; attempts to eliminate Palestinian identity, 174; attempts to implicate Haj Amin in murder of Abdullah, 163; backs revolt within Fatah, 306, 307; clashes with Palestinians, 240–247; Communist Party declared illegal in, 171; confrontations with Palestinian organizations, 237–250; co-opts some Palestinian leadership, 151; deterioration of relations with Fatah, 239–245; ends relations with PLO, 248, 249; includes residents of West Bank in elections, 161; Islamic Liberation Party in, 171–173; Muslim Brotherhood in, 175–177; neutralization of Palestinian organizations in, 246; "open bridges" policy with Israel, 268; Palestinian refugees in, 148–151, 306–308; Palestinians dismissed from army, 260; plans to incorporate territory from War of 1948, 110; Popular War of Liberation in, 237–250; reconciliation negotiations with PLO, 248; refusal to recognize Government of All Palestine, 128; regulation of imams in, 172; state of emergency in, 244; takes control of Popular Front for the Liberation of Palestine bases, 241; threatens to withdraw from Arab League if Government of All Palestine is represented, 161; in War of 1948, 114, 115tab, 117; in War of 1967, 222
Jordanian Communist Party, 171, 230
Jordanian Legion, 108, 109
Journal of the Palestinian Oriental Society, 79
Jubran, Salem, 274
al-Julani, 'Abd al-Halim, 13

al-Jumayyil, Pierre, 261n4, 279, 280, 283
Junbalat, Kamal, 194, 258, 285

Kamal, Wasif, 48, 80n12, 81n15, 87
Kanafani, Ghassan, 175, 204, 259
Kan'an, Tawfiq, 79
Karameh Day, 238–239
Kardush, Mansour, 186
Karkar, Gurget, 64
al-Karmi, 'Abd al-Karim, 76, 77
Katan, Henri, 87
Kaywan, Muhammad, 276
al-Kayyali, 'Abd al-Wahab, 20, 133
al-Kayyali, Majid, 357
al-Khadra, Subhi, 66, 94
Khalaf, Karim, 269
Khalaf, Salah, 180, 194–195, 196, 197, 198, 202, 224, 225, 239, 244, 248, 258, 259, 260, 264, 297, 301, 319
al-Khaldi, Husayn Fakhri, 45
Khalf, Karim, 250
al-Khalidi, Ahmad Samih, 72
al-Khalidi, Husayn Fakhri, 40, 125
al-Khalidi, Rasem, 87
al-Khalidi, Walid, 134
Khalifa, 'Abd al-Rahman, 176
Khalifa, Ahmad, 229
al-Khalil, Sa'id, 66
al-Khalil, 'Umar, 48
al-Khalili, 'Ali, 131
Khalla, Kamil Mahmoud, 20, 133
Khamis, Yusuf, 183
Khammash, Rawhi, 160
Khas, Muhammad, 178
al-Khatabi, 'Abd al-Karim, 128
al-Khatib, 'Umar, 203
Khawarij (Seceders), 22n7
al-Khayri, Khalusi, 48, 80n12
Khomeini, Ayatolla, 325
Khouri, Tawfiq, 199
Khuri, Muwaffaq, 156
al-Kilani, Rashid 'Ali, 25, 27, 48, 104
Kulthum, Um, 58
Kusa, Ilyas, 41, 214n114
Kuwait: as center of independent Palestinian activity, 197

Labib, Mahmoud, 55
Land: Arab self-development of, 68; sales to Jews, 60, 65–68
Land Day, 6, 275–276

390 Index

Lebanon: Arabic press in, 74; armistice with Israel, 129; Army of Free Lebanon in, 284, 285, 287; attempts to limit activities of Fatah, 256; Cairo Treaty and, 256–258; cease-fire agreement in, 284; Christians in, 156; Citizenship and Immigration Act in, 280; civil war in, 194, 279–291; Clashes of May 1969 in, 256; conflict with PLO, 279–291; declining status in Arab world, 257; Department for Refugee Matters in, 156; departure of PLO from, 289–291; Fatah military presence in, 255–261; Haj Amin in, 12, 15, 25; intervention by Egypt in, 256; intifada in, 257; invaded by Israel, 289–291; local popular support for Palestinians, 257; opposition to growing Fatah presence, 256; Palestinian refugees in, 148, 156–157, 304–306; PLO in, 255; resists attempts by Fatah to reoccupy positions in, 306; in War of 1948, 112, 114, 115tab, 116, 117; young refugees take revenge on local populations in, 258

Liberation Army, 79, 137n40; arena of operation, 102, 103; composition, 99, 100; deployment, 102–104; disorder in, 100, 101; failure of, 103, 104; in fight against partition, 98–102; inability to defend Arab population, 109; lack of motivation/discipline, 100, 101; in War of 1948, 114, 123

Libya: support for Palestinian organizations, 257, 266

Literature, 76–78, 132, 133, 274; historical, 132, 133, 134

Little Triangle, 143, 145, 190, 208n7

London Convention (1939), 42

al-Madani, Rashed, 221
al-Madani, Wajih, 232
al-Madi, Mahmoud, 11
al-Madi, Mu'in, 13, 26
Mahamid, Hashem, 156
Mahmoud, Nur al-Din, 114, 118
Makhus, Ibrahim, 203
Makki, Fakhri, 178
Malul, Nisim, 74
Mansur, Tamim, 356
Mapai Party, 182, 276

Mapam Party, 183
Maragha, Musa, 295
Maraka, Fakhri, 107
Mardam, Jamel, 42
Mas'ad, Joseph, 353
Masalha, Nur al-Din, 134
al-Masri, Nimr, 171
The Masses (journal), 171
McMichael, Harold, 31
Mecca Agreement, 343
Meir, Golda, 250
Memoirs of a Chicken (al-Husayni), 78
Mi'ari, Muhammad, 156, 276, 308, 313n41
Mifrig, Fu'ad, 47
Milson, Menahem, 272
al-Miqdadi, Darwish, 26, 79, 80n12, 81n15
Mir'at al-Sharq (newspaper), 74
Mirror of the East (newspaper), 3
More Land, Less Arabs (al-Din), 134
Movement for the Reform of Fatah, 296
Movement of the Earth, 185
Movements: armed youth, 54; labor, 59–63; pan-Arab, 3, 26, 27; reform, 61
Mu'addi, Jabr Dahish, 213n107
Mubarak, Hosni, 299, 300, 304, 351, 352
Mufti. *See* al-Husayni, Mufti Haj Amin
al-Mughannam, Mitil, 63
Muhammad, 'Abd al-Rahim al-Haj, 76, 77, 81n15; death of, 14; leads revolt of 1936-1939, 12
Muhsin, Zuhir, 264, 265, 280
Murqus, Nimr, 17, 31
Musa, Comrad. *See* al-Hiliw, Radwan
Muslim Brotherhood, 49, 50; alliance with Haj Amin, 162, 164; branches of, 194–195; charitable works by, 49, 50; collaboration with communists, 179–180; crisis with Egyptian regime, 162; in fight against partition, 96, 97; in Gaza Strip, 179–181; generation of Hamas and, 322; infiltration of Palestine by, 50; in Jordan, 175–177; in Palestine, 175–177; relations with Syrian Social Nationalist Party, 51; shift to military activities, 50; Train of Mercy project, 180; in War of 1948, 114, 175; in West Bank, 169
Muslim-Christian associations, 3, 53

Muslim Higher Council, 4, 5, 66, 128, 171
Mussolini, Benito, 28
Mustafa, Hassan, 78
Mustafa, Khaled 'Ali, 160
Mustafa, Salah, 189
Muways, Hanna, 310
al-Muzayyin, Sa'id, 197
"My Homeland" (Tuqan), 77

al-Nabhani, Taqi al-Din, 171, 172
al-Nabulsi, Sulayman, 171, 193
al-Nahhas, Mustafa, 35, 86
Najib, General Muhammad, 144
al-Najjada, 68
al-Najjar, Muhammad Yusuf, 194–195, 197, 198, 257, 258, 259, 260
The Nakba, 85–135; aftermath of, 160–168, 168–186; defining, 130; recollections of, 130–135
Nakhla, 'Issa, 87
Nakhlah, Ilyas, 213n107
The Naksa, 141–208
al-Naqrashi, Mahmoud Fahmi, 113, 128, 162
Naser, Kamal, 260
al-Nashashibi, Fakhri, 11, 14
al-Nashashibi, Fawzi, 56
al-Nashashibi, Muhammad Is'af, 78
al-Nashashibi, Naser al-Din, 166
al-Nashashibi, Raghib, 11
Nashashibi Defense Party, 66
Nashashibi-led group: elimination during partition, 94; in revolt of 1936–1939, 10
Nassar, Fu'ad, 45, 47, 60, 134, 169, 170, 171
Nassar, Najib, 2
Nassar, Sadij, 63, 64
Nasser, Gamal Abdel, 97, 164, 194, 202; attempted assassinations of, 180; claims Arabs incapable of resolving conflict through force, 223; clash with King Husayn, 174; death of, 245; in establishment of PLO, 166; establishment of United Arab Republic by, 165; intervention in Lebanon, 256; intervention in PLO conflict with Jordan, 244, 245; nationalization of Suez Canal by, 164, 193; pan-Arabism of, 165; recognition of Fatah, 233; reluctance to recognize

Palestine Liberation Army, 205; rivalry with Iraqi president, 129, 185; success against Baghdad Alliance, 193; transitions from defense to deterrence, 239
Nasser, Kamal, 208, 242
National Association of Arab Academics, 274
National Coalition, 301
National Committee of Arab High School Pupils, 274
National Committee of Arab Mayors, 310
National Committee of Arab Students, 274
National Committee of Heads of Arab Local Councils, 274, 275
National Defense Party, 11; withdrawal from Arab Higher Committee, 11, 12
National Democratic Assembly, 354
National Guidance Committee, 270, 271
Nationalism: of labor unions, 61; nurtured by Arab Scouts, 56, 57; Palestinian, 58, 273; pan-Arab, 58, 273
National Liberation Front, 226
National Liberation League, 45–47, 169, 170, 178
National Union, 166
Nation's Fund, 40, 62, 65–70
al-Natsha, Hafiz 'Abd al-Nabi, 175–177
al-Natsha, Rafiq, 197, 216n160
Netanyahu, Benjamin, 339
Newcomb, Colonel S. F., 32
New Communist List (Rakah), 184
Nimr, Walid, 247
Niqula, Jabra, 45
al-Numayri, Ja'far, 245
Nurallah, 'Atef, 56
Nusayba, Anwar, 126, 140n87
Nuwayhid, 'Ajaj, 75, 143

October Uprising, 340
Olympics, Munich (1972), 259
On the Hijaz Railway (al-Husayni), 78
Operation Cast Lead, 343
Operation Danny, 119
Operation Hiram, 123
Operation Horev, 123
Operation Litani, 286–287
Operation Policeman, 120–121
Operation Sinai (1956), 189
Operation Spring of Youth, 216n160

Operation 'Uvda, 123
Operation Yoav, 123, 142
Orthodox Scouts Society, 53
Oslo Accords (1993), 7, 291, 337, 341
Ottoman Law of Association, 172

Palestine: anger at Arab countries for conduct in War of 1948, 194–195; Arabic press in, 73–75; competition among Arab countries for dominance in, 86; conflict with Zionism, 1, 2; demands for independence, 60; factionalism in, 4, 5, 85–87; family-based factions in, 4, 5; Husayni-led group in, 5; ideological political parties in, 45–52; intellectual middle class in, 5; lack of modern national forms of organization in, 5; Muslim Brotherhood in, 175–177; Nashashibi-led group in, 5; need for support from Arab world, 2; political definition of, 3; post–World War II education system, 70–73; post–World War II poetry and literature in, 76–78; pre–World War II, 25–36; reaction to UN Resolution 181, 90–91; rejection of partition plans, 79, 80; revival of armed conflict and, 186–195; Revolt of 1936-1939 and, 9–21; scientific research in, 78, 79; threat posed by Jewish immigration, 2; three triangles of development in, 6; willingness to cede territory to Jordan if Jews are removed, 142; working class in political activity in, 5
"Palestine for the Palestinians," 8n10
Palestine Liberation Army (PLA), 189, 202, 221, 231–233, 263; establishment of, 166, 204–206; propaganda value of, 205, 206
Palestine Liberation Organization (PLO): accepts UN resolutions, 302; affiliation of new mayors of occupied territories with, 268–270; armed organizations assume control of, 223, 224; attacked by Israel in Lebanon, 289–291; bases in Lebanon, 257; Central Council, 320; collapse of defense during Israeli attack, 294; conflict over participation in political process with Israel in, 265, 266; conflict with King Husayn, 175; conflict with Lebanon, 279–291; demands immediate war of liberation from Israel, 223; departure from Lebanon, 289–291; dependence on Israeli economy, 268; diplomatic strategies, 319–320; drawn into Lebanon civil war, 280–282; efforts to revive status in West Bank and Gaza Strip, 268; elements acting against Arafat, 295; ends relations with Jordan, 248, 249; establishes status as sole representative of Palestinian people, 267; establishment of, 163–168; expedites establishment of Palestine Liberation Army, 205; expulsion from Beirut, 7; in First Intifada, 7; frustration with Egyptian reluctant to provide aid, 232; gives control to Fatah, 233–234; interprets position of Arab governments as withdrawal from commitments, 223; in Iraq, 159; military presence in Lebanon, 255; objections to Sadat's peace endeavors, 286; realization that Arab states could not put an end to occupations by Israel, 268, 269; rebellion against Arafat, 293–304; receives revenues from liberation tax on residents of Gaza Strip, 206; recognition of, 7; refusal to forego Cairo Treaty, 261; regains strength in first intifada, 317–320; relations with Fatah, 203; relations with Israel, 7; relations with Soviet Union, 320; relations with Syria, 281; relinquishes strategy of violence and assassinations, 259, 260; rise in status due to increasing pragmatism, 269; supports Cairo Treaty, 257; tries to overthrow King Husayn, 244; in Tunis, 7; use of Islamic motifs, 338; Voice of Palestine Radio and, 206; in War of October, 263–267; war with Hamas, 7
Palestine Popular Liberation Front, 236n39
Palestine Rescue Committee, 96
Palestine Royal Commission, 10, 11; partition plan offered by, 16; recommendations for partition by, 12
Palestinian: bitterness over military involvement of Arab League,

110–111; clashes with Jordan, 240–247; conflicts with Great Britain, 29; demands for suspension of Jewish immigration to Palestine, 34; diaspora distinctions, 168, 169; embarrassment at Arab League usurping of right to select representatives, 87; feelings of alliance with Ottoman system, 1, 2; historical narrative of The Nakba, 130–135; identity, 1, 2; Land Day, 275–276; national state, 1; objections to partition plans, 85, 86; refugees, 147–148; rejection of any compromise, 34; rejection of Peel Commission plan, 10, 11; relations with Lebanese Christians, 258; representation in parliament of Jordan, 161, 162; support for Allies by, 31; support for Arab Spring, 351, 352
Palestinian Authority (PA): establishment of, 7, 338; Fatah identification with, 339; intergenerational struggle for control of, 338; internal fissures in after death of Arafat, 338, 339; views on situation in Syria, 354
Palestinian Communist Party (PCP), 45–47, 77, 300, 301, 317, 318; in Gaza Strip, 178–179; inclusion of Arabs and Jews in, 45
Palestinian Liberation Front, 229, 230, 300
Palestinian Liberation Front-Way of Return, 232
Palestinian Mujahidin, 323
Palestinian National Charter, 167, 168, 324
Palestinian National Council (Algiers 1982), 126, 175, 224, 295, 301
Palestinian National Front, 179, 271
Palestinian National Guard, 189, 190, 205
Palestinian national movement, 4; absence of leadership in, 39; after Nakba, 85–135; alliance with Axis powers in World War II, 27, 28, 29; al-Najjada in, 53–55; Arabic press and, 73–75; Arab League and, 35, 36, 41–43; armed youth movement, 54, 55, 56; Ba'ath Party in, 52; confrontations with Jordan, 237–250; consolidation of, 2; cultural clubs in, 57–59; damage due to failure of Revolt of 1936-1939, 39; deep divisions in, 4; design on entangling Arab countries in all-out war against Israel, 221; destruction of institutions of society after War of 1948, 168, 169; economic and social aspects of, 64–70; educational system, 70–73; effect of Arab Spring on, 347–358; failure of rehabilitation from Revolt, 64–70; fight for Palestinian land after partition, 91–110; increasing Arabization of, 32; internal consensus in, 10; keeping Arab states from dominance of Palestinian cause, 264, 265; labor movement and trade unions in, 59–63; lack of trust in Arab governments in, 224; main axes of after Oslo Accords, 341–344; Muslim Brotherhood in, 49, 50; to Naksa, 141–208; nationalist foundations of, 2; national stream vs. Islamist stream, 341–344; need for definition of goals in practical, realistic manner, 265; objections to partition plans, 62; poetry and literature in, 76–78; popular forces in, 52–64; Popular War of Liberation, 237–250; post–Nakba rehabilitation efforts, 160–163, 168–186; post–World War II to War of 1948, 39–80; post–World War II weakness, 39; principle of armed struggle in, 173, 174; recognition of June 1967 borders, 134; reinstatement of Arab honor in, 238–239; rejection of UN Resolution 242 in, 264; relinquishes status as local movement, 26; research and texts in, 78, 79; restoration of territory and return of refugees in, 266; revival of armed conflict, 186–195; rural-urban issues, 64–65; scouting in, 56, 57; split with former allies Iraq and Transjordan, 27; Syrian Social Nationalist Party in, 50–52; transition to belligerent outlook, 230, 231; and UN Resolution 181, 90–91; war of liberation modeled on Vietnamese experience, 224; War of October and, 263–267; in West Bank, 169–177; during World War II, 29–32
Palestinian National Union, 166

Palestinian organizations: assaults on kibbutzes by, 266; calls for removal from Lebanon, 261; demonstrations by, 266; hijackings, 243, 259, 286; hostage-taking, 266; Islamic, 326; in Israel, 273–275; in Jordan, 237–250; in Lebanon, 279–291; "perseverance" funds provided by Arab countries and, 271; rejection organizations, 296; in War of 1967, 221–234. *See also* Palestinian national movement; individual organizations
Palestinian Red Crescent, 272
Palestinian Research Center, 133
Palestinian Revolutionary Organization, 202
Palestinian Scouts Association, 44
Palestinian Sports Association, 56
Palestinian Storm Units, 231
Palestinian Student Association, 180
Palestinian Student Union, 216n160
Palestinian-Arab minority in Israel, 144–147; defining, 145; perceived as security issue, 146; regarded as "time bomb," 146; residential areas of, 146
Pan-Arabism, 3, 26, 27, 35, 43, 48, 58, 99, 133, 143, 158, 174, 273
Pan-Islamic Conference (1931), 162, 163
Partition (plans and resolution), 11; Arab objections to, 85, 86; cause of internal dissent in Palestinian organizations, 46, 47; factionalism and, 85–87; "hidden hand" in, 86; military sphere, 94–98; objections to, 62; of Peel Commission, 12, 16; political sphere, 92–94; United Nations and, 47, 50, 87–91
Pasha, 'Azzam, 121
Pasha, Ibrahim, 1
Path of Return Society, 198
Peace (newspaper), 74
Peel Commission, 10, 11; partition plan offered by, 16; recommendations for partition by, 12
Peled, Matityahu, 285, 308, 313n41
People's Republic of China, 227
Phalange, 258, 261n4, 279, 280
Pioneers of Islam, 325
Pioneers of Self-Sacrifice, 167
Pioneers of the Popular War of Liberation, 236n39
Pioneers of the Students (bulletin), 178

"Poem of a Shahid" (Muhammad), 77
Poetry, 76–78
Popular Arab Front, 185
Popular Democratic Front for the Liberation of Palestine, 230
Popular Front for the Liberation of Palestine-General Command, 230, 265, 266, 301; use of suicide bombers, 230
Popular Front for the Liberation of Palestine (PFLP), 229, 238, 243, 246, 248, 261, 266, 271, 282, 296, 300, 317; announces armed struggle against Israel through guerilla warfare, 194; clashes with Jordan, 241, 242; in Gaza Strip, 247; relations with various Arab governments, 229, 230; Special Unit, 259; split within, 230
Popular Resistance Committees, 231
Popular Resistance (journal), 170
Progressive Dialogue, 351
Progressive List for Peace, 308

Qaddafi, Muammar, 295
al-Qaddumi, Farouq, 196, 224, 225, 243, 248, 285, 297
al-Qaddumi, Hani, 197, 216n160
al-Qaddumi, Jamel, 56
Qahwaji, Habib, 186
Qarrash, Ya'qub, 323
Qasem, 'Abd al-Karim, 129, 164, 165, 175, 194
Qasem, 'Abd al-Sattar, 354, 355
Qasmiyya, Khayriyya, 133
al-Qassam, Shaikh 'Izz al-Din, 41, 104, 325; development of political Islam and, 6; in revolt of 1936-1939, 12; symbol of armed participation, 5
al-Qawasmi, Fahd, 302
al-Qawiqji, Fawzi, 10, 99, 102, 103, 114, 123
Qushta, Jamil, 160
Qutb, Sayyid, 325

Rabin, Yitzhak, 285, 339
Radio Ramallah, 143
Ramlawi, Ibrahim, 54
al-Rantisi, 'Abd al-'Aziz, 322, 325
Rashid, Fawzi, 13
Rawhi, Husayn, 4
al-Rayyis, Munir, 198

Reagan Plan, 301, 307
Refugees: assistance contingent on relinquishment of property in place of origin, 154; due to War of 1948, 141; in East Bank, 149–150; economic issues for, 147, 148, 151, 152, 158; estimated number of, 147, 148, 156, 157, 158; expelled from villages during War of 1948, 155; in Gaza Strip, 151–152, 177–181; income sources for, 149, 150; insistence that status is temporary, 141, 148; "integration" and "assimilation" of, 148, 149, 150, 151, 155, 156, 157, 159–160, 168, 169; internal, 153, 155, 156; in Iraq, 158–160; in Israel, 152–156, 181–186, 308–311; in Jordan, 148–151, 306–308; lack of basic freedoms for, 156–157; in Lebanon, 156–157, 304–306; loss of hope of return to original homes after War of 1967, 155, 156; Palestinian in diaspora, 147–148; perceived as foreigners, 156; present absentees, 153; prevented from becoming permanent residents, 156; prevented from returning to villages, 153, 154; restrictions on, 158; in Syria, 157–158; in West Bank, 150–151
Rejection Front, 266, 267, 285–286, 287
Religious Adherence Association, 58
Republic of Fakhani, 287–289
The Resistance (journal), 178, 230
Revenge (journal), 173, 174
Revolt of 1936–1939, 6, 9–21; Arab Higher Committee in, 10; becomes civil war, 14; British sanctions during, 14, 18; Central Jihad Committee, 18; coalitions in, 10, 11; confiscation of property and, 18; diplomatic efforts stage in, 10–12; disastrous effect on Palestinian society, 18; disintegration stage of, 14–15; establishment of governing agencies during, 13; as Events of 5796–5799, 21n1; fellahin subordination of cities and, 17; firsthand accounts of, 18–20; general strike stage, 9–10, 57; halts emergent modernization processes, 18; height of, 12–14; Holy Jihad Committee in, 13; Husayni-led group in, 10, 13; as inspiration to Palestinians, 15, 21; internecine conflicts in, 13; legacy of, 15–18; Nashashibi-led group in, 10, 11; Palestinian recollection/historiography and, 18–21; peace bands in, 13, 14; post-revolt leadership clashes in, 16–18; professional accounts of, 20–21; regional commanders of, 13; social schisms, 16–18; use of leadership in the field in, 13; youth element takes control in, 16, 17, 18
Revolution for the Liberation of Palestine: Command Council, 232
al-Rihani, Najib, 58
al-Rimawi, Qasem, 106
Roke, Alfred, 40, 42
Rogers, William, 242
Ruwayha, Amin, 26

Sa'ad, Ahmad, 156
Sa'ada, Anton, 50, 51
al-Sa'adi, Ahmad, 232
Saba, Fu'ad, 40, 42, 66
Saba', Sa'id, 79
al-Sabbagh, Salah al-Din, 26
Sacrificing Pioneers Organization, 236n39
al-Sa'd, Farid, 48, 80n12
al-Sadat, Anwar, 269, 270, 271, 272, 284, 304; denounced as "traitor to Arab cause," 285; peace initiative by, 285–286
Saddam Hussein, 7, 303, 326
Sadeq, Muhammad Ahmad, 233
al-Sa'di, Shaikh Farhan, 77
The Sad Sisters (Sidqi), 78
Safa, Muhammad, 100
Safwat, General Isma'il, 94, 99, 108, 109
al-Saghyyer, Ziyad, 296
al-Sahli, Nabil, 349
Sham'un, Kamil, 192
Sahyoun, Yusuf, 126, 140n87
al-Sa'id, Fahmi, 26
al-Sa'id, Nuri, 27, 28, 41, 42, 164; Blue Book Plan by, 32, 34–35
al-Sakakini, Khalil, 4, 78
Salah, 'Abd al-Latif, 40
Salah, Nimr, 282
al-Salah, 'Abd al-Qader, 171
al-Salah, Rashid, 280
Salam, Sa'ib, 261

Salameh, 'Ali Hassan, 13, 14, 18, 104, 106, 107, 108, 109, 258, 259, 260
al-Salfiti, Fahmi, 230
Salman, Mahmoud, 26
Salvation Organization, 81n29
al-Sarraj, 'Abd al-Hamid, 193
al-Sarraj, Jamil, 128
Sartawi, 'Isam, 236n39, 242
Sason, Moshe, 155
Saudi Arabia: resentment of Haj Amin in, 36; rivalry with Jordan, 112; sends assistance to PLO in Syrian conflict, 283; in War of 1948, 112, 114, 115tab
Sawwan, 'Abbas, 156
Saydam, Mamduh, 227
Sayigh, Yazid, 196, 201, 222, 264, 300, 321, 327
Sayil, General Sa'd, 294
Sayigh, Anis, 259
al-Sayyid, 'Ali, 197
Schultz, George, 290, 304
Second immigration (1904), 2
Second World Trade Union Conference of 1945 (Paris), 60, 62
Secret of the Disaster (al-Hawwari), 132
al-Serjany, Ragheb, 328
Shabib, Kamil, 26
Shadid, Tawfiq, 196
Shahin, Rushdi, 171
al-Sha'ir, 'Abdallah, 13
al-Sha'ir, Muhammad, 255
al-Shak'ah, Bassam, 269, 270, 271
Shammut, Isma'il, 199
Shaqaqi, Dr. Fathi, 325, 327
Sharon, Ari'el, 247, 272, 290, 303, 340
al-Shawwa, 'Izz al-Din, 80n12
al-Shawwa, Rashad, 80n12
Shertok, Moshe, 139n69
al-Shihabi, Zulaykha, 63
Shihada, Boulos, 3
al-Shishkali, Adib, 100
al-Shu'aybi, 'Azmi, 318
Shufani, Ilyas, 20
al-Shuqayri, Ahmad, 48, 166, 167, 168, 202, 205, 221, 222, 223, 231, 232, 233
Shuwqayr, Shawkat, 94
Sidqi, Najati, 78
al-Siksik, 'Abd al-Rahman, 43
Sinai Plan, 179
Socialist Nationalist Party, 174
Society for Improvement and Development, 65

Society of Arab Ladies, 63
Society of Female Solidarity, 63
Society of Good Attributes, 49
So That We Will Not Forget (al-Khalidi), 134
Soviet Union: Arafat asks aid from, 286; relations with PLO, 320; support for UNSCOP, 90; trade union affiliation with, 61
Spirit of Youth group, 55
Strikes: by Arab Higher Institution during partition discussions, 88; for improvement of working conditions for Arab vs. Jewish workers, 59; for International Commission of Inquiry, 62; in Lebanon, 257; over UN Resolution 181, 90; in Revolt of 1936-1939, 9–10, 57
Struggle Apparatus, 204, 205
Struggle of the Workers (bulletin), 178
Suez Canal, 224; nationalization of, 164, 193
al-Sukhun, Mamduh, 48, 80n12, 81n15
Sulayman, Shaikh Salih Salim, 155
Summit of Resistance and Steadfast Perseverance (1977), 285, 286
Suwaydani, Ahmad, 203
Suwwan, 'Umar, 180
Syria: Arabic press in, 74; armistice with Israel, 129; asks Arafat to leave country, 297, 298; Ba'ath Party in, 181, 236n39, 354; conflicts with PLO, 280–284; forbids incursions into Israel from its borders, 225; forces Arafat to leave base, 293, 294; founding of Ba'ath Party in, 52; infiltration of Israeli borders by, 192; intervention in PLO conflict with Jordan, 244, 245; Palestine decreed part of, 51; Palestinian refugees in, 148, 157–158, 356, 357; refusal to allow PLO infiltration of Israel through Syrian borders, 232; secret preparations for War of October, 263; struggle to overthrow Assad, 353–358; support for Assad regime in, 355, 356; supports rebellion against Arafat, 296; suppression of Fatah and, 207–208; unwritten alliance with Israel, 299; in War of 1948, 112, 114, 115tab, 116, 117
Syrian Club, 58
Syrian National Action League, 26

Syrian Social Nationalist Party, 50–52; decrees that Palestine is part of Syria, 51; relations with Haj Amin, 51

Tabbara, Bahjat, 94
Taha, Muhammad 'Ali, 156, 259
Taha, Sami, 60, 61, 62
Tajammu' Party, 354
al-Tal, Abdullah, 133
al-Tal, Wasfi, 173, 174, 175, 248, 258
al-Tamimi, Amin, 42
al-Tamimi, Rafiq, 79
al-Tamimi, Rajab Bayyud, 172
al-Tamimi, Subhi, 221
Tawfiq, Husayn, 193
Tawtah, Khalil, 4, 79
Tempest of the Western Wall, 57, 73
Ten Plagues Operation, 123
Thabit, Sa'id, 26
Thurayya (al-Husayni), 78
Tlas, Mustafa, 281
Toma, Emil, 45, 47, 134, 183
Tomorrow (journal), 45
Trade: bureaus, 64–65; unions, 59–63
Train of Mercy project, 180
Transjordan. *See* Jordan
Treaty of Hudaybiyah, 337
Truth About the Issue of Palestine (Haj Amin), 132
Truth of the Matter (newspaper), 74
Tubi, Tawfiq, 45, 47
Tuqan, Ibrahim, 76
Tuqan, Sulayman, 126
al-Turk, Fayiz, 232

'Ubayd, Diyab, 213n107
'Ubayd, Mu'iz, 197
al-'Umar, Dahir, 1
Unaffiliated Young, 68
Unified National Leadership, 322, 326
Unions: Arab Workers' Congress, 60, 61; Arab Workers' Union, 59, 60, 61, 61tab; attacks against, 62; Council of Trade Unions, 61, 62; credit, 64; merchant, 65; pan-Arab, 65; professional, 65; trade, 59–63
United Arab Command, 205, 218n179
United Arab Kingdom, 248, 249, 250
United Arab Republic (UAR), 165, 166, 193; dissolution of, 158
United Nations, 319; in Arab-Israeli conflict, 286, 287; Arafat speaks at, 267; declared situation in Israel a "threat to world peace," 120; Resolution 181, 90; resolution on partition of Palestine, 47, 50, 79, 80, 85, 87–91
United Nations Relief and Works Agency (UNRWA), 148, 149, 209n21
United Nations Resolution 242, 304
United States, 341; consents to include PLO in peace talks, 304; facilitates withdrawal of PLO from Lebanon, 291; support from King Husayn for, 172
Unity Clubs, 57
Unity (journal), 45, 46, 47
UN Relief and Works Agency, 180
UN Special Committee on Palestine (UNSCOP), 88, 89; lack of agreement on implementation of recommendations, 89; terms of recommendations, 89
'Urabi, Yusuf, 208
Urbanization, 64; post-revolt, 16; in rehabilitation phase, 64

Village Sons Movement, 276
Village Views (Mustafa), 78
Voice of Palestine Radio, 206

Wahba, Yusuf, 58
Wahid, Muhammad, 160
al-Wahidi, Fayiz, 178
Waldheim, Kurt, 285
War of 1948, 15, 16; Arab defeat in, 141; Arab League and, 47; armistice agreements, 129; attempts at mediation in, 118; Battle of the Ten Days in, 119; cessation of, 129; combat forces in, 114; Egypt in, 112, 114, 115tab, 116, 117, 118; entrance of Arab countries into, 110–124; establishment of state of Israel, 110–113; fighting for the land, 91–110; first stage of fighting in, 116–118; first truce in, 118; historiography of, 129–135; Holy Jihad Army in, 104–110; involvement of Arab countries in, 110–113; Iraq in, 114, 115tab, 116, 117; Jordan in, 114, 115tab, 117; last stage, 122–124; Lebanon in, 114, 115tab, 116, 117; Liberation Army in, 98–104, 114, 123; military sphere, 94–98; Muslim Brotherhood in, 114; Operation

Danny, 119; Operation Hiram, 123; Operation Horev, 123; Operation Policeman, 120–121; Operation Uvda, 123; Operation Yoav, 123, 142; Palestinian national movement and, 39–80; Palestinian refugees and, 141; partition and, 85–91; plan of action, 114; political sphere, 92–94; Saudi Arabia in, 114, 115tab; second truce, 120–121; Syria in, 114, 115tab, 116, 117; Ten Plagues Operation, 123; vested interests of Arab countries in, 110–113
War of 1967, 205; approaches to, 222–223; Arab defeat in, 221–234; Battle of Karameh, 224; defeat ends Palestinian trust in Arab governments, 224; defeat of Arab armies in, 133; extinguishment of hope of return for refugees, 155, 156; rise of Fatah in, 223–224
War of October: Palestinians and, 263–267
Warrad, Fa'iq, 171
al-Wazir, Khalil, 194–195, 196, 197, 198, 199, 202, 224, 225, 227, 239, 247, 258, 318
al-Wazzan, Shafiq, 290
Weitz, Yosef, 154, 155
West Bank: annexed by Jordan, 110, 141–144, 169, 170; Communist Party in, 171; Islamic Liberation Party in, 169; Israel in, 190; Jordanian Communist Party in, 169; Muslim Brotherhood in, 169; National Liberation League in, 169, 170; Palestine Liberation Organization control of, 7; Palestinian refugees in, 148, 150–151; PLO efforts to revive status in, 268; political organization/activities in, 169–177
White Paper (1939), 15, 16, 32, 85
Women's organizations, 63–64
World Muslim Conference (1950), 163
World War II: Arabs in, 29–32; Jews during, 28, 29; Palestinian alliance with Axis powers, 27, 28, 29, 32; Palestinian national movement during, 29–32

Yadin, General Yig'al-, 155
al-Yahya, 'Abd al-Razzaq, 221, 232
Ya'ish, Farid, 80n12, 81n15

al-Yamani, Ahmad Husayn, 204
Yanni Yanni, 214n114
Yasin, Shaikh Yusuf, 32
Yasin, Subhi, 167, 236n39
Yassin, 'Abd al-Hamid, 78
Yassin, Shaikh Ahmad, 323, 325
Yemen: coup in, 194
Young Arab Organization, 55
Young Egypt Party, 128
Young Men's Christian Association (YMCA), 58
Young Men's Muslim Association, 41
Young Muslim Association, 58
Young Muslims Movement, 309
Young Muslim Society, 128
Young Palestinians for Change, 350–351
Young Turks, 2
Yousef, Nasser, 338
Youth Congress Party, 66
Youth of Revenge, 194–195
Yusuf, Naser, 227

Zaki, 'Abbas, 203
Zallum, 'Abd al-Qadim, 172
al-Za'nun, Salim, 180, 197
Zawati, Hamad, 104
Zayadin, Ya'qub, 171
Zaydan, Muhammad, 313n46
Zayyad, Tawfiq, 274, 276
al-Zayyat, Muhammad, 194
al-Zibri, Abu 'Ali Mustafa, 204, 229, 243
Zionism, 16, 52, 54, 62; in Arabic press, 74; conflict with Palestinians, 50; differentiated from Judaism, 46; in historical narrative, 132; international, 91; objections to, 60; pre-state, 6; relations with Arab citizens in Israel, 182–183; during revolt of 1936-1939, 11; Revolt of 1936-1939 and, 20
Zionist-Palestinian conflict, 5; British role in, 27; brought to United Nations, 85; discussion at workers' conferences, 60
al-Zirakli, Khayr al-Din, 58
Zu'abi, 'Abd al-'Aziz, 183
al- Zu'abi, Sif al-Din, 213n107
Zu'aytir, Akram, 13, 18, 19, 20, 21n5, 26, 27, 28, 40, 75, 79, 132, 174
Zu'aytir, Wa'il, 259
Zu'ayyin, Yusuf, 203
Zu'bi, Nayif, 18
Zurayq, Qustantin, 47, 130

About the Book

Mustafa Kabha plumbs the complex story of the Palestinian people, from the revolts of 1936–1939 to the present, focusing on their efforts to establish a viable independent state—and the internal factors that have thwarted them.

With unparalleled access to primary sources, as well as secondary material in Arabic, Hebrew, and English, Kabha provides an abundance of new information in a sweeping historical context. Uniquely combining his overarching narrative with the narratives of the multiple Palestinian communities throughout the Middle East, he makes a groundbreaking contribution to our understanding of the political, social, and cultural dimensions of Palestinian history.

Mustafa Kabha is head of the Department of History, Philosophy, and Judaism at the Open University of Israel. He has published numerous books and articles in Arabic, English, and Hebrew, and his publications in English include *The Palestinian Arab In/Outsiders: Media and Conflicts in Israel* and *The Palestinian Press as Shaper of Public Opinion*.